ARMENIA

BUSINESS AND INVESTMENT OPPORTUNITIES YEARBOOK

VOLUME 2

LEADING EXPORT-IMPORT, BUSINESS, INVESTMENT OPPORTUNITIES AND PROJECTS

International Business Publications, USA
Washington DC, USA - Armenia

ARMENIA

BUSINESS AND INVESTMENT OPPORTUNITIES YEARBOOK

VOLUME 2 LEADING EXPORT-IMPORT, BUSINESS, INVESTMENT OPPORTUNITIES AND PROJECTS

UPDATED ANNUALLY

Cover Design: **International Business Publications, USA**

We express our sincere appreciation to all government agencies and international organizations which provided information and other materials for this yearbook

2016 Edition Updated Reprints International Business Publications, USA
ISBN

This yearbook provides basic information for starting or/and conducting business in the country. The extraordinary volume of materials covering the topic, prevents us from placing all these materials in this yearbook. For more detailed information on issues related to any specific investment and business activity in the country, please contact Global Investment Center, USA Please acquire the list of our business intelligence and marketing reports and other business publications. We constantly update and expand our business intelligence and marketing materials. Please contact the center for the updated list of reports on over 250 countries.

in the USA: **Global Investment Center, USA.**
P.O.Box 15343, Washington, DC 20053
Phone: (202) 546-2103, Fax: (202) 546-3275, E-mail: rusric@erols.com

For additional analytical, marketing and other information please contact Global Investment Center, USA

Printed in the USA

ARMENIA

BUSINESS AND INVESTMENT OPPORTUNITIES YEARBOOK

VOLUME 2

LEADING EXPORT-IMPORT, BUSINESS, INVESTMENT OPPORTUNITIES AND PROJECTS

TABLE OF CONTENTS

ARMENIA: BUSINESS AND DEVELOPMENT PROFILES

ARMENIA: STRATEGIC PROFILE

Capital and largest city	Yerevan 40°11′N 44°31′E40.183°N 44.517°E
Official languages	Armenian
Official written language	Eastern Armenian
Official script	Armenian alphabet (Reformed orthography)
Ethnic groups ()	• 97.9% Armenian • 1.3% Yazidis • 0.5% Russian • 0.3% other
Demonym	Armenian
Government	Semi-presidential republic
- President	Serzh Sargsyan
- Prime Minister	Hovik Abrahamyan
Legislature	National Assembly
Formation and independence	
- Traditional date	2492 BC
- Hayasa-Azzi	1500–1290 BC
- Arme-Shupria	1300s–1190 BC
- Urartu	860–590 BC
- Orontid Dynasty	6th century BC
- Kingdom of Greater Armenia united under the Artaxiad Dynasty	190 BC
- Arsacid Dynasty	52–428 AD
- Bagratid Armenia	885 AD
- Kingdom of Cilicia	1198–1375 AD
- Independence from the Soviet Union	23 August 1990 (declared) 21 September 1991 (referendum)
Area	
- Total	29,743 km² (141st) 11,484 sq mi
- Water (%)	4.71
Population	
- 2011 census	3,018,854 134th)
- Density	101.5/km² (99th) 262.9/sq mi
GDP (PPP)	2013 estimate
- Total	$20.831 billion

- Per capita	$6,128
GDP (nominal)	2013 estimate
- Total	$10.325 billion
- Per capita	$3,037
Gini	30.9 medium
HDI	0.730 high · 87th
Currency	Dram (դր.) (AMD)
Time zone	UTC (UTC+4)
Drives on the	right
Calling code	+374
Patron saint	St. Gregory the Illuminator
ISO 3166 code	AM
Internet TLD	.am

Armenia officially the **Republic of Armenia** is a mountainous country in the South Caucasus region of Eurasia. Located at the crossroads of Western Asia and Eastern Europe, it is bordered by Turkey to the west, Georgia to the north, the *de facto* independent Nagorno-Karabakh Republic and Azerbaijan to the east, and Iran and the Azerbaijani exclave of Nakhchivan to the south.

Armenia is a unitary, multi-party, democratic nation-state with an ancient cultural heritage. The Satrapy of Armenia was established in the 6th century BC, after the fall of Urartu. In the first century BC the Kingdom of Armenia reached its height under Tigranes the Great. Armenia became the first state in the world to adopt Christianity as its official religion, in the early years of the 4th century (the traditional date is 301 AD). For this reason, Armenia is often referred to as the "first Christian nation." An Armenian principality and later a kingdom, known as Cilician Armenia, existed on the coast of the Mediterranean Sea between the 11th and 14th centuries.

Between the 16th and early 19th century, the traditional Armenian homeland composed of Eastern Armenia and Western Armenia came under rule of the rivaling Ottoman and Persian Empires, often being passed between the former and the latter during the course of centuries, with all its native peoples inside it. By the mid 19th century, Eastern Armenia had been conquered by Russia over Persia, while most of the western parts of the traditional Armenian homeland still remained under Ottoman rule. During World War I, the Armenians living in their ancestral lands in the Ottoman Empire were systematically exterminated in the Armenian Genocide. After almost 600 years of statelessness, Armenia was able to become independent in 1918; however, the First Republic of Armenia, surrounded by hostile countries, was Sovietized in 1920. Between 1922 and 1991, Armenia was part of the Soviet Union. The modern Republic of Armenia became independent in 1991.

The Republic of Armenia recognizes the Armenian Apostolic Church, the world's oldest national church, as the country's primary religious establishment. Armenians have their own unique alphabet, which was invented by Mesrop Mashtots in 405 AD.

Armenia is a member of the Council of Europe and the Collective Security Treaty Organization. Armenia supports the de facto independent Nagorno-Karabakh Republic, which was proclaimed in 1991

Current issues: Armenia's leaders remain preoccupied by Armenia's nine-year old conflict with Azerbaijan over the Nagorno-Karabakh enclave. Although a cease-fire has been in effect since May 1994, the sides have not made substantial progress toward a peaceful resolution. President TER-PETROSSIAN's latitude on the issue may be further constrained by his controversial reelection in September 1996.

When supporters of the main opposition candidate stormed the parliament following the announcement of TER-PETROSSIAN's victory, MVD forces were called in to restore order. The subsequent political standoff between government and opposition supporters diminished in late 1996 as the government has gradually attempted reconciliation. Despite these political problems, the Armenian government has been pursuing its aggressive economic reform program, although implementation of its privatization program stalled in late 1996.

GEOGRAPHY

Location: Southwestern Asia, east of Turkey
Geographic coordinates: 40 00 N, 45 00 E
Map references: Commonwealth of Independent States

Area:
total : 29,800 sq km
land: 28,400 sq km
water: 1,400 sq km

Area - comparative: slightly smaller than Maryland

Land boundaries:
total: 1,254 km
border countries: Azerbaijan-proper 566 km, Azerbaijan-Naxcivan exclave 221 km, Georgia 164 km, Iran 35 km, Turkey 268 km

Coastline: 0 km (landlocked)
Maritime claims: none (landlocked)
Climate: highland continental, hot summers, cold winters

Terrain: high Armenian Plateau with mountains; little forest land; fast flowing rivers; good soil in Aras River valley

Elevation extremes:
lowest point: Debed River 400 m
highest point: Aragats Lerr 4,095 m

Natural resources: small deposits of gold, copper, molybdenum, zinc, alumina

Land use:
arable land : 17%
permanent crops: 3%
permanent pastures: 24%
forests and woodland: 15%
other: 41%

Irrigated land: 2,870 sq km
Natural hazards: occasionally severe earthquakes; droughts

Environment - current issues: soil pollution from toxic chemicals such as DDT; energy blockade, the result of conflict with Azerbaijan, has led to deforestation when citizens scavenged for firewood; pollution of Hrazdan (Razdan) and Aras Rivers; the draining of Sevana Lich, a result of its use as a source for hydropower, threatens drinking water supplies; restart of Metsamor nuclear power plant without adequate (IAEA-recommended) safety and backup systems

Environment - international agreements:
party to : Biodiversity, Climate Change, Nuclear Test Ban, Wetlands
signed, but not ratified: Desertification

Geography - note: landlocked

PEOPLE

Population: 3,433,629

Age structure:
0-14 years: 27% (male 476,375; female 456,723)
15-64 years: 65% (male 1,088,103; female 1,134,649)
65 years and over: 8% (male 115,135; female 162,644)

Population growth rate: -0.33%
Birth rate: 13.59 births/1,000 population
Death rate: 8.6 deaths/1,000 population
Net migration rate: -8.32 migrant(s)/1,000 population

Sex ratio:
at birth: 1.05 male(s)/female
under 15 years: 1.04 male(s)/female
15-64 years: 0.96 male(s)/female
65 years and over: 0.71 male(s)/female
total population: 0.96 male(s)/female

Infant mortality rate: 40.4 deaths/1,000 live births

Life expectancy at birth:
total population: 66.9 years
male: 62.69 years
female: 71.32 years

Total fertility rate: 1.71 children born/woman

Nationality:
noun: Armenian(s)
adjective: Armenian

Ethnic groups: Armenian 93%, Azeri 3%, Russian 2%, other (mostly Yezidi Kurds) 2%
note: as of the end of 1993, virtually all Azeris had emigrated from Armenia

Religions: Armenian Orthodox 94%

Languages: Armenian 96%, Russian 2%, other 2%

Armenia

C. I. S.
GEORGIA
AZERBAIJAN
TURKEY
IRAN
Tetri-Tskaro
Rustavi
Mameuli
Ozero Paravani
Akhalkalaki
Kazreti
Bogdanovka
Kura
Çıldır
Çıldır Gölü
Kalinino
Uzunlar
Akstafa
Kazakh
Mingechaurskoye Vodokhranilishche
Tauz
Idzhevan
Spitak
Kumayri (Leninakan)
Kirovakan
Dilizhan
Kars
Gyandzha (Kirovabad)
Artsvashen
Maralik
Sevan
Razdan
Charentsavan
Ashtarak
Kamo
Ozero Sevan
Akhuryan
Arpaçay
Kağızman
Aras
Echmiadzin
Oktemberyan
Yerevan
Zod
Martuni
Nagorno-Karabakhskaya AO
Agdam
Artashat
Iğdır
Ararat
Mount Ararat
Dzhermuk
Stepanakert
Karakose
Lachin
Doğubayazıt
Angekhakot
Il'ichevsk
Goris
NAKHICHEVANSKAYA ASSR
Mākū
Nakhichevan'
Kafan
Dzhul'fa
Qareh Ziā'od Dīn
Jolfā
Megri
Āq Chāy
Autonomous oblast (AO) boundary
Autonomous republic (ASSR) center
Autonomous oblast (AO) center
Railroad
Road
Armenia has no internal administrative divisions.
0 25 50 Kilometers
0 25 50 Miles
802084 (R00138) 8-92

Literacy:
definition: age 15 and over can read and write
total population: 99%
male: 99%
female : 98%

GOVERNMENT

Country name:
conventional long form: Republic of Armenia
conventional short form: Armenia
local long form: Hayastani Hanrapetut'yun
local short form: Hayastan
former: Armenian Soviet Socialist Republic, Armenian Republic

Government type:
republic

Capital:
name: Yerevan
geographic coordinates: 40 10 N, 44 30 E
time difference: UTC+4 (9 hours ahead of Washington, DC, during Standard Time)

Administrative divisions:
11 provinces (marzer, singular - marz); Aragatsotn, Ararat, Armavir, Geghark'unik', Kotayk', Lorri, Shirak, Syunik', Tavush, Vayots' Dzor, Yerevan

Independence:
21 September 1991 (from the Soviet Union)

National holiday:
Independence Day, 21 September (1991)

Constitution:
previous 1915, 1978; latest adopted 5 July 1995; amended 2005 (2013)

Legal system:
civil law system

International law organization participation:
has not submitted an ICJ jurisdiction declaration; non-party state to the ICCt

Suffrage:
18 years of age; universal

Executive branch:
chief of state: President Serzh SARGSIAN (since 9 April 2008)
head of government: Prime Minister Hovik ABRAHAMYAN (since 13 April 2014)

cabinet: Council of Ministers appointed by the prime minister

elections: president elected by popular vote for a five-year term (eligible for a second term); election last held on 18 February 2013 (next to be held February 2018); prime minister appointed by the president based on majority or plurality support in parliament; the prime minister and Council of Ministers must resign if the National Assembly refuses to accept their program
election results: Serzh SARGSIAN reelected president; percent of vote - Serzh SARGSIAN 58.6%, Raffi HOVHANNISIAN 36.7%, Hrant BAGRATIAN 2.2%, other 2.5%

Legislative branch:

unicameral National Assembly (Parliament) or Azgayin Zhoghov (131 seats; members elected by popular vote, 90 members elected by party list and 41 by direct vote; to serve five-year terms)
elections: last held on 6 May 2012 (next to be held in the spring of 2017)
election results: percent of vote by party - RPA 44%, Prosperous Armenia 30.1%, ANC 7.1%, Heritage Party 5.8%, ARF (Dashnak) 5.7%, Rule of Law 5.5%, other 1.8%; seats by party - RPA 69, Prosperous Armenia 37, ANC 7, Heritage Party 5, ARF (Dashnak) 5, Rule of Law 6, independent 2

Judicial branch:
highest court(s): Court of Cassation (consists of the court chairman and organized into a criminal chamber and a civil and administrative chamber, each with a court chairman and 2 judges); Constitutional Court (consists of 9 judges)
judge selection and term of office: Court of Cassation judges nominated by the Judicial Council, a 9-member body of selected judges and legal scholars; judges appointed by the president; Constitutional Court judges - 4 appointed by the president, and 5 elected by National Assembly; judges of both courts can serve until retirement at age 65
subordinate courts: 2 Courts of Appeal (for civil cases and for criminal and military cases); district courts; Administrative Court

Political parties and leaders:
Armenian National Congress or ANC (bloc of independent and opposition parties) [Levon TER-PETROSSIAN]
Armenian National Movement or ANM [Ararat ZURABIAN]
Armenian Revolutionary Federation ("Dashnak" Party) or ARF [Hrant MARKARIAN]
Heritage Party [Raffi HOVHANNISIAN]
People's Party of Armenia [Stepan DEMIRCHIAN]
Prosperous Armenia [Gagik TSARUKIAN]
Republican Party of Armenia or RPA [Serzh SARGSIAN]
Rule of Law Party (Orinats Yerkir) [Artur BAGHDASARIAN]

Political pressure groups and leaders:
Aylentrank (Impeachment Alliance) [Nikol PASHINIAN]
Yerkrapah Union [Manvel GRIGORIAN]

International organization participation:
ADB, BSEC, CD, CE, CIS, CSTO, EAEC (observer), EAPC, EBRD, FAO, GCTU, IAEA, IBRD, ICAO, ICC (NGOs), ICRM, IDA, IFAD, IFC, IFRCS, ILO, IMF, Interpol, IOC, IOM,

IPU, ISO, ITSO, ITU, MIGA, NAM (observer), OAS (observer), OIF, OPCW, OSCE, PFP, UN, UNCTAD, UNESCO, UNIDO, UNIFIL, UNWTO, UPU, WCO, WFTU (NGOs), WHO, WIPO, WMO, WTO

Diplomatic representation in the US:
chief of mission: Ambassador Tatoul MARKARIAN (since 26 May 2005)
chancery: 2225 R Street NW, Washington, DC 20008
telephone: (202) 319-1976
FAX: (202) 319-2982
consulate(s) general: Glendale (CA), Los Angeles

Diplomatic representation from the US:
chief of mission: Ambassador John HEFFERN (since 6 October 2011)
embassy: 1 American Ave., Yerevan 0082
mailing address: American Embassy Yerevan, US Department of State, 7020 Yerevan Place, Washington, DC 20521-7020
telephone: [374](10) 464-700
FAX: [374](10) 464-742

Flag description:
three equal horizontal bands of red (top), blue, and orange; the color red recalls the blood shed for liberty, blue the Armenian skies as well as hope, and orange the land and the courage of the workers who farm it

National symbol(s):
Mount Ararat; eagle; lion

National anthem:
name: "Mer Hayrenik""(Our Fatherland)

lyrics/music: Mikael NALBANDIAN/Barsegh KANACHYAN
note: adopted 1991; based on the anthem of the Democratic Republic of Armenia (1918-1922) but with different lyrics

ECONOMY

After several years of double-digit economic growth, Armenia faced a severe economic recession with GDP declining more than 14% in 2009, despite large loans from multilateral institutions. Sharp declines in the construction sector and workers' remittances, particularly from Russia, led the downturn. The economy began to recover in 2010 with 2.1% growth, and has grown even faster in the three years since then.

Under the old Soviet central planning system, Armenia developed a modern industrial sector, supplying machine tools, textiles, and other manufactured goods to sister republics, in exchange for raw materials and energy. Armenia has since switched to small-scale agriculture and away from the large agroindustrial complexes of the Soviet era. Armenia's geographic isolation, a narrow export base, and pervasive monopolies in important business sectors have made it particularly vulnerable to the sharp deterioration in the global economy and the economic downturn in Russia. Since August 2011, Armenia has experienced a sharp currency depreciation. Armenia has only two open trade borders - Iran and Georgia - because its borders with Azerbaijan and Turkey have been closed since 1991 and 1993, respectively, as a result of Armenia's ongoing conflict with Azerbaijan over the separatist Nagorno-Karabakh region. Armenia is particularly dependent on Russian commercial and governmental support and most key Armenian infrastructure is Russian-owned and/or managed, especially in the energy sector.

The electricity distribution system was privatized in 2002 and bought by Russia's RAO-UES in 2005. Natural gas is primarily imported from Russia but construction of a pipeline to deliver natural gas from Iran to Armenia was completed in December 2008, and gas deliveries expanded after the April 2010 completion of the Yerevan Thermal Power Plant. Armenia's severe trade imbalance has been offset somewhat by international aid, remittances from Armenians working abroad, and foreign direct investment.

Armenia joined the WTO in January 2003. The government made some improvements in tax and customs administration in recent years, but anti-corruption measures have been ineffective and the economic downturn has led to a sharp drop in tax revenue and forced the government to accept large loan packages from Russia, the IMF, and other international financial institutions. Amendments to tax legislation, including the introduction of the first ever "luxury tax" in 2011, aim to increase the ratio of budget revenues to GDP, which still remains at low levels. Armenia will need to pursue additional economic reforms and to strengthen the rule of law in order to regain economic growth and improve economic competitiveness and employment opportunities, especially given its economic isolation from two of its nearest neighbors, Turkey and Azerbaijan.

GDP (purchasing power parity):
$20.61 billion (2013 est.)
country comparison to the world: 133
$19.7 billion (2012 est.)
$18.38 billion (2011 est.)
note: data are in 2013 US dollars

GDP (official exchange rate):
$10.44 billion (2013 est.)

GDP - real growth rate:
4.6% (2013 est.)
country comparison to the world: 65
7.2% (2012 est.)
4.7% (2011 est.)

GDP - per capita (PPP):
$6,300 (2013 est.)
country comparison to the world: 148
$6,000 (2012 est.)
$5,600 (2011 est.)***note:*** data are in 2013 US dollars

Gross national saving:
16.2% of GDP (2013 est.)
country comparison to the world: 103

13.2% of GDP (2012 est.)
16.1% of GDP (2011 est.)

GDP - composition, by end use:
household consumption: 84.7%
government consumption: 13%
investment in fixed capital: 22.7%
investment in inventories: -0.9%
exports of goods and services: 23.6%
imports of goods and services: -43.1%
(2013 est.)

GDP - composition, by sector of origin:

agriculture: 20.6%
industry: 37.3%
services: 42.1% (2013 est.)

Agriculture - products:
fruit (especially grapes), vegetables; livestock

Industries:
diamond processing, metal-cutting machine tools, forging and pressing machines, electric motors, tires, knitted wear, hosiery, shoes, silk fabric, chemicals, trucks, instruments, microelectronics, jewelry, software, food processing, brandy, mining

Industrial production growth rate:
3.9% (2013 est.)
country comparison to the world: 76

Labor force:
1.394 million (2013 est.)
country comparison to the world: 133

Labor force - by occupation:
agriculture: 44.2%
industry: 16.8%
services: 39% (2008 est.)

Unemployment rate:

17.3% (2012 est.)
country comparison to the world: 1528.4% (2011 est.)

Population below poverty line:
35.8% (2010 est.)

Household income or consumption by percentage share:

lowest 10%: 3.7%
highest 10%: 25.4% (2008)

Distribution of family income - Gini index:

30.9 (2008)
country comparison to the world: 114
44.4 (1996)

Budget:
revenues: $2.677 billion
expenditures: $2.707 billion (2013 est.)

Taxes and other revenues:
25.6% of GDP (2013 est.)
country comparison to the world: 119

Budget surplus (+) or deficit (-):
-0.3% of GDP (2013 est.)
country comparison to the world: 50

Public debt:

37.7% of GDP (2013 est.)
country comparison to the world: 99
41.4% of GDP (2012 est.)

Fiscal year:
calendar year

Inflation rate (consumer prices):
6.2% (2013 est.)
country comparison to the world: 179
2.6% (2012 est.)

Central bank discount rate:
$NA (11 January 2012)
country comparison to the world: 39
7.25% (2 December 2008)
note: this is the Refinancing Rate, the key monetary policy instrument of the Armenian National Bank

Commercial bank prime lending rate:
16.5% (31 December 2013 est.)
country comparison to the world: 26
17.23% (31 December 2012 est.)
note: average lending rate on loans up to one year

Stock of narrow money:
$1.418 billion (31 December 2013 est.)
country comparison to the world: 140
$1.352 billion (31 December 2012 est.)

Stock of broad money:
$2.051 billion (31 December 2013 est.)
country comparison to the world: 149
$1.829 billion (31 December 2012 est.)

Stock of domestic credit:
$4.355 billion (31 December 2012 est.)
country comparison to the world: 117
$3.548 billion (31 December 2011 est.)

Market value of publicly traded shares:
$132.1 million (31 December 2012 est.)
country comparison to the world: 109
$139.6 million (31 December 2011)
$144.8 million (31 December 2010 est.)

Current account balance:
-$720.6 million (2013 est.)
country comparison to the world: 112
-$1.052 billion (2012 est.)

Exports:
$1.653 billion (2013 est.)
country comparison to the world: 145
$1.588 billion (2012 est.)

Exports - commodities:
pig iron, unwrought copper, nonferrous metals, diamonds, mineral products, foodstuffs, energy

Exports - partners:
Russia 19.6%, Germany 10.7%, Bulgaria 9.1%, Belgium 8.9%, Iran 6.9%, US 6.1%, Canada 6%, Georgia 5.7%, Netherlands 5.6%, Switzerland 5% (2012)

Imports:
$3.459 billion (2013 est.)
country comparison to the world: 140
$3.656 billion (2012 est.)

Imports - commodities:
natural gas, petroleum, tobacco products, foodstuffs, diamonds

Imports - partners:

Russia 20%, Germany 11%, Bulgaria 9%, Belgium 9%, Iran 6.5%, US 6.1%, Canada 5.9%, Netherlands 5.6%, Georgia 5.6%, Switzerland 5.2% (2012 est.)

Reserves of foreign exchange and gold:
$1.863 billion (31 December 2013 est.)
country comparison to the world: 125
$1.799 billion (31 December 2012 est.)

Debt - external:
$7.839 billion (31 December 2013 est.)
country comparison to the world: 105
$7.633 billion (31 December 2012 est.)

Exchange rates:
drams (AMD) per US dollar -
410.5 (2013 est.)
401.76 (2012 est.)
373.66 (2010 est.)
363.28 (2009)
303.93 (2008)

ENERGY

Electricity - production:
7.432 billion kWh (2011 est.)
country comparison to the world: 102

Electricity - consumption:
5.8 billion kWh (2011 est.)
country comparison to the world: 108

Electricity - exports:
1.36 billion kWh (2011 est.)
country comparison to the world: 53

Electricity - imports:
246 million kWh (2010 est.)
country comparison to the world: 86

Electricity - installed generating capacity:
3.472 million kW (2010 est.)
country comparison to the world: 85

Electricity - from fossil fuels:
55.6% of total installed capacity (2010 est.)
country comparison to the world: 141

Electricity - from nuclear fuels:
10.8% of total installed capacity (2010 est.)

country comparison to the world: 16

Electricity - from hydroelectric plants:

33.5% of total installed capacity (2010 est.)
country comparison to the world: 67

Electricity - from other renewable sources:

0.1% of total installed capacity (2010 est.)
country comparison to the world: 106

Crude oil - production:
0 bbl/day (2013 est.)
country comparison to the world: 149

Crude oil - exports:
0 bbl/day (2013 est.)
country comparison to the world: 78

Crude oil - imports:
0 bbl/day (2013 est.)
country comparison to the world: 152

Crude oil - proved reserves:
0 bbl (1 January 2013 est.)
country comparison to the world: 103

Refined petroleum products - production:
0 bbl/day (2013 est.)
country comparison to the world: 118

Refined petroleum products - consumption:
45,300 bbl/day (2011 est.)
country comparison to the world: 102

Refined petroleum products - exports:

32 bbl/day (2010 est.)
country comparison to the world: 122

Refined petroleum products - imports:
46,550 bbl/day (2010 est.)
country comparison to the world: 71

Natural gas - production:
0 cu m (2013 est.)
country comparison to the world: 98

Natural gas - consumption:
2.1 billion cu m (2013 est.)
country comparison to the world: 78

Natural gas - exports:
0 cu m (2013 est.)
country comparison to the world: 57

Natural gas - imports:
2.1 billion cu m (2013 est.)
country comparison to the world: 47

Natural gas - proved reserves:
0 cu m (1 January 2013 est.)
country comparison to the world: 109

Carbon dioxide emissions from consumption of energy:
11.74 million Mt (2011 est.)

COMMUNICATIONS

Telephones - main lines in use:
584,000
country comparison to the world: 92

Telephones - mobile cellular:

3.223 million
country comparison to the world: 128

Telephone system:
general assessment: telecommunications investments have made major inroads in modernizing and upgrading the outdated telecommunications network inherited from the Soviet era; now 100% privately owned and undergoing modernization and expansion; mobile-cellular services monopoly terminated in late 2004 and a second provider began operations in mid-2005
domestic: reliable modern fixed-line and mobile-cellular services are available across Yerevan in major cities and towns; significant but ever-shrinking gaps remain in mobile-cellular coverage in rural areas
international: country code - 374; Yerevan is connected to the Trans-Asia-Europe fiber-optic cable through Iran; additional international service is available by microwave radio relay and landline connections to the other countries of the Commonwealth of Independent States, through the Moscow international switch, and by satellite to the rest of the world; satellite earth stations - 3 (2008)

Broadcast media:
2 public TV networks operating alongside more than 40 privately owned TV stations that provide local to near nationwide coverage; major Russian broadcast stations are widely

available; subscription cable TV services are available in most regions; Public Radio of Armenia is a national, state-run broadcast network that operates alongside about 20 privately owned radio stations; several major international broadcasters are available (2008)

Internet country code:
.am

Internet hosts:
194,142
country comparison to the world: 73

Internet users:
208,200
country comparison to the world: 138

TRANSPORTATION

Airports:
11
country comparison to the world: 154

Airports - with paved runways:
total: 10
over 3,047 m: 2
2,438 to 3,047 m: 2
1,524 to 2,437 m: 4
914 to 1,523 m: 2 (2013)

Airports - with unpaved runways:
total: 1
914 to 1,523 m: 1 (2013)

Pipelines:
gas 2,233 km (2013)

Railways:
total: 869 km
country comparison to the world: 96
broad gauge: 869 km 1.520-m gauge (818 km electrified)
note: some lines are out of service (2009)

Roadways:
total: 7,705 km (2012)
country comparison to the world: 143

MILITARY

Military branches:
Armenian Armed Forces: Ground Forces, Air Force and Air Defense; "Nagorno-Karabakh Republic": Nagorno-Karabakh Self-Defense Force (NKSDF) (2011)

Military service age and obligation:
18-27 years of age for voluntary or compulsory military service; 2-year conscript service obligation; 17 year olds are eligible to become cadets at military higher education institutes, where they are classified as military personnel (2012)

Manpower available for military service:
males age 16-49: 805,847
females age 16-49: 854,296 (2010 est.)

Manpower fit for military service:
males age 16-49: 644,372
females age 16-49: 717,272 (2010 est.)

Manpower reaching militarily significant age annually:
male: 23,470
female: 21,417 (2010 est.)

Military expenditures:
3.92% of GDP (2012)
country comparison to the world: 12
3.87% of GDP (2011)
3.92% of GDP (2010)

TRANSNATIONAL ISSUES

Disputes - international:
the dispute over the break-away Nagorno-Karabakh region and the Armenian military occupation of surrounding lands in Azerbaijan remains the primary focus of regional instability; residents have evacuated the former Soviet-era small ethnic enclaves in Armenia and Azerbaijan; Turkish authorities have complained that blasting from quarries in Armenia might be damaging the medieval ruins of Ani, on the other side of the Arpacay valley; in 2009, Swiss mediators facilitated an accord reestablishing diplomatic ties between Armenia and Turkey, but neither side has ratified the agreement and the rapprochement effort has faltered; local border forces struggle to control the illegal transit of goods and people across the porous, undemarcated Armenian, Azerbaijani, and Georgian borders; ethnic Armenian groups in the Javakheti region of Georgia seek greater autonomy from the Georgian Government

Refugees and internally displaced persons:
refugees (country of origin): 11,090 (Syria - ethnic Armenians) (2013)
IDPs: 8,400 (conflict with Azerbaijan over Nagorno-Karabakh) (2009)
stateless persons: 35 (2012)

Illicit drugs:
illicit cultivation of small amount of cannabis for domestic consumption; minor transit point for illicit drugs - mostly opium and hashish - moving from Southwest Asia to Russia and to a lesser extent the rest of Europe

IMPORTANT INFORMATION FOR UNDERSTANDING ARMENIA

PROFILE

OFFICIAL NAME: Republic of Armenia

GEOGRAPHY

Area: 29,800 sq. km. (11,500 sq. mi.); slightly larger than Maryland. Cities: *Capital*--Yerevan.
Terrain: High plateau with mountains, little forest land.
Climate: Highland continental, hot summers, cold winters.

PEOPLE

Nationality: *Noun*--Armenian(s). *Adjective*--Armenian.
Population (unofficial est.): About 2.6 million (Government of Armenia is currently conducting a census, with results due early 2002).
Ethnic groups: Armenian 95%; Kurd 2%; Russian, Greek, and other 3%.
Religion: Armenian Apostolic Church (more than 90% nominally affiliated).
Languages: Armenian (96%), Russian, other.
Education: *Literacy*--99%.
Health: *Infant mortality rate*--20/1,000. *Life expectancy*--72 years.
Work force (1.6 million): *Industry and construction*--30%; *agriculture and forestry*--35%; *other*--35%.

GOVERNMENT

Type: Republic.
Constitution: Approved in 1995 referendum.
Independence: 1918 (First Armenian Republic); 1991 (from Soviet Union).
Branches: *Executive*--president (head of state) with wider powers relative to other branches, prime minister (head of cabinet), Council of Ministers (cabinet). *Legislative*--unicameral National Assembly (parliament). *Judicial*--Constitutional Court.
Administrative subdivisions: 10 marzer (provinces) in addition to the city of Yerevan, which has the status of a province.
Political parties: Republican Party of Armenia, Armenian Peoples Party, Agro-Technical Peoples Union (formerly Stability Faction), Constitutional Rights Union, Armenian National Movement, National Democratic Union, Republic Party, Social Democratic Union, Liberal Democratic Party, Ramkvar-Christian Democratic Party, Communist Party of Armenia, National Accord Party, Armenian Revolutionary Federation-Dashnaktsutyun, Country of Laws (Orinats Yerkir) Party, plus 84 registered marginal parties, many of which are now dormant.
Suffrage: Universal at 18.

U.S.-ARMENIAN RELATIONS

The dissolution of the Soviet Union in December 1991 brought an end to the Cold War and created the opportunity to build bilateral relations with the New Independent States (NIS) as they began a political and economic transformation. The U.S. recognized the independence of Armenia on December 25, 1991, and opened an embassy in Yerevan in February 1992.

The United States has made a concerted effort to help Armenia and the other NIS during their difficult transition from totalitarianism and a command economy to democracy and open markets. The cornerstone of this continuing partnership has been the Freedom for Russia and Emerging Eurasian Democracies and Open Markets (FREEDOM) Support Act, enacted in October 1992, under which the U.S. to date has provided nearly $1.2 billion in humanitarian and technical assistance for Armenia.

In addition, the U.S. has played a leading role in the Minsk Group, which was created in 1992 by the Conference of Security and Cooperation in Europe--now the Organization for Security and Cooperation in Europe (OSCE)--to encourage a peaceful, negotiated resolution to the conflict over the Nagorno-Karabakh region. That conflict has cost several thousand lives, created nearly one million refugees and displaced persons, and caused economic hardships for Armenia.

U.S.-ARMENIAN ECONOMIC RELATIONS

In 1992 Armenia signed three agreements with the U.S. affecting trade between the two countries. The agreements were ratified by the Armenian parliament in September 1995 and entered into force in the beginning of 1996. They include an "Agreement on Trade Relations," an "Investment Incentive Agreement," and a treaty on the "Reciprocal Encouragement and Protection of Investment" (generally referred to as the Bilateral Investment Treaty, or BIT). Armenia does not have a bilateral taxation treaty with the U.S. The 1994 Law on Foreign Investment governs all direct investments in Armenia, including those from the U.S.

Approximately 70 U.S.-owned firms currently do business in Armenia, including such multinationals as Procter & Gamble, M&M-Mars, Xerox, Dell, and IBM. Recent major U.S. investment projects include the Hotel Armenia, the Hotel Ani; a Greek-owned Coca-Cola bottling plant; petroleum exploration by the American-Armenian Exploration Company; upgrading of the wine and brandy production at Ararat winery; a large perlite mining and processing plant; and the joint venture Jermuk, which produces one of the more popular brands of mineral water in Armenia.

U.S. SUPPORT TO BUILD A MARKET ECONOMY

The U.S. continues to work closely with international financial institutions like the International Monetary Fund (IMF) and the World Bank to help Armenia in its transition to a free-market economy. Armenia has embarked upon an ambitious reform program, which has allowed a gradual transition from humanitarian aid toward more developmental assistance. U.S. economic assistance programs, primarily under the administration of the U.S. Agency for International Development (USAID), have three objectives: to help create a legal, regulatory, and policy framework for competition and economic growth in energy, agriculture, housing, and other sectors; to promote fiscal reform; and to develop a competitive and efficient private financial sector. Other agencies, including the State Department, Peace Corps, Department of Treasury, Customs Service, and the Department of Defense also sponsor various assistance projects. The U.S.-Armenia Task Force, established in 2005, is a bilateral commission that meets every 6 months to review the progress and objectives of U.S. assistance to Armenia.

Specific USAID programs focus on the development of a private sector and small and medium-size enterprises, including microcredit programs; energy sector reform, including preparation for privatization of energy distribution companies; democracy and good governance programs, including the promotion of a well-informed and active civil society; social sector reform, including funding for medical partnerships and social insurance programs; and earthquake zone assistance, which provides housing and economic reactivation for victims of the 1988 earthquake.

The U.S. Department of Agriculture Marketing Assistance Project (MAP) provides advisory services and support to private farmers in all Armenian provinces, facilitates the formation of farmer associations and marketing initiatives, provides micro-credits for agricultural producers, and has laid the groundwork for several agribusiness associations. The U.S. Department of Agriculture's (USDA) Cochran Fellowship Program provides training to Armenian agriculturists. USDA and USAID also have launched efforts to revive production and export of Armenian vegetables, fruits, and other agricultural products.

U.S. Humanitarian Assistance

Over the past decade the U.S. has provided $1.2 billion in assistance to Armenia, the highest per capita amount in the NIS. Humanitarian aid originally accounted for up to 85% of this total, reflecting the economic effects caused by Turkish and Azerbaijani embargoes related to the Nagorno-Karabakh conflict, destruction in northern Armenia left from the devastating 1988 earthquake, and the virtual paralysis of most of the country's factories.

As conditions in Armenia have improved, with the stabilization of the economy and increased energy production--including the restarting of the Armenian Nuclear Power Plant at Metsamor--U.S. assistance programs have moved away from humanitarian goals to longer term development ones. Nevertheless, humanitarian programs, which make up approximately 15% of total assistance in fiscal year 2001, still provide an important source of food, medical supplies, and other necessary items to needy Armenians.

U.S. Support To Achieve Democracy

Technical assistance and training programs have been provided in municipal administration, intergovernmental relations, public affairs, foreign policy, diplomatic training, rule of law, and development of a constitution. Specific programs are targeted at promoting free and fair elections, strengthening political parties, and promoting the establishment of an independent judiciary and independent media. This includes financing for programs that support civil society organizations, local non-governmental organizations (NGO) capacity building, National Assembly professional development, and local and community-level governance.

State Department and USAID educational exchange programs play an important role in supporting democratic and free-market reforms. Assistance in the translation and publication of printed information also has been provided. Exchange programs in the U.S. for Armenian lawyers, judges, political party members, business people, government officials, NGO activists, journalists, and other public figures focus on a range of topics, including the American judicial and political system, privatization, specific business sectors, the media, and civil society. The State Department has funded an ongoing project to provide Internet connectivity to schools at various levels throughout the country; these centers provide both educational and community-building opportunities.

USAID has funded international and domestic groups to monitor national elections. USAID has also funded programs to educate voters and to strengthen the role of an array of civic organizations in the democratic process.

PRINCIPAL U.S. EMBASSY OFFICIALS

Ambassador-- Richard M. Mills, Jr.

Ambassador Richard M. Mills, Jr., a career member of the U.S. Foreign Service, most recently served as the Deputy Chief of Mission at the U.S. Embassy in Beirut, Lebanon from 2012 to 2014.

Deputy Chief of Mission--Joseph Pennington
Political/Economic Chief--Steve Banks
Assistance Coordinator--Daniel Renna
Consular Officer--Robin Busse
Management Officer--Robert Frazier
Regional Security Officer--Gordon Goetz
USDA Marketing Assistance Project Director--Sean Carmody
USAID Director--Robin Phillips
Public Affairs Officer--Thomas Mittnacht

The U.S. embassy in Yerevan, Armenia is at 18 Marshal Bagramyan; tel: 3741-54-3900 or 3741-52-4661; fax: 3741-52-0800.

HISTORICAL HIGHLIGHTS

Armenia first emerged into history around 800 BC as part of the Kingdom of Urartu or Van, which flourished in the Caucasus and eastern Asia Minor until 600. After the destruction of the Seleucid Empire, the first Armenian state was founded in 190 BC. At its zenith, from 95 to 65 BC, Armenia extended its rule over the entire Caucasus and the area that is now eastern Turkey, Syria and Lebanon. For a time, Armenia was the strongest state in the Roman East. It became part of the Roman Empire in 64 BC and adopted a Western political, philosophical, and religious orientation.

In 301 AD, Armenia became the first nation to adopt Christianity as a state religion, establishing a church that still exists independently of both the Catholic and the Eastern Orthodox churches. During its later political eclipses, Armenia depended on the church to preserve and protect its unique identity. From around 1100 to 1350, the focus of Armenian nationalism moved south, as the Armenian Kingdom of Cilicia, which had close ties to European Crusader states, flourished in southeastern Asia Minor until conquered by Muslim states.

Between the 4th and 19th centuries, Armenia was conquered and ruled by, among others, Persians, Byzantines, Arabs, Mongols, and Turks. For a brief period from 1918 to 1920, it was an independent republic. In late 1920, the communists came to power following an invasion of Armenia by the Red Army, and in 1922, Armenia became part of the Trans-Caucasian Soviet Socialist Republic. In 1936, it became the Armenian Soviet Socialist Republic. Armenia declared its independence from the Soviet Union on September 21, 1991.

GOVERNMENT AND POLITICAL CONDITIONS

Armenians voted overwhelmingly for independence in a September 1991 referendum, followed by a presidential election in October 1991 that gave 83% of the vote to Levon Ter-Petrossian. Ter-Petrossian had been elected head of government in 1990, when the Armenian National

Movement defeated the Communist Party. Ter-Petrossian was re-elected in 1996. Following public demonstrations against Ter-Petrossian's policies on Nagorno-Karabakh, the President resigned in January 2002 and was replaced by Prime Minister Robert Kocharian, who was elected President in March 2002. Following the assassination in Parliament of Prime Minister Vazgen Sargsian and parliament Speaker Karen Demirchian and six other officials, on October 27, 2003, a period of political instability ensued during which an opposition headed by elements of the former Armenian National Movement government attempted unsuccessfully to force Kocharian to resign. Kocharian was successful in riding out the unrest. The next presidential elections are slated for 2003.

The unicameral parliament (also called the National Assembly) is dominated by a coalition, called "Unity" (Miasnutyun), between the Republican and Peoples Parties and the Agro-Technical Peoples Union, aided by numerous independents. Dashnaksutyun, which was outlawed by Ter-Petrossian in 1995-96 but legalized again after Ter-Petrossian resigned, also usually supports the government. A new party, the Republic Party, is headed by ex-Prime Minister Aram Sargsian, brother of the late Vazgen Sargsian, and has become the primary voice of the opposition, which also includes the communists, the National Accord Party of Artashes Geghamian, and elements of the former Ter-Petrossian government.

The Government of Armenia's stated aim is to build a Western-style parliamentary democracy as the basis of its form of government. However, international observers have questioned the inherent fairness of parliamentary and presidential elections and constitutional referenda since 1995, citing polling deficiencies, lack of cooperation by the electoral commission, and poor maintenance of electoral lists and polling places. Observers noted, though, that opposition parties and candidates have been able to mount credible campaigns and proper polling procedures have been generally followed. Elections since 2002 have represented an improvement in terms of both fairness and efficiency, although they have not met international standards. The new constitution of 1995 greatly expanded the powers of the executive branch and gives it much more influence over the judiciary and municipal officials.

The observance of human rights in Armenia is uneven and is marked by serious shortcomings. Police brutality still goes largely unreported, while observers note that defendants are often beaten to extract confessions and are denied visits from relatives and lawyers. Public demonstrations usually take place without government interference, though one rally in November 2005 by an opposition party was followed by the arrest and imprisonment for a month of its organizer. Freedom of religion is not always protected under existing law. Nontraditional churches, especially the Jehovah's Witnesses, have been subjected to harassment, sometimes violently. All churches apart from the Armenian Apostolic Church must register with the government, and proselytizing is forbidden by law. The government's policy toward conscientious objection is in transition, as part of Armenia's accession to the Council of Europe. Most of Armenia's ethnic Azeri population was deported in 1988-89 and remain refugees, largely in Azerbaijan. Armenia's record on discrimination toward the few remaining national minorities is generally good. The government does not restrict internal or international travel. Although freedom of the press and speech are guaranteed, the government maintains its monopoly over television and radio broadcasting.

Principal Government Officials

resident--Serzh Sargsian
Prime Minister--Tigran Sargsian
Foreign Minister--Edward Nalbandian
Defense Minister--Seyran Ohanian
Ambassador to the U.S.--Tatoul Markarian
Ambassador to the UN--Armen Martirosian

Armenia's embassy in the U.S. is at 2225 R Street, NW, Washington, DC, 20058; tel: 202-319-1976 or 202-319-2983; fax: 202-319-2984.

DEFENSE AND MILITARY ISSUES

Armenia established a Ministry of Defense in 1992. Border guards subject to the Ministry patrol Armenia's borders with Georgia and Azerbaijan, while Russian troops continue to monitor its borders with Iran and Turkey.

The Conventional Armed Forces in Europe (CFE) Treaty was ratified by the Armenian parliament in July 1992. The treaty establishes comprehensive limits on key categories of military equipment, such as tanks, artillery, armored combat vehicles, combat aircraft, and combat helicopters, and provides for the destruction of weaponry in excess of those limits. Armenian officials have consistently expressed determination to comply with its provisions. Armenia has provided data on armaments as required under the CFE Treaty. There are indications that Armenia is trying to establish mechanisms to ensure fulfillment of its arms control obligations. Armenia is not a significant exporter of conventional weapons, but it has provided substantial support, including materiel, to separatists in Nagorno-Karabakh.

In March 1993, Armenia signed the multilateral Chemical Weapons Convention, which calls for the eventual elimination of chemical weapons. Armenia acceded to the nuclear Non-Proliferation Treaty as a non-nuclear weapons state in July 1993. The U.S. and other Western governments have discussed efforts to establish effective nuclear export control systems with Armenia.

FOREIGN RELATIONS

Armenia is a member of the Commonwealth of Independent States, the United Nations, the Council of Europe, the Organization for Security and Cooperation in Europe, NATO's Partnership for Peace, the North Atlantic Cooperation Council, the International Monetary Fund, and the International Bank for Reconstruction and Development.

NAGORNO-KARABAKH

In 1988, the territory of Nagorno-Karabakh, a predominantly ethnic Armenian enclave within Azerbaijan, voted to secede and join Armenia. This eventually developed into a full-scale armed conflict. Armenian support for the separatists led to an economic embargo by Azerbaijan, which has crippled Armenia's foreign trade and restricted its imports of food and fuel, three-quarters of which transited Azerbaijan under Soviet rule.

Peace talks in early 1993 were disrupted by the seizure of Azerbaijan's Kelbajar district by Nagorno-Karabakh Armenian forces and the forced evacuation of thousands of ethnic Azeris. Turkey in protest then followed with an embargo of its own against Armenia. A cease-fire was declared between Azeri and Armenian/N-K forces in 1994 and has been maintained by both sides since then in spite of occasional shooting along the line of contact between the two. All Armenian governments have thus far resisted domestic pressure to recognize the self-proclaimed independence of the "Nagorno-Karabakh Republic," while at the same time announcing they would not accept any peace accords that returned the enclave to Azerbaijani rule. Some 750,000 ethnic Azeris who fled during the Karabakhi offensives still live as internally displaced persons in Azerbaijan, while roughly 400,000 ethnic Armenians who fled Azerbaijan since 1988 remain refugees, although around 35,000 have accepted Armenian citizenship since 2002.

Negotiations to peacefully resolve the conflict have been ongoing since 1992 under the aegis of the Minsk Group of the OSCE. The Minsk Group is currently co-chaired by the U.S., France, and Russia and comprises Armenia, Azerbaijan, Turkey, the U.S., several western European nations, and representatives of the Armenian and Azeri communities of Nagorno-Karabakh. The talks have focused on the status of Nagorno-Karabakh, the return of refugees, the lifting of blockades, the withdrawal from occupied territories, and the status of the Lachin corridor, which connects Nagorno-Karabakh to Armenia.

Karabakhi Armenians, supported by the Republic of Armenia, now hold about 15% of Azerbaijan and have refused to withdraw from occupied territories until an agreement on the status of Nagorno-Karabakh is reached. Armenia and Azerbaijan continue to observe the cease-fire which has been in effect since May 1994, and in late 1995 both also agreed to OSCE field representatives being based in Tbilisi, Georgia, to monitor the cease-fire and facilitate the peace process.

ECONOMY

Currency	554 Dram = 1 Euro
Fiscal year	Calendar year
Trade organisations	CIS, WTO
	Statistics
GDP	$10.066 billion (nominal, 2012 est.) $19.649 billion (PPP, 2012 est.)
GDP growth	▲7.2% (2012 est.)
GDP per capita	$2.991 (nominal, 2012 est.) $5,839 (PPP, 2012 est.)
GDP by sector	agriculture (19.2%), industry (40.8%), services (40%) (2012 est.)
Inflation (CPI)	5.8 % (2013)
Population below poverty line	35.8% (2010 est.)
Gini coefficient	30.9 (2008)
Labour force	1.194 million (2011 est)
Labour force by occupation	services (44.2%), industry (16.8%), agriculture (39%) (2008 est.)
Unemployment	17.3% (2012)
Main industries	diamond-processing, metal-cutting machine tools, forging-pressing machines, electric motors, tires, knitted wear, hosiery, shoes, silk fabric, chemicals, trucks, instruments, microelectronics, jewelry manufacturing, software development, food processing, brandy
Ease-of-doing-business rank	32nd
	External
Exports	▲$1.602 billion (2012)
Export goods	pig iron, unwrought copper, nonferrous metals, diamonds, mineral products, foodstuffs, energy
Main export partners	Russia 19.6% Germany 10.7% Bulgaria 9.1% Belgium 8.9% Iran 6.9% United States 6.1% Canada 6.0% Georgia 5.7% Netherlands 5.6% Switzerland 5.0% (2012 est.)
Imports	▲$3.656 billion (2012)
Import goods	natural gas, petroleum, tobacco products, foodstuffs,

	diamonds
Main import partners	Russia 24.8% China 9.4% Germany 6.2% Iran 5.2% Ukraine 5.1% Turkey 5.0%
Gross external debt	$6.435 billion
Public finances	
Public debt	42.1% of GDP
Revenues	$2.2 billion
Expenses	$2.5 billion
Economic aid	$302 million (ODA)
Foreign reserves	▲US$2.021 billion

Armenia is the second most densely populated of the former Soviet republics because of its small size. It is situated between the Black Sea and the Caspian Sea, bordered on the north and east by Georgia and Azerbaijan and on the south and west by Iran and Turkey.

Until independence, Armenia's economy was based largely on industry—chemicals, electronic products, machinery, processed food, synthetic rubber and textiles; it was highly dependent on outside resources. Agriculture accounted for only 20% of net material product and 10% of employment before the breakup of the Soviet Union in 1991. Armenian mines produce copper, zinc, gold and lead. The vast majority of energy is produced with imported fuel, including gas and nuclear fuel (for its one nuclear power plant) from Russia; the main domestic energy source is hydroelectric. Small amounts of coal, gas and petroleum have not yet been developed.

Like other former states, Armenia's economy suffers from the legacy of a centrally planned economy and the breakdown of former Soviet trading patterns. Soviet investment in and support of Armenian industry has virtually disappeared, so that few major enterprises are still able to function. In addition, the effects of the 1988 earthquake, which killed more than 25,000 people and made 500,000 homeless, are still being felt. Although a cease-fire has held since 1994, the conflict with Azerbaijan over Nagorno-Karabakh has not been resolved. The consequent blockade along both the Azerbaijani and Turkish borders has devastated the economy, because of Armenia's dependence on outside supplies of energy and most raw materials. Land routes through Azerbaijan and Turkey are closed; routes through Georgia and Iran are adequate and reliable. In 1992-93, the GDP had fallen nearly 60% from its 1989 level. The national currency, the dram, suffered hyperinflation for the first few years after its introduction in 1993.

Armenia has registered strong economic growth since 1995 and inflation has been negligible for the past several years. New sectors, such as precious stone processing and jewelry making and communication technology (primarily Armentel, which is left from the USSR era and is owned by external investors). This steady economic progress has earned Armenia increasing support from international institutions. The International Monetary Fund (IMF), World Bank, EBRD, as well as other international financial institutions (IFIs) and foreign countries are extending considerable grants and loans. Total loans extended to Armenia since 1993 exceed $800 million. These loans are targeted at reducing the budget deficit, stabilizing the local currency; developing private businesses; energy; the agriculture, food processing, transportation, and health and education sectors; and ongoing rehabilitation work in the earthquake zone.

Continued progress will depend on the ability of the government to strengthen its macroeconomic management, including increasing revenue collection, improving the investment climate, and accelerating privatization. A liberal foreign investment law was approved in June 1994, and a law on privatization was adopted in 1997, as well as a program on state property privatization. The government has made major strides toward joining the World Trade Organization. By 1994, however, the Armenian government had launched an ambitious IMF-sponsored economic liberalization program that resulted in positive growth rates in 1995-2005. Armenia joined the World Trade Organization (WTO) in January 2003. Armenia also has managed to slash inflation, stabilize its currency, and privatize most small- and medium-sized enterprises. Armenia's unemployment rate, however, remains high, despite strong economic growth. The chronic energy shortages Armenia suffered in the early and mid-1990s have been offset by the energy supplied by one of its nuclear power plants at Metsamor. Armenia is now a net energy exporter, although it does not have sufficient generating capacity to replace Metsamor, which is under international pressure to close. The electricity distribution system was privatized in 2002. Armenia's severe trade imbalance has been offset somewhat by international aid, remittances from Armenians working abroad, and foreign direct investment. Economic ties with Russia remain close, especially in the energy sector. The government made some improvements in tax and customs administration in 2005, but anti-corruption measures have been more difficult to implement. Investment in the construction and industrial sectors is expected to continue in 2006 and will help to ensure annual average real GDP growth of about 13.9%

Armenia is the second most densely populated of the former Soviet republics. It is a landlocked country between the Black and the Caspian Seas, bordered on the north and east by Georgia and Azerbaijan and on the south and west by Iran and Turkey. Up until independence, Armenia's economy was based largely on industry--chemicals, electronic products, machinery, processed food, synthetic rubber, and textiles--and highly dependent on outside resources. Agriculture accounted for only 20% of net material product and 10% of employment before the breakup of the Soviet Union in 1991. Armenian mines produce copper, zinc, gold, and lead. The vast majority of energy is produced with imported fuel, including gas and nuclear fuel (for its one nuclear power plant) from Russia; the main domestic energy source is hydroelectric. Small amounts of coal, gas, and petroleum have not yet been developed.

Like other New Independent States, Armenia's economy suffers from the legacy of a centrally planned economy and the breakdown of former Soviet trading patterns. Soviet investment in and support of Armenian industry has virtually disappeared, so that few major enterprises are still able to function. In addition, the effects of the 1988 earthquake, which killed more than 25,000 people and made 500,000 homeless, are still being felt. Although a cease-fire has held since 1994, the conflict with Azerbaijan over Nagorno-Karabakh has not been resolved. The consequent blockade along both the Azerbaijani and Turkish borders has devastated the economy, because of Armenia's dependence on outside supplies of energy and most raw materials. Land routes through Azerbaijan and Turkey are closed; routes through Georgia and Iran are inadequate or unreliable. In 1992-93, GDP fell nearly 60% from its 1989 level. The national currency, the dram, suffered hyperinflation for the first few years after its introduction in 1993.

Nevertheless, the Government of Armenia, helped by the cease-fire that has been in effect in Nagorno-Karabakh since 1994, has been able to carry out wideranging economic reforms which paid off in dramatically lower inflation and steady growth. Armenia has registered strong economic growth since 1995, building on the turnaround that began the previous year, and inflation has been negligible for the past several years. New sectors, such as precious stone processing and jewelry making, information and communication technology, and even tourism are beginning to supplement more traditional sectors such as agriculture in the economy.

This steady economic progress has earned Armenia increasing support from international institutions. The IMF, World Bank, EBRD, as well as other IFIs and foreign countries are extending considerable grants and loans. Total loans extended to Armenia since 1993 exceed $800 million. These loans are targeted at reducing the budget deficit, stabilizing the local currency; developing private businesses; energy; the agriculture, food processing, transportation, and health and education sectors; and ongoing rehabilitation work in the earthquake zone.

Continued progress will depend on the ability of the government to strengthen its macroeconomic management, including increasing revenue collection, improve the investment climate, and accelerate the privatization process. A liberal foreign investment law was approved in June 1994, and a Law on Privatization was adopted in 1997, as well as a program on state property privatization. The government has made major strides toward joining the World Trade Organization.

ENVIRONMENTAL ISSUES

Armenia is trying to address its environmental problems. It has established a Ministry of Environment and has introduced a pollution fee system by which taxes are levied on air and water emissions and solid waste disposal, with the resulting revenues used for environmental protection activities. Armenia is interested in cooperating with other members of the Commonwealth of Independent States (a group of 12 former Soviet republics) and with members of the international community on environmental issues. The Armenian Government is working toward closing the Armenian Nuclear Power Plant as soon as alternate energy sources can be identified.

TRAVEL AND BUSINESS INFORMATION

The U.S. Department of State's Consular Information Program provides Consular Information Sheets, Travel Warnings, and Public Announcements. **Consular Information Sheets** exist for all countries and include information on entry requirements, currency regulations, health conditions, areas of instability, crime and security, political disturbances, and the addresses of the U.S. posts in the country. **Travel Warnings** are issued when the State Department recommends that Americans avoid travel to a certain country. **Public Announcements** are issued as a means to disseminate information quickly about terrorist threats and other relatively short-term conditions overseas which pose significant risks to the security of American travelers. Free copies of this information are available by calling the Bureau of Consular Affairs at 202-647-5225 or via the fax-on-demand system: 202-647-3000. Consular Information Sheets and Travel Warnings also are available on the Consular Affairs Internet home page: http://travel.state.gov. Consular Affairs Tips for Travelers publication series, which contain information on obtaining passports and planning a safe trip abroad are on the internet and hard copies can be purchased from the Superintendent of Documents, U.S. Government Printing Office, telephone: 202-512-1800; fax 202-512-2250.

Emergency information concerning Americans traveling abroad may be obtained from the Office of Overseas Citizens Services at (202) 647-5225. For after-hours emergencies, Sundays and holidays, call 202-647-4000.

Passport information can be obtained by calling the National Passport Information Center's automated system ($.35 per minute) or live operators 8 a.m. to 8 p.m. (EST) Monday-Friday ($1.05 per minute). The number is 1-900-225-5674 (TDD: 1-900-225-7778). Major credit card users (for a flat rate of $4.95) may call 1-888-362-8668 (TDD: 1-888-498-3648). It also is available on the internet.

Travelers can check the latest health information with the U.S. Centers for Disease Control and Prevention in Atlanta, Georgia. A hotline at 877-FYI-TRIP (877-394-8747) and a web site at http://www.cdc.gov/travel/index.htm give the most recent health advisories, immunization recommendations or requirements, and advice on food and drinking water safety for regions and countries. A booklet entitled Health Information for International Travel (HHS publication number CDC-95-8280) is available from the U.S. Government Printing Office, Washington, DC 20402, tel. (202) 512-1800.

Information on travel conditions, visa requirements, currency and customs regulations, legal holidays, and other items of interest to travelers also may be obtained before your departure from

DEVELOPMENT STRATEGY AND BUSINESS OPPORTUNITIES[1]

OBJECTIVES AND PRIORITIES

The Sustainable Development Program (SDP) had three sets of objectives:

* Reduction of poverty in 2008-2021 to the extent that poverty will not be a problem of economic development, and extreme poverty will be totally eliminated and will no longer be a significant social phenomenon.

* Elimination of human poverty and ensuring accelerated human development, as a result of which, in a few years, the country should have moved from the group of countries with average human development to the group of countries with high level of human development[1].

* Mitigation of disproportions of the territorial development and acceleration of economic growth of underdeveloped regions by developing and implementing a relevant territorial policy.

12. In order to achieve the mentioned objectives, SDP envisaged three sets of priority strategies:

* Economic policy for ensuring sustainable and accelerated economic growth; * Active social and income policy for vulnerable groups of population (including the poor); * Modernization of governance system, including improved effectiveness of state governance and ensuring accelerated growth of the resource envelope at the disposal of the state.

SDP economic policy priorities focused on ensuring accelerated, sustainable and poor-oriented economic growth and consisted of two groups: framework and direct or investment policies.

Framework policy is the same for all participants of the relevant sector and does not include the use of public funding for achieving policy objectives.

The basis for SDP economic policy was an approach, which assumed that the quality of the growth environment (business environment and investment climate in particular), freedom to enter the market, prevention of abuse by economic entities having dominant or monopoly position and promotion of competition, labor all foreign and sustainable domestic macroeconomic policy, have a decisive role in ensuring accelerated and sustainable economic growth.

Framework economic policy priorities included the design and introduction of the main elements and institutions of knowledge-based economy, as well as the institutional

[1] According to UNDP Human Development Index which is published in the annual Human Development Reports.

modernization of the country, which also can be considered as the environment where economic growth takes place.

Direct or investment policy assumes the financial intervention of the state for achieving policy goals and has an interventionist nature.

The direct economic policy of SDP was to make only those investments from public financial resources, either fully or partially, which currently or in the near future, cannot be made by the private sector, but are necessary for ensuring economic growth and aim to eliminate the bottlenecks of the economy. Thus, the main priorities of the direct policy were public investments in infrastructure sectors.

Another priority of the direct policy was investments within the framework of Public-Private Partnership, which would be necessary for attracting foreign investment, as well as mitigating disparities of regional development.

The targeted social policy, which was the second strategic priority of the SDP, was a mix of direct and framework policies, where the direct policy assumed the accelerated growth of the public funding in the corresponding sectors, and the framework policy was directed to considerable improvement of the quality, conditions and accessibility of services provided to the population in the social sector.

The active social policy covered the following sectors:

* Social assistance, where the priority is the allocation of family benefits, as the main tool for eradicating extreme poverty. The main objective of the framework policy was to continuously improve the targeting of family benefits, and the goal of the direct policy was to increase family benefits to around 70 percent of the poverty line.

* Social insurance, where the priority of the direct policy was the sharp increase of pensions up to the value of the minimum consumer basket, and the framework policy aimed to move labor pensions to the budget, as well as establish the foundations for funded pension and its gradual introduction.

* Social infrastructures, where the priorities of the direct policy were the accelerated increase in the volumes of public funding for basic social services (including education and healthcare), and the main priority of the framework policy was to improve the accessibility, effectiveness and quality of services by continuing the comprehensive reforms in the sector.

* Income policy, where the direct policy aimed to ensure the accelerated growth of primary incomes in the budgetary and social infrastructure sectors. The main priority of the framework policy was the use of the set value of minimum wage as one of the main tools for significantly reducing the number of “working poor” and the later elimination of this group of population.

Improving the effectiveness of the state governance sector, at all levels of governance, which is the third strategic priority of the Sustainable Development Program, is also a mix of direct and framework policies, where the direct policy aims to continually increase the volumes of resources at the disposal of the state, and the framework policy describes and lists the measures, which will ensure the mentioned increase, as well as significantly increase the effectiveness of the state and the quality of and access to services provided by the state, as well as the level of accountability to citizens.

The framework policy for increasing the volume of resources at the disposal of the state[2] should have focused on significantly improving tax and customs administration and disclosure and reduction of shadow economy.

The framework policy for public expenditures aims to improve their distribution and technical effectiveness, in particular, through transition to results-based and program budgeting.

The priorities of the framework policy for enhancing the effectiveness of state governance are the drafting and introduction of a new effective anticorruption strategy, maximum possible transparency of decisions made by the state and ensuring active participation of the civil society in the process of decision-making, in particular through the introduction of electronic management and information systems at all levels (e-government, e-management, etc.).

GENERAL DEVELOPMENT TRENDS

The Sustainable Development Program was approved by the Decree of the Government of Armenia No. 1207-N dated 30 October 2008, right at the outset of the global financial and economic crisis. The crisis could not have been taken into account during the drafting of the program and its spread throughout the world in 2008-2009 could not have no impact on Armenia's economy and have no influence the process of SDP implementation and achievement of its indicators. Thus, the crisis, by itself, became the main factor justifying the revision of SDP.

The economic growth model is Armenia formed prior to the crisis (2003-2008) was based on foreign financing (direct foreign investment, official and private transfers), the volumes of which grew year-to-year. As a result, in conditions of double-digit economic growth, imports grew rapidly, the competitiveness of local industrial products in the domestic market declined, non-agricultural employment rates did not grow, and the relative and absolute volumes of exports shrunk.

In conditions of declining competitiveness of the industry and the relative decrease in exports, the main engine of economic growth in the country was construction and services sectors, the combined share of which in the GDP increased from 50.1 percent in 2003 to 56.4 percent in 2007 and 59.3 percent in 2008, while the combined share of industry and agriculture in the GDP declined from 44 percent in 2003 to 29.6 percent in 2008.

Considering that the model of economic growth based on foreign financing and the resulting increase in domestic demand cannot be maintained in the long run, the SDP envisaged a gradual transition to an economic growth model based on the accelerated increase in the volumes of exported goods and services, as a result of which the country would gradually become less dependent on foreign financing and the share of construction in GDP would decline gradually.

The impact of global financial and economic crisis emerging in September 2008 reached Armenia in the fourth quarter of 2008, when the GDP produced in the quarter declined by 1.2 percent compared to the same period in 2007, and the decline continued in 2009 resulting in

[2] It was assumed that the accelerated growth of the volumes of resources at the disposal of the state, at 0.3-0.4 percentage points of GDP annually, should take place without a heavier tax burden.

a 14.1 percent drop in GDP. The crisis ended in 2010, when 2.2 percent year-on-year GDP growth was recorded in Armenia, and the global economy, of which also Armenia entered the recovery phase.

The recovery continued in 2011-2013. Thus, during that period average growth was 5.1 percent: Main contributors to the growth were the services (including trade) – 2.2 percentage points, agriculture – 2.0 percentage points and industry – 1.4 percentage points. The construction sector continued to have negative contribution to GDP (-1 percentage point).

At the same time economic crisis has brought in new global challenges, which have created necessity to revise country's long-term development strategy in correspondence to the post-crisis realities, the main of which are as follows:

As a result of the global economic crisis, the sectoral structure of economy changed significantly and the share of construction has visibly declined because of the increase in the share of all other macro-sectors. It is, on the one hand, more stable compared to the pre-crisis structure, since it is less dependent on the volumes of foreign financing, and on the other hand, unlike the previous development model, it cannot ensure very high growth rates, because of the sharp decline in construction and its contribution to economic growth.

The sharp decline of the volumes of foreign financing (Sum of net foreign direct investments, private and official transfers) by about 31 percent in 2009-2011 has made it significantly difficult to continue the 2003-2007 economic growth model based on the increase in domestic demand in current conditions.

At the same time, a new challenge is created by the fact, that until now economic growth in Armenia does not lead to increased employment:

The preconditions and causes of economic growth without increased employment in Armenia after independence can be divided into two groups:

1) In 1994-2003, during the recovery growth, the main factor behind the significant decline in employment and changes to its structure was the transition process, since the new economic structure had a lower level of demand for jobs, compared to the former structure which was being dismantled and transformed.

2) In 2003-2008, the rapid economic growth did not result in increased employment, because the growth in the newly formed economic sectors was assured mainly as a result of higher productivity, and consequently higher incomes from employment, while employment continued to shrink in sectors inherited from the USSR, as well as in social infrastructures.

3) In 2008-2009, there was a decline in employment as a result of economic crisis, due to the decline of production in new sectors, particularly in construction, and the subsequent job losses.

1) The first one is based on objective reasons resulted from transition processes and impact of corresponding factors is gradually diminishing and in the current phase of development, where the new structure of the economy has already been formed and the old Soviet era sectors have practically transformed or disappeared, they can no longer be considered as crucial or decisive.

2) Secondly, the absence of adequate coordinated policies aimed at increasing jobs. In the previous long-term strategic programs creation of jobs was considered one of the priorities of economic policy; however the application of relevant direct policy tools was either not in place or had fragmented nature. Particularly, the policy of creation of jobs and reduction of unemployment in those strategies was based on the assumption that the role of the state in that sector should be limited to improvement of business environment and investment climate, promotion of competitiveness, restriction of abuse of dominant or monopoly position and public investments should be directed only at infrastructure maintenance and improvement. Improvement of public administration sector was viewed as an important precondition for employment growth, including reduction of public regulations and their simplification, combating corruption, improving effectiveness and quality of public services.

Nonetheless, starting from 2008 these approaches have been significantly revised and institutionalized and in addition to framework policy and activities aimed at improvement of business environment and investment climate, the government has implemented activities financially supporting business and individual sectors. At the same time, clarification of the scope of the said activities in medium-and long-term perspectives, is still on the agenda.

Another important reason for developing a new strategic program was the change of views on both economic policy and its toolset, which was demonstrated during the global economic crises and continues until now, emphasizing the importance of increasing the state regulatory role and the direct policy.

ARMENIA DEVELOPMENT STRATEGY (ADS) PRIORITIES AND MAIN OBJECTIVE

THE ADS TIME COVERAGE AND PRIORITIES

The ADS covers the period of 2014-2025 and is the country's main socioeconomic development strategy and the basis for medium-term, sectoral and other program documents.

Being the primary guide of the Government, ADS is based on the following four priorities:

1) Priority 1. Growth of employment; 2) Priority 2. Development of human capital; 3) Priority 3. Improvement of social protection system; and 4) Priority 4. Institutional modernization of the public administration and governance.

During the first five years of ADS, employment growth will be recognized a key priority, highlighting activities aimed at creation of quality, well-paid jobs3. The activities of the RA Government will be directed at the creation of possibilities for everyone to get fair income according to the working efforts exerted.

Activities aimed at *development of human capital* will be geared at enhancing the scope, quality and accessibility of primary services (including healthcare, education, science, culture and primary infrastructures) with a special emphasis on nature-human relationships and harmonious development as well. The activities aiming at personal development of the citizen of RA, his/her professional growth, civic education and enhanced cultural level will be always under the strong focus of the Government, fostering the willingness of each person to live in the homeland.

Activities aimed at *improvement of the social protection system* will be geared at improvement of the effectiveness of current systems (including improvement of the targeting) and creation of the basis for financial stability in the long-term, ensuring provision of comprehensive social guarantees, essential reduction of social risks and reduction of poverty. At the same time, activities will be implemented in the medium term to gradually transit from delivery of primarily monetary social aid to vulnerable population groups to provision of needs-based complex packages of social assistance. Implementation of the program will guarantee for each member of the society the strong feeling of being protected and socially secured by the own state.

Activities aimed at *institutional modernization of the public administration system* will adhere to the adopted fundamental policies and will be geared at improving the public efficiency, growth of public resources and their targeted use, improvement of service quality and accessibility, reduction of corruption, transparency of decision-making, and increased civil society participation in these processes.

[3] Quality job ensures physical and psychological well-being of the employed person, as well as creates sense of job satisfaction.

ADS MAIN OBJECTIVE, POLICY DIRECTIONS AND TARGETS

The main objective of the ADS is increase in employment through creation of quality and well-paid jobs.

Employment increase will be the measurable outcome of implementation of the sustainable economic growth policy. Policies ensuring sustainable economic growth, which creates new quality jobs, have systemic nature, i.e. they will flow from the priority of the primary objective by promoting its achievement or at least not hampering it.

Highlighting the importance of framework policies aimed at main program objective, they will be complimented by financial, credit and monetary tools geared at increase of jobs and reduction of unemployment.

In monetary policy these tool will be aimed at increasing accessibility and affordability of borrowings.

Along with framework policy aimed at increase of the country's international competitiveness, as well as improvement of business environment and investment climate, a special importance will be given to modern industrial and export with direct interventionist elements aimed at job creation.

When designing such policies sector specifics and conditions of job creation will be taken into consideration. Particularly the policy will differ based on labor-intensive and modern academic sectors. Special emphasis will be placed on regional specifics of employment which will be viewed within direct regional development intervention mechanisms.

Unlike the previous economic development phases, when economic growth was ensured mainly due to work productivity increase, the planned activities will result in the following picture: during 2014-2025 in non-agriculture sector of economy about 4/5 of percentage point of economic growth will be ensured through productivity and 1/5 through employment growth. In industry, which will be the one of the main sectors contributing to increase in employment, the growth proportions will be 3/4 and 1/4, correspondingly.

As a result of the implemented activities it is expected to achieve the following targets of employment growth in non-agriculture sector:

Employment growth of around 60 thousand by 2017 vs. 2012,

Employment growth of around 135 thousand by 2021 vs. 2012, and

Employment growth of around 220 thousand by 2025 vs. 2012.

In addition to employment growth, an increase in formality of non-agriculture employment is envisaged as well, which is planned to reach 78% in 2017, 80% in 2021, 83% in 2025, as compared to 73% recorded in 2011.

Apart from employment growth, the program envisages also employment structure changes (Figure 1) due to the fact that around 50% of employment growth will be assigned to industry and construction sectors. As a result it is expected that in 2025 the share of industry in nonfarm employment will increase by around 3.5 percentage points as compared to 2012, and will make up 22.4% and the share of construction will increase by 2.5 percentage points reaching 12% in 2025..

Figure 1. Non-farm employment in 2011-2025

Expansion of jobs in industry will be ensured mainly by creation of quality jobs, characterized as above-medium productivity and salary job places.

Expansion of jobs in construction will be ensured through recovery of economic growth in the sector (in average, 6.0-6.5% annually), as well as framework policy promoting increase of employment formality and reduction of shadow activity in the sector.

As for employment in the services sector, here also absolute employment increase is expected, though at a slower rate, which will reduce the share of employment in services in the structure of non-farm employment. Projections of such developments are explained with the fact that along with sectors that have big potential of growth and expansion in the services sector (in particular, information technologies and tourism infrastructures) there are sectors with employment surplus as well.

Viewing employment growth as the main socioeconomic development objective for the coming years, **the income policy action**s and measures will be designed with the logic, that salary increase should not exceed the productivity increase, thus not allowing increase of the unit labor costs[4], which is critical for the increase of the country's international competitiveness.

At the same time, the minimum salary acierated increase policy will be implemented, one of the main goals of which is drastic reduction of working poor. This policy will result in net minimum to average salary ratio sharp growth, reaching around 40 % in 2014 (versus 26.8% in 2012) and this level will be retained until 2025. With planned increase by 2017 net minimum salary will make up around 160% of the upper poverty line, reaching 240% in 2025 as compared to 88% in 2012.

[4] Unit labour costs (ULC) measure the average cost of labour per unit of output and are calculated as the ratio of total labour costs to real output.

MACROECONOMIC FRAMEWORK

MAIN MACROECONOMIC DEVELOPMENTS

The actual developments of macroeconomic indicators, particularly the rates of economic growth, have significantly deviated from the scenario forecasted for macroeconomic indicators by the Sustainable Development Program, which is largely result of the impact of the global financial and economic crisis of 2008. In Armenia, as well as numerous other countries, development programs were replaced by anti-crisis programs because of the uncertainties of medium-term and long-term forecasts. Already in 2009, the application of the principle of following MTEF and long-term development programs, which was exercised for a continuous period not only in Armenia, but also in a number of other countries, was temporarily halted. Formerly, prominent international organizations revised their short-term economic forecasts 1-2 times per year, while in 2009 those organizations revised their forecasts repeatedly[5].

The considerable worsening of the global economy had a negative impact especially on countries with open economies, including Armenia. The main reason behind the relatively deeper decline in Armenia were the specific structural characteristics of economic growth in Armenia -the high rates of economic growth in 2000-2008 were the result of the unprecedented growth of non-export sectors, specialty construction, which was the result of the sharp increase in capital inflow into Armenia and concentration of the capital in the construction sector. The evidence proving that fact is that 10.5 percentage points of the 14.1 percent decline recorded in 2009 was the share of the construction sector. But it is important to note that regardless of the serious decline recorded in 2009, it was possible to avoid macroeconomic destabilization in the post crisis period due to the coordinated monetary and fiscal policies, and economic growth tendencies were recorded already in 2010-2013. Characteristically, the structure of economic growth considerably improved as well with a larger share of export sectors, which will give a new quality and sustainability to the formation of future economic growths. Nonetheless, it must be noted that after the crisis and high rates of economic growth, the Armenian economy was naturally make the transition to lower rates of economic growth, which will nevertheless be of higher quality and more resistant to shocks, which is very important considering the uncertainties of current global economic developments.

The above mentioned characteristics of economic development are reflected in the development of different sectors of the economy, as well as directions of the enacted macroeconomic policy.

THE REAL SECTOR

In the pre-crisis period of 2003-2008, an average annual economic growth of 12 percent with the participation of all the main sectors of economy was recorded in Armenia, but the main contribution to the GDP was made by non-export sectors of the economy[6] at an annual average of 8.3 percent. As a result, in 2003-2008, the share of non-export sectors of the economy significantly increased in the structure of the GDP -rising from around 47 percent of

[5]For example, the team drafting the IMF published World Economic Outlook report changed economic growth/decline indicators for the European Union four times in the period of December 2008 to June 2009. [6]Non-export sectors are services and construction sectors.

the GDP to 59 percent. However, during the crisis and the following years, the structure of economy was adjusted and the share of export sectors of the economy increased. In 2009, an unprecedented high rate of economic decline was recorded in Armenia at 14.1 percent, and later in 2010-2013 growth rates were recorded in the economy at an average of 4.4 percent, which was a modest, but qualitatively different growth compared to the pre-crisis era and was characterized by the relatively higher diversification of structure of economy.

The share of the construction sector in the GDP increased and reached 25.3 percent in 2008, with an accelerated increase of the share in GDP (on average 26 percent in 2003-2008). The unprecedented growth of construction in the pre-crisis period was mainly due to private investment, especially the increase in the volume of housing construction. The reason behind the construction boom was monetary transfers from abroad and, in parallel, the higher rates of increase in savings of the population compared to previous years[7]. Naturally, because of the significant decline in monetary remittances in 2009, the construction sector recorded a serious drop of 41.6 percent. After the crisis, the construction sector did not recover its former high levels and as of 2013 continued to decline. Thus, during 2010-2013 construction sector declined on average by 4.2 percent annually. As a result, the share of construction in GDP in 2013 was 10.3 percent. But characteristically, after the crisis, despite the decline in private housing construction, the share of industrial construction aimed at the real sector improved and recorded a growing trend.

The share of services in the GDP in 2008 amounted to 33.7 percent because of the high level of demand for services in the preceding five years, which, in its turn, was the result of the high rate of growth of incomes. In the pre-crisis period (2003-2008), the average growth rate of the sector amounted to 12.2 percent, which was mainly the result of growth in non-export subsectors – trade, transport and communication, as well as the financial mediation sector. The decline in services during the crisis was relatively modest at 3.3 percent and was mainly impacted by trade, transport and communications subsectors. In 2010-2013, services increased on average by 5.1 percent, serving as one of the engines for GDP. In 2010-2013 as well, the growth in services was based on the above-mentioned subsectors, but compared to the pre-crisis period, the role of trade declined and the contribution of services related to export in the total growth of the services sector increased to some extent.

The industrial sector had the smallest share in the GDP in 2008 (the average growth in 20032008 amounted to 3.8 percent), which was the result of a number of factors. First, during the economic upturn in 2006, the industrial sector had a 2.5 percent decline, the main cause of which was the 11 percent decline in the production volumes of electricity, gas, water and steam, as well as the decline in the production volumes of processing industry subsectors, in particular chemical production, diamond processing and tobacco production. In addition, the growth of the industrial sector throughout the mentioned period was stifled due to the unfavorable export price environment. During the crisis, the industrial sector had a 6.9 percent decline, mainly as a result of the reduced demand in the global and domestic markets and the decline in foodstuff and construction material productions. After the crisis, growth in foodstuff and beverages production, as well as mining and metallurgy, contributed to the industrial growth, which was impacted by the anti-crisis policy implemented by the government, creation of a relatively favorable price environment for exports (currency exchange rate and international prices of raw materials), and the global economic recovery. Characteristically, the

[7] The high growth rates of monetary remittances in the mentioned period resulted in the manifestation of the "Dutch disease". As a result of the continuous growth of remittances, the real effective exchange rate appreciated and reduced export competitiveness. As a result, the profitability of non-export sectors -construction and services, increased, and investments were channeled to those sectors.

share of industry in GDP in 2011 amounted to 17.1 percent, compared to the 14.2 percent planned by the Sustainable Development Program for that year, whereas in 2013 it reached 17.4 percent.

The share of agriculture in the GDP in 2008 was small and exceeded only the share of industry. In the preceding period, the growth of the sector (on average 7.4 percent in 2003-2008) was the result of higher intensity in the sector and natural climatic conditions. During the crisis, agriculture was the only sector recording a growth rate (6 percent). However, 2010 was a turnaround year for agriculture because of the unfavorable natural climatic conditions, as a result of which the sector recorded a decline of 16 percent, mainly because of the decline in the crops farming subsector. In 2011, the sector began to recover as a result of favorable natural climatic conditions in the number of programs implemented by the government[8] and made the highest contribution to the economic growth. The sector continued to grow in 20122013, and the value added of the sector increased on average by 8.8 percent annually with respect to the preceding year. The share of agriculture in GDP in 2011 amounted to 20.3 percent, compared to the 14.2 percent planned by the Sustainable Development Program.

Under the above-mentioned pre-crisis developments, the accelerated growth of the construction sector and the high initial share of the services sector in the GDP had resulted in reduced shares of the industrial and agricultural sectors in GDP. After the crisis, the structure of economy changed. The construction sector, which was the main engine of economic growth in the preceding period, shrunk and state continues to shrink as a percentage of GDP. As a result, in 2010-2013, the contribution of sectors with better perspectives and export potential to the GDP increased, and the share of construction declined by 15 percentage points compared to the level in 2008 and amounted to 10.3 percent.

As a result of the high rates of economic growth and large volumes of remittances received from abroad, changes had taken place in the ratio of consumption and savings in the pre-crisis period, national savings were increasing, the major part of which, basically bypassing the financial sector, became investments. In those conditions, the volumes of especially private investments were increasing, including investments in the housing construction sector. As a result, the share of investments and national savings in the GDP increased in 2008 amounting to 41 percent and 32 percent respectively. During the crisis, the share of investments in the GDP declined sharply mainly because of the decline in the volume of private monetary remittances, and national savings declined even to a larger extent. In 2010-2013, investments continued to shrink parallel to the decline in the volumes of housing construction. National savings have also declined compared to the pre-crisis period, but certain improvement is noticed since 2011.

As a result of the mentioned economic development trends, the per capita GDP in US dollars in 2008 amounted to 3606 US dollars, compared to 740 US dollars in 2002. But it declined sharply in 2009 and started to recover gradually in the post-crisis period – 3,447 US dollars in 2013.

[8] In 2010-2011, the government initiated a number of measures – the subsidizing of interest rates on credits, ensuring the market chain for agricultural products, seed production for wheat and barley, development of organic agriculture, development of local bio-fertilizers, refurbishment of agricultural machinery.

PRICES

Consumer price increase (12 months) in 2008-2013, amounted to an average annual of 5.8 percent, compared to the planned annual 4 (+/-1.5) percent. Price increase was mainly result of the global financial and economic crisis and the rapid changes of natural climatic conditions impacting the agricultural sector, as well as due tariff increase for energy resources. In 2008, the main reason for deviation from the forecasts of price rises was the price increases of food, including cereals and vegetable and animal fat, as well as fuel, especially in the first nine months, while in 2009, despite the price drops recorded in the first nine months, price rises were the result of higher prices of food and non-food goods in the international markets because of the more active global economy at the end of the year and the impact of the implemented expansive monetary-credit and tax-budgetary policies. And the consequences of these developments continued also in 2010.

Characteristically, the environment of price rises further worsened in 2010, because of the reduced demand for agricultural products and higher tariffs for certain utility services. As a result, only 7.5 percentage points of the 9.4 percent price increase (12 months) in 2010 was due to food price rises, where around five percentage points of price rise was recorded due to higher prices of domestic agricultural products and more than two percentage points of price rise was recorded due to higher prices of imported food products.

Nonetheless, in 2011, especially at the end of the year, the price rise environment became softer, as a result of which the price rise for the 12 months of the year was within the target value. Contributing factors were the reduced international prices of basic raw material and food products due to slower global economic growth and deepening of debt problems in the Eurozone, stricter monetary-credit conditions introduced at the beginning of the implemented year and the preventive tax-budgetary policy, as well as larger supply of agricultural products. 2012 was favorable in terms of inflationary developments as 12 months' inflation was around the midpoint of the target and its corridor's lower bound – 3.2 percent. In 2013 increase in energy tariffs brought it inflationary pressure in the first half of the year which was mitigated in the second half also due to mild contractionary macroeconomic environment and inflation was close to its target's upper bound -5.6 percent.

EXTERNAL SECTOR DEVELOPMENTS

In 2008-2009, developments of the export sector of the economy were predominantly impacted by the decline in global demand for specialty nonfood products resulting from the financial and economic crisis, rapid worsening of Armenia's trade conditions and the reduction of foreign currency inflows into the country mainly due to lower level of remittances.

At the same time, the relatively lower rates of actual consumption did not result in significant reductions in the volume of imports, which together with the decline in the volume of private remittances, has resulted in a sharp increase in the current account deficit. The current account deficit in 2007 amounted to 6.7 percent of the GDP, while in 2008 it increased sharply up to 11.8 percent -constituting 1,382 million US dollars. At the same time, in 2008, the inflow of capital and funds somewhat increased amounting to a total of 1,147 million US dollars. As a result, there was a deficit of payment balance in 2008, which resulted in reduced net external assets of the Central Bank.

Despite certain improvement of the trade balance, because of the sharp decline of GDP, the deficit of current account as a share of GDP further worsened in 2009 amounting to 16.2

percent of the GDP. Nonetheless, due to the recovery of the global economy, formation of optimistic expectations and implementation of the package of anti-crisis measures by the government, the current account began to improve in 2010, amounting to 14.8 percent of the GDP.

The improvement trends of the current account continued in the following years, coming down to 9.1 percent of GDP in 2013. The share of export increased from 15.1 percent in 2008 to 25.1 percent in 2013, while if mining and non-precious metals production and precious stones exports are excluded, the share of export amounted to 18.6 percent of the GDP (compared to 9.1 percent in 2008).

PUBLIC FINANCE

2008 was unprecedented with regard to a collection of tax revenues and tax administration – the revenue/GDP ratio of the consolidated budget increased by 1.7 percentage points amounting to 20.7 percent. But already 2009, as a result of further deepening of the consequences of the crisis, the drop in GDP reduced the volume of the internal resource base of the state and public expenditures were threatened.

In conditions of lower rates of tax collection, the government applied for external assistance in order to prevent a sharp decline in expenditures. Due to funds received from international structures and the Russian Federation, social expenditures were made to the full extent, avoiding a sharper decline in GDP and significant worsening of social conditions, as well as a considerable increase in the level of unemployment. A significant portion of the received funds were channeled to the most important sectors of the economy and development of infrastructures, partially through sub-loans. As a result, despite the reduced ratio of taxes/GDP of the consolidated budget in 2009 down to 20.5 percent, the expenditures/GDP ratio increased by seven percentage points amounting to around 30.2 percent.

Naturally, indicators for the deficit and external debt also rose. The level of deficit/GDP in 2009 constituted 7.5 percent, which was in unprecedented indicator in Armenia's history. Overcoming the further deepening of the consequences of the financial crisis, in conditions of the recovery of the economic growth rates in 2012-2013, the government made the transition to the exit strategy, as a result of which indicator for deficit shrunk considerably amounting to only 2.8 percent of the

GDP in 2011. Due to efficient fiscal policy decline of the deficit continue also in 2012-2013 and it reached to 1.6 percent of GDP in 2013. In 2008-2011, on average, regardless of the consequences of the crisis, as a result of improved tax administration, budget revenues of the consolidated budget as a share of GDP were higher compared to the actual level in 2007 as well as the planned levels for 2008-2011. Improvement of tax administration continued also in 2012-2013 contributing to high rates of tax collection.

In particular, the average ratio of actual tax revenues/GDP in 2008-2011 was 1.8 percentage points higher than the same indicator for 2007. Naturally, the average expenditures/GDP ratio for the mentioned period was significantly higher than planned level at 22.1 percent and amounted to 27.3 percent. As in previous years, in 2012-2013 also the major part of budget revenues came from tax revenues. During the last two years tax revenues to GDP ratio improved by 2.9 percentage points reaching 24.0 percent in 2013, while public expenditures to GDP increased by 0.6 percentage points with respect to 2011 constituting 27.4 percent in 2013.

The increased share of social expenditures, which was particularly significant in 2009, can be noted as one of the main changes to the expenditure structure. In the structure of

expenditures share of expenses on commodities and services has increased. At the same time it is worth to note that share of public capital investments decreased. In particular increased volumes of external public debt were comparable to the capital investments made during these years.

Public debt. As already mentioned, the external public debt of Armenia significantly increased during the crisis and post-crisis years, amounting to 35.7 percent of the GDP in 2009 and 34.7 percent and 37.5 percent in 2010 and 2013 respectively, but, due to external assistance, it became possible to avoid shocks in the financial system, as well as create conditions for restoring economic growth rates.

PROJECTIONS OF 2014-2025 MACROECONOMIC FRAMEWORK

For the forecasting of the macroeconomic framework of the program, the directions and objectives of reform programs of the government, including pension reforms, as well as the main priorities for enhancing the competitiveness of the country -competitiveness of the economy, capacity building for human capital and economic institutions, were taken into account. The experience of the crisis revealed that the main precondition for sustainable development of the economy is the effective structure of the economy based on the development of export-oriented sectors.

At the same time, program forecasts have taken into account macroeconomic developments for 2013 and other existing programs, while macroeconomic forecast indicators for 2014-2017 contained in the midterm planning documents and other target indicators have been approximated. As a result, the approaches to the forecasts presented in the program are specifically different from the forecasts made in previous long-term programs. The main difference is that the macroeconomic framework presented in the program is somewhat more optimistic, since the main macroeconomic indicators are brought closer to target indicators, thus requiring more effort from the state governance system to achieve the target indicators, which will result in more accelerated development in income generation and poverty eradication.

The main precondition for expanding the possibilities for poverty eradication and income redistribution will still be the long-term sustainable economic growth. Increase in the number of jobs, production of goods corresponding to modern international competition requirements and training of specialists will, on the one hand, result in higher incomes from employment, and on the other hand, will contribute to a larger basis for state budget revenues and will expand the possibilities of the policy for redistribution of incomes implemented by the state.

Considering the developments of the Armenian economy in the previous years, the behavior of factors impacting the development, as well as the progress of reforms for strengthening the institutional basis of the economy, Armenian economy has recovered and in 2013 has surpassed the pre-crisis period level. For the forthcoming 12 years it is forecasted that the economy will continue to develop at sustainable rates, ensuring around 5.5 -6.5 percent of annual growth rate.

From 1994 up to the crisis, the Armenian economy grew continuously, on average at almost 9 percent annual growth rate. And in 2003-2008, economic growth accelerated and amounted to an annual average of 12.0 percent. Although the economy declined as a result of the crisis, but as a result of the policy for promoting exports, the enactment of which started in 20102011, in the long run, it will be characterized by quite high and export-oriented economic indicators. At the same time, during the program period nominal average annual GDP growth

in US dollars will be around 9 percent, as a result of which GDP per capita will triple in 2025 compared to the level in 2013 and will constitute about 9,500 US dollars.

During the crisis period significantly expansive tax-budgetary policies were implemented in all countries in crisis, including Armenia, the result was a substantial increase in Armenia's foreign debt, as a result of which ensuring the necessary conditions for debt stability has become especially important for sustainable development of the economy. Based on the above-mentioned, international organizations and governmental bodies in Armenia attached importance to the necessity of resolving the issue and medium-term and long-term analyses of debt sustainability were conducted. Concluding the assessments of all the analyses, it can be stated that baseline scenarios for all the models used for analysis did not identify any serious threats, although models signaled the need for enacting a policy for reducing debt in the coming years. Nonetheless, shock tests conducted under the baseline scenario reveals that situation worsens but does not result in instability, and the stability of public debt is more sensitive to national currency depreciation and lower GDP growth rates. The long term low level of GDP growth rate is the main factor having a negative impact on fiscal stability. Consequently, the first priority of macroeconomic stability is to ensure high rates of economic growth, which, in its turn, will prevent the depreciation of national currency, since GDP growth assumes larger the amount also with regard to the national currency, which can counteract the depreciation pressures. Another conclusion of the analyses is also important, according to which the level of debt stabilizes more rapidly if the growth of tax revenues is faster than the growth of GDP, considering the fact that Armenia has such a possibility, since the assessed potential level of tax revenues is for from the level of actually collected taxes. The mentioned analyses have also served as the basis for forecasts of the macroeconomic environment, as a result of which, under the forecast of macroeconomic developments at the basis of the program and the planned directions of tax-budgetary policy, risks related to repayment of debt will continue to be at a low level in the long run. Characteristically, after the stabilization of the primary deficit of the budget in the medium-term, significant adjustments for deficit reduction in the long term would not be necessary for maintaining the low level of risks related to repayment of debts. This means that in case of possible economic instability, the tax-budgetary policy will have some flexibility from the viewpoint of promoting economic growth if necessary. However, for the near future years, the tax-budgetary policy is limited with regard to the promotion of economic growth and thus the monetary-credit policy should be more flexible, maintaining, at the same time, a high level of coordination with the tax-budgetary policy.

The following developments are forecasted with regard to the main macroeconomic indicators:

1) **The real sector.** In the planned period of 2014-2025, the GDP will have a growing trend, the rate of which will exceed the average rate of the period 2012-2011 and will be in the range of 5.5-6.5 percent. These developments will take place as a result of the following planned changes to the existing sectoral structure of the GDP. The export sector in the structure of the GDP will have the leading role and will be the engine of economic growth, mainly thanks to the industrial sector, as well as the services sector, and will serve as the sector promoting economic activity. Incentives of economic growth will gradually move to sectors operating based on expanded capital and scientific potential. In other words, high productivity sectors will gradually take the lead[9].

[9] The experience of development of countries in the global economy reveals that countries' economies undergo a number of transformations in their development process. The first one is the development of production of import substitutes. The subsequent one is the growth of exports at the expense of labor-intensive sectors (competitively

2) **Consumer prices.** Considering the recent developments in the global market, some slowdown of global economy development rates, as well as the instability of the geopolitical situation, it is forecasted that the price rises environment will be formed under various economic factors which will result in a possible continuation of price rises fluctuations. At the same time, it is generally forecasted that the impact of those factors on price rises will be balanced. Developments of the domestic economy, in conditions of certain decline in consumption growth and accelerated increase in savings, will also have a balanced impact on the price rise environment. After anticipated price level increase in 2013 due to gas price growth, the forecasted price rise will be within the target value at around 4 percent in 2014-2015. The long-term effective management of price rises will be ensured by continuing to follow the principle of price rise targeting adopted by Central Bank, which has proven to be effective also in the period of financial and economic crisis, when it was necessary to implement a flexible monetary-credit policy. The Customs Union membership's initiated process will contribute to more predictable price levels, as it will become possible to avoid sharp changes in the prices of energy resources. Within the process of stabilization of global economic conditions and the transition of the Armenian economy from low value added to high value added production (more expensive goods), which will be achieved through the development of the industrial sector, it is planned to decrease the difference between the value of the GDP deflator and the CPI in the long run.

3) **Structure of GDP by expenditure components.**

The share of investments will be stabilized in the upcoming 12 years at the level of 26-27 percent of GDP. At the same time, it is expected that in the forecast period, the trend which began after the crisis will be prevalent in the investment structure – capital non-industrial construction (especially dwellings and buildings) will decline, reflecting the GDP sectoral developments mentioned above. In the mentioned situation, investments as a share of GDP will exceed the level recorded in post-crisis years, and the level of industrial investments will be adequate for the development of other sectors of the economy. This means that investments as a share of GDP, amounting on average to 24.1 percent in 2010-2012, will increase in the long run reaching on average 26.6 percent and will contribute to more effective and industrial investments.

4) **Monetary sector.**

Forecasts of the monetary sector indicators have been made based on the assumption that the medium-term price rise should remain within the range of the target value of 4 (+/-1.5) percent, as well as the need for meeting the demand for money that would be necessary based on the forecast of external and domestic economic environment. In these conditions, a further increase in the level of financial mediation has been planned, although in slower rates, which, however, in conditions of the accelerated growth as a share of GDP, will result in a decline in the velocity of money circulation and higher level of monetization of the economy. It is expected that the level of dollarization of the economy will decline down to its pre-crisis level. It is also planned to further expand the diversity of monetary tools and the volume of the financial market, while transition to funded pension system and measures aimed at increase of corporate governance quality will contribute to that goal. Under these trends, savings in Armenian drams will have more accelerated growth compared to savings in foreign currency. On the other hand, the

lower wages), then it is the transition from labor-intensive sectors to capital-intensive sectors, and the last phase of the transformation of the economy is the transition from capital-intensive sectors to high-technology or so-called knowledge-based sectors. The mentioned scenario was used for macroeconomic forecasts at the basis of the ADS, i.e. transition from labor-intensive sectors to capital-intensive and then knowledge-based economy.

improved quality of banking services parallel to the reduction of the gray sector of the economy, the increase of demand for money would be mainly in other forms than cash money. As a result, the share of cash in money supply would gradually decrease in the favor of non-cash money, amounting to around 17 percent in 2025. At the same time, the level of monetization of the economy reaches to 45.5 percent in 2025.

5) **External sector.**

The external sector developments will be impacted mainly by domestic economy development, continuation of the qualitative changes to the structure of economy, as well as the process of integration of the Armenian economy into regional cooperation formats and international economy in general. In particular, these developments will be crucially conditioned upon processes associated with Armenia's membership in the Customs Union with Russia, Belarus and Kazakhstan. Membership in this Customs Union will provide to local producers easier access to a consumers' market with more than 170 mln population. Given that quality criteria on this product and services market being more achievable for the local producers, already in short term in a number of markets Armenian products will gain its competitive and constant position. ON the other hand, membership in the Customs Union will enable cheaper import of energy resources, which will boost competitive supply from local market. In particular it is expected that integration process will be quite smooth and fast given common historical, language, cultural and behavioral background of Armenia and the countries involved in the Union. In the mid and long term perspective Armenia will have a real possibility to carry out expanded external economic activities.

On the one hand possibility of enjoying "GSP+" privileged trade regime granted by European Union, and on the other hand advantages of Customs Union membership will create important preconditions for becoming a specific crossroad for EU-Customs Union economic relations and trade flows. Within this context, it is forecasted that export will grow relatively faster compared to import, in particular due to significant increase in the volumes of export-oriented industrial production. In these conditions, the increased demand for imported items will basically coincide with GDP growth rates. Under the mentioned development, in the coming years, the negative balance of goods and services as a share of GDP will gradually decrease amounting to around 4.5 percent in 2025 compared to 24.8 percent recorded in 2012, and the reflect the impact of the high rate of growth of the more productive sectors of the economy, which will also result in larger exports of competitive goods and services. It is forecasted that the ratio of current account deficit/GDP will have almost the same behavior. The current account will gradually improve up to 2025 and by the end of planning period will be around

3.8 percent of GDP. These developments will be in line with the formation of higher levels of savings compared to investments, resulting from accelerated growth of incomes at the disposal of the population, and lower levels of foreign debt as a percentage of GDP.

6) **Fiscal sector indicators.**

Long-term forecasts for fiscal indicators were done based on the fact that fiscal policy should be anti-cyclic, i.e. when the economic growth slows down it should be growth promoting and vice versa. However, developments oblige (explanation of this obligation is presented in box 1) to implement a fiscal policy for debt stabilization in the medium term, which limits economy expanding impact of fiscal policy . Given these limitations the deficit will be decreased in the midterm and will fluctuate around and 2.0 percent of GDP, as a result of which it would become possible to smoothly decrease the indicator for public debt as a share of GDP, and tax revenues as a share of GDP will continually so that the debt can be stabilized more quickly. As for the long-term, anti-cyclical fiscal policy will be possible, under the conditions of tax revenues growth of 0.3-0.4 percentage points of GDP annually. In the programming period the level of public capital expenditures will be from 1.5 to 2.5 percentage points higher than the levels of deficit, which will create sustainable basis for long-term economic growth.

Table 1. ADS macroeconomic framework: projection of main indicators

Indicators	2011	2012	2013	2014	2017	2021	2025
	Actual	Actual	Prelim.			Projections	
(in percent of GDP, unless otherwise indicated)							
National income and prices							
Real GDP, year-on-year % change	4.7	7.2	3.5	5.5	6.1	6.4	6.5
Gross Domestic Product, million US dollars	10,142	9,950	10,416	10,928	12,759	19,141	28,753
Gross Domestic Product, billion drams	3,778	3,998	4,267	4,700	6,232	9,350	14,045
Per capita GDP, US dollars	3,358	3,290	3,447	3,589	4,171	6,252	9,441
GDP deflator, year-on-year % change	4.3%	-1.2%	3.2%	4.4%	4.0%	4.0%	4.0%
Investments and savings							
Investments	27.9	23.8	20.8	24.5	26.7	27.2	26.9
General government	5.4	4.0	3.6	3.5	3.1	4.0	4.2
Other	22.5	19.8	17.2	21.0	23.6	23.2	22.7

National savings	16.0	12.2	10.5		16.1	21.5	21.3	23.2
General government	1.2	0.9	0.6		1.0	1.3	2.2	2.9
Other	14.8	11.3	9.9		15.1	20.2	19.1	20.3
Fiscal sector								
Consolidated budget								
Total revenues and grants	24.5	24.8	25.8%		24.9%	25.0%	26.5%	27.9%
of which: Tax revenues	21.1	22.5	24.0		23.8%	24.3%	25.9%	27.4%
Grants	1.6	0.5	0.3		0.4%	0.3%	0.2%	0.1%
Total expenditures	27.3	26.3	27.4%		27.4%	26.8%	28.2%	29.3%
Current expenditure	22.5	22.8	27.4%		27.4%	23.7%	24.2%	25.1%
Capital Expenditure	4.8	3.6	24.2%		23.9%	3.1%	4.0%	4.2%
Overall balance	-2.8	-1.5	-1.6%		-2.5%	-1.8%	-1.8%	-1.3%
Public debt								
Domestic debt	5.8	6.4	6.6		6.3	7.4	10.8	12.7
External debt	36.4	37.7	37.5		36.6	34.4	24.5	18.7
Total debt	42.2	44.1	44.1		42.9	41.8	35.3	31.4
External sector								
Exports	23.7	24.5	25.1		26.3	31.7	33.0	34.7
Imports	47.3	49.3	49.1		47.7	46.8	42.8	39.2
Current account balance	-10.9	-11.2	-9.1		-8.3	-5.2	-5.9	-3.8

89. Forecasts of the development of economic sector were made with consideration for certain sectoral changes to the economy. In 2014-2025, the increase in the share of export sectors – industry, as well as agriculture, which began after the crisis, will continue. Before the crisis, economic growth was led by construction and services sectors, where the increase in supply was mainly a reflection of that demand formed in the economy, while the increase in productivity of the nation sectors is limited in the long run[10]. Instead of that, export sectors of the economy are forced to work with higher productivity in order to be competitive, and consequently are more promising from the viewpoint of ensuring long-term economic growth.

[10]Another proof is the assessments received from regression analysis, according to which construction and services sectors are largely dependent on the volumes of remittances from abroad.

In 2014-2025, the mentioned trends will change to some extent, as a result of a number of structural factors. First, capital investments in industry made in previous years will begin to gradually pay back through increasing productivity, as a result of which the development of the economy and industry in particular, as well as other capital intensive sectors, will accelerate. At the same time, due to increased demand for services provided to the industry and more complicated structure of the economy as it develops, the high rates of increase in added value of services will continue. On the other hand, the growth of industrial sectors of the economy will be followed by higher wages, which will result in the return of Armenian citizens who have left for seasonal work abroad, which in its turn will impact the volume of remittances from abroad. In the light of the above mentioned the following developments are expected:

In 2014-2025, the average growth rate of value added created in industry will exceed the GDP growth rate being at a rate of about 8 percent per year. As a result, in the mentioned period, the share of the added value of the sector in the GDP will stabilize at an average of around 1920 percent. These trends will be manifested in investments made in the sector, and consequently also the acceleration of growth rates of productivity.

Considering the specific nature of agriculture, high rates of growth of the agricultural sector are not expected in the entire forecast period, but the productivity of agricultural sector, as well as the volumes of export, will increase. The average indicator for changes to productivity will be around three times higher than changes to productivity in the pre-crisis period. In 20142025, the added value of the sector will increase by 3.5-4 percent annually.

In 2014-2025, the average annual growth rate of the value added created in the construction sector will be 6.2 percent, and the share of the sector in the GDP will be around 10 percent. Moreover, after the expected decline in 2013, for the first half of the programming period the average growth rate of the sector will be more modest at around 6.0 percent.

In 2014-2025, the added value the services sector will continue to grow at a high rate at around 6-6.5 percent annually, which is somewhat faster than the GDP growth rate. As a result, the share of this sector in the GDP by 2025 will grow by 1.2 percentage points compared to 2013 level reaching 42.3 percent.

The continuation of such high rates of economic growth, naturally, will not have an inertial nature. That will be necessarily also conditioned by the implementation of a number of structural measures for strengthening the institutional basis of the economy, such as improving the business environment, increasing the effectiveness of investment policy, activities contributing to higher productivity and export sectors and consequently increased competitiveness, as well as development of institutions for increasing educational and scientific potential. Developments planned by the macroeconomic framework of the strategy, by main sectors of economy, are presented in Table 2.

7. FORECASTING RISKS

96. Since forecasting covers the entire economy, the risks also reflect the entire spectrum of economic risks correspondingly. Internal risks can be tentatively divided into two groups. The first group includes risks associated with implementation of reforms, such as problems associated with certain public policy in ensuring competitiveness, reforming business environment and other areas. The second group encompasses undesirable structural reforms in economy (e.g. deepening revenue inequalities, worsening quality of bank credit portfolio, etc.).

Table 2. Development of economy by sector: projections of main indicators

Indicators	2011	2012	2013	2014	2017	2021	2025
	Actual	Actual	Prelim.			Forecast	
GDP by sector, billion drams							
Industry	647.8	687.5	741.6	829.0	1,160.7	1,860.7	2,979.3
Agriculture	767.9	764.0	818.8	889.2	1,116.7	1,524.7	2,046.8
Construction	491.1	489.0	438.5	485.4	645.4	957.7	1,441.3
Services	1,458.9	1,599.0	1,761.7	1,941.3	2,582.1	3,902.1	5,946.1
Net indirect taxes	412.3	458.1	506.3	555.2	727.2	1,104.7	1,631.6
Gross domestic product	3,777.9	3,997.6	4,266.8	4,700.1	6,232.2	9,349.9	14,045.1
Structure of GDP by sector, percent of total							
Industry	17.1	17.2	17.4	17.6	18.6	19.9	21.2
Agriculture	20.3	19.1	19.2	18.9	17.9	16.3	14.6
Construction	13.0	12.2	10.3	10.3	10.4	10.2	10.3
Services	38.6	40.0	41.3	41.3	41.4	41.7	42.3
Net indirect taxes	10.9	11.5	11.9	11.8	11.7	11.8	11.6
Gross domestic product	100	100	100	100	100	100	100
Growth rates by sector, year-on-year percent change							
Industry	13.6	7.0	4.9	6.9	8.2	8.1	8.2
Agriculture	14.0	9.5	8.1	4.0	4.0	3.8	3.5
Construction	-12.2	3.3	-11.2	6.0	6.0	6.5	6.5
Services	4.7	6.5	5.3	5.6	6.3	6.8	6.8
Net indirect taxes	3.8	9.9	2.9	5.0	5.5	6.0	6.0
Gross domestic product	4.7	7.2	3.5	5.5	6.1	6.4	6.5

As regards the mentioned risks, it is critical to identify specific risks for each sphere and/or program, as well as qualitative assessment of the likelihood of their impact and manifestation and definition of the risk management mechanism.

As for the internal environment, there is also a non-human factor related risk, i.e. the risk of unfavorable natural and climate conditions, which if persists, will have a negative impact on the planned agriculture growth.

A number of nature and technology driven risks are specific to RA territory and realization of those will disrupt the normal economic development process putting the country into a crisis.

The risks related to forecasts are associated with external economic factors of not less importance. It must be noted that Armenia, as a small country with an open economy, reacts rapidly to economic developments in partner countries. As a result, the main risks of forecast are largely dependent on macroeconomic changes in the global economy. At the same time, it is important to take into account that the main risks are assessed for the medium-term and long-term assessment is not available.

Another group of external risks is associated with the membership of Armenia in Customs Union with Russia, Belarus and Kazakhstan and Armenia's decision not to sign Association Agreement with EU and refuse participation in the Deep and Comprehensive free trade area. Decrease in investment attractiveness for European investors, possible need to revise relations with WTO other parties, as well as possible difficulties associated with the export to EU market (in particular for mining products, which have small share in country's overall GDP but have large portfolio in export structure) may cause negative expectations among the local producers in the short and mid term perspective and urge them to change strategic development plans. In particular, as a result of diminishing external financing (due to decrease in budget assistance

and investment projects by EU) internal risks may emerge with respect to finalization of already initiated and/or planned reform projects.

The global economy continues to develop under significant uncertainties, which, in case of possible emerging risks, forces us to assess the possible deviations from forecasts at the basis of the program and the necessary steps for neutralizing those risks. In this regard, the main influences on the Armenian economy might emerge from adverse developments in the economies of Customs Union member states or further deepening of the debt crisis in the European Union. This situation can directly or indirectly reflect on the economic growth, price rise environment, currency exchange rates and other macroeconomic indicators.

It should be taken into account that even in the worst-case scenario of the deepening of the European Union crisis; the global economy will not be impacted as severely as during the crisis of 2008-2009. But the possible new crisis can be manifested in a longer period of time, but to a lesser amplitude, which will allow for implementing more flexible anti-crisis measures.

Customs Union member and Armenia's main economic partner – Russia's economy is particularly sensitive to volatility of prices on international energy resources markets. Decrease growth rate trend of Russia's economy in 2013 may have its adverse effect on Armenia's economy as well.

At the same time, USA and Japan continue facing strong fiscal policy stability problems, which are expressed in form of fiscal adjustment timing uncertainty. This may lead to negative expectations among investors adversely impacting the economic growth rates in those countries. As a result, demand for goods exported from Armenia may diminish and the prices for metals may go down.

RISK IMPACT DIRECTIONS

Though economic activity level worldwide has increased in the second half of 2013, the risks which might result in slower global economy growth still persist and can directly or indirectly impact the Armenian economy. Eurozone has begun to grow after a period of decline, but debt issues in some of European countries still persist and can cause decline in economic growth in European countries, which can be transferred to Armenia's economy in the ways considered right below.

Direct impacts will be the result of lower rates of export to bilateral trade partners in the Customs Union (mainly Russia) and European Union (mainly the Eurozone), as well as reduced volumes of capital investments from them. The share of the European Union in Armenia's trade turnover 2013 amounted to 27.8 percent, whereas Russia's share was around 24.3 percent. While the share of EU and Russia in total foreign investments for the same year was around 51.2 percent. Apart from that share of Russia in the net inflow of non-commercial remittances amounted to 92.3 percent in 2013. Thus, delay of common solution to structural problems in Eurozone and deepening of Russia's stagnation trends will impact the economic activity in Armenia through the mentioned channels.

The indirect impacts can be due to risk of economic activity decline in developed countries conditioned upon low inflation levels in those countries (mainly Eurozone) and crisis in the European Union will spread specially to countries with huge volumes of trade with the European Union, including Russia, where the share of trade turnover with the European Union in 2011 amounted to around 48 percent. On the other hand, slower rates of economic growth in Eurozone to higher extent and in Russia in lesser extent can have adverse impact on the

overall global demand. If in these conditions, the US also implements a more preventive tax-budgetary policy, then the decline in the global demand will become more substantial. These developments will also impact the demand for mainly nonfood goods in international market, and consequently their international prices will drop. These developments will result in the worsening of trade conditions for Armenia and the decline of exports in dollar terms, which will slow down the economic growth rate. Also due to mentioned factors investment prospects will decline and can cause decrease of foreign investments in Armenia.

As a result, developments related to global risks impacting Armenia directly or indirectly can slow down the rates of economic growth, as well as depreciate the Armenian dram.

RISK MANAGEMENT

Formalisation of necessary preventive measures and their consistent implementation is important for the management of catastrophic events, including technology driven and natural disasters.

The risks described above can introduce changes to the forecasts at the basis of the macrocosmic scenario of the program, which can be reflected on the level of revenue, and the latter will have an impact on the rate of improvements related to the level of poverty. Consequently, it is important that all steps focus on maintaining economic growth, since the slowing of economic growth will firstly, threaten the objectives of the program, secondly, will disrupt fiscal stability (paragraph 87) and thirdly, declaration of economy growth will at the same time to neutralize the risk of foreign currency appreciation. Thus, ensuring the program forecasted level of economic growth is a priority for neutralizing risks, i.e. tax-budgetary and monetary-credit policies should aim to promote economic growth. In this regard:

1) First, the country should quickly diagnose the threats and be prepared for a non-severe but medium-term European economic crisis. With respect to this problem, the country already has some experience with regard to the application of mechanisms and tools. However, the lessons of the previous crisis revealed that capacities for quick diagnosis and response are not available.

2) Second, the tax-budgetary policy should have possible alternative directions for quick replenishment of possible additional financial demand, and if necessary also with a surplus, but, at the same time, maintaining the fiscal stability.

3) Third, the monetary-credit policies should be flexible so that it can relax monetary-credit conditions one step ahead of the emerging signs of the risks, but, at the same time, maintaining the fiscal stability.

4) Fourth, recent developments in transition countries may cause risk of financial flows changes and this must be permanently under the focus.

112. It is also important to note that, during the financial and economic crisis in 2008-2009, the tax-budgetary possibilities were adequate for implementing an expansive economic policy, but the possibilities of tax-budgetary tools for counteracting the upcoming crises are quite limited (see paragraph 87), and thus, in order to expand the economy, priority should be given to the use of tax-credit tools.

ADS ECONOMIC DEVELOPMENT STRATEGY

ECONOMIC DEVELOPMENT FRAMEWORK POLICIES

The ADS economic policy geared at creation of quality jobs is a mixture of coordinated use of various framework and direct policies and their respective toolsets.

An important element of framework policy is the macroeconomic environment, which is described in details in Chapter 3. The framework policies used up to now, such as improvement of the quality of business environment and investment climate, promotion of investments and competitiveness, preventing abuse of dominant or monopoly position of economic entities and their effective control, strengthening of financial intermediation, etc. will be maintained in the frames of the current program.

Their main result, in addition to creation of favorable conditions for economic growth, will include increase of the country's international competitiveness as the main aggregate estimate of the framework policies' implementation effectiveness.

8.1. COUNTRY'S INTERNATIONAL COMPETITIVENESS AS AN INTEGRAL INDICATOR OF FRAMEWORK POLICIES

International competitiveness is the country's productivity level, which depends on the institutional level of the country (quality of institutions), productivity factors, as well as policies enacted(The Global Competitiveness Report 2011 – 2012 World Economic Forum). Based on the above-mentioned, enhancing the international competitiveness of the country means increasing the productivity, which depends on the quality of institutions and policies, as well as improvement in productivity factors, and consequently is the main precondition for creating quality modern jobs.

Country's international competitiveness level will be calculated using the benchmarks of annual Global Competitiveness Report published by Global Economic Forum and the methodology for their calculation(For international comparison of benchmarks the last report "The Global Competitiveness Report 2013 – 2014 World Economic Forum 2013"). According to that report, in 2013 Armenia ranked 79 among 148 countries, with overall international competitiveness index value of 4.1 (maximum is 7 and minimum is 1)(According to the two previous reports, Armenia in 2012 ranked 82 among 144 countries and 92nd in 2011 among 142 countries).

A total of 113 benchmark indicators are calculated for all countries characterizing 12 "pillars" of the economy -institutions and their quality, infrastructures, macroeconomic environment, healthcare and basic education, higher education and human resources training, goods market efficiency, labor market efficiency, financial markets development, technological readiness level, market size, business sophistication level, innovation level.

Thus, this system of benchmark indicators almost totally characterizes the economic situation and policy, including also social policy on education and healthcare and can be a very good tool for assessing the results and the quality of the enacted policy in comparison with other countries.

It is envisaged that policy drafted and enacted in programming period and its expected results will enhance the international competitiveness of the country significantly and improve the indicators for all the 12 "pillars". In particular, in 2017 Armenia shall rank 65-70 with an overall international competitiveness index of 4.20-4.25, and in 2025 its rank shall be 50-55 with an overall index value of 4.35-4.40.

BUSINESS ENVIRONMENT AND INVESTMENT CLIMATE

In the program period, the continuous improvement of business environment and investment climate will remain the main priority of the state framework policy to increase the employment, and will be will be aimed at facilitating the establishment of businesses and investments and reducing significantly undue state intervention. From the viewpoint of foreign strategic investment attraction steady growth of investors' protection level is important.

The benchmark indicators of the World Bank "Doing Business" annual reports, both for individual sectors as well as for the overall quality of the business environment, will be used as a toolset for planning and assessing the policy measures undertaken to improve the business environment[11].

Effective protection of investors' interests and further development of corporate governance are important also in the light of introduction of compulsory funded pension scheme in Armenia since 2014. The effectiveness of the system will largely depend upon demand by corporate sector for longterm money. Transparent management system is a necessary condition for existence of such demand, which will enable large companies to attract investments not only from pension funds, but also from other participants of the financial market.

Despite the large number of activities aimed at improvement of business environment during the recent years and reduction and simplification of state regulations, only in the recently published Doing Business 2013 Report, Armenia succeeded in improving its position both in terms of overall business environment quality indicator and with respect to previously problematic sectors' indicators. Similar trend was observed in the last "Doing Business 2013" report. Thus, according to 2014 indicator Armenia occupies the 37th position for the integral ease of doing business indicator (vs. 55th position recorded in 2012). More serious progress was recorded in tax administration (103rd position vs. 153 in 2012) and investment protection (22nd position vs. 97 in 2012).

Further improvement of indicators, particularly of those already enjoying comparatively high ranks, will be conditioned with the enforcement level of already acting laws.

It is worth underlining that the negative dynamics observed for the previous years was not because of the deterioration of business environment in Armenia, but due to faster compared to Armenia reforms of the business environment in a number of developing and developed countries[12].

Taking into account the abovementioned, the main priority of the government in this area will be the stark acceleration of the reforms, particularly for the indicators for which Armenia occupies low ranks (tax and customs administration, contract enforcement). The main target is

[11] Data from the last "Doing Business 2014" (published in 2013) report will be used as the basis for forecasting

performance indicators. [12] According to the methodology, negative movement in the country's position may be observed even if there are reforms implemented. This may happen in particular, when wider reforms were implemented in the countries occupying adjacent positions in the ranking.

that Armenia ranks among 20 leading countries in 2017 and among 15 countries with the most favorable business environment in 2025 (as of 2012).

Regarding the investment climate, the planning and progress assessment of the policies implemented will be based on the benchmark indicators of BEEPS[13] surveys implemented by the World Bank and the European Bank for Reconstruction and Development.

The comparison of the BEEPS-2009 and BEEPS-2005 surveys' results reveals that notwithstanding the change in classifications of the main barriers for the entrepreneurship and the investments have changed[14], according to the enterprises' opinions there has not been recorded an overall improvement in the effectiveness of state governance and regulations from the viewpoint of businesses, despite the obvious progress in some spheres[15].

In the frames of ADS a target indicator of investment environment reforms is Armenia's position among ECA countries, which is defined based on aggregated indicator of investment climate (The aggregate indicator is calculated as the summary of cumulative describing all seven sectors. The latter were calculated as the sum of values of indicators describing these sectors. The indicators' values have been calculated as ECA countries' average and the difference of that indicator related to ECA average). It is expected that in 2017 Armenia will be among the second top 5 countries and in 2025 among the first top 5 (among 26 countries).

The main policy elements for continuous improvement of business environment and investment climate for the upcoming years will be the following ones:

1) significant reduction in direct contacts of businesses and citizens with the state through the introduction of interagency electronic information exchange systems 2) asaone-time measure reduction and simplification of state regulations (by about 50%) relating to businesses and citizens

3) implement inspections system reform, particularly rationalize their number and functions, and pay greater focus on education and training of human resources, introducing contemporary training processes and evaluation standards.

4) complete implementation of regulatory impact assessment, which will allow for avoiding new regulations creating additional burden 5) regular study of the business regulation and investment climate best practices and their introduction in Armenia with consideration for specific local characteristics.

Improvement of the competitive environment plays a critical role in further development of business and investment environment. According to the Global Competitiveness Index Armenia has recorded a positive shift with respect to indicators of intensity of local competition and effectiveness of the anti-monopoly policy. Though recent years saw significant increase of the role and position of the State Commission for the Protection of Economic Competition (SCPEC), nonetheless legislative issues/loops and lack of resources limit effective enforcement of competition policy.

As a rule existence of economic entities with dominant or monopoly position and high rate of concentration hinder the formation and consequent development of competitive

[13] Data from the last BEEPS 2009 report will be used as the basis for forecasting performance indicators.

[14] In particular, the first top three issues in 2005 were tax administration, tax rates and access to financial resources,

while in 2009 the issues are as follows: tax rates, access to financial resources and corruption. Crimes, robberies and

disorderly conduct, which were the last factor by importance in 2005, became fourth in 2009.

[15] In particular tax administration, which was considered the main hindrance to the development of businesses in

2005, ranked seventh in 2009, and certification and issuing of permissions moved from the sixth placed to the 14th.

environment. High concentration rate in some product markets in Armenia has also objective reasons, such as geographical position of RA, closed borders, small economy, high transportation costs that make more efficient larger entities. At the same time there are institutional problems that affect the well functioning of markets for goods and services related to restrictive regulation, distortive state aid, and ineffective enforcement of competition rules and public procurement systems.

134. Effective competition policies and competition protection should not be limited only to the SCPEC activities but should also concern other line ministries and sectoral regulators in order to ensure pro-competition policies in all sectors of the economy. This also requires consistent reforms in addressing problems such as independence of judicial bodies and their capacity building to enable them examine anti-trust cases in line with international practice. It is necessary to improve enforcement of policies in various fields. Widening mechanisms for detecting anti-competitive agreements and regulation of state aid which limits competition will be favorable for the improvement of competition environment in products' and services' markets. In this respect the role of the SCPEC in enabling market competition will continue to remain critical, which makes crucial widening the scope of authorities of the SCPEC and capacity building of its staff. At that, the following measures are singled out to be implemented through relevant legislative changes and revision of the SCPEC functions. Main reforms should include the following:

1) Improve the competition legislation and its enforcement. The RA Law "On preservation of economic competition" and the changes in the normative acts based on this law must be aimed at: a) define unified approach of imposing fines based on the turnover of the economic entity in the previous year and ensure their accordance to international practice, b) improve fines payment mechanisms, c) clarify main provisions of the law, explain nature of anticompetitive agreements and the provisions relating to definition and abuse of dominant position, concentrations, unlawful

competition practices and administrative actions applied to such entities, d) strengthen the investigation powers of the SCPEC (e.g. wider power to conduct unexpected checks -dawn raids).

2) SCPEC needs to move away from focusing on price fluctuations in favor of focusing on actual and potential barriers to entry and market contestability (including during public procurement), given that besides prices, other factors determine effective competition, such as the economic characteristics of the production process, the functioning of the supply chain, and the strategic behavior of firms. As a result, the level and behavior of prices do not necessarily indicate the intensity of competition, and it becomes necessary to look at market behavior.

3) Widen SCPEC's advocacy mandate to prevent possible anticompetitive interventions and regulations by state authorities which do or might limit, prevent or prohibit economic competition or result in unlawful competition practices. It is necessary to promote a better understanding of competition principles vis-à-vis other government bodies, public procurement officials and judges. Expansion of the mandates of the Commission in reviewing all sectoral policies and legal acts from the competition point of view is required and and it is to enable the suspension by the Commission of decisions or orders (already issued or in draft) by other public administration bodies which restrict competition.

4) Strengthen the state aid legal provisions and their enforcement to minimize potential distortive effects on competition.

5) Introduce transparency and access to data to guarantee competitive neutrality between market participants to avoid market distortions.

6) Remove barriers to entry and competition and mainstream competition principles within broader government policies.

The Government will pursue the goal of revealing and eliminating obstacles hampering access to the market for both domestic producers and importers.

In order to assess the improvements of competitive environment two figures from Sixth Pillar of the Global Competition Index were taken as an indicator (goods market efficiency), i.e. the intensity of local competition and effectiveness of anti-monopoly policy. Armenia, being in the group of countries in the transition from first to second (efficiency driven) stage, in spite of serious improvement of position in 2013 with respect to previous year, is still far from desired level. Thus, for the intensity of local competition indicator Armenia occupies 102nd position, while for the efficiency of anti-monopoly policy 97th among the total of 148 (in 2012 for the mentioned indicators Armenia was holding 130th and 116th positions accordingly among a total of 144 countries).

It is expected that implementation of activities geared at improvement of the general framework policies and the competition level will result in the following improvements: in 2017 Armenia's rank in intensity of local competition will range between 4.7-.4.9, which for 2013-2014 will correspond to 80-90 position and in 2025 the country will have an indicator between 5.0 and 5.1 (60-70 position for 2013-2014 ranking). Value of efficiency of antimonopoly policy will show similar improvement.

MONETARY POLICY AND FINANCIAL INTERMEDIATION DEEPENING

The main indicators of monetary policy for 2012, taking into account the GDP decline in 2009-2010, were basically in line and in relative terms (as a percentage of GDP) even exceeded SDP forecasts. The observed indicators suggest that the economy's financial sector, not having significant external obligations, recovered from the crisis more rapidly compared to the real sector.

In particular, the money supply at the end of 2012 amounted to 33.7% of the GDP, compared to 29.6% forecasted by the SDP, whereas the domestic bank loans constituted 39.8% of the GDP, compared to 25.3% forecasted by the SDP.

Interest rate spread (difference of deposit and loan interest rates) has also outperformed SDP forecasts – it was 5.9% by the end of 2012 (SDP forecast – 7.8%), but nonetheless remaining high compared to international standards. Considering the importance of credit resources for job creation, the Government and the Central Bank policy should be targeted at decrease of the intereset rate spread, aiming to reduce it to 3-4% by the end of programming period. The Central Bank in terms of policies has got as a constraint its primary function of controlling level of prices. But it plays an important role in achieving ADS targets, while a number of important policies and reforms, such as new pension system, banking sector supervision, enhancing financial literacy are under the CBA mandate. As a result cooperation between the Government and the Central Bank will have a crucial importance to achieve the targets.

In particular, Central Bank's policy must be directed at developing non-banking institutions

– lending agencies and insurance companies, as well as at promoting further development of the stock market.

When it comes to banking regulation, it should take into account the collusion possibilities among the banks and must implement a clear policy for promoting competition. Measures

directed at the promotion of competition must not anyhow endanger stability of the financial system and must be implemented at the detriment of consumers' interests.

It is necessary to investigate the main reasons for banking spread remaining at such a high level. In particular, it is important to discover the factors which are not directly associated with the financial system, such as existence of problems in the collateral evaluation process of lending transaction, lack of competition in the economy or lack of transparency due to weak corporate governance that translates into higher riskiness of borrowing organizations.

Thus, regardless of the rapid development of the financial sector and the banking sector in particular, the new policy, maintaining the current development rates, should mainly aim to significantly reduce the prices of financial resources. In this regard the transition to mandatory contributive pension system is expected to produce positive effect, since in mid-term period investments made by fund managers within the territory of Armenia will create favorable conditions for decrease of interest rates.

PUBLIC REVENUES POLICY

In recent years the policy implemented in the taxation and customs spheres was aimed at the solution of the following two important issues:

1) expansion of the tax base and thus ensuring the necessary tax revenues for state and community budgets;

2) creation of favorable business environment for businesses.

The investigation of the experience of countries that have had successful results from their public revenue policy reveals that by application of efficient models of tax and customs systems it is possible to enact a balanced policy which will contribute to the creation of preconditions for implementation of the above mentioned objectives in parallel.

The principles of the RA public revenues policy are derived from the overall direction of the social-economic policy being implemented and its logic. In particular, when drafting and implementing public policies in the tax and the customs sectors the following targets are always accounted for: ensuring sustainable and long-term economic growth, promotion of investment, improvement and modernization of the production-technical basis of the economy, fair distribution of incomes among different social groups of the population.

The modest level of tax revenues collection, which is also reflected in the tax/GDP ratio, has always been and continues to be the main challenge of the public revenues system. In the future, the reorientation of the state revenues policy and the strengthening of country's fiscal position become objective necessities and serious challenges.

The study of possibilities and limitations for the additional tax revenues collection reveals that additional tax revenues, and thus expansion of the economy potential, will be ensured with the following two directions:

1) change of the sectoral structure of the economy ensuring the prevalence of more taxable sectors

2) selection of types of taxes with additional potential (not yet used) for tax revenue collection and revision of the tax policy with regard to those taxes, so that horizontal and vertical justice principles of taxation are further strengthened and the optimum level of taxation is defined.

Considering that the transformation of the sectoral structure of the economy assumes the implementation of systemic changes, long-term development, as well as the fact that the priorities of the economic policy might not require the development of taxable sectors, but rather sectors with higher significance from the viewpoint of the long-term and sustainable development of the national economy (which do not have large potential for ensuring tax revenues), it is more realistic that additional tax revenues, until 2025, are linked to the selection of tax types with additional potential for collection of tax revenues as well as with the improvement of their tax base and taxation procedures. In this regard, the selection of property and excise taxes is more realistic, taking into account that their role and potential in the current tax system are significantly undervalued.

Within the abovementioned context, until 2025, the public policy in the taxation system will attach special importance to implementation of horizontal and vertical equity principle of the taxation, increase in tax administration efficiency in the context of business environment and application of grounded tax rates.

Horizontal equity principle of the taxation envisages application of similar rules and regulations to the taxpayers operating in identical economic circumstances. Main directions for implementing the mentioned principle will be:

1) Narrow the frames of currently applied tax exemptions. Decrease of particularly those exemptions must be emphasized, which are not approved to be suitable according the results of "cost-benefit" analyses. That is, all those tax exemptions, as a result of application of such the "benefits" accruing to the consumers and the business entities are not commensurate with the "costs" incurred by the state (tax income foregone by the state), must be gradually diminished. At the same time granting new exemptions to separate taxpayers or to the group of taxpayers must

be in exceptional cases and be derived from the country's strategic development objectives and programs.

2) Maximum broadening of the tax base. Specific measures must be taken to eliminate disparities of tax burden among different spheres of the economy. Particularly steps will be taken to eliminate VAT exemptions for some non-margin based services provided in the financial services sector, taking into account best international practice in this field.

3) Expanding the circle of goods subject to excise tax. Studies of the international experience in excise tax policy revealed that the circle of goods subject to excise tax in our country is relatively limited and thus has certain potential for expansion. The government has already adopted the policy for expanding the circle of goods subject to excise tax and will continue to carry out this policy in the medium-term. And the selection of goods subject to excise tax will be made in a way that will ensure the full accomplishment of the purpose of excise tax – limiting the consumption of harmful goods, redistribution of incomes in the society and ensuring tax revenues for the state budget.

153. Implementation of taxation vertical equity principle will enable the state to collect additional financial resources in order to carry out its social programs at the expense of population share with relatively higher income and to solve other problems of social nature. Main directions for strengthening vertical equity principal of the taxation will be:

1) Higher taxation of visible wealth. To implement the vertical equity principle the taxation of visible wealth or luxury will be applied. In this regard, the Government of the RA attaches high importance to the taxation of the visible wealth. Moreover, the first step has been taken with the legislative amendments in force since 1st of January, 2012, when the luxury cars has been included in the list of goods subject to excise tax. With this regard, the future steps of the Government of RA will be aimed at defining the luxury criteria of the property and application of higher tax rates to the properties satisfying those criteria.

2) Introduction of capital gain taxation. The new value (capital gain) emerging as a result of transactions with the securities, acquisition and disposal of real estate property is substantially similar to all other types of values arising as a result of other types of passive income. Consequently, capital gain must be taxed similar to the other types of passive income. In this regard, legislative amendments in the forthcoming years must be directed at the improvement of the capital gain taxation procedures (particularly for the residents of RA).

To create a viable mechanism of taxing both the visible wealth and the capital gain it is very important to implement regular and massive re-evaluation of the real estate properties with the purpose of decreasing the gap between their cadastral and market values to the possible extent and as a result broaden the property tax base.

Revisions of the tax legislation must be aimed at further improvement of the business environment in RA as a logical continuation of the activities being undertaken during the recent years. Main target of this policy direction must be at least the preservation of the competitiveness and attractiveness of our tax system in the region. In this regard, it is very important, that prospective legislative amendments are directed at the elimination of irrelevant and economically ungrounded limitations for the taxpayers. Main directions for the implementation of these principles are:

1) Specification of the procedures of returning to the taxpayers in a specified time period the conditional overpayments (debit balances) arising as a result of VAT calculations.

2) Determination of jointly accepted principles of calculating the VAT liabilities.

3) Improving the system of delaying the dates of VAT payments calculated by customs bodies at the date of import.

From the viewpoint of business environment, great importance is attached also to further improvement of tax administration. In this regard use of new toolsets should, to the extent possible, exclude putting additional burden on taxpayers including the time and human resources needed to meet the new requirements. In addition, further improvement of the administration and the use of new tools should be coupled with clear evaluation of their effectiveness.

Refraining from further tightening of tax administration and transition to risk based supervision is considered as a factor for improving business environment. The main approach in the improvement of tax administration is that tax control tools will be applied to those taxpayers which are identified as risky based on the results of analysis carried out. This will ensure targeted and efficient tax control. Other taxpayers will enjoy minimum level of tax control interventions. As a consequence, for 2014-2015 period tax to GDP ratio is expected and to stabilize around 23.8 percent. Another administrative improvement direction is considered to be identification of tax evasion cases, in particular putting special emphasize on cases when the breach of laws and regulation is carried out with the special purpose of evasion. It is expected to decrease the size of informal economy, to foster culture of autonomous tax liabilities calculations and payments by the taxpayers, to ensure fair and competitive economic environment.

Tax rates are one of the main tax policy tools and must be determined in such a way, that:

1) Their application would be maximum neutral for the business activities. In cases, when the taxation object is the economic rent, neutrality can be achieved directly, while for the remaining types of taxes the rates must be neutral to the possible extent.

2) They would be harmonized to the possible extent with the tax rates applied in CIS and in the countries which are competitors of RA in the respective spheres. Moreover, for the spheres considered to be priority for the economy of the Republic of Armenia the comparisons in tax policies, including the tax rates, must be implemented with respect to the countries which are leaders in those spheres. In all types of comparisons effective tax rates must considered, which take into account the taxation factual rules and all kinds of allowances.

3) The goods which have low price elasticity of demand and which are not primary consumption goods (mainly goods subject to excise tax such as alcoholic drinks, cigarettes, fuel) should be taxed with relatively higher rates, taking into account that price increase of those products due to tax factors will not cause drastic changes in the market conditions.

Taking into consideration the economic development strategy, an important element of tax policy will be mechanisms for development of special tax and customs regimes (exemptions, diversified administrative treatment) for priority economic sectors, as an important component of direct policy toolset in those sectors.

Until 2025, as a result of the implementation of an effective tax policy in the above-mentioned directions, it is expected:

1) to increase considerably the shares of property tax in the overall composition of tax revenues. In particular, it is expected to increase the ratio of property tax/GDP from 0.4% to 0.7%;

2) starting from 2016 to increase tax revenue collection by 0.3-0.4 percents of GDP annually;

3) to combine the continuous improvement of the business environment in the Republic of Armenia with the strengthening of the country's fiscal position, and thus ensuring the stability of the fiscal system;

4) to increase the financial stability of local communities, contributing to the implementation of more responsive, targeted and effective programs and application of the relevant tools for resolving social-economic problems of at the community level.

Customs policy is the next important element of public revenue system. At the same time, customs policy has a direct impact on the business environment by affecting the efficiency of across border trade transactions.

The revisions of the legislation regulating customs relationships in the Republic of Armenia in the forthcoming years will be based on the revised Kyoto Convention "Simplification and Harmonization of Customs procedures" adopted in 1999 and at the same time will be oriented towards Armenia's membership in Customs Union and subsequent implementation of responsibilities assumed as a party to Eurasian economic community.

Improvement of the risk management system might be an important input for the enhancement of the business climate as well as for the increase in the efficiency of customs bodies' operations. In particular, application of the simplified and faster customs procedures for the conscientious and not risky business entities will decrease the customs clearance time and will enable the customs body to use the administrative resources with higher efficiency.

In the context of customs system development an important issue is also the improvement of the customs post clearance control system taking into account that the latter can contribute to the minimization of control at the customs border on the date of import. In this sense, it is noteworthy that the gradual transfer of some control functions from the customs border and their adaptation in the frames of post clearance control systems is in line with the international experience in this sphere and can be successfully implemented also in our country.

Apart from the legislative and procedural reforms, special importance will be paid to the infrastructure improvement. Bavra-Bagratashen-Gogavan border improvement program as well as the implementation of integrated border management system will be finalized. Those are very important both for the overall success of the export oriented industrial policy and the development of tourism.

POLICIES FOR VARIOUS SECTORS AND AREAS

According to the concept of this program, direct policies will be implemented along with the framework ones, and these direct policies will contribute to the long-lasting, jobs creating economic growth.

Given the economic development goal, as well as the potential for jobs creation, the direct policies will be geared at creation of jobs in relevant sectors, branches and areas, through creation of adequate conditions for their development and elimination of obstacles.

The peculiarities of each sphere will dictate the special policy and the policy enacted will differ from sector to sector. Taking into account the short-and long-term potential for job creation, as well as the input in ensuring quality economic growth, the program's priority sectors and areas subject to the direct policies include:

1) Industry and export promotion;

2) Tourism development;

3) Information technologies' sector development

4) Agriculture and rural development

5) SME creation and ensuring their adequate activities;

Direct policies will complement the corresponding framework policies for business environment and investment climate improvement as well as competitiveness promotion. The mixture of direct and framework policies will be the main tool for job creation in the economy and will be implemented using PPP (public-private partnership) tools, in particular through direct involvement of private sector in the sectoral and branch development policy.

At the same time direct policies should create relevant environment for development of innovative and knowledge-based economy. Policies oriented at export and promoting development of IT already assume promotion of innovative measures. However direct policies promoting innovative developments cover not only priority sectors but will be implemented throughout the entire economy.

1. INDUSTRY AND EXPORT PROMOTION

Classical industrial policy is a mixture of framework and direct policies of interventionist nature, which aims to create new economic sectors and enterprises, protect them from external competition, as well as ensure and expand export possibilities. Armenia has never had such policy developed and implemented[16].

In a wider sense[17], the industrial policy is a part of the state's sector policy. The sector policy, in its turn, is interventionist policy promoting growth and development of different economy sectors, where the level of state intervention is determined based on specific aspects of development, the level of competitiveness of those sectors, as well as the nature and necessity of government regulation.

The economic crisis revealed the serious problems of the Armenian economy's real sector competitiveness. Before that the economic policy was based on the creation of favorable framework conditions for the development of the private sector. But the deep structural problems of the economy, limitations for the growth and the export, low level of business sophistication and innovations (which are confirmed by the estimations of Global competitiveness report) called for the necessity of states active participation in correcting the "market failures".

In the period preceding this program, the relative decline in the volumes of exports of goods and services (as a share of GDP) continued, while the relative and absolute volumes of imports increased. In the crisis year of 2009, the absolute volumes of both exports and imports declined considerably, although recovering in the post-crisis year of 2011.

Export and import volumes in 2008-2011 are significantly far from the SDP plan indicators and the accelerated growth of exports planned by SDP happened only in 2011 (27.7% increase in exports with respect to the previous year, and 10.7% increase in volume of imports), which was mainly the result of higher prices for main groups of goods exported from Armenia processed food (40.3% increase), metals (9.7% increase), mining products (30% increase), precious stones and metals (46.5% increase).

During 2006-2012 period 90 to 95 percent of exports constituted 10 large product groups (three of which -live animals and products of animal origin, products of plant origin and vegetable and animal oil -are presented as agricultural products) (Table 3).

Certain elements of industry or more precisely interventional 'direct' policy were applied by the government in 2009-2010 in industry, construction and financial sectors of economy in order to protect them from crisis consequences.

Table 3. Exports actual structure, by main product groups in 2007-2012, % of total exports

	2007	2008	2009	2010	2011	2012
				% of total		
Total	100	100	100	100	100	100
Agricultural products	2.2	3.0	5.0	3.8	4.0	4.9
Processed food	12.5	15.9	14.0	12.6	13.8	18.5
Mining products	15.1	16.3	20.5	29.5	30.3	29.2
Construction materials	1.8	1.3	1.9	1.5	1.3	1.3
Chemical products, plastics, rubber	1.8	3.4	2.3	2.4	1.5	1.8
Precious and semiprecious stones and metals	18.1	16.4	14.8	12.9	14.7	12.5
Non precious metals and products made of them	33.9	32.8	32.5	31.9	27.3	24.8
Machinery, equipment and mechanisms	3.4	3.8	3.0	2.9	2.5	3.0
Other*	11.2	7.1	6.0	2.5	4.6	4.1

**Total, according to trade statistics*

Source: calculated based on NSS of RA data.

It is worth to be underlined that for all the product groups mentioned above, including those which are primarily exported products, Armenia is a net importer.

One of the main export risks is the extreme concentration, both by products and by geographical destinations. In 2012, three product groups -mining products, food products and non-precious metals and items manufactured from them amounted to more than 70 percent of total export. On the other hand, three largest trade partners – Russia, Bulgaria and Belgium

– accounted for 38.8% of total exports in 2012. Thus the export promotion policy must be directed at the diversification of the export both in terms of product groups and geographical destinations.

Based on the country's development specifics during 2003-2008, the 2009-2011 crisis and post-crisis realities, ADS considers the export, its advanced growth and correspondingly drastic increase of its role and importance, as the main driving force for the development during the period of 2014-2025.

With adoption of its industrial policy strategy aimed at Armenia's export, approved by the 2011 Government Protocol Decree N 49, the Government of Armenia announced implementation of its new industrial policy. According to the strategy, the export-oriented industrial policy of Armenia includes a group of well-balanced and phase activities aimed at enhancing spheres with potential of developing export and improvement of international competition, which is targeted at export expansion and diversification. The long-term goal of the export-oriented industrial policy is development of new driving areas of economic growth by enhancing development of currently exporting area and those with export potential. Development of processing branches and complexes is seen as the direct target of industrial policy.

The guiding vision of industrial policy is to make Armenia a country producing high-value and knowledge-based goods and services, anchored on the creative human capital. Implementation of this vision requires phase approach assuming gradual transition from resource-intensive industry to those based on capacities and skills, afterwards focusing more on knowledge-based industries in the long-term perspective. Given the importance of systemic development of the economy the industrial strategy is viewed in the context of comprehensive economic development vision and priorities of development of other spheres of economy.

The initial stage of the strategy includes the following processing industry sub-branches: diamond cutting, goldsmithery, producing of watches, light industry, brandy and wine production, pharmaceuticals and biotechnologies, production of canned foodstuff, production of mineral waters and juices, engineering/precise engineering, processing of non-ferrous mineral. State support in each area will be temporary, according to preliminarily defined targets and gradually new areas may be involved over time.

Membership in Customs Union is crucial for export promotion. In particular it is important to take steps in the period preceding the official membership to the Union for achieving favourable regulations and developing projects that will enable full utilization of export growth and diversification potential.

It is expected that most job places in the sphere of industry will be created in the above branches with maximal potential on the basis of replacement of export or import.

The industrial policy will be implemented through sector strategies and relevant triennial action plans, which will be approved by sector councils and the Industrial Council by the Prime Minister. The industrial policy will be implemented by application of general actions and special toolkits.

Implementation of general actions aimed at creation of favorable environment and improvement of productivity (improvement of business regulating environment, ensuring favorable external regimes, elimination of trade obstacles, modernization of infrastructures, promotion of foreign investments)

Application of special toolkits to include the following:

1) Special tax and customs regimes

a) Special tax and customs regimes for exporting companies, b) Deferred VAT for goods imported under investment goods and programs, c) A number of free trade zones with use of PPT toolkit (particularly on the area of

Zvartnots airport and Mars company) with application of relevant tax and customs regimes.

2) Financial support and ensuring access to financing:

a) Loans at special terms (e.g. for investments aimed at implementation of quality

assurance system, export expansion, creation of jobs), b) Provision of export guarantees, c) Provision of credit guarantees, d) Own capital funding, e) Participation in investment funds.

3) Access to markets:

a) Identification of goods with export potential and potential partners, b) Presentation and protection of interests of exporters through trade

representations, c) Support to participation in exhibitions, d) Organization of incoming and outgoing business visits and conferences, e) Branding of countries and specific sectors in target markets, f) Support to involvement of trade representatives in target markets.

4) Capacity building/increase of competitiveness:

a) Co-funding of human resources training programs, b) Provision of technical and financial assistance to companies in implementation of internationally recognized quality assurance systems, c) Support to sharing technologies and knowledge, including using potential and contacts of the Diaspora.

5) Promoting research studies and developments:

a) Foundation of technoparks and industrial parks, b) Provision of grants for joint researches and developments by companies and higher educational institutions, c) Creation of venture funds.

Special sector support tools and structures will be created within the framework of sector development strategies. In 2012 the Industry Development Fund and the Armenia Export Financing Insurance Company were created within the framework of the industry policy.

In terms of improvement of the effectiveness of export promotion and foreign investments attraction policies and activities a key role is assigned to implementation of functional mechanisms for agreement of cross-structure activities, considering the alternative of creation of a relevant unified structure over time. Among possible advantages of this approach are development of an agreed policy, maximally effective use of capacities, and the application of the 'single-window' principle.

As a result of accelerated exports growth policy and imports moderate suppression policy[18] it is planned to essentially reduce dependence of the country from external financing during the program period, by bringing the products and services balance deficit to 15,1% of the GDP by 2017 as opposed to 24,8% in 2012, followed by 9.8% in 2021 and 4.5% in 2025.

Figure 3. Exports, imports and balance of goods and services in 2012-2025, % of GDP

At the same time, during the forecasted period, the openness of the country's (Is measured as the ratio of the foreign economic turnover of the country to the GDP) economy will not change significantly, as along with the increase in exports volume the import will relatively decrease. This indicator will fluctuate around 74-78% percent of GDP during the programming period, as opposed to 73.8% in 2012.

Economic growth in some sectors and branches will occur due to expansion of the domestic demand (including import substitution).

Main tools for moderate import suppression policy under liberal external economic policy conditions will include:

1) Relevant monetary policy which should not be aimed at import promotion but be rather neutral in that regard.

2) Import replacement policy which by applying different tools will support the local producers. In particular, increase in transparency and efficiency of public procurement can be an example of such a tool.

2. TOURISM DEVELOPMENT

Incoming tourism is Armenia's second export line item after mining and metal industry and covers more than half of services export. In addition, about 20 thousand people are employed in the spheres of incoming, outgoing and domestic tourism, which totals around 3% of non-agricultural employment.

The incoming tourism will retain its role as the second export sector and will cover around 24% of export throughout implementation of ADS. It is estimated that the number of directly tourism-related jobs will increase by 7.7 thousand compared with 2011 and during the programming period will continue to constitute 3.0% of non-agricultural jobs.

Table 4. Tourism sector development in 2011-2025

	2011	2017	2021	2025
Incoming tourism, thous. persons	757.9	1351.2	1907.3	2692.3
Index, 2008=100	100.0	178.3	251.6	355.2
Outgoing tourism, thous. persons	715.0	1232.9	1677.3	2282.0
Index, 2008=100	100.0	172.4	234.6	319.2
Incoming tourism expenses, mln. USD	513.0	1030.0	1573.7	2404.5
% of total export	21.6	25.5	24.9	24.1
Outgoing tourism expenses, mln. USD	513.5	1130.2	1869.0	3090.7
% of total import	10.7	18.9	22.8	27.4
Employment in tourism sector, thous. persons	20.6	23.9	26.0	28.3
% of non-agricultural employment	2.9	3.0	3.0	3.0

Source: Calculated based on NSS, Ministry of Economy publications, World Bank World Development Indicators 2010, 2011, 2012 yearbooks, ADS forecasts.

ADS envisages that incoming and outgoing tourism will keep their growth rates of 20082012, around 8-9 percent, which will result in the number of incoming tourists reaching 1,35 million in 2017, and 2.7 million in 2025 as opposed to 758 thousand in 2011.

The main sector policy directions ensuring the abovementioned high development rates in the sector of tourism will be the improvement of relevant infrastructures through PPP toolsets, particularly the policies of reduction of high transport costs related to entry to and exit from Armenia.

Diligent implementation of already initiated strategies on touristic centers' development (Jermuk, Tsakhkadzor, Dilijan and others) will play an important role. Implementation of such projects is important from the viewpoint of balanced development of the regions.

The latter policy includes implementation of 'open sky' approach with involvement of low-cost airline companies, demonopolization of railway market, and ensuring competitiveness, creation and upgrading of tourism infrastructures out of Yerevan, as well as promotion of involvement of international hotel operators.

On 23rd of October, 2013 RA Government approved the Project on ensuring competitive and sustainable air transportation services in Armenia and program implementation measures. According to the project Armenia is implementing air transportation liberalization and adopting open air policy. Facilitation of air transportation creates additional possibilities for economic development given the existing strict constraints on land transportation. Positive impact on GDP and employment is expected as a result of implementing the newly declared policy, which is mainly due to expected increase in financial resources obtained from tourism. Open air will have positive economic impact on majority of beneficiaries. In particular the new policy in the field will promote incoming tourism and diversification of its geography. On top of that, Armenian Diaspora will have more possibilities to strengthen the ties with the homeland, both by private and business visits. The airport will have higher turnover of flights and can involve higher frequency flights, offering decreased fees as well as assisting in marketing of new routes. Business sector representatives will have more convenient conditions (in terms of times and expenses) and extended possibilities for business communications.

3. INFORMATION TECHNOLOGIES DEVELOPMENT

In 2000 information technologies (IT) were recognized one of the priority branches of Armenian economy and its development will be an essential contribution to the transition towards knowledge-based economy.

In 2008 the RA Government adopted a new 10-year IT sector development strategy which includes objectives of infrastructure development, increase in the quality of IT sector graduates, creation of venture and other financial mechanisms for the start-ups, etc. Among particular goals of the new strategy are building of new technoparks and incubators, creation of a big venture fund, expansion of local market for local IT products and services, increase the volume of foreign direct investments.

In the period preceding the ADS the Government participated in a number of initiatives aimed at achieving the above goals. In 2007 the National Instruments Corporation founded an engineering and research office in Yerevan. In 2008 the Gyumri technopark construction was initiated and it is currently in the process. The latter hosts the regional software development laboratory of D-Link International. In May 2011, within the framework of the Cooperation Memorandum signed between RA Government and Microsoft Corporation, the Microsoft Innovations Center was opened in Yerevan, which is aimed at creation of an environment promoting development of professional skills and capacity building through application of Microsoft tools and programs.

The mentioned and other initiatives launched by the government, as well as the active participation of the private sector resulted in significant growth of IT sector indicators in 2011 compared with 2008. Particularly, the total revenue increased by 84%, whereas the share of IT sector in GDP reached 2% in 2011 versus 1% in 2008. The number of employed in the sector increased by 38% and by around same percentage productivity growth was recorded.

During ADS implementation period direct policies in IT sector will include: 1) Continuation of establishment of technoparks, incubators and other IT infrastructures being implemented through PPP toolsets, 2) Support to universities in implementation of modern curricula and acquisition of

necessary laboratories, through promotion of their cooperation with private sector, 3) Implementation of favorable tax policy promoting export potential in the sector, 4) Implementation of state-support programs for SMEs and start-ups involved in the IT

sector, including access to markets, professional trainings and ensuring access to information, 5) Direct support to IT companies offering innovative products or services.

206. In addition to general framework policies, implementation of direct policies in the sector is expected to contribute to the creation of 10 to 15 thousand new jobs by 2025. Export will increase along with the sector growth: it is expected to export around 60% of products in 2017. The share of IT sector in GDP will be around 6-7% in 2025. ADS forecasts are in line with target indicators set in 2008 IT sector strategy and take into account the dynamics of recent years.

4. AGRICULTURE AND RURAL DEVELOPMENT

9.4.1 SECTOR OVERVIEW

In 2012 value-added in agriculture accounted for 19.1 % of the GDP, while combined with agriculture processing it comprised around 26% of GDP. As of 2012 the gross agriculture produce makes up AMD 764 bln (equivalent of USD 1.9 bln), with plant cultivation counting for 60% and animal husbandry 40%. Agriculture shares a unique place in the country's food security. Today, in terms of energy value, the self-sustainability of first-need foodstuffs comprises around 60 %.

Out of total 915 communities of Armenia 866 are rural (around 36.0% of the country population resides in villages), hence agriculture plays an important strategic role also in terms of rural area development. As of 2012, agriculture employs 437.2 thousand people, which accounts for 37% of the country's total employment and 80% of rural area employment. In the external commodity turnover structure the share of vegetable-and animal-origin products in 2011 was 18.6, and in the structure of exported goods -17.8%. According to 2012 data, these indicators improved reaching 19.9 and 22.6% correspondingly.

Recognizing agriculture as a priority sector is dwelled on two principle reasons. Firstly, agriculture is the key link of the food industry value chain, which is one of the sub-branches with export potential. Secondly, development of agriculture is critical for increase of productivity and creation of non-agricultural jobs in rural areas, thus contributing to balanced regional development.

The lion's share of revenues of the rural population comes from agriculture products and hired labor. Hence, poverty in this sector is largely contingent on agriculture development.

According to the 2012 land balance data arable lands covered 448.4 thousand hectares and the areas under crops 304.2 thousand hectares (Figure 4), meaning that 144.2 thousand hectares of arable lands are not used at their designated purpose, and the level of designated use is 67.8 % as opposed to 63.0 % recorded in 2010. Poor use of arable lands is essentially dependent on the lack of financial resources of businesses employed in agriculture, low profitability, difficult access to machine works, fragmented land parcels, difficulties in marketing agricultural products, etc. In some boarder communities, designated use of arable lands is affected by dangers associated with borderline land cultivation. In addition, out of

232.9 thousand ha irrigable lands of the country only around 155 thousand ha are actually irrigated.

BUSINESS FRAMEWORK AND FOREIGN INVESTMENT REGIME

GENERAL LEGAL FRAMEWORK FOR BUSINESSES

(a) Types of business structures

1. Since its accession to the WTO, there has been no significant change to Armenia's general legal framework for businesses. The principal laws for establishing and conducting business are the Civil Code (Chapter 5) and the Law on State Registration of Legal Entities of 2001.

2. Other legislation that affects businesses includes, *inter alia*, the Law on the Protection of Consumer Rights of January 2002, the Law on Foreign Investments of July 1994, and the Law on Bankruptcy of December 2006. Under these rules, foreign companies and individuals are subject to the same procedures and requirements as Armenian nationals. There are no restrictions for the participation of foreigners in legal entities established in Armenia, except as listed in section (ii) below.

3. In order to start a business, Armenian nationals and foreigners are required to establish a legal entity or to register as a private entrepreneur (sole proprietorship) . According to the Civil Code, a legal entity may be either a profit-making commercial organization, or a non-profit organization. A commercial organization may take the form of a company (limited or supplementary liability, or an open or closed joint-stock company), a business partnership (general or limited partnership) or a cooperative. A foreign company may also establish a branch or a representative office in Armenia (Table V.1) .

Principal business structures and selected requirements

Type of registration	Fee (dram)	Selected rules and requirements
Limited liability companies		
State Register	12,000	Governed by Law on Limited Liability Companies of 24 October 2001, as amended
Registration of the company name in State Register	5,000	Shareholders are not liable for the obligations of the company
Tax Service Register	Free	No minimum capital requirements
Supplementary liability companies		
State Register	12,000	Governed by the Civil Code of 28 July 1998, as amended
Registration of the company name in State Register	5,000	Shareholders bear subsidiary liability for the company's obligations with their personal wealth, in a multiple of the

		value of their contributions
Tax Service Register	Free	No minimum capital requirements

Joint-stock companies (JSCs)

State Register	12,000	Governed by Law on Joint Stock Companies of 2001
Registration of the company name in State Register	5,000	JSCs may be open (i.e. with no limit to the number of shareholders and with shares freely traded - referred to as OJSC) or closed (i.e. with a limited number of shareholders – referred to as CJSC) . A closed company may have a maximum of 49 shareholders
Tax Service Register	Free	No minimum capital requirements

Sole proprietorship

State Register	12,000	Governed by Civil Code of 28 July 1998, as amended
Tax Service Register	Free	No minimum capital requirement. No nationality or residency requirements

Source: WTO Secretariat, based on Armenian legislation; and American Chamber of Commerce in Armenia online information, "Company Registration". Viewed at: http://www.amcham.am/index.cfm?objectid=7F6CA7F0-4150 - 11DE-90400003FF3452C2.

4. All business entities must apply for registration in the State Register of Legal Entities. [1] In addition, certain activities, such as the production and sale of pharmaceutical products, require licences (Chapter III(6)) . Within one month of receiving its certificate of registration, a legal entity must register with the regional offices of the tax and statistical agencies, and companies that wish to import goods must also register with their regional customs office (Chapter III(1)) . In July 2009, the Government eliminated the mandatory requirement for a company's seal, which used to cost dram 6,000 (some US$17) at the regional tax office. [2]

5. According to the authorities, Armenian legislation was amended in 2009 and minimum charter capital requirements were eliminated for all types of legal entities, with the exception of financial institutions (Chapter VI(4)(ii)) .

6. Armenia ranked 43rd out of 183 economies analysed in the World Bank's Ease of Doing Business Index for 2010 (an improvement from 50th place in the 2009 Index) . [3] According to the World Bank the improvement was particularly noticeable in the stages starting a business (ranking improved from 65th in 2009 to 21st in 2010) and trading across borders (improved from 136th to 102nd) . In terms of starting a business, the number of procedures (6) declined (from 9), and the average amount of time needed to start a standard medium-size company decreased from 18 to 15 days. The authorities indicate that regulatory changes introduced in 2009 have reduced the number of procedures to 5 and the time needed to 7-9 days. Moreover, in order to continue to expedite and simplify the process of starting a company, the Government expects to inaugurate a business centre providing one-stop-shop services for registration of legal entities. [4]

(b) Corporate taxation

1. A profit tax, at the rate of 20%, applies to all commercial organizations. Resident companies are taxed on worldwide profits, while non-resident companies are taxed only on profits generated

in Armenia or attributable to a business carried out by a branch in Armenia. During 2003-07, foreign companies were entitled to apply for a profit tax break consisting of a reduction in the profit tax due in the two subsequent fiscal years. The reduction was for the full amount of the foreign investment in a given year. This tax break was not extended to investments undertaken from 2008. The authorities could not provide information on the number of foreign companies that benefited from this tax break or the amount of tax revenue forgone.

2. Companies are also subject to property tax on buildings and automotive vehicles. The property tax is based on the cadastral value of the buildings as a sliding scale starting at 0.1% of the value over dram 3 million and rising to 1% for the value over dram 40 million. Property tax on vehicles is also a sliding scale based on engine power. For cars [5] the rate is dram 200 per horsepower (1 hp = 0.735 kW) up to 120 hp, while, at the top end (i.e. vehicles of 251 hp or more), the rate is set at dram 500 per hp and an additional dram 1,000 per hp for each horsepower over 150 hp. [6]

3. Armenia has signed tax treaties for the avoidance of double taxation with 36 countries. [7]

FOREIGN INVESTMENT REGIME

1. The Ministry of Economy (ME) is responsible for implementing investment policy in Armenia. Promotion of foreign and local investment is undertaken by the Armenian Development Agency (ADA), a government body chaired by the Prime Minister. [8] The ADA is the primary contact for foreign investors and is responsible for helping them to set up a business in Armenia, by providing assistance for project implementation and liaison with other government agencies, such as the State Register of Legal Entities (see above) . It also provides information on investment opportunities in the country, and on investment-related regulations.

2. Foreign direct investment into Armenia is officially encouraged and seen by the Government as one of the key aspects of its economic development policy. During the review period, the Government offered two direct incentives exclusively to foreign investors: (i) a profit tax break (see above); and (ii) a tariff exemption on the importation of certain capital inputs (Chapter III(4)) . According to the authorities, Armenia's current investment policy seeks to remove administrative barriers, complete the legal framework that regulates investments, and develop the infrastructure that promotes investment. [9] However, despite the infrastructure projects carried out via both public and private investments since 2006, key areas, such as transport and telecommunications (Chapter VI) still need to keep pace with the general economic development achieved during the review period.

3. The Law on Foreign Investments of 31 July 1994 is the main legislation governing foreign investments in Armenia. No significant amendments were made to the Law during the review period. The Law guarantees national treatment to foreign investors. Foreign investment is defined by the Law as investments with no less than 30% of foreign participation at the moment of foundation.

4. There are no legal restrictions to the participation of foreign investors in any economic activity in Armenia. The only exception is set by the Constitution [10], which denies foreign citizens and persons without citizenship the right to own land in Armenia. However, foreigners are allowed to use land through lease contracts with an Armenian counterpart. Furthermore, foreigners have the right to own real estate properties built on Armenian land, and to exploit renewable and non-renewable natural resources on the basis of concession contracts granted by the Government.

5. Nevertheless, the legislation grants the Government the power to limit and prohibit foreign investment for national security concerns. The authorities indicated that this provision was not used during the review period.

6. The Law on Foreign Investments guarantees that, in the event of amendments to the legislation on foreign investment, the law in force at the time the investment was made can, upon the request of a foreign investor, continue to be applied for a maximum of five years from the date of the investment. The Law also restricts the ability of the Government to confiscate or nationalize the property of foreign investors and, where it might occur, requires full compensation. Foreign investors and employees are guaranteed the right to freely repatriate their property, profits, and other goods legally earned as a result of investments or as compensation for services.

7. Armenia has signed bilateral treaties on reciprocal promotion and protection of investments with 44 countries. [11] It is also a signatory of the International Convention on Investment Disputes, which allows for resolution of disputes by the International Centre for the Settlement of Investment Disputes (ICSID) . [12]

8. Under the General Agreement on Trade in Services (GATS) Armenia has scheduled no limitations to foreign investment with respect to both market access and national treatment for practically all activities, with the exception of a few specific services activities (Chapter VI(4)) .

STATE TRADING, STATE-OWNED ENTERPRISES, AND PRIVATIZATION

1. Armenia notified the WTO that it does not maintain any state-trading enterprise in accordance with the provisions of GATT Article XVII and the Understanding on the Interpretation of Article XVII. [13]

2. During the period under review, Armenia continued to privatize its remaining state-owned enterprises. From January 2003 to November 2009, 283 large and medium-scale companies were privatized, mainly in the agriculture, transport, communication, energy, and mining sectors. These privatizations generated some US$110 million in public revenues for the State. At end 2009, state participation in the economy was limited to 400 companies fully or partially owned by the State: of these approximately 300 are in health care, education, and military activities, while the other 100 are non-operational small companies awaiting liquidation. [14]

3. Armenia's current privatization policy differs from the one adopted up to 2002 as it focuses on enhancing the competitiveness and efficiency of commercial organizations through the divestiture of the State's share in them. Before 2002, the Government sought to maximize cash returns, consolidate market reforms, develop the stock market, and introduce corporate governance principles to public enterprises. The authorities state that tendering, open share subscriptions, and direct sales to strategic investors were the methods of privatization adopted during the review period. [15] Since privatization started in the 1990s, 1,937 companies have been privatized through 175 tenders, 677 direct sales, and 1,085 open subscriptions.

INCENTIVES

1. Armenia provides some support to the agriculture sector but this is limited due to scarce budgetary resources (Chapter VI(1)) . The Armenian Development Agency promotes Armenian exports abroad, but does not provide direct financial or tax incentives (Chapter IV(5)) . Otherwise, the authorities indicated that the State does not provide any significant incentives to its domestic producers.

COMPETITION AND PRICE POLICIES

(i) Competition policy

1. According to the European Commission, Armenia's legal and institutional framework on competition is relatively well established, but the powers of the Armenian competition authority remain limited. [16] Evidence suggests that, in practice, the level of competition is low in a number of product markets, such as meat, beer, hen eggs, granulated sugar, butter, petrol, diesel fuel, cement, and other construction materials. [17]

2. Armenia's competition legislation comprises the Constitution, the Civil Code of 1998, and the Law on Protection of Economic Competition of 6 November 2000, as amended. The Law applies equally to foreign and domestic companies, including state-owned enterprises, in all economic sectors. Since January 2001, the State Commission for the Protection of Economic Competition (the Commission) has been responsible for safeguarding competition; the Commission is administratively, but not financially, independent. [18]

3. The Commission is composed of a chairman and six other members appointed by the President of Armenia for a five-year tenure. According to the Law on Protection of Economic Competition of 2000, the Commission must protect and promote economic competition in order to bring about the development of businesses and the protection of consumer rights. In order to achieve this objective, the Commission has the authority to, *inter alia*, disaggregate companies that abuse their dominant position, amend or revoke contracts between economic agents that contradict the Law, and impose penalties on companies and their managers, as well as on public officials, in the event of infringement. In April 2007, a number of amendments to the Law were introduced giving the Commission the power to inspect, impose stricter sanctions for infringements, and control the impact of state aid on competition. The mechanisms to implement the control over state aid have not yet been defined by late 2009. [19]

4. The Commission publishes annual programme reports on its activities and keeps a centralized register of economic entities with a dominant position. During 2003-08, the Commission adopted a total of 794 decisions, some of which resulted in the imposition of sanctions totalling about US$2 million. The number of decisions adopted and the value of sanctions imposed grew significantly between 2003 and 2005 and stayed fairly constant thereafter. In 2008, the courts received 22 claims from the Commission to ensure the enforcement of its adopted decisions (one of which was partially rejected), as well as 14 appeals against decisions taken by the Commission. In August 2009, 48 economic entities with dominant positions in 108 product markets were registered in the centralized log [20]; some are the same markets identified by the Commission as lacking competition in 2006 (see above) .

5. The Law on Protection of Economic Competition of 2000 defines dominant position as a situation where a company: has no competitors; or is not exposed to any substantial competition; or has a market share equal to or greater than one third. The parties involved in an act of concentration must, before the concentration comes into practice, submit a declaration if, in the preceding fiscal year: the joint or individual value of assets was at least dram 3 billion (some US$8.5 million); or participants operate in the same product market and the joint or individual value of their assets was greater than dram 1 billion. According to the Law, any concentration leading to a dominant position is prohibited except when it promotes consumers interests and/or fosters the development of competition in that particular market. Where a declaration is required, the parties must await the decision of the Commission, which must be made within 90 days if it is to impose terms and conditions or prohibit the concentration altogether.

6. Armenian legislation grants economic entities and government bodies the right to appeal a Commission decision before the courts. It also gives the Commission the right to initiate court

proceedings if one of its decisions is not implemented. Furthermore, damages that are caused to an economic entity or other persons due to anti-competitive practices analysed by the Commission must be compensated by the infringer.

7. It could be argued that Armenia's legislation on intellectual property rights indirectly promotes competition as it allows parallel imports of patented and copyright protected products (see section (6) below) . However, there are no studies that measure the economic impact of these provisions.

8. As in other regulatory areas, the Armenian authorities have been working with the European Commission on harmonizing Armenia's competition legislation with EU's; according to the European Commission, the process is not yet fully complete. [21]

9. Armenia and other 11 CIS member states founded the CIS Interstate Council of Antitrust Policy in 2000 and signed a Contract on "Maintaining of Agreed Antimonopoly Policy". The State Commission is also collaborating closely with international organizations, such as competition experts at the OECD and the International Competition Network. Moreover, Armenia has signed cooperation agreements in the field of competition with Moldova, Romania, and Ukraine. [22]

(ii) Price policy

1. Armenia eliminated all its price controls before it acceded to the WTO. Prices of certain services provided by utility companies, including telecommunications, and distribution of electricity, gas, and water are controlled by the Government through the Public Services Regulatory Commission, in order to correct for externalities caused by natural monopolies (Chapter VI(3) and (4)(iii)) .

GOVERNMENT PROCUREMENT

1. Since its accession to the WTO, Armenia has adopted a new Law on Procurement and implemented its secondary regulations (see below) . The Government estimated that public procurement represented 10.6% of GDP in 2008, and that, in nominal terms, it had grown at an annual average rate of 22% since 2003. [23] Many of the Government's large purchases are connected to projects funded by international financial donors. [24]

2. Armenia is not a signatory to the WTO Plurilateral Agreement on Government Procurement (GPA) . In acceding to the WTO, Armenia indicated that it would become an observer to the GPA and that it would start negotiations to join the Agreement. [25] During the review period, some preparatory work was done and it was reported that its legislation and practices are GPA-compatible in most respects, although some areas require further work, particularly relating to bid protest/domestic review procedures and other institutional requirements. [26] In October 2009, Armenia presented its initial offer and started negotiations with other WTO Members to join the GPA. [27]

3. None of Armenia's preferential trade agreements contains specific provisions on government procurement.

4. Armenia's main laws governing government procurement are the Law on Procurement, which entered into force in January 2005; Government Decree No. 853-N of 5 June 2008; and Instruction No. 426 of 25 April 2005, issued by the Ministry of Finance. [28] The Law states that international agreements signed by Armenia, take precedence over domestic provisions. The Law on Procurement covers purchases of all types of goods, works, and services (including rent and lease contracts) procured by State and local Government bodies, State or community

agencies, non-profit organizations, the Central Bank, and enterprises with over 50% State and/or community ownership. [29] The authorities state, however, that the Government adopted a new "Procurement System Reforms Strategy" in April 2009, seeking to amend the current legislation to include provisions on procurement by public-private partnership agreements and private utilities companies that operate under exclusive rights granted by the State.

5. The Government's procurement policy aims to broaden the circle of participants and to foster a competitive, efficient, transparent and non-discriminating procurement process. Armenia has opted for legislation that favours the use of the lowest price as the sole award criterion, mainly in order to curb corruption.

6. The Law does not contain any provision to promote domestic suppliers or local content, and it explicitly guarantees equal rights for foreign providers. However, the choice of procurement method (see below) may in certain circumstances disfavour foreign suppliers.

7. From an institutional perspective, government procurement is the responsibility of the Ministry of Finance; the State Procurement Agency (SPA), which is a semi-autonomous Government body under the Ministry of Finance; and procuring entities (including local governments) . The Ministry of Finance is responsible for procurement policy and regulation. The SPA is responsible for the actual conduct of procurement in collaboration with procuring entities, and for signing all contracts concluded through open tenders. The role of procuring entities (i.e. budget spending units) is to: prepare technical specifications, delivery schedule, and payment terms; establish tender committees; and supervise contract performance and contractual payments. A joint study by the EU and the OECD noted that the lack of institutional capacity of procuring entities can justify centralizing procurement in the SPA. However, the study also pointed out that it may be necessary to re-evaluate this situation in the future and preferably assign more freedom and responsibility to the contracting authorities themselves. [30] Under the "Procurement System Reforms Strategy", the role of the SPA will be re-defined in the near future and more freedom and responsibility will be given to contracting authorities, including contract signature.

8. Armenian legislation allows for the following methods of procurement: open tender; closed tender; restricted tendering; request for quotations; competitive negotiations; and single-source procurement. Open tenders can be periodic or targeted. A periodic tender involves procurement of periodically used or recurrent items from a list compiled by the Ministry of Finance. All other items are procured using targeted tendering. Under the Law, open tender is the preferred method of procurement, but the Law also defines exceptions. For example: closed tenders may be used if the procurement involves state secrets (e.g. military purchases); restricted tendering may be applied due to technical specifications of the procurement item; and single-source may be used in cases of urgent need, of a complementary order or due to copyright or licence restrictions.

9. According to official estimates, the use of open tendering increased to 78% of the total value awarded in 2008 (Table V.2) . [31] Nevertheless, according to Transparency International, single-source procurement has been abused in the areas of education, health, and culture. [32]

Procurement methods, 2006-08

Procurement method	Procurement processes			Share of total value (%)		
	2006	2007	2008	2006	2007	2008
Open tender (periodic)	74	98	59	21.0	17.4	23.1

Open tender (targeted)	448	655	865	50.9	40.9	54.9
Restricted	0	0	0	0.0	0.0	0.0
Two stage	7	10	0	..	..	..
Competitive negotiations	60	403	124	10.9	32.2	10.9
Request for quotations	138	146	114	1.1	0.4	0.4
Single source	703	638	496	16.1	9.1	10.7
Total	1,423	1,940	1,658	100.0	100.0	100.0

10. Contract notices for open tenders must be published in the *Official Journal on Procurement* at least 30 days prior to the deadline for bid submission. If the amount is higher than US$7.7 million [33], notices must be published at least 40 days prior to the deadline, and suppliers are entitled to request the invitation to tender in English. In practice, open tenders and their respective awarded contracts are also published electronically at the SPA's website in Armenian, English, and Russian, as well as on TV and radio. If the price of the procurement contract is higher than dram 1 million [34] (some US$2,860) the contracting agency must publish an announcement on the Ministry of Finance website after the contract is signed. The authorities indicate that the minimum periods between publication and deadline for bid submission have been respected since 2005.

11. For periodic tenders the legislation requires a registration system or a permanent list of qualified providers. With regard to qualification criteria, the Law establishes general suitability as well as capacity requirements for providers. [35] These criteria must, in principle, be applied equally to domestic and foreign suppliers. Prequalification procedures are defined in Article 6 of the Law. Moreover, Article 12 requires the publication of a "black list" of providers whose managers have been convicted of wrongdoing in the previous three years. [36] In November 2009, the black list, published on the website of the Ministry of Finance, listed 13 providers. [37]

12. Armenia has been trying to put in place an electronic procurement system since its accession to the WTO; however, the work is still in progress. [38] The efficient implementation of an e-procurement system will require a significant improvement in the telecom infrastructure, particularly broadband accessibility throughout the country (Chapter VI(4)(iii)) .

13. According to Article 27 of the Law, the evaluation and award criteria must be part of the content of invitations sent to suppliers. Suppliers participating in tendering proceedings must provide a tender security of 2% of the proposed contract price, as specified in the invitation. No later than 15 days after the last day for tender submission the SPA is required to announce the results of the tender procedure, publicly, or to declare the tender proceeding invalid. Unsuccessful bidders have the guaranteed right to obtain, on the day of the announcement of the results, pertinent information, in writing, concerning the reasons why they were not selected. [39] In 2008, some 20% of all tenders were declared invalid. [40]

14. The Law determines that any person is entitled to appeal against the actions and decisions of the SPA and/or other procuring entity. The appeal may be made administratively, before the authorized procurement appeals body, or judicially, in the courts. The authorized procurement appeals body, a semi-autonomous body under the Ministry of Finance, must reach a final decision within 20 days of receipt of an appeal. Possible appeal decisions are set out in Article 53

of the Law. The authorized body has the power to suspend the procurement proceedings until the appeal decision is made. The "Procurement System Reforms Strategy" foresees the creation of an appeal system independent from the Ministry of Finance. The system would include an appeal body with a varied membership (including academics, NGO members, retired judges, and private-sector representatives) . Such a body would improve confidence in terms of fairness and transparency.

15. In 2006-08, 79 appeals were filed before the Ministry of Finance (12 in 2006, 14 in 2007, and 53 in 2008); 51% succeeded in overturning or modifying the procurement decision. None of the unsuccessful appeals was judicially brought before a court. [41]

INTELLECTUAL PROPERTY RIGHTS

(i) General aspects

1. Armenia is a member of the World Intellectual Property Organization (WIPO) and has signed a number of international agreements on intellectual property rights. [42] However, it is not a signatory of the Patent Law Treaty, the Singapore Treaty on the Law on Trademarks, the Trademark Law Treaty, or the International Convention for the Protection of New Varieties of Plants. The authorities noted, however, that recent amendments to Armenia's Law on Trademark and the new Law on Patents (see below) have prepared the way for it to join these treaties in the near future. Armenia is a member of the Eurasian Patent Office. [43]

2. Armenia has notified the Agency of Intellectual Property (Agency) as the contact point under Article 69 of the TRIPS Agreement. [44] The Agency was established as a separate division acting within the Ministry of Economy, in 2002, following the merger of the Patent Office and the National Agency of Copyright. The Agency is responsible for policy formulation and implementation in industrial property and copyright, including processing applications for patent protection, and trade mark and design registration. It has a cooperation agreement with the European Patent Office (EPO) . The collection and payment of copyright royalties are carried out by the non-governmental organization ARMAUTHOR. [45] All intellectual property (IP) rights disputes are dealt with in the courts, in accordance with the legislation.

3. None of the nine free-trade agreements to which Armenia is a signatory contains TRIPS-plus clauses or any specific provisions regarding IP rights.

4. During the review period, trade in IPR-intensive goods (i.e. information technology (ITA) products, pharmaceuticals, beverages, and copyright based products) as a percentage of total trade increased by 3.1 percentage points, to reach 10.9% of Armenia's total trade in 2008 (approximately 5.5% of GDP) . This gain was underpinned by significant increases in imports of ITA products and in imports and exports of beverages (Table AV.1) .

5. Statistics are not available on the value of royalties and licence fees paid to or received from abroad during the review period.

(ii) Regulatory framework

1. The general objectives of Armenia's IP rights policy are to promote innovation and IP commercialization, and to provide effective economic rights protection to IP owners. Armenia notified its main IP laws to the WTO in 2003 and 2008 [46] and the legislation was reviewed in the TRIPS Council in 2004-05. [47]

2. During the review period, Armenia adopted new laws on copyrights and patents, and amended its law on trade marks. Armenia's main IP legislation covers the major areas referred to in the TRIPS Agreement (Table V.3) .

3. The new Law on Copyright and Related Rights, which entered into force in June 2006, introduced new provisions to further harmonize Armenian legislation with EC Directives. Amongst other things, it extended the economic rights from 50 to 70 years after the author's death, and broaden the coverage to include the rights of makers of databases. However, the authorities noted that implementation of the new Law remains a challenge.

4. The Law on Inventions, Utility Models and Industrial Designs, which entered into force in January 2009, replaced the Law on Patents of 2004. The objectives of the new Law are to modernize and simplify Armenian legislation, and to bring it more into line with provisions of the TRIPS Agreement and relevant EC Directives.

Overview of intellectual property rights protection, 2009

Law: scope	Term	Comments, limitations, and exclusions
Copyright and related rights		
Law on Copyright and Related Rights of 15 June 2006: literary, choreographic, audiovisual, decorative, photographic, architectural and scientific works, works of fine arts, translations and adaptations of works, maps, computer programs and databases	Lifetime of author or last co-author plus 70 years (including audiovisual works and computer programs) Collective works, anonymous or pseudonymous works, 70 years from disclosure or first publication Performers and producers of phonograms and films, 50 years from date of fixation	No registration is required for protection By the mere fact of creation, the author has original ownership of the right in the work, which includes the economic and moral rights defined in the Law Expressions of traditional folklore, daily news, official documents, state emblems, and political speeches are not protected
Patents (incl. utility models)		
Law on Inventions, Utility Models and Industrial Designs of 10 June 2008: any invention susceptible to industrial application, and any new and industrially applicable solution that concerns production or a method (i.e. utility model)	20 years from filing of application, extendable for a maximum of 5 years	Protection through registration of a patent The law does not provide for protection of scientific discoveries and theories, conventional signs, algorithms, and mental processes Plant and animal varieties, use of human embryos and processes of modifying genetic identity are not patentable
Industrial designs		
Law on Inventions, Utility Models and Industrial Designs	5 years from date of filing of application, possibility of	Protection through registration The protection conferred does

of 10 June 2008: any solution defining the outward appearance of an article, which is novel and original	renewal up to a total of 25 years	not include elements or characteristics of the design that serve only to obtain a technical effect
Layout-designs of integrated circuits		
Law on the Legal Protection of Topographies of Integrated Circuits of 3 February 1998: original layout-designs	10 years from the earlier of: the date of first use or the date of registration	Protection through registration Ownership rights may be transferred by agreement, either fully or partially, to other natural persons or legal entities
Trade marks and trade names		
Law on Trademarks, Service Marks and Appellations of Origin of 20 March 2000, as amended: any mark, sign, word or combination of these elements capable of distinguishing a product or service in trade	10 years from filling of application, indefinitely renewable for 10-year periods Use of the mark not compulsory	The following, inter alia, may not be registered: general designations; generally recognized symbols and terms; marks that are identical, similar, or alike to used marks; geographical designations that individualize wines that have not been produced in the place in question Foreigners must manage registration of trade marks through patent attorneys registered with the Agency of IP
Geographical indications		
Law on Trademarks, Service Marks and Appellations of Origin of 20 March 2000, as amended: appellations of origin	10 years from filling of application, indefinitely renewable for 10-year periods	Protection through registration Applicants may appeal against an examiner's decision
New plant varieties		
Law on Selection Achievements of 23 November 1999: new plant varieties	20 years from date of registration of the selection achievement in the State Register For varieties of grapevines and ornamental, fruit or forest trees, protection is granted for 25 years	Armenia is not a signatory of the UPOV; the National Assembly is expected to discuss a draft Law on the Protection of New Plant Varieties in 2010
Protection of undisclosed information		

information		
Articles 141, 1,164, 1,165, 1,166 of the Civil Code of 28 July 2000, and Law on Protection of Economic Competition of 15 December 2000: industrial and commercial secrets	Indefinitely	Persons who by illegal means have received secret information are obliged to compensate for losses caused Data subject to state registration and contained in state statistical reports may not be considered undisclosed information

Source: WTO Secretariat.

5. The authorities stated that a separate draft Law that will broaden the coverage of rights related to geographical indications (GIs) was sent to the National Assembly at the end of 2009. They also noted that the 2008 amendments to the Law on Trademarks, Service Marks, and Appellation of Origin of 2000 were not sufficient to clarify certain aspects of the Law and that a draft of an entire new law was presented to the National Assembly at the end of 2009.

6. During 2003-08, applications for the protection of inventions and utility models from national applicants increased while applications by foreigners declined; and applications for the protection of industrial designs from national applicants stayed constant while applications from foreigners increased. The approval rate of applications (i.e. percentage for which a patent was granted) is higher for nationals than for foreign applicants of inventions, and higher for both national and foreign applicants of utility models and industrial designs relative to inventions. With respect to patents in general, it seems that foreigners rushed to apply for protection after Armenia independence and lost their interest in more recent years. On the other hand, foreign interest in registering trade marks and trade names in Armenia has remained strong throughout the entire period. In 2008, nearly half of the 1,189 trade marks and 8,099 trade names registered were in the name of foreign applicants (under the national procedure [48]) . At end-2009, four appellations of origin were registered in Armenia for different kinds of mineral water; while alcoholic drinks were registered as trade marks rather than of appellations of origin. The new Law (see above) is expected to change both situations. [49]

7. The Agency's fees for legal protection of industrial property rights are identical for nationals and foreigners. [50]

8. Compulsory licences to use a protected invention, utility model or industrial design may be granted by court decision in cases of: national security or health emergencies; abuse of patent rights; or if the rights have not been used for four years after the filling of application (or three years from granting of patent certificate) . The person asking for the licence must prove that efforts were made to conclude a contract with the right holder on reasonable commercial terms and that such efforts failed within a reasonable period. Compulsory licences have a limited duration, may not be transferred, and may not be used to export. In the case of semiconductor technologies, a compulsory licence may be granted only for exclusively non-commercial use and for prevention of unfair competition. [51] No compulsory licences were granted during 2003-09.

9. Armenia's current IP legislation has provisions that allow parallel importation of patented protected products as well as copies of fixed performances and of fixation of a film. [52] During the review period, the authorities received, but did not react to, some complaints against parallel importation from distributors that want exclusive rights over their respective product markets. The authorities state that, given the small scale of Armenia's economy and the low level of

competition in numerous consumer product markets (see section (4) above), it may be beneficial to the economy to permit parallel imports.

(iii) Enforcement

1. Armenia submitted its Checklist of Issues on Enforcement to the WTO in 2004. [53]

2. Armenian civil courts are empowered to order the payment of damages and court expenses, as well as other remedies envisioned in the TRIPS Agreement. The Courts of First Instance also have authority where necessary, to take the provisional measures envisioned in Article 50 of the TRIPS Agreement. Foreigners enjoy the same rights as Armenian nationals. [54] Section 10 of Armenia's Civil Code establishes provisions for the enforcement of IP rights protection, with the exception of the Law on Copyright, which also carries enforcement provisions. Furthermore, the Criminal Code of 2003 establishes different fines and prison terms for infringement of each of the main IP rights.

3. Customs authorities (SRC) do not have *ex officio* power to inspect shipments for counterfeit goods. On the other hand, a holder of any IP right may submit a suspension request to the SRC in order to prevent the release of the product from customs; this measure does not apply to goods in transit. [55] The authorities noted that the SRC did not receive any such request during the period under review.

4. Although Armenia has adopted extensive and carefully written legislation on IP rights, it has been reported that counterfeit goods circulate reasonably freely within Armenia, and that effective enforcement of IP rights remains a challenge. [56]

DEVELOPMENTS IN TRADE AND INVESTMENT

MERCHANDISE TRADE

(a) Composition of trade

1. The composition and direction of Armenia's merchandise trade during the period 2003-08 are presented in Appendix tables AI.1 through AI.6; these are based on information from the United Nations' Comtrade database.

2. Armenia's total trade (imports plus exports and re-exports) increased at an average annual nominal rate of 23% over 2003-08; as a proportion of GDP, trade decreased from 67.1% in 2003 to 43.3% in 2008. Over the same period, imports grew faster than exports, with the trade deficit increasing from US$0.6 billion in 2003 to US$3.1 billion in 2008; imports represented on average 69% of total trade. Furthermore, Armenia's terms of trade have improved significantly, due, *inter alia*, to sharp increases in the price of copper and ferro-alloys, while gas prices remained fairly stable, and prices of manufacturing goods, in general, decreased. [21]

3. During the review period, re-exports represented on average 17% of total exports (Tables AI.1 and AI.2) . Re-exports covered a wide range of products, but the majority consisted of coffee (re-exported mainly to Russia and Georgia), non-electrical machines, textiles (re-exported mainly to the United States), clothing, jewellery and gold (re-exported mainly to Europe); processed diamonds are not counted as re-exports. The authorities noted that Armenia's relatively liberal trade regime (mainly low tariffs) and the high value of some of these commodities, more than compensate for high transportation costs, making re-exports economically feasible.

4. Armenia's export basket has historically been concentrated in mineral products and processed diamonds. Although there has been some diversification (the share of processed diamonds in total exports dropped from 50% in 2003 to 15% in 2008) the export basket continues to be concentrated in a handful of products and somewhat biased towards goods with high value relative to weight, due to high transport costs (see below) . In 2008, four groups of products (i.e. spirits, copper, ferro-alloys and diamonds) represented approximately 70% of total exports (Table AI.3) .

5. The composition of imports remained practically unchanged in general terms during 2003-08 (Table AI.4) . Close to 59% of Armenia's imports were manufactured goods in 2008. Amongst manufactures, imports of rough diamonds fell significantly while imports of machinery and transport equipment increased. Imports of iron and steel grew tenfold in nominal value terms and doubled in relative importance, underpinned by strong demand from the construction sector.

6. Both exports and imports are affected by Armenia's closed borders with Turkey and Azerbaijan. This diplomatic conundrum has increased transport costs, and made Armenia highly dependant on Georgia's transportation routes. High and volatile transportation costs hinder Armenia's integration into international production chains and networks, and its capacity to create new export products that are economically sensible. Thus, trade would be expected to grow and diversify should the borders re-open and transport links be re-established.

(b) Direction of trade

1. The direction of Armenia's merchandise trade changed somewhat during 2003-08. Russia remained Armenia's main trading partner, accounting for 20% of exports and 20% of imports in 2008. If the other countries of the Commonwealth of Independent States (CIS) are added, the share of total trade increased to 31.2% in 2008. The share of total trade with the European Union (EU27) remained high, and the European Union as a group was Armenia's largest trading partner, accounting for nearly 35% of total trade in 2008. However, trade with specific Member states of the EU changed as trade with Belgium (and Israel) fell dramatically due to the reduction in diamond processing, while exports to Germany and the Netherlands increased considerably (Table AI.5) . Exports to the United States declined in total value terms and as a percentage of total exports, mainly due to the lack of demand as a result of the economic crisis.

2. The share of the EU27 in imports declined during the period under review, while the share of the CIS and Asia increased. In particular, imports from China increased tremendously making it Armenia's second largest provider of imported goods after Russia (Table AI.6) . Among others, imports from China include consumer products in general, furniture, textiles, shoes, and electronics. Although Armenia has nine free trade agreements in force with CIS countries, trade diversion is unlikely to be significant given that nearly three quarters of tariff lines are duty-free.

(ii) Trade in services

1. During 2003-08, Armenia's services exports grew slower than services imports, worsening the deficit in the balance of trade in services, which represented 11% of the total trade balance deficit in 2008 (Table I.6) . In particular, the contribution of transportation and insurance services (mainly freight) to the trade deficit has tripled, in part reflecting Armenia's landlocked nature and closed borders. Trade in tourism services was the fastest growing subsector during the review period, and tourism became Armenia's largest generator of services export earnings. Surprisingly, given the recent real estate boom, Armenia imported little in the way of construction services.

Trade in services, (US$ million)

	2003	2004	2005	2006	2007	2008[a]
Balance of trade in services	-68.3	-98.9	-119.9	-130.4	-212.5	-327.1
Services exports	207.4	332.6	411.1	484.7	580.0	645.0
Transportation	73.0	73.6	92.2	102.3	132.9	137.7
Freight	46.2	43.2	58.0	59.2	83.3	76.8
Tourism services	72.7	171.5	219.9	270.7	304.9	330.5
Communication	16.7	23.8	28.2	22.9	41.4	62.1
Construction	7.9	11.9	10.6	9.9	11.2	14.3
Insurance	7.4	9.2	11.8	14.8	14.7	15.5
Other services	29.7	42.6	48.4	64.1	74.9	84.9
Services imports	-275.7	-431.5	-531.1	-615.6	-792.6	-972.1
Transportation	-151.3	-178.7	-211.6	-231.9	-361.3	-486.7
Freight	-116.6	-118.3	-147.2	-183.9	-267.8	-369.0
Tourism services	-67.0	-178.9	-236.3	-286.1	-294.3	-324.0
Communication	-10.9	-12.9	-13.9	-16.5	-17.2	-20.1
Construction	-3.1	-3.3	-2.8	-3.2	-3.8	-5.2
Insurance	-15.4	-18.4	-23.7	-28.7	-48.9	-72.8
Other services	28.0	-39.3	-42.8	-49.2	-67.1	-81.3

FOREIGN DIRECT INVESTMENT

1. Inflows of foreign direct investment (FDI) grew at annual average rate of 38.9% between 2003 and 2008, and the net stock of FDI in Armenia reached US$3.4 billion in December 2008 (Table I.7) . This was driven by large increases of FDI in telecommunications and financial services, as well as the electricity sector since 2006; together these accounted for approximately 59% of the total FDI stock in 2008 (Chapter VI) . Inflows of FDI into the food and beverages industry doubled over the review period, while investment in other manufacturing industries fell dramatically to US$3.6 million in 2008.

FDI inflows and stock, (US$ million)

	Gross inflows	Net stock Dec. 2008

	2003	2004	2005	2006	2007	2008	
FDI by economic sector							
Agriculture	0.0	0.0	0.0	0.0	0.0	22.9	24.5
Mining	12.2	42.9	98.4	66.0	80.9	33.8	218.9
Food and beverages	12.9	34.7	26.4	11.4	21.2	25.4	237.9
Other manufactures	73.4	5.1	8.3	6.5	4.3	3.6	122.7
Tourism, retail, and wholesale trade	8.2	7.8	9.5	19.6	24.9	6.5	103.2
Construction	1.1	1.0	4.4	6.4	1.0	1.6	20.4
Real estate activities	4.2	13.0	30.8	40.1	29.9	29.6	179.1
Electricity, gas, and water supply	3.8	32.3	0.1	142.9	222.8	476.3	1,008.3
Telecommunications and post	10.1	43.2	56.1	61.9	149.4	157.8	650.6
Financial services	67.7	20.5	28.8	29.5	93.0	123.6	365.8
Transport services (incl. pipelines)	3.6	24.4	14.9	33.6	18.2	201.1	291.1
Other service activities	20.7	10.3	26.1	18.7	29.8	42.1	201.7
FDI by country of origin							
Russia	68.4	52.4	12.5	153.9	339.5	735.4	1,914.0
EU	36.2	124.7	193.4	147.5	130.0	203.4	717.9
France	9.4	28.4	20.2	16.1	18.7	84.5	261.8
Argentina	3.6	24.4	11.2	33.6	18.2	87.7	175.4
United States	10.8	12.2	16.5	38.3	30.8	23.9	171.0
Canada	11.3	3.4	0.9	17.9	0	0.0	98.8
Other countries	87.3	18.1	69.0	47.0	159.4	74.1	362.3
Total	217.7	235.2	303.7	436.7	675.3	1,124.5	3,424.6

Source: WTO Secretariat, based on information from the National Statistical Service of the Republic of Armenia.

2. FDI in transportation services surged in 2008 as the construction of the gas pipeline between Armenia and Iran started. Real estate activities attracted US$32.6 million on average during 2005-08, suggesting that the contribution of the diaspora to the recent construction boom was twofold: via remittances and FDI.

3. Russia is by far the main source of FDI capital inflow into Armenia, accounting for 50% of the inflows in 2007, and 65% of inflows and 56% of the stock in 2008. The EU is the second largest source, particularly France, followed by Argentina and the United States. Not coincidentally, these countries all host large Armenian immigrant populations.

TRADE AND INVESTMENT POLICY FRAMEWORK

1. As in other states of the former Soviet Union, Armenia's economy contracted sharply after independence. In addition, at that time it was still suffering the effects of the Spitak Earthquake in December 1988, which killed 25,000, left about 500,000 homeless and was responsible for the closure of the nuclear power plant. The conflict in Nagorno-Karabakh and the subsequent closure of the borders between Armenia and Azerbaijan, and between Armenia and Turkey, added to the economic difficulties.

2. The collapse of the rouble and the introduction of the Armenian dram in November 1993 marked the start of a return to economic stability. With IMF support, the Armenian Government started to stabilize the economy through an ambitious reform programme, which included Armenia's 1993 application to accede to the GATT and, in 1995, the WTO.

3. With the assistance of the European Union under the Partnership and Cooperation Agreement between Armenia and the European Union (signed in 1996), the European Neighbourhood Action Plan (adopted in November 2006), the Country Strategy Paper 2007-2013 and the National Indicative Programme Armenia has undertaken a comprehensive reform of much of its legislation, institutions and policy implementation to bring them into line with those of the EU. The objective of much of the reform is to improve trade and economic ties with the EU to the point where Armenia can establish a a deep and comprehensive free-trade area with the Union.

4. At the same time, Armenia has maintained its existing network of free-trade agreements with other nine CIS countries and is exploring the possibility of improving its economic relations with its neighbour Iran.

GENERAL INSTITUTIONAL FRAMEWORK

(i) Branches of government

1. Following the collapse of the Soviet Union and a referendum of its citizens, Armenia became an independent republic in 1991. The Constitution was adopted by a nationwide referendum on 5 July 1995, and a number of amendments were made through another referendum on 27 November 2005. [1] The amendments to the Constitution improved the distribution of powers among the presidency, Government, and National Assembly, and provided greater independence to the judiciary. State power is to be exercised based on the principle of the separation of the executive, legislative, and judicial powers. The Venice Commission of the Council of Europe assisted the Armenian authorities in preparing the draft amendments before they were put to the referendum in 2005. [2]

2. According to the Constitution, the head of state is the President who is elected for a five-year term with a maximum of two consecutive terms. The last Presidential election was held in

February 2008. The President's responsibilities are set out in Article 55 of the Constitution. Amongst other things, he represents the country in international relations, is the commander-in-chief of the armed forces, and is responsible for making a number of key official appointments. These official appointments include:

- the Prime Minister, who must be the person enjoying the confidence of the majority of Deputies in the National Assembly or, failing that, the greatest number of deputies;
- the members of the Government, upon the recommendation of the Prime Minister;
- four members of the Constitutional Court (there are a total of nine members plus a president) [3];
- two legal scholars to the Council of Justice (there are another nine members of the council elected by the General Assembly of Judges and two more appointed by the National Assembly) [4];
- the presidents and judges of the Court of Cassation, upon the recommendation of the Council of Justice. (The Court of Cassation is, the highest judiciary body in Armenia except for constitutional issues);
- judges of the courts of Appeal and First Instance, upon the conclusion of the Council of Justice; and
- as Commander-in-Chief of the armed forces, the office of the Highest Command of the armed and paramilitary forces.

3. The President also recommends candidates for the posts of Chairman of the Central Bank, Chairman of the Control Chamber, and the Prosecutor General, who are appointed by the National Assembly. On the recommendation of the Prosecutor General, he also appoints the deputies to this post.

4. The head of Government is the Prime Minister, who chooses the ministers and the Vice Prime Minister for appointment by the President. The Government is responsible for policy development and implementation through ministries and other public institutions. At end-November 2009, there were 18 Ministers; one of who, the Minister of Territorial Administration, is also the Vice Prime Minister.

5. Legislative power is vested in the unicameral National Assembly, which consists of 131 deputies elected for five-year terms. The last elections were held in May 2007. In addition to its main role of debating and voting on proposed legislation, the Assembly also appoints the Chairman of the National Assembly's Oversight Office and the President of the Constitutional Court, and elects the Human Rights Defender (the Armenian equivalent of an ombudsman), which requires a two-thirds majority of the National Assembly.

6. The court system in Armenia is based on the Judicial Code (in effect since 1 January 2008 and amended in February 2009) . There are Common Jurisdiction Courts of First Instance, then Civil and Criminal Courts of Appeal and, at the highest level, the Court of Cassation and the Constitutional Court. [5]

7. The Common Jurisdiction Courts of First Instance are responsible for civil cases involving claims of up to 5,000 times the minimum monthly salary. The Civil Court of Appeal has jurisdiction to hear civil cases for claims above this threshold, bankruptcy cases, and non-property disputes specified by procedural law. [6] Eight, out of a total of 30, civil court judges are

designated to hear bankruptcy cases. The appeals may only be based on evidence presented in the first court. For non-constitutional issues, the highest court is the Court of Cassation.

8. The Constitutional Court is responsible for determining the constitutionality of domestic legislation and the conformity with the Constitution of treaties before they are sent to the National Assembly for ratification. Its responsibilities also include resolving disputes regarding national elections or referenda, and determining whether there are grounds to impeach the President.

(ii) Institutional powers in WTO-related matters

1. In Armenia, a treaty enters into force after the Constitutional Court has declared it to be in conformity with the Constitution and after it has been ratified by the National Assembly. Under Article 6 of the Constitution, all domestic legislation in Armenia must conform to the Constitution. Therefore, in cases of conflict, the Constitution and treaties prevail over domestic legislation

2. Since June 2002 the *Official Bulletin of the Republic of Armenia* and the *Bulletin for Departmental Normative Acts of the Republic of Armenia* have, between them, published all new legislation including: international agreements, laws enacted by the National Assembly, Decrees and Orders of the President, Resolutions of the National Assembly, Resolutions of the Government and the Prime-Minister, and Orders of ministers and governors.

3. On 17 December 1993, Armenia applied to accede to the GATT under Article XXXIII of GATT 1947. It applied to accede to the Organization on 31 January 1995, under Article XII of the Agreement Establishing the WTO. [7] It became the 145th Member of the WTO on 5 February 2003, 30 days after it had been confirmed that the Protocol of Accession had been ratified by the National Assembly.

4. The Ministry of Economy has responsibility for most aspects of policy affecting international trade in goods and services. [8] It replaced the Ministry of Trade and Economic Development by Presidential Decree on 21 April 2008. The Armenian Development Agency was established in 1998 to assist investors, including export promotion activities (Chapter IV(5)) . The Agency is governed by a board with the Prime Minister as Chairman. Relevant government ministries and the private sector (for example the Union of Manufacturers and Entrepreneurs) are also represented on the Board.

5. Sanitary and phytosanitary measures are the responsibility of a number of ministries. The Ministry of Agriculture is responsible for measures relating to animal and plant health. The Ministry of Healthcare is responsible for food safety and the Ministry of Environmental Protection for threats to the environment (Chapter III(9)) . Technical regulations and standards are the responsibility of various governmental bodies within the Ministry of Economy (Chapter III(8)) .

6. The Armenian Central Bank is responsible for the development, approval, and implementation of monetary policy programmes, and issuing the currency. It also has the authority to license and supervise the activities of credit institutions in Armenia and, since 1 January 2006, has been the regulator and supervisor of the financial market. [9] Under the amendments to the Constitution in 2005 and the amendments to the Law on Central Bank, the Central Bank is independent (Chapters I(2) and VI(4)(ii)) .

7. The privatization programme is the responsibility of the Government's Department of State Property Management (Chapter V(2)) .

8. A number of public institutions are responsible for public policy on investment and its implementation in Armenia: the Ministry of Economy is responsible for investment generally and for improving Armenia's investment rating; the Business Support Council, for reducing

administrative barriers and regulations on investment; the Armenian Development Agency (ADA), for implementing investment policy; and the Securities Commission regulates the securities market. [10] The Law on Foreign Investments of July 1994 is the principle legislation. No significant restrictions are applied to foreign investors, and no significant direct incentives are offered to foreign investors over local ones, but investment is encouraged through ADA assistance with procedures, and through a general policy to encourage investment from domestic sources or from abroad. For more details (Chapter V(1)(ii)) .

9. Armenia is a landlocked country and two of its four borders are closed. Thus, although transport policy is the responsibility of the Ministry of Transport and Communication, the larger political issues affecting the country have a much greater impact on transport than the roads and railways to Georgia and Iran. Road and rail infrastructure depends on available funds, both through the domestic budget and from foreign donors (Chapter VI(4)(iv)) .

10. The State Revenue Committee is responsible for collection and administration of taxes, including: customs valuation; tariffs; rules of origin, and border controls (Chapter III(1)) .

11. The Agency of Intellectual Property was created in 2002 within the Ministry of Economy, and it is responsible for policy formulation and implementation with respect to intellectual property rights (Chapter V(6)) .

INSTITUTIONAL REFORMS

1. During the accession process a number of important institutional reforms took place covering many aspects of the economy, including: adoption of the obligations of Article VIII of the IMF Agreement (Sections 2, 3, and 4); new system for income, value-added, and property taxes; adoption of bound tariffs; and continuation of the privatization programme.

2. Before and since acceding to the WTO in 2003, Armenia has been pursuing a policy of reform in the legal, administrative and institutional areas. Although the most important legal changes were the 2005 amendments of the Constitution, other reforms in national legislation have continued, including several that directly affect trade. The reforms in legislation included: the 2001 Law on Licensing which simplified import and other licensing procedures; the 2002 Law on Anti-Dumping and Countervailing Measures; the 2001 Law on Protection of Domestic Market, which established the legal basis for safeguard measures; and the 2004 Law on Veterinary Practice. The institutional reforms included: the establishment of the State Revenue Committee in 2008 (Chapter III(1)); the changes to the structure of the courts made in 2008 (see above); and the extension of the regulatory role of the Central Bank (Chapter VI(4)) .

3. The World Bank has identified several areas where reforms are needed to remove constraints to economic growth, including several issues linked to the efficiency of the public sector and the reduction of corruption. [11]

4. In the past few years, Armenia has been taking steps to address political and public accountability. In addition to the reforms in the judiciary and in the Customs Office (Chapter III(1)), penalties for tax evasion were increased and higher audit standards for public bodies were introduced. However, according to the World Bank, surveys of public and business opinion have repeatedly shown tax and customs, education, and anti-corruption policy as the main areas of concern. [12] In addition, despite being ranked 43rd out of 183 countries in the World Bank's Ease of Doing Business Index, Armenia's performance varied considerably from one category to another, for example, it was ranked 5th for registering property and 153rd for paying taxes. [13]

5. In Transparency International's 2009 Corruption Perceptions Index, Armenia was 120th out of 180 countries, a decline from 99th place in 2007 [14]; according to the Global Corruption Barometer it scored particularly badly for confidence in the judiciary. [15] This view is supported by other reports. [16] The new Judicial Code of 2008 is meant to address many of the issues concerning public perception of corruption in the judiciary. In addition, the authorities are preparing an anti-corruption strategy, which is expected to focus on rules for the conduct of public servants and managing conflicts of interest. It will also address the interaction between the public and private sectors, not only at central government level, but also at agency level. A third element of the strategy will include improved accountability in terms of both how the public service operates and its use of resources.

MAIN TRADE AGREEMENTS

6. Armenia's trade policy is predominantly focused on trade with the EU and with members of the Commonwealth of Independent States (CIS), which together represented 68% of imports and 87% of exports (including re-exports) in 2008. It is also heavily influenced by the closed borders with Turkey and Azerbaijan. According to reports, this has greatly limited trading opportunities and increased the costs of exports and imports, and has restricted economic growth in Armenia. Opening the borders would benefit Armenia although it has been stated that there would be some adjustment costs for some sectors.

World Trade Organization

(a) Accession to the WTO [18]

1. During the process for its accession to the WTO in 2003, Armenia had a relatively straightforward tariff structure with nearly all tariffs at rates of 0% or 10%; it also had a largely open and non-discriminatory trade and investment regime. However, the accession process required substantial legislative changes to bring domestic policies into line with WTO rules.

2. Upon accession, it bound the entire Schedule in *ad valorem* terms with rates ranging from 0% to 15% (Chapter III(4)) with each product listed individually. It also joined in a number of zero-for-zero initiatives, including: agricultural equipment, chemicals, most construction equipment, medical equipment, most paper, pharmaceuticals, steel, and ITA.

3. Armenia also undertook to abide by the rules applicable to developed country Members. It did not undertake any commitments on tariff quotas and did not reserve the right to use the special agricultural safeguard for any agricultural products. On subsidies to agriculture, Armenia undertook: not to seek recourse to the investment, input, and diversification subsidies provided for under Article 6.2 of the Agreement on Agriculture for developing countries; accepted, with effect from end 2008, a de minimis limit of 5% of the value of agricultural production for calculating its Current Total Aggregate Measurement of Support [19]; and bound its export subsidies at zero. Furthermore, it undertook to remove, by the end of 2008, an exemption from VAT which applied to basic agriculture products and veterinary drugs.

4. Other changes to customs and related procedures included: replacing the *ad valorem* customs fee of 0.3% by a uniform fee of US$6.50 for customs processing and a specific weight-related fee of US$0.55 per tonne for freight inspection; changing the origin principle of charging VAT and excise tax on imports, which exempted imports from CIS countries, to the destination principle to comply with Article I of GATT; and amending the Customs Code to allow for greater use of transaction value as a basis for customs valuation.

5. Armenia did not apply any quantitative restrictions to imports or exports before or after acceding to the WTO. However, a number of products are subject to import prohibitions for health, security, and environmental reasons. In the accession process Armenia also undertook to apply excise duties in a way that ensures that similar products are subject to the same levels of duties.

6. In services, Armenia's commitments cover all sectors except postal services and, not surprisingly for a landlocked country, maritime services. However, it maintains limitations on the right of foreign natural persons to own land as well as several other sector-specific restrictions. Service suppliers, like all businesses in Armenia, are required to register with the State Register of Legal Entities.

(a) Participation in the WTO

7. Armenia has a Permanent Mission to the United Nations Office and other International Organizations at Geneva which currently has one diplomat, the Permanent Representative, who is responsible for trade and economic issues including: WTO matters; and economic and trade matters in other international Organizations based in Geneva (for example, UNCTAD, WIPO and UPOV) . In addition, he is responsible for issues relating to bilateral trade between Armenia and Switzerland.

8. In the negotiations under the Doha Development Agenda, Armenia is a member of the group of recently acceded Members (RAMs) and has participated in its proposals. In the most recent draft of modalities for agriculture, Armenia has been listed, along with some other RAMs [20], as a small, low-income RAM with an economy in transition; therefore, it would be entitled to additional flexibility relative to that provided for other recently acceded Members. Similarly, in the most recent draft of modalities for market access for non-agriculture products, Armenia, along with some other RAMs [21], would be entitled to greater flexibility than that provided for other recently acceded Members.

9. Armenia has been particularly active in the negotiations on trade facilitation where, as part of various groups, it has submitted several proposals, mostly on the transit of goods. [22] As of end-2009, it had not submitted an offer on services. According to the authorities, it has not been active in the services negotiations because it had already made extensive commitments in this area in its accession to the WTO. Armenia has started negotiations to accede to the Government Procurement Agreement. The authorities stated that, although it has not actively participated in many meetings, it is a member of the RAMs group, through which it has participated in the negotiations. Furthermore, as a small country with limited resources, it has to focus its efforts where they are most needed.

10. Following the administrative reorganization under which the Ministry of Economy replaced the Ministry of Trade and Economic Development (MTED), an agency was created with responsibility for notifications to the WTO. The Ministry of Economy is responsible for the agency

11. Since accession, Armenia has not been involved in any disputes under the WTO's dispute settlement mechanism.

Generalized System of Preferences

12. Armenia has GSP arrangements with Canada, Japan, Norway, Switzerland, and the United States. [23] Since 1 January 2009, it has had GSP+ status with the European Union. [24]

(i) European Union [25]

13. In addition to being eligible for the European Union's GSP+ arrangement, Armenia has a number of agreements with the EU covering a broad range of political, social, cultural and economic issues. The Partnership and Cooperation Agreement between the EC and Armenia was signed in April 1996 and entered into force in July 1999. Following the outcome of the European Council of 14 June 2004, the countries of the South Caucasus entered into the framework of the European Neighbourhood Policy. Following a Country Report published in March 2005, an Action Plan was discussed between the Commission and the Armenian Government and adopted in November 2006. [26] The five-year Action Plan is intended to help, *inter alia*, improve trade and economic integration with the EU including through the alignment of laws and regulations. It includes a number of objectives relating to trade, such as improving the administrative capacity of the customs administration and setting up a mechanism for consultations with the trading community. It also requires monitoring of compliance with WTO rules in the framework of existing WTO rules and procedures. The Country Strategy Paper for 2007-13 and the National Indicative Programmes provide technical assistance from the EU to Armenia to meet a number of goals, including: good governance; regulatory reform; administrative capacity building; and poverty reduction.

14. Implementation of the ENP Action Plans are intended, *inter alia*, to assist development in Armenia, and the other countries of the South Caucuses (Azerbaijan and Georgia), so that they can negotiate, implement, and sustain a deep and comprehensive free-trade area with the EU. [27] Such an agreement would cover more than tariffs and rules of origin. It would require close alignment with the EU of Armenia's trade-related laws and their implementation in many areas, including: sanitary and phytosanitary measures; technical barriers to trade; and intellectual property. A feasibility study for such an agreement, completed in May 2008, concluded that it would benefit Armenia, but that Armenia was not ready, at that stage, to enter such an FTA. [28] However, the authorities stated that Armenia's implementation of the current Action Plan and the Country Strategy Plan was contributing to the reform and improvement of institutional structures which should, in the foreseeable future, enable Armenia to start negotiations on establishing a deep and comprehensive free-trade area with the EU.

Commonwealth of Independent States

15. The Report of the Working Party on the Accession of the Republic of Armenia to the WTO states that the Treaty of Economic Union between the Heads of State of the Commonwealth of Independent States (CIS) in 1993 was a framework document and that the specifics of preferential trading relationships should be defined in the bilateral free-trade agreements. [29] The Report of the Working Party also states that Armenia had concluded and ratified seven free-trade agreements. [30]

16. At the end of 2009, Armenia had nine FTAs in force, all them with its CIS partners: Belarus, Georgia, Kazakhstan, Kyrgyz Republic, Moldova, Russian Federation, Tajikistan, Turkmenistan, and Ukraine. Of these, only five have been notified to the Committee on Regional Trade Agreements. [31] The agreements effectively apply duty-free treatment to all merchandise imports into Armenia from these countries but they do not cover trade in services, investment or government procurement.

Other agreements

17. Armenia, along with Albania, Azerbaijan, Bulgaria, Georgia, Greece, Moldova, Romania, the Russian Federation, Serbia, Turkey and Ukraine, is a member of the Organization of the Black Sea Economic Cooperation (BSEC) . The BSEC is a multilateral, economic initiative aimed at encouraging cooperation in the Black Sea region. [32] Armenia has had an MFN trade agreement with Iran since 1997 [33], and has been exploring the possibility of entering into negotiations to with the objective of achieving closer economic ties.

MEASURES AFFECTING MARKET ACCESS FOR GOODS

CUSTOMS PROCEDURES

1. The State Revenue Committee (SRC) is responsible for, *inter alia*, tax revenue collection and customs administration. The SRC was established in August 2008, after the merger between the State Tax Service and the State Customs Committee, as an independent government body that reports directly to the Prime Minister. Armenia has been a member of the World Customs Organization since 1992.

2. Armenia's customs regime is based on the Customs Code of 1 January 2001, last amended in 2008, and detailed customs import procedures are laid down in Government Decree No. 236 of 2001. The Customs Code grants the SRC the authority to apply administrative fines, arrest suspects, and confiscate goods in cases of infringements of customs regulations. Decisions by the SRC, as well as other action or inaction by customs authorities, may be appealed to the SRC or to the courts. The SRC has powers to inspect and/or detain goods entering Armenia or in transit if it suspects (generally as a result of a complaint) that the goods infringe intellectual property rights or constitute illicit substances (Chapter V(6)) .

3. Under Armenian legislation, engaging in entrepreneurial activities, including foreign trade, without State registration is prohibited. Natural persons may import limited quantities of goods for personal use [1], but to sell those goods they must be registered as a sole entrepreneur. [2] Thus, to import goods commercially, an importer must be a legal entity registered in the State Registry of Armenia, including a branch or an official representative of a foreign company (Chapter V(1)) . Moreover, an importer must register with its local custom office by presenting its registration with the State Registry, tax identification number, and company charter.

4. Customs clearance may be carried out by the importer or by a licensed customs broker (agent); the latter must be an Armenian national. [3] All goods imported commercially must be declared to customs within ten days after arrival in the Armenian customs territory, and they remain under customs control during this period, although not necessarily under physical control. Customs clearance must be done at the customs office where the legal entity (i.e. the importer) is registered (see above), with the exception of goods entering via the Yerevan International Airport, in which case they must be cleared at the airport.

5. In 2007, an amendment to the Customs Code introduced post-clearance controls, through which the SRC may review customs declarations submitted during the last three years. The authorities noted that during 2008, when it was first applied, 60 post-clearance controls were carried out by the SRC, and that the assessment criteria depended on the risk profile of the imported good.

6. During the review period, Armenia continued to modernize its customs administration through the creation of a more effective tax collection authority, the SRC (see above), and by improving its electronic system. Though not yet compulsory, the on-line customs declaration system has been perceived as having helped to improve efficiency and curb corruption. Furthermore, the 2008 upgrade of the customs' software system has simplified and expedited certain customs procedures related to valuation (see section (2) below) . [4]

7. The upgraded electronic system includes a traffic light (channel) system at the border. Goods passing through the green channel cross the border without any verification; if the red channel is selected, the import is subject to documentary verification and physical examination; for the yellow channel, only documentary verification is necessary. In 2008, the green channel was

selected in 66% of all import declarations, the red and yellow channels each accounted for 17%. [5]

8. The Customs Code establishes that imports of up to dram 50,000 (US$142) are directed to a customs express system, independently of their means of transport. Imports of higher value must follow regular customs procedures. Furthermore, the authorities indicated that in 2009 a specialized customs house was established for goods imported via post or courier operators, regardless of their value.

9. In accordance with its WTO accession commitment [6], Armenia did not implement a preshipment inspection system during the review period, and the authorities stated that there were no plans to do so.

10. According to studies by the World Bank, it took on average 24 days to complete the customs clearance process in 2008, a 35% decrease compared with 2005 (first year available) . [7] On the other hand, the number of documents needed to import goods into Armenia increased from six in 2005 to nine in 2008 [8], and the cost of importing a container was higher than the average in Eastern Europe and Central Asia. These three factors combined ranked Armenia in 143rd place out of 181 countries in good practice for trading across borders. In 2009, the number of documents that must be presented at customs clearance was reduced to three: custom declaration; invoice; and the contract for international carriage of goods by road (CMR note) . [9]

CUSTOMS VALUATION

1. The SRC is responsible for applying the regulations on customs valuation. The regulations are set out in Articles 74 to 96 of Armenia's Customs Code of 2001 and in Decree No. 2170 of 5 December 2002. [10]

2. In general terms, Armenia's regulations on customs valuation appear to be in line with the Agreement on Implementation of Article VII of GATT 1994 (the Customs Valuation Agreement or CVA), although, in 2003, the Government acknowledged that more efforts were needed to improve the transparency with which those rules were implemented by customs authorities. [11] During the review period, the Government sought to improve transparency by enhancing the customs electronic system and expediting the determination of customs value. Nevertheless, it has been reported that there is still room for improvement in the implementation of the CVA. [12]

3. Under-declaration of transaction value is a persistent problem in Armenia. The authorities indicate that this is why the use of transaction value has been low throughout the review period, although it is the authorities' preferred method of valuation. Nevertheless, although an exact figure was not available, they stated that there had been a significant increase in the use of transaction value when compared with 2003 when it was used in only 25% of cases. [13]

4. In 2003 Armenia replied to the Checklist of Issues relating to Article 22 of the CVA concerning the implementation and administration of the Agreement. [14] Among other things, Armenia noted that, in accordance with Article 1.2(a) of the CVA, Article 95 of its Customs Code grants the importer the right to demand a written explanation of the valuation decision and the method used by customs authorities, and requires a response within five working days of submission of the written request. It also noted that importers have the right to appeal the decision to the superior customs bodies or to the court; the superior customs body must make its decision regarding the appeal, and inform the applicant within one month. [15] In practice, the majority of the appeals brought forward by importers during 2003-08 related to the rejection of the transaction value by customs authorities. [16]

5. With reference to Article 1.2 of the CVA, Armenia noted that, under Paragraph (2)(d) of Article 87 of its Customs Code, the transaction price is accepted between related persons as long as the relationship did not influence the price. [17] Furthermore, an importer has the option of proving the relationship did not influence the price by the "circumstance of sale" or the "test value" methods. [18]

6. In 2008, the Armenian Customs Code was changed to allow an importer whose documentation is incomplete to use bank guarantees to cover the duties resulting from a disputed customs value. In all cases, the bank guarantee must cover the 30-day period allowed to the superior customs authority to reach a final decision. While importers may obtain bank guarantees directly from the banks, the authorities noted that they were rarely used (15 cases in 2008), as the banks were reluctant to provide them.

7. The exchange rate applied by the customs authorities is derived from the daily foreign exchange auctions held by the Central Bank of Armenia (Chapter I) . These rates are published in the press and posted every day in accounting offices of the customs bodies. [19]

RULES OF ORIGIN

1. The rules of origin applied to all goods entering Armenia (i.e. non-preferential and preferential) have been notified to the WTO. [20] The SRC is responsible for verifying certificates of origin and investigating the origin of goods without a certificate.

2. For non-preferential trade, in cases where more than one country participates in the production of the goods, the two main criteria for determining origin are: (a) a change in the first four digits of tariff classification; or (b) a minimum value added corresponding to 30% of the final value of the good. Article 160 of Armenia's Customs Code defines the products that should be considered as wholly obtained in one country. In accordance with its WTO accession commitments, Armenia has amended Paragraph 2 of Article 167 of its Customs Code in order to bring it into compliance with the requirements of Article 2(h) and Annex II of the WTO Agreement on Rules of Origin. [21]

3. Although the legislation establishes that the absence of a certificate of origin cannot be used as a basis to forbid the transportation of goods through customs border [22] , this rule is not applied in exceptional cases, such as when the imported good is subject to an emergency SPS measure.

4. Armenia applies preferential rules of origin under all its trade agreements that are in force: i.e. Belarus, Georgia, Kazakhstan, Kyrgyz Republic, Moldova, Russian Federation, Tajikistan, Turkmenistan, and Ukraine.[23] In 2008, 7.1% of all import declarations presented a certificate of origin in order to benefit from preferential treatment under one of these agreements. [24]

5. The rules of origin applicable for trade under these preferential agreements were established in the Decision on the Rules for the Determination of a Country of Origin of Goods, adopted on 30 November 2000 by the Council of Heads of the CIS Governments. [25] According to this decision, in order to receive preferential treatment the goods must be exported and imported by residents of the CIS signatory parties, which implies that foreign-owned companies can be denied preferential treatment if they, or their subsidiaries, are not registered in the CIS free-trade area. [26] A good is considered to be originating in a signatory party if it: is wholly obtained in the Parties; has undergone a change in tariff classification at the heading level (four-digit); or complies with the product-specific rules of origin included in the CIS decision. [27]

6. Armenia's preferential rules of origin allow for diagonal cumulation between CIS countries that ratified the CIS FTA. Thus, all parts and materials originating in the CIS area are automatically considered originating if incorporated in a good imported into Armenia.

(4) TARIFFS

1. On 5 January 2009, Armenia deposited with the Secretary General of the World Customs Organization its instrument of accession to the International Convention on the Harmonized Commodity Description and Coding System (Harmonized System, HS) . [28]

(ii) MFN applied tariff

1. The Armenian Customs Tariff applied in 2009 is based on the HS2007 classification. Import duties are levied on the c.i.f. value of goods. The 2009 MFN tariff schedule contains 5,864 lines at the eight-digit level, of which 0.5% are non-*ad valorem* duties (Table III.1) . Armenia applies MFN tariffs to all WTO Members.

Structure of the tariff schedule, 2003 and 2009

		2003	2009	Final bound
1.	Total number of tariff lines	5,842	5,864	5,864
2.	Non-ad valorem tariffs (% of all tariff lines)	0.4	0.5	0.0
3.	Non-ad valorem with no AVEs (% of all tariff lines)	0.4	0.5	0.0
4.	Tariff quotas (% of all tariff lines)	0.0	0.0	0.0
5.	Duty-free tariff lines (% of all tariff lines)	72.8	72.6	36.7
6.	Average tariff rate of dutiable lines (%)	9.9	9.8	13.5
7	Simple average tariff rate (%)	2.7	2.7	8.5
8.	Bound tariff lines (% of all tariff lines)	100.0	100.0	100.0

Note: Since *ad valorem* equivalents could not be estimated, respectively 23 and 29 tariff lines in 2003 and 2009 have been considered as empty (no rate) .
Source: WTO Secretariat calculations, based on data provided by the Armenian authorities.

2. The structure of the 2009 MFN applied tariff is simple: 72.6% of all lines are duty-free; 26.6% subject to a 10% tariff; 0.3% subject to a 6.5% tariff; and 0.5% subject to specific duties. The 6.5% tariff rate applies to 16 tariff lines corresponding to tubes, pipes, hoses, and fittings therefore of plastic (HS code: 3917) . Armenia's tariff structure does not have international tariff peaks (rates greater than 15%) .

3. Non-*ad valorem* import tariffs apply to 19 lines covering alcoholic beverages and 10 lines covering tobacco products. The authorities indicate that these import tariffs are calculated together with the corresponding VAT and excise tax (see section (5) below) and collected from the importer in a single payment, and, therefore, it is not possible to estimate *ad valorem* equivalents (AVEs) of the import tariff. Nevertheless, the authorities also indicate that as part of the Government's fiscal reform strategy, it planned to substitute all specific duties by *ad valorem* rates in January 2011.

4. Not including the tariff lines subject to specific duties, the global average applied MFN tariff remained constant over the review period at 2.7% (Table III.1), and was one of the lowest among WTO Members. The percentage of tariff lines that are duty-free and the average tariff rate of dutiable lines also remained constant.

5. Tariffs contributed to only 6% of total tax revenue collection in 2008 and are, therefore, of minor importance to fiscal policy (Chapter I(3)) . [29]

6. At 6.6%, the average tariff for agricultural products (WTO definition) is three times higher than for non-agricultural products (2.2%) . About 78.2% of the tariff lines for non-agricultural products are duty free, compared to 32.5% for agricultural products (WTO definition) . The relatively high tariff protection granted to agricultural products was in place during the entire review period (Chapter VI(1)) .

7. The activities (ISIC Rev.2 classification) with the highest average tariff rates (i.e. with the lowest percentage of products subject to duty-free rates) are those producing: fishing products; manufactured foods (particularly soft drinks, cocoa confectionary, canned fruits and vegetables, and meat, dairy, and fish products); carpets and rugs; leather products and footwear; furniture and fixtures, except of metal; manufactured plastic products; pottery and china; structural clay products; electrical appliances; and sporting goods (Table AIII.1) . [30] Some of these activities are also subject to technical regulations (see section (8) below) .

8. Armenia does not administer tariff quotas or any type of seasonal tariffs.

9. Armenia's import tariff reveals noticeable, although not large, "v-shaped" escalation. There is negative escalation between unprocessed and semi-processed products (4.1% and 0.4% respectively), mainly due to relatively high protection of agricultural raw materials. On the other hand, there is positive escalation between semi-processed and fully processed products (average of 3.6% for fully processed products) (Table III.2) . The authorities indicate that the structure of the tariff schedule was defined in the early 1990s, in part as the result of discussions regarding its industrialization policy at that time.

Summary analysis of MFN tariff, 2009

Analysis	No. of lines[a]	No. of lines used	Applied 2009 rates			Bound rates	Imports 2008 (US$ million)
			Simple avg. tariff (%)	Range tariff (%)	CV	Simple avg. tariff (%)	
Total	5,864	5,834	2.7	0-10	1.6	8.5	4,101.2[b]
HS 01-24	741	712	7.8	0-10	0.5	14.9	745.1
HS 25-97	5,123	5,122	2.0	0-10	2.0	7.6	3,353.1
By WTO definition[c]							
Agriculture	711	682	6.6	0-10	0.7	14.7	738.0
Live animals and	93	93	7.5	0-10	0.6	14.9	103.2

products thereof							
Dairy products	20	20	10.0	10	0.0	15.0	26.9
Coffee and tea, cocoa, sugar, etc.	125	125	8.1	0-10	0.5	14.8	190.5
Cut flowers and plants	34	34	5.3	0-10	1.0	15.0	6.1
Fruit and vegetables	157	157	9.9	0-10	0.1	15.0	59.0
Grains	16	16	0.0	0	n.a.	15.0	110.5
Oil seeds, fats, oils, and their products	77	77	5.6	0-10	0.9	13.4	67.7
Beverages and spirits	39	20	10.0	10	0.0	15.0	70.6
Tobacco	17	7	1.4	0-10	2.6	15.0	86.2
Other agricultural products	133	133	1.7	0-10	2.2	14.6	17.3
Non-agriculture (incl. petroleum)	5,153	5,152	2.2	0-10	1.9	7.7	3,360.2
Fish and fishery products	115	115	9.5	0-10	0.2	15.0	8.9
Mineral products, precious stones, and precious metals	351	351	4.0	0-10	1.2	10.9	701.3
Metals	620	620	0.2	0-10	7.4	5.2	401.2
Chemicals and photographic supplies	909	909	0.4	0-10	4.8	0.4	393.6
Leather, rubber, footwear, and travel goods	189	189	2.8	0-10	1.6	13.4	79.1
Wood, pulp, paper, and furniture	278	278	1.3	0-10	2.6	3.2	200.2
Textiles and clothing	856	855	3.9	0-10	1.2	10.9	163.3
Transport equipment	146	146	2.7	0-10	1.7	9.2	289.5
Non-electric machinery	725	725	0.3	0-10	5.3	9.3	382.7

Electric machinery	456	456	3.2	0-10	1.5	9.4	269.2
Non agricultural articles n.e.s.	503	503	3.8	0-10	1.3	10.2	101.9
By ISIC sector[d]							
Agriculture, hunting, forestry, and fishing	299	299	5.4	0-10	0.9	13.9	206.4
Mining	103	103	1.2	0-10	2.8	10.7	326.5
Manufacturing	5,461	5,431	2.6	0-10	1.7	8.2	3,561.7
By stage of processing							
Raw materials	643	642	4.1	0-10	1.2	12.3	688.6
Semi-processed products	1,787	1,787	0.4	0-10	4.6	3.8	793.3
Fully-processed products	3,434	3,405	3.6	0-10	1.3	10.3	2,616.4

Source: WTO Secretariat estimates, based on WTO IDB database; imports data from UNSD, Comtrade database.

Tariff bindings

1. Armenia has bound its entire tariff schedule. All tariff bindings are *ad valorem*, including the 29 lines covering tobacco products and alcoholic beverages, for which bound *ad valorem* equivalent rates were calculated (at a rate of 15%) . In 2009, the overall average bound rate was 8.5%, with rates ranging from 0% to 15%. With the exception of the 29 tariff lines for which applied AVEs could not be calculated (see above), all other applied tariffs are below their corresponding bound levels.

Tariff concessions

1. Article 104 of Armenia's Customs Code lists all goods that are exempt from the payment of duties, such as goods imported within the framework of humanitarian aid or charity programmes and sample quantities of goods imported for exhibitions, international fairs, and similar events.

2. Armenia also grants tariff concessions on goods in transit, goods temporarily imported, and imports intended for re-export (Chapter IV(4)) .

3. In addition, goods imported to supplement the charter capital of enterprises with foreign investments are exempt from the payment of tariffs. The specific goods for which this rule applies are listed in Government Decree No. 720 of 7 August 2001. If the goods are sold in the domestic market within three years of importation the importer must pay the customs tariff, including the calculated penalty for delayed payment. [31]

Tariff preferences

1. The provisions of the nine free-trade agreements (FTAs) in force with some of Armenia's CIS commercial partners (Chapter II(4)) are simple with respect to tariff liberalization [32]: there are no

liberalization schedules and all goods, without exception, became duty free from the moment the respective FTAs entered into force. In 2008, 31% of the total value of Armenia's imports came from these CIS partners (Chapter I(5)) . However, trade diversion was much smaller than this figure would suggest given that 75% of this preferential trade would have been granted duty free treatment anyway. [33]

CHARGES AFFECTING IMPORTS

(i) Charges applied exclusively to imports

1. Besides tariffs, imports are subject to: a customs formalities fee of dram 3,500 (US$10); and a customs inspection and recording fee of dram 1,000 (US$2.9) for each cargo weighing less than one ton and dram 300 (US$0.9) for each additional ton of cargo. Goods transported through pipelines and electricity cables are subject to a customs inspection fee of dram 500,000 (US$1,500) . [34] When customs formalities and/or inspections are carried out elsewhere than in places determined by the Customs Authorities or during non-working days, the customs fees are doubled. Importers also have to pay dram 1,000 for each document (form) provided by the Customs Authorities.

2. In addition, importers may incur other customs user fees depending on the services supplied by Customs, such as accompaniment of transit shipment and warehousing services. The SRC is responsible for administering and collecting all customs fees.

(ii) Indirect taxes

1. With few exceptions (see below), all imports are subject to the payment of a VAT of 20%, and alcoholic beverages, tobacco products, and fuels are also subject to an excise tax. In 2007 (latest year available), VAT collected represented half of total tax revenue or the equivalent of 7.9% of GDP, while VAT collected from imports represented 65% of total VAT collection. In the same year, excise tax collected represented 1.3% of GDP, although the percentage collected from imports could not be calculated. [35]

2. The SRC is responsible for administering and collecting all taxes applied to imports.

3. According to the Law on VAT of 1997, as amended, and the Law on Excise Tax of 2000, as amended, the principle of destination prevails in Armenia and MFN treatment is ensured.

(b) VAT

1. VAT is levied on all economic activities, including the importation of goods and services, with the exception of those subject to simplified taxation (i.e. companies with taxable turnover of less than dram 58.4 million (US$167,000) in a calendar year) . The taxable base is the value of good and services (usually the invoice amount) delivered, excluding VAT paid on purchases by the supplier, and it should include, if applicable, the value of the excise tax. For imported goods, the taxable base is the sum of their customs value, customs duty, and any excise tax levied at the time of importation.

2. Armenia applies the credit method of levying VAT, that is, the VAT paid to suppliers is deducted from the VAT collected from customers. VAT on imported goods is levied at the point of importation by customs officials and must be paid within ten days after importation. For imported goods that have been previously exported from Armenia by VAT taxpayers for the purpose of processing or repair abroad, the taxable base is the value of processing and repair that has been

paid or, when this is impossible to define, the difference between the customs value after processing and repair and the customs value declared at the time of export. [36]

3. The standard rate of VAT is 20% but several types of transactions are exempted or zero rated: exemption covers only the final transaction before consumption or export, while zero rating removes VAT paid at all stages. Zero rating includes: exported goods and services provided outside Armenia; goods in transit through Armenia; and processing and assembly of goods provided by foreign residents and exported. Exemptions include: education services and material; scientific research; chemicals and fertilizers used in agriculture; insurance, reinsurance and banking services; sales of precious and semi-precious stones and products; services imported for humanitarian and charitable purposes; and maintenance of equipment used in international transport (Chapter VI(4)(iv)) . [37] The legislation also establishes a list of products (in general terms, goods subject to a tariff rate other than duty free) for which the importer is obliged to pay the VAT during customs clearance, while for all other products VAT may be paid under the same regime applied to domestic sales. [38]

4. In order to comply with its WTO obligations, in January 2009 Armenia eliminated the discriminatory treatment that exempted domestic agricultural output sold by farmers and sales of domestic veterinary drugs from the payment of VAT.

(c) Excise tax

1. Excise tax is an indirect tax levied on domestically produced and imported alcoholic beverages, tobacco products, petrol, and diesel fuels (Table III.3) . The tax rate varies according to the product and in most cases is defined as a specific rate. For *ad valorem* excise duties on goods produced in Armenia the tax it is based on the sales prices without VAT. For *ad valorem* excise duties on imported goods, the tax is calculated on the basis of their customs value without VAT and customs duties/tariffs. Excise tax on imports must be paid during customs clearance, and in practice (though not established in the Law) is calculated and paid together with the respective tariff and VAT (see section (4) above) .

Excise tax rates, 2009

HS No.	Product description	Taxable base	Tax rate (dram)
2203	Beer	1 litre	70
2204	Wine of fresh grapes	1 litre	10%, but not less than dram 100/litre
2205	Vermouth and other wine of grapes flavoured with plants or aromatic extracts	1 litre	500
2206	Other fermented beverages (e.g. cider, perry)	1 litre	180
2207	Undernaturated ethyl alcohol and alcoholic drinks with more or equal to 80% alcohol content	1 litre (by recalculation of 100% spirit)	600
2208	Undernaturated ethyl alcohol and alcoholic drinks with less than 80%	1 litre	30%, but not less than dram 380/litre

	alcohol content		
2403	Other manufactured tobacco	1 kilogram	1,500
2709	Crude oil and oil products	1 tonne	27,000
2711	Oil-gas and other carbohydrate gases (except for natural gas, HS 2711.11/21)	1 tonne	1,000

Note The average exchange rate for the first half of 2009 was dram 1 = US$350.

Source: Armenian Law on Excise Tax of 2000.

IMPORT PROHIBITIONS, RESTRICTIONS, AND LICENSING

1. Armenia notified the WTO that it did not maintain quantitative restrictions during the period under review.[39]

2. Armenia maintains import prohibitions on a limited number of products for health, security, or environmental reasons, on: all kinds of weapons and ammunition; explosives; army equipment and components; narcotics and psychotropic substances; and pornography. In addition, Armenia prohibits the importation as well as the transit through Armenian territory of any nuclear material, nuclear-related equipment or substances emitting ionizing radiation. [40]

3. Armenia notified to the WTO its Law on Licensing of 30 May 2001, which established general licensing provisions, including those applied to imported goods. [41] Armenia also notified Government Decree No. 2012 of 14 November 2002 on Making Amendments to the Government Decree No. 581 of 20 September 2000, and Public Services Regulatory Commission Decree No. 24 of 3 April 2002 on Approval of the Temporary Order of the Licensing for Import and Export of Natural Gas and Electrical Energy in the Power Engineering Sector. [42]

4. Under Armenia's 2001 Law on Licensing, there are two types of licences: simple and compound (i.e. automatic and non-automatic) . The simple licence should be issued by the Ministry of Economy within three days of submission of a request, and does not require the approval of the licensing commission. The compound licence, on the other hand, may be issued up to 30 days after submission and may only be issued on the basis of the conclusions drawn by a licensing commission. A list of activities subject to licensing is provided in Chapter VII of the Law. Various government agencies are responsible for issuing the different types of licences.

5. During the period under review, Armenia eliminated import licensing requirements on radio-electronic devices within the frequency range above 9 KHz and below 400 GHz, as well as requirements applied to imports of medicines and herbs. [43] Furthermore, Armenia notified the requirement (from 2002) of a licence to import botanical collections, wild animals, and zoological collections. [44] In October 2008, Armenia replied to the questionnaire on import licensing procedures stating that it applied non-automatic licensing procedures on imports of natural gas and electricity, and automatic licensing on imports of fireworks and diamonds. [45]

(7) CONTINGENCY MEASURES

1. The Department of Trade and Effective Markets, of the Ministry of Economy (ME) [46] is responsible for initiating and conducting investigations with respect to anti-dumping (AD), countervailing (CV), and safeguard measures. [47] Moreover, the ME is responsible for proposing

to the Government the application of provisional and final duties/safeguards, and for publicizing the rules on unfair trade practices.

(ii) Anti-dumping and countervailing measures

1. Armenia notified the WTO that it did not adopt AD or CV duty actions during the period under review. [48]The authorities indicated that informal complaints were made during the review period, but none resulted in an investigation.

2. The Law on Anti-Dumping and Countervailing Measures of 19 June 2002, defines dumping, subsidies, and the rules for the implementation of AD and CV duties. [49] In addition, Armenia adopted Decree No. 1770-N on "the approval of the order on receiving necessary information for determination of normal value of a product" of 30 November 2006. [50] The Committees on Anti-Dumping Practices and on Subsidies and Countervailing Measures have examined the 2002 Law; two Members posed questions, to which Armenia provided written replies. [51] At the end of 2009, these Committees had not yet examined Decree No. 1770-N.

3. In its replies to the questions posed by Members in the WTO Committees, Armenia asserted that it applies the lesser duty rule and that Armenian legislation does not provide for the payment of interest on a security disbursement refunded after a negative final determination. [52] Armenia also clarified that under the 2002 Law, the provisions of AD, but not those on CV, apply to agricultural products. [53]

4. Article 2.2 of the Law on AD and CV measures determines that provisions stipulated in international agreements take precedence over those established in the law. Furthermore, any interested party may seek review of final determinations, interim reviews, and refund determinations taken by the ME to the Courts of Armenia, as provided for in other Armenian legislation.

5. An affected domestic industry may request the initiation of an administrative subsidy or dumping investigation only if it has the support of domestic producers accounting for at least 25% of total production of the product under investigation. The ME may initiate an investigation *ex officio*.

6. Article 63 of the law prohibits the simultaneous application of an AD measure and a CV measure to compensate for the same situation of dumping and subsidization. However, there are no provisions in Armenian legislation against a safeguard and an AD or CV measure being applied simultaneously to the same product.

7. Article 11 of the law establishes special provisions for cases where the exporting country involved in the investigation is a non-market economy.

(iii) Safeguard measures

1. Armenia has not taken any safeguard action since its accession to the WTO in 2003. The authorities indicated that they received no formal complaints and that no investigations were initiated during the review period.

2. The legal basis for Armenia's application of safeguard measures is set out in the Law on Protection of Domestic Market of 18 April 2001. [54] The Committee on Safeguards examined the law and only one Member submitted questions, which Armenia answered directly. [55]

3. The 2001 Law states that a safeguard measure may only be applied if it is determined that the investigated product is imported in such increased quantities and conditions that cause or

threaten to cause serious injury to the domestic industry. Safeguard measures may involve the imposition of: tariff increases; tariff quotas; quantitative restrictions; or any combination of the three measures.

4. Safeguard measures may have a maximum duration of four years, which may be extended for a further period of four years. However, measures with duration of more than one year must be liberalized progressively as provided for in the legislation.

5. The domestic producers or their representative, provided they account for more than half of the total production of like or directly competitive products under investigation, are entitled to request the initiation of an investigation. The ME may also initiate an investigation *ex officio*.

6. Provisional safeguard measures may be applied for a maximum of 180 days. If after investigation, the ME concludes that increased imports do not cause serious injury to the domestic industry, the excess duties paid during the application of the provisional measure must be refunded within three months of the decision.

7. There are no provisions relating to safeguard measures within the framework of Armenia's free-trade agreements.

TECHNICAL REGULATIONS AND STANDARDS

1. Issues related to technical regulations and standards are the responsibility of different governmental bodies within the Ministry of Economy (ME) . Armenia notified the WTO that the Department of Standardization, Metrology and Conformity Assessment of the ME had accepted the Code of Good Practice for the Preparation, Adoption, and Application of Standards in July 2003. [56] The National Institute of Standards (SARM), a closed joint stock company under the ME, is Armenia's TBT enquiry point. [57] Among other things, the SARM coordinates the activities of standardization technical committees in Armenia. The ME also overlooks the work of the National Institute of Metrology, the Quality Inspectorate, and the Accreditation Agency.

2. The WTO Notification Agency under the ME is responsible for complying with Armenia's notification obligations under the TBT Agreement (Chapter II) . Under Armenian legislation, various ministries may prepare and adopt a technical regulation.

3. Although Armenia has not yet signed the voluntary memorandum of understanding with ASTM International, it has been a member of the International Standardization Organization (ISO) since 1997.

4. In 2006, Armenia submitted a notification on its technical assistance needs with respect to the TBT Agreement. [58] In the same year, the World Bank organized training seminars in Armenia to discuss TBT issues, and since then representatives of the Armenian Government have participated in several WTO courses on the subject.

5. Armenia has notified its main legislation regulating its national metrology, standardization, and conformity assessment systems. [59] The Law on Ensuring Uniformity of Measurement, adopted on 26 May 2004, regulates the relationship between governmental bodies and private enterprises, and defines the processes of metrological testing and calibration. The Law on Standardization, as modified by the Law on making Additions and Amendments to the Law on Standardization adopted on 26 May 2004, regulates the principles of development and application of technical regulations and normative documents on standardization. According to the authorities, together with Decree No. 9 of 11 January 2000 on Preparation, Adoption and Application of Technical Regulations, the Law on Standardization defines standards and technical regulations in

compliance with the respective definitions in Annex 1 to the TBT Agreement. The Law on Conformity Assessment, adopted on 26 May 2004, defines the legal basis and procedures of licensing of those who participate in the process of conformity assessment. [60]

6. Armenia notified the WTO that, in 1996, it concluded an agreement on mutual recognition of certificates and cooperation in the sphere of standardization, metrology, and certification with Ukraine. [61] Armenia also signed similar agreements with Belarus, Bulgaria, Georgia, Iran, Kazakhstan, Kyrgyz Republic, Moldova, Russian Federation, and Tajikistan. In addition, Armenia has simple cooperation agreements on issues related to standards and technical regulations with China, India, and Slovakia.

7. As in other trade policy areas, Armenia is working closely with the European Commission to bring its regulatory and standards' systems into conformity with the EU system. In 2007, for example, Armenia became a member of the European Committee for Standardization. According to the European Commission, Armenia has made significant progress in the last few years with respect to the harmonization of TBT legislation, however more needs to be done to improve the quality of training and of TBT-related infrastructure. [62]

8. According to Government Decree No. 9 on Development and Adoption of Technical Regulations of May 2000, international standards should be used as the basis for the preparation of technical regulations, taking into account geographical, climate, and technological differences. Technical regulations should establish product consumptive characteristics and requirements rather than structural (design), technological or operational principles. When the content of a technical regulation is not in accordance with the relevant international standard (or if the standard does not exist), and if the developed technical regulation can have an impact on trade, the ME must: publish a notice in the *Official Bulletin*, notify the drafted technical regulation to WTO Members, and allow no less than 60 days for comments. However, if the technical regulation deals with urgent matters of consumer safety, environmental protection or national security, the decree allows the ME to omit these steps and notify the WTO of the adoption of an urgent technical regulation; in any case, comments from WTO Members must be taken into consideration.

9. Decree No. 9 also establishes the mechanisms to review and eliminate technical regulations that no longer serve their initial purpose. In 2009, some ten technical regulations were amended. [63]

10. Since its accession in 2003, Armenia has notified 70 technical regulations to the WTO, of which 67 are still in force; the vast majority (60) are available in English. [64] Armenia allowed on average 43 days for comments from other WTO Members, and respected the six-month period between publication and entry to force for at least half of the notifications. The products mainly affected by these notified measures were foodstuffs, electrical equipment, detergents, cement, tobacco, and fuels. Armenia did not adopt urgent measures during the review period.

11. Under Decree No. 9 of 2000, the Ministries authorized to adopt technical regulations are also authorized to consider technical regulations from other trading partners as equivalent if they do not contravene Armenian legislation. In practice, no foreign technical regulations have been accepted as equivalent.

12. The Testing Laboratory of the SARM carries out tests with the purpose of attestation, if requested by private persons or if ordered by public bodies. In addition, there are 64 accredited testing laboratories in Armenia. [65] Government Decree No. 1170-N on "Attestation schemes used for obligatory certification of products or services" of August 2004 establishes the criteria for selecting procedures laboratories should adopt in each case.

13. Product certification can be compulsory or voluntary. The Law on Conformity Assessment provides that compulsory assessment should be implemented in accordance with the requirements of specific technical regulations. Compulsory certification activities are coordinated by the Ministry of Economy, which is responsible for accrediting certification bodies. Certification is conducted by the 19 accredited certification bodies. One of these certification bodies is the SARM, which was accredited as a product, services, quality, and environmental management systems certification body, and is allowed to carry out related conformity assessment activities. [66] Sampling is the procedure most used by certification bodies.

14. Decree No. 976 on the Mandatory Conformity Assessment of Products and Services of 29 August 2008, which replaced Decree No. 239 of July 2004, lists the products subject to compulsory conformity assessment and defines their respective requirements. The number of products was reduced from 65 in 2003 to 17 in 2009; the list includes fish and fish products, vegetable oils, bread and bakery products, toys, radio equipment, and firearms. Certificates are issued based on sample testing, analysis of production systems, quality system certification, or supplier declaration depending on the specific certification. Mandatory certification procedures, as well as fees imposed, are the same for imported and domestically produced goods.

15. In the specific case of pharmaceutical products, both domestic and foreign firms require import permission from the Ministry of Health, which must be preceded by an application for a licence to perform pharmaceutical activities in general. The cost of obtaining the import permission is dram 20,500 (some US$59) and of the licence is dram 200,000 (US$570) . According to the authorities, the procedure of granting import permission is not discretionary and is aimed at verifying the compliance of the medicines with technical regulations, as well as their quality; decisions must be made within ten days of receipt of an application. Permission to import is not transferable among importers. [67] Imported pharmaceutical products, like domestic medicines, must be registered with the Ministry of Health; veterinary vaccines and serums must be registered with the Ministry of Agriculture. [68]

16. The provisions of the Law on Conformity Assessment of 2004 on first- and second-party assessments and on market surveillance are not very clear nor detailed, and could therefore be improved in a future legislature review.

17. In accordance with the Law on Standardization of 2004, Armenian national standards are voluntary. A quarterly *Standard's Guide* and annually *Catalogue on Standards and Certifications* are published by SARM.[69] Standards are adopted by consensus among the interested parties (i.e. SARM, certification bodies, industry representatives, and NGOs), all of which receive a copy of the draft standard and are given time for comments and suggestions.

SANITARY AND PHYTOSANITARY MEASURES

1. In January 2005, the GOST system of standards and sanitary and phytosanitary regulations used in the Soviet Union was *de jure* abolished in Armenia. It is now progressively bringing its sanitary and phytosanitary standards into convergence with the EU. Armenia adopted the Law on Veterinary Practice in October 2005, the Law on Food Safety in November 2006, the Law on Plant Protection and Plant Quarantine in November 2006 (renamed as the Law on Phytosanitary in May 2009) (Table III.4) . The Ministry of Agriculture is responsible for food safety, the veterinary state inspectorate [70], and phytosanitary issues.

2. Armenia became a member of the CODEX Alimentarius Commission in 1994; it has established a local contact point in the Ministry of Agriculture, but not a CODEX Alimentarius National Commission. [71] Since 2007, the contact point for the CODEX Alimentarius has been the responsibility of the International Affairs and Marketing Department of the Ministry of Agriculture.

This Department is responsible for coordinating the activities of the CODEX Alimentarius Commission at the national level and for co-operation with other public agencies with responsibility for food safety, such as the Ministry of Health. The Strategy for Sustainable Development of the Agriculture Sector (approved by Resolution No. 682-N in November 2006), states that CODEX should be the basis for further development of national norms and standards related to food safety. In addition, the authorities stated that, in the absence of a national measure, Armenia uses measures that conform to standards, recommendations and/or guidelines of the responsible international organization.

Legislation and institutions for SPS, 2009

Legislation	Date of legislation	Responsible institutions
Agreement on co-operation between CIS members on veterinary issues	July 1994	Ministry of Agriculture
Law on Food Safety	November 2006	Ministry of Agriculture implements state control over food safety issues related to enforcement of veterinary and plant quarantine norms Ministry of Health is responsible for sanitary norms and hygiene rules
Law on ensuring sanitary and epidemiological safety of the population	November 1992	Hygienic and Epidemiological Inspectorate of the Ministry of Health
Law on Veterinary Medicine	October 1999	Cattle Breeding Inspectorate of the Ministry of Agriculture
Law on Plant Protection and Plant Quarantine (renamed as the Law on Phytosanitary)	November 2006 (May 2009)	Plant Quarantine and Farming Inspectorate of the Ministry of Agriculture
Law on Standardization	November 1999 and amendments of May 2004	Ministry of Trade and Development
Law on Veterinary Practice	October 2005	Ministry of Agriculture
Resolution No. 59-N: numbering and registering livestock and farm animals	January 2004	Ministry of Agriculture
Resolution No. 426-N: implementation of veterinary sanitary testing of meat and production from the slaughter of animals	March 2004	Ministry of Agriculture

Resolution No. 1228-N: state veterinary control during international and inter-state transportation of veterinary consignment	August 2004	Ministry of Agriculture

Source: European Commission; World Bank; and information provided by the Armenian authorities.

3. Armenia became party to the International Plant Protection Convention (IPPC) in June 2006. [72] It is also a member of the European and Mediterranean Plant Protection Organization (EPPO) . Armenia became a member of the World Organisation for Animal Health (OIE) in 1997. [73]

4. The Ministry of Agriculture is responsible for all aspects of food safety in the import and export of foodstuffs except for transport and hygiene, which are under the Ministry of Health. Although imports of food do not require licences, all imported food must be sampled and tested in laboratories before importation is permitted.

5. Imports of plants and plant materials must be accompanied by phytosanitary certificates from the country of origin. Clearance at the border is only provisional: imported plant materials must then be taken to an authorized customs clearing site near Yerevan for final inspection and sampling before full clearance is given. Planting breeding material requires a further inspection and approval from the Ministry of Agriculture.

6. All imports of animals require veterinary certificates from the Ministry of Agriculture. This certificate requires a corresponding certificate from an officially recognized veterinarian in the exporting country showing that the animal complies with Armenian requirements for vaccinations, absence of parasites, and comes from an area recognized by the OIE as free of pests and diseases listed in Armenian legislation. Imports are subject to sampling and testing.

7. In 2005, budget funds were provided for the construction of three combined border checkpoints and basic laboratory equipment for the Plant Quarantine and Farming and Veterinary State Inspectorates. However, lack of resources poses a severe problem for the SPS regime, not only for imports but also internally. [74]

8. In the WTO, Armenia has submitted 24 notifications to the SPS Committee: 22 regular notifications; and 2 emergency notifications (both relating to avian influenza) . Of the regular notifications, four specifically provided 60 days for comments and ten notified measures already in force on the date the notification was circulated.

MEASURES DIRECTLY AFFECTING EXPORTS

CUSTOMS PROCEDURES AND CHARGES

1. The State Revenue Committee (SRC) is responsible for customs procedures with respect to exports as well as for imports (Chapter III(1)) . According to Article 128 of the Customs Code, all goods exported from Armenia are subject to customs declarations. Goods must be declared at the regional customs office closest to the exporter's location, with the exception of goods exported via Yerevan International Airport, which must be declared at the airport customs office.

2. In principle, the procedure is simple: a declaration form is submitted to the customs official, who is responsible for verifying its completeness as well as the validity of the supporting documentation.

3. Armexpertiza, an organization founded by the Chamber of Commerce and Industry of Armenia, is responsible for issuing four different certificates of origin for Armenian exports depending on their destinations: (i) for all destinations; (ii) for CIS countries governed by CIS Resolution of November 2000 (Chapter III(3)); (iii) for CIS countries not governed by the Regulation; and (iv) for countries that provide GSP preferences to Armenian exports. [1] Exporters have complained that certification of origin is a costly and complicated procedure, as even small quantities of exports are subject to sample analyses. [2]

4. According to the World Bank's Doing Business Project 2009, it took on average 30 days to complete export customs procedures in 2008 for a standardized cargo. [3] However, Doing Business 2010 has shown an improvement: the average time has been reduced to 17 days, the number of documents reduced from 6 to 5, and the average cost for a standard container reduced from US$1,746 to US$1,731.

5. There are no registration requirements for exporters.

6. The Customs Code establishes that exports are subject to payment of customs service fees in the same way as imports (Chapter III(5)) .

7. Armenia does not maintain minimum prices for exports.

EXPORT TAXES

1. The Customs Code provides for an export tax (i.e. customs duties), however the applied rate for all goods was zero throughout the review period.

EXPORT PROHIBITIONS, RESTRICTIONS, AND LICENSING

1. Armenia prohibits exports of all kinds of weapons and ammunition, explosives, army equipment and components, narcotics and psychotropic substances, and pornographic material. Armenia does not apply trade embargoes other than those imposed by UN Security Council Resolutions.

2. Armenia applies licensing requirements on exports of pharmaceutical products to ensure public health and safety, of rare animal and plants, and of objects considered part of the national heritage. Export permission procedures for pharmaceutical products are the same as those for imports and are regulated by the same legislation. To obtain an export permit, a company must obtain a pharmaceutical licence (needed for all activities related to pharmaceutical products) . Both the export permit and the licence for pharmaceutical products are issued by the Ministry of Health (Chapter III(6)) . Exports of rare animals and plants included in Armenia's *Red Book* require permission from the Ministry of Nature and the Environment. [4] Exports of objects considered of interest to the national heritage must be authorized by the Ministry of Culture. [5]

DUTY AND TAX CONCESSIONS

1. Under Armenian legislation, indirect taxes (i.e. VAT and excise tax) are zero rated on all exports. In addition, the Customs Code provides for exemptions from tariff duties for imports that enter under one of the following import regimes for products to be re-exported: temporary imports

for processing; temporary import; import into free trade zones; and re-export. [6] Imports under these regimes have one year to be exported or tariff duties are levied. However, although provided for in the Customs Code, as at mid 2009, no free trade zones or other special economic zones have been established in Armenia.

2. During the review period, some exporters complained of delays in obtaining VAT refunds from the Government. [7] The authorities have undertaken improvements by: (i) meeting the statutory 90-day processing deadline for all VAT refund claims filed in 2009; (ii) clearing the stock of late refund claims; (iii) implementing risk management approaches (i.e. taxpayers with good compliance histories get fast-track refunds, while risky cases face pre-refund audits); (iv) implementing a forecasting system to guarantee that funds will be available; and (v) submitting legislation to Parliament to strengthen penalties for false refund claims. [8] Furthermore, at the end of 2009 a draft law was before the National Assembly that would make tax refunds, in general, automatic after three months. The authorities expect the new law to be in force in 2011 and to be applied to tax refunds incurred during 2010.

EXPORT FINANCE, INSURANCE, AND PROMOTION

1. There is no government institution in Armenia providing export finance, insurance, or guarantees. Moreover, there are no government lending schemes or official credit lines distributed via private financial institutions designed to support exporters.

2. Trade finance is provided by large private banks, which in some cases work in association with international financial institutions such as the European Bank for Reconstruction and Development (EBRD), the International Finance Corporation (IFC), and the International Bank for Reconstruction and Development (IBRD) . For example, Armeconombank (an Armenian privately owned bank) and the EBRD have been carrying out a trade facilitation programme under which letters of credit are issued when a credit line is already available to the exporter. [9]

3. The authorities state that Armenia does not provide subsidies contingent on export performance nor does it have any export processing zones.

4. The Armenian Development Agency (ADA), established in 1998, is the government agency responsible for export promotion. The ADA helps Armenian exporters to find markets for their products, performs market studies, and seeks out partners for joint ventures aimed at increasing the volume of exports. It also organizes international conferences, business forums, trade fairs, and exhibitions. ADA's budget totalled some US$809,000 in 2009, of which 45% was funded by the Government's fiscal budget and 55% from the "Foreign Investment and Export Facilitation Project" financed by the World Bank and the International Development Association. [10]

TRADE POLICIES BY SECTOR

AGRICULTURE

1. Soon after Armenia's independence in September 1991, 864 collective and state farms were privatized and about 321,000 private farms created. [1] By 2006 the number of private farms had increased to about 340,000, as more public land was privatized by open tender. Farms are not only small in size (the average is about 1.4 ha), they are also fragmented, with about 1,200,000 parcels of land shared among the 340,000 farms. The size varies considerably from 0.62 ha in the irrigated Ararat Marz to 3.8 ha in the extensive crop and livestock raising Syunik Marz. If agriculture is to develop further, farms and holdings will need to be consolidated in order to

achieve economies of scale. A major impediment to consolidation and a functioning land market was poor registration of land parcels and the issuance of titles. During the review period, a project sponsored by the World Bank and supported by other donors has greatly improved this situation, and most land parcels have now been surveyed and registered, and titles have been issued. [2]

2. Agriculture contributed an average of 18.8% to Armenia's GDP during 2004-08, and made up about 46% of employment (Chapter I(1)) . However, in addition to the problems associated with farm structure, the growth and competitiveness of the sector is restricted by various topographic and climatic factors; for example, most of the land is at an altitude of over 1,000 metres; and over two thirds is on slopes of 6° or more. Armenia is a net food importing country and the structural and other limitations to agricultural development mean that agriculture is unlikely to be the main engine for economic growth. [3] Nevertheless, even if the rest of the economy continues to grow at a faster pace, agriculture will remain an important part of employment and GDP (Chapter I) . Furthermore, several food processing sub-sectors, such as alcoholic and non-alcoholic beverages and cheese, have good potential for development using agricultural raw materials.

3. The immediate post independence period saw a sharp decline in gross value of production and an even sharper decline in net production as the newly privatized farms focussed on self-sufficiency rather than sales. The recovery in the late 1990s was stunted by drought, and it was not until about 2002 that the value of agricultural production recovered to the level of ten years earlier. [4] Since then the gross value of production has increased steadily (Table VI.1) .

4. In general, the production patterns of specific commodities follow a similar path to the general pattern for gross agriculture production, except with greater year-on-year variation. That is, there was a sharp decline in the early 1990s; recovery; another drop in production in the late 1990s; and then an unsteady but sustained increase in production. Given the very small size of agriculture holdings in Armenia it is not surprising that production increases have been greatest for the most labour-intensive products – fruits and vegetables. The recovery since 2002 has been particularly strong for apples, grapes, potatoes, tomatoes, and vegetables. Other more extensively produced products also recovered, but to a lesser extent (Table VI.2 and Chart VI.1) .

5. Despite the limitations mentioned above, there is considerable potential for increasing agricultural productivity, for example, through improved irrigation. Armenia has about 7.4 billion m^3 of water resources annually, and uses around 2.5 billion m^3 for irrigation. However, much of the irrigation system was constructed before independence and relies heavily on electrically powered pumping, which has high running costs and is inefficient. Switching to more efficient gravity systems is very capital expensive. Nevertheless, some tens of millions of dollars have been invested in increasing the capacity of Alpine water reservoirs over the past five years, but it is difficult to quantify precisely how much has been spent and more is needed to better exploit the potential for irrigation.

6. Another impediment to agricultural development is the lack of available finance (section (4)(ii) below) . Some finance has been provided through various loan schemes, some supported by donors and non-governmental organizations. However, according to the authorities, the absence of a national income insurance scheme means banks perceive loans to farmers as high risk even though over 95% of loans are repaid. In addition, Armenian banks have limited resources. Thus, banks are reluctant to lend to farmers, and loans to agriculture represent only 5.5% of value added in the agriculture sector. The Agricultural Cooperative Bank of Armenia – Crédit Agricole (ACBA) has 37 branches in Armenia, including 5 in Yerevan, and a customer base of around 350,000.

7. The uncertainty about foreign ownership of land in Armenia may reduce the level of investment from abroad. Article 31 of the Constitution states that foreign citizens and persons

without citizenship shall not have the right to own land except in cases prescribed by law. Although it is possible for foreigners to lease land (Chapter V(1)(ii)), the prohibition on foreigners owning land is likely to deter foreign investment in agriculture.

8. Armenia is a net food-importing country. The main imports are wheat, meat, tobacco products, and distilled alcoholic beverages. As would be expected, given its size and geographic proximity, Russia is the principal source for some of the main imports: out of a total of US$88.7 million in wheat imports in 2008, 82% were from Russia; and out of total imports of US$24.1 million in safflower, sunflower, and cottonseed oil 57% were from Russia. However, for meat: the United States is the main supplier of poultry meat (61% of a total of US$39.1 million); India is the main supplier of frozen bovine meat (95% of a total of US$21.6 million); and Brazil is the main supplier of meat of swine (59% of a total of US$20.7 million) . Armenia's main agriculture export is brandy most of which goes to Russia (85% of a total of US$141.4 million) . [5]

9. According to the authorities, Armenia has no quantitative restrictions on exports or imports. Available budgetary funds for agriculture are concentrated on pest and disease control, marketing and promotion services, and infrastructure (Table VI.3) . Several measures are supported by the World Bank or governmental aid programmes: in 2007 measures to combat avian influenza were supported by the World Bank and Japan, and the World Bank supported marketing and promotion services, as did the International Fund for Agriculture Development.

10. Agriculture policy is the responsibility of the Ministry of Agriculture, which includes the central administration and provincial-level inspection staff. In addition, each province has an agricultural department that is separate from the Ministry. The Ministry of Agriculture is responsible for seven research centres covering the main agriculture sectors and issues, such as: agriculture and plant protection; agri-chemistry and reclamation; cattle breeding and veterinary; fruit growing and wine making; vegetable-gourds; and industrial crops. The Academy of Agriculture of Armenia and the Armenian State Agrarian University plus other governmental and private educational and research institutions provide technical training and research facilities.

Domestic support measures, 2003-07

(Dram million)

	2003	2004	2005	2006	2007
Green Box					
General services					
Research	53	75	57	155	166
Pest and disease control	1,223	1,308	1,175	1,537	2,275
Extension and training services	202	191	296	445	389
Inspection services	42	11	14	14	14
Marketing and promotion services	1,042	3,805	25	4,033	4,642
Infrastructure	3,918	3,304	550	896	1,162

Public stockholding for food security	0	0	695	0	0
Direct payments					
Disaster relief	1,023	330	343	594	0
Structural adjustment assistance	564	0	0	0	0
Amber Box					
Non-product-specific					
Assistance to land users up to 7 ha.[a]	0	0	0	0	166
Assistance for nitrogen fertilizer acquisition	0	0	0	0	150
Total domestic support	8,068	9,025	3,154	7,674	8,964

a WTO document G/AG/N/ARM/16 , 4 July 2008, refers to assistance to land users of up to 7 "acres". The Armenian authorities confirmed that this should read "hectares".

Source: WTO documents G/AG/N/ARM/2 , 14 April 2004; G/AG/N/ARM/5/Rev.2 , 4 August 2006; G/AG/N/ARM/9 and Corr.1, 4 August 2006 and 2 November 2006; G/AG/N/ARM/12 , 11 June 2007; and G/AG/N/ARM/16 , 4 July 2008.

11. The Ministry of Agriculture is also responsible for the agriculture extension service, which operates through ten support centres. Until 2005, funding for the service was provided by the World Bank's Agricultural Reform Support Project (ARSP) . [6] Since then the State budget has provided for the support centres.

12. In 2002, it was reported that the absence of an overall strategy for agriculture development was Armenia's most serious agriculture policy problem. [7] Since then, the Strategy for Sustainable Development of the Agriculture Sector was approved by Resolution No. 682-N in April 2004, and the Strategy for Sustainable Development of Agriculture was approved by Resolution No. 826-N in November 2006. The main objectives of these strategies are to: achieve sustainable agricultural development; improve food security; and increase rural incomes. These objectives are to be achieved by: increasing production and profitability; making more efficient use of factors of production; improving food safety; and improving rural infrastructure. [8] The next review of agriculture policy will take place in 2010.

MINING

1. Mining is an important part of Armenia's economy. It accounted for 2.6% of GDP in 2006 (latest year available), and 26% of exports (including re-exports) in 2008. Significant deposits of molybdenum, copper, and gold are present along with smaller deposits of lead, silver, and zinc. In addition, there are commercial deposits of industrial minerals including basalt, diatomite, granite, gypsum, limestone, and perlite (Table VI.4) . All mineral deposits belong to the State, which has the power to grant investigation, prospecting, and exploitation licences.

2. In 2005 there were 17 mining and metallurgical enterprises operating in Armenia. In addition to extracting minerals, Armenia produces aluminium foil and has an important diamond-processing industry, both based on imported raw materials. RUSAL of Russia owns the aluminium foil plant, Armenal, and has invested over US$100 million in the plant over the past few years. Production capacity is about 25,000 tonnes of foil per year, which is equivalent to about 12% of all foil produced in the CIS countries. There are also significant exports of iron and

steel, which were reported as either transhipments or scrap as there is no domestic steel industry. [9]

3. Armenia was a major producer of minerals in the Soviet Union. However, for a number of years after independence, production effectively halted as a result of the Armenian energy crises and economic instability. With the economic reforms of the mid 1990s, production resumed and the Government started to privatize all mining companies, a process that was essentially completed in 2004. The decline in minerals prices in international markets in 2008 led to a decline in production in Armenia. However, as prices recovered, Armenia resumed expansion of production and exports of minerals in 2009.

4. Several foreign enterprises have invested in the mining sector in Armenia. A consortium of companies led by Cronimet of Germany took over the Zangezur copper-molybdenum plant and has invested US$200 million in improving facilities. Production is expected to reach 18,000 tonnes of copper and 4,000 tonnes of molybdenum concentrates annually. The Kajaran copper-molybdenum mine was privatized in December 2004 and ore-processing had increased to about 12.5 million tonnes in 2008. The United States-based Comsup Commodities purchased the Agarak Cu-Mo plant in 2003 and is reported to have invested US$3.5 million in 2004-05. The Armenian Copper Programme (ACP), a private Armenian copper mining and smelting enterprise, is evaluating the Teghout copper-molybdenum deposit. The ACP also owns and operates the Alaverdi smelter, the largest in the region, which produces up to 10,000 tonnes of blister copper from concentrate. Several companies are developing other copper, molybdenum, gold, zinc, and other mineral deposits in Armenia. [10]

5. A number of problems confront the mining sector. In particular, transport cost are high because most production is located in the south and carried overland, via Georgia, to Black Sea ports for export. Poor mineral recovery rates and environmental issues related to mining were also a problem according to a 2003 ECE report. [11] However, the authorities noted that since 2001, nature-use charges in Armenia have increased from dram 322.2 million to dram 3,986.3 million in 2008. In addition, since 2005, based on the terms of their mining licences, mining companies have begun transfers to the Special Environment Protection fund for the recultivation of land damaged by mining activities. At end-October 2009, total transfers stood at dram 271.5 million. Transport costs are also being addressed through the North-South Road Corridor Investment Program, which will cross Armenia from south to north then through Georgia to Poti and Batumi on the Black Sea. The Program's supporters include the Asian Development Bank. [12]

6. The Ministry of Energy and Nature Resources is responsible for regulating the mining sector, including: issuing licences; and monitoring exploration and production. Environmental controls are the responsibility of the Ministry of Nature Protection. Armenia's mining sector is regulated by the Subsoil Code and the Law on Concessions of 2003 plus subsequent amendments and implementation regulations. [13] The authorities noted that, with a view to improving conditions for exploration and exploitation of minerals, they are elaborating a new Subsoil Code, which will replace the current Subsoil Code and the Law on Concessions.

7. The current Concession Law makes provision for various types of prospecting and mining licences, which may not be sold but may be transferred with the approval of the Ministry of Energy and Nature Resources.

8. Between 2004 and 2009, 680 investigation licences and 600 mining licences were granted. Licence fees depend on the type of licence and the mineral being exploited. On average investigation licences cost dram 50,000 per year while exploitation licences are dram 10 million per year for metals, dram 1 million per year for non-precious stones, and dram 500,000 per year for non-metallic mining.

9. According to the authorities, there are no restrictions on foreign enterprises obtaining licences for exploration or mining. They pointed out that the mining regulations are meant to attract foreign investment and that there has been considerable investment in the sector from abroad.

10. Armenia introduced a tax on the exploitation of natural resources in 1999 at 1.5% of turnover for gold, silver, and platinum; 1.3% for copper and molybdenum; 1.0% for lead and zinc; and 6% for precious stones. [14]This was amended in the Concessions Law of 2003 to a variable royalty which depends on the profitability of the enterprise. The basic royalty is set at 1% of sales. An additional royalty is levied once profitability (revenue less costs) exceeds 25% of total revenue. The additional royalty is levied at an incremental rate of 0.1% up to a maximum additional royalty of 0.8%. [15]

ENERGY

(i) Overview

1. The only domestically produced primary energy in Armenia is electricity from hydroelectric plants. Out of a total annual primary energy supply of 2,586 thousand tonnes of oil equivalent (ktoe), 1,372 ktoe are from natural gas, 688 ktoe are from nuclear power, 394 ktoe from petroleum products, 157 ktoe from hydro electricity plants, and 1 ktoe from renewable sources. Although Armenia imports nearly all its primary energy needs, it is a net exporter of electricity, with net exports of 27 ktoe. [16]

2. The Medzamor Nuclear Power Plant (NPP) uses fuel imported from Russia. Armenia has no oil or gas production or any oil refineries. Although the country has not been systematically explored for hydrocarbon deposits, efforts over the past 50 years or so have not resulted in any commercial finds. There are some coal fields and shale oil deposits in various locations but it is not clear whether any are commercially viable, and as of end-2009, none are being exploited. [17] Import tariffs on electricity, coal and petroleum products are bound at 5% (all products in HS chapter 27) in Armenia's Schedule but the applied tariffs were zero in early 2009.

3. Before independence, Armenia received its energy supplies, including all gas, oil, and nuclear fuel, from Russia and Turkmenistan and, until 1979, Iran. The electricity system was operated jointly with Georgia and Azerbaijan. The situation changed radically in the late 1980s and early 1990s. The Medzamor NPP, commissioned in the late 1970s, was shut down in 1989 due to concerns with seismic vulnerability following the earthquake in 1988. [18] Gas supplies arriving via Azerbaijan stopped in 1991. As a result of the turmoil of the early 1990s energy supply fell by 83% between 1991 and 1994. To address the energy crises, one of the two units of the Medzamor nuclear power plant was re-opened in 1995 following extensive improvements. [19]Gas supplies via Georgia replaced those that came via Azerbaijan.

4. The Ministry of Energy and Natural Resources is responsible for energy policy. The legal framework for the energy sector is set out in the Energy Law of 1997, as amended, and the Law on Energy Saving and Renewable Energy of 2004. Public policy is also set out in the Energy Sector Development Strategy adopted by the Government of Armenia in 2005. [20] The main objectives set out in the Strategy paper include to:

□□□ provide reliable energy supply at low cost to all customers;

□□□ improve energy conservation;

□□□ avoid energy import sources that threaten the security and economy of Armenia;

□□□ ensure the safe operation of the nuclear power plant to 2016 or such time as it can be replaced and decommissioned without unacceptable economic, ecological, and energy security impact; and

□□□ ensure an ecologically and financially sustainable energy supply.

5. Public policy for energy generally, and electricity in particular, has been further developed in the Least-Cost Generation Plan for 2006, and a new energy programme approved by the Government in 2007. The 2006 Plan focussed on: improving safety at the Medzamor NPP and decommissioning it by 2016; construction of a new nuclear power plant; and energy conservation and the development of renewable energy. In addition, the plan emphasized projects to minimize the costs to consumers of decommissioning Medzamor. [21]

6. Armenia is a partner in the EU INOGATE energy programme between the EU, the littoral states of the Black and Caspian seas and their neighbouring countries. The objectives of the programme are to: work towards converging energy markets on the basis of the EU's internal energy market; enhance energy security; support sustainable energy development; and attract investment.

(ii) Electricity

1. Armenia has installed electrical capacity of about 3,149 MW, of which 2,420 MW is available, while peak loads were about 1,204 MW in 2008. However, much of the capacity is old and inefficient. Some of it needs to be replaced and much of it needs to be upgraded. The total capacity of the thermal power plants (TPP) is 1,754 MW, provided by Hrazdan TPP and Yerevan TPP. Hydroelectric power is similarly concentrated: out of a total installed capacity of about 960 MW most is supplied by the Sevan-Hradzdan Cascade and the Vorotan Cascade. All electricity from nuclear power is provided by the Medzamor nuclear power plant with an installed capacity of 407.5 MW (from Unit 2; Unit 1 is not operational) (Table VI.5) . [23]

2. Considerable investment is taking place in the electricity sector. Construction of a new 250 MW combined-cycle energy unit on the Yerevan TPP started in July 2008 with the assistance of a loan from the Japan Bank for International Co-operation, and construction is under way on a 450 MW gas-steam thermal unit on Hrazdan. Similarly, investment in transmission to help trade in electricity is taking place with a 400 kV line between Armenia and Georgia, and a 400 kV line between Armenia and Iran.

Main electricity plants, 2009

Power plant	Type	Owner	Main stockholders	Installed capacity (MW)
Hrazdan	Thermal (natural gas and oil)	Hrazdan Energy Company (RazTES) OJSC	Wholly owned by the Federal Agency for Management of Federal Property of the Russian Federation	1,110
Yerevan	Thermal (natural gas and oil)	Yerevan Thermal Power Plant CJSC	..	550

Sevan-Hrazdan Cascade	Hydro	International Energy Corporation CJSC	InterRAO UES is a wholly owned subsidiary of RAO UES Russia	559
Vorotan Cascade	Hydro	Vorotan Complex of HPP CJSC	State owned	404
Medzamor	Nuclear	State owned financial management by InterRAO UES	InterRAO UES is a wholly owned subsidiary of RAO UES Russia	407
Dzorhek	Hydro	Ministry of Defence	State owned	27
Small hydroelectric plants	Hydro	Private ownerships	Private owners	89
Lori-1	Wind	High-voltage Electricity Network CJSC	State owned	3
Total	n.a.	n.a.	n.a.	3,149

.. Not available.
n.a. Not applicable.
Source: Hrazdan Energy Company online information. Viewed at: http://www.raztes.am/eng/index.htm ; Yerevan Thermal Power Plant Cjsc online information. Viewed at: http://yerevantpp.com/hom ; NTI online information, "Armenia Profile: Nuclear facilities": Viewed at: http://www.nti.org/e_research/profiles/Armenia/Nuclear/facilities_metsamor.html; and information provided by the Armenian authorities.

3. Armenia has considerable potential to produce more electricity from renewable resources. There are 70 small hydroelectric plants operating with an installed capacity of 89 MW; in January 2009, building licences were issued for 64, and more are foreseen, along with several major plants. Armenia also has the first wind plant in the Trans-Caucasus region, the Lori-1 power plant; a second, the Iran-Armenia Wind Farm, is under construction. There are also opportunities for electricity production from solar and geothermal power sources. Initial geological and geophysical exploration in Jermaghbyur has been promising and drilling works are expected to start in 2010.

4. In 2002, all distribution companies were merged into a single entity, the Electricity Network of Armenia (ENA), which was privatized that same year with ownership passing to a British offshore-registered enterprise, Midland Resources Holding Ltd. In September 2005, the Armenian Government authorized Midland Resources to dispose of its stake. The current owner of ENA is InterRAO UES of Russia. [24]

5. The Public Services Regulatory Commission (PSRC) is responsible for setting the price of utilities (electricity, natural gas, thermal energy, water, and electronic communications) in Armenia. In April 2009, for the first time in 11 years, it increased the average tariff for all customer groups for electricity by an average of 24.4%. The tariffs vary from dram 17 per kWh for 35 kV connections night-time rate to dram 30 per kWh for residential customers (including VAT) . [25] It also approved price increases for natural gas and water.

6. The PSRC is also responsible for setting the price for sales by the generators of electricity to the distribution company. To encourage production, purchase of electricity produced by renewable sources (small hydropower plants, wind, and biomass plants) at preferential tariffs rates is mandatory for distributors. The rates, including VAT, are: dram 37.66 per kWh for wind; dram 39.36 per kWh for biomass from biomass plants; dram 20.55 per kWh for small hydro plants constructed on natural water flows; dram 13.7 per kWh for hydro plants constructed on the irrigation system; and dram 9.13 per kWh for small hydro plants constructed on drinking-water pipes. A licence, issued by the PSRC, is required to import or export electricity and natural gas. The PSRC also issues licences for generation, transmission, and distribution of electricity and thermal power, transport and distribution of natural gas; calculates and approves payments for usage of the railway infrastructure; sets tariffs for universal post services; and sets tariffs for mandatory technical supervision of transport vehicles.

(iii) Gas

1. Armenia has an underground natural gas storage facility, which is used for energy security and seasonal adjustment of gas flows. The sole gas distribution and transmission company, ArmRosGasprom CJSC (ARG), is 80% owned by Russia's Gazprom and 20% by the Government of Armenia through the Ministry of Energy and Natural Resources. All natural gas used in Armenia is imported from Russia through Georgia. ARG buys the gas from Gazprom at a price of US$154 per 1,000 m^3, which was fixed in April 2009 until April 2010 when a new agreement will be negotiated.

2. Construction of a 720 mm natural gas pipeline between Iran and Armenia was completed in December 2008. ARG intends to purchase the pipeline. ARG is also investing in electricity generation through the rehabilitation and modernization of the 5th unit of the Hrazdan TPP, which is under construction.

3. The PSRC sets the retail price for gas; this is currently at US$215 per 1,000 m^3 for customers that use 10,000 m^3 per month or more and dram 96 per m^3 for other users (including VAT in both cases) .

(iv) Urban heating

1. In the Soviet era Armenia had extensive urban district heating systems. However, with the crises of the early 1990s coverage collapsed from 35% of urban residential areas in 1989 to 10% in 2003 and has not been rebuilt. [26] To a large extent, the urban heating system is being replaced indirectly by the expansion of the gas distribution system, while the Government is also implementing a 2002 Urban Heating Strategy based on gas-based heating and distributed heat.

2. On 13 April 2006 the Government adopted Decision No. 609-N "The Principal Projects on Rehabilitation of Power and Thermal Supply by Utilization of Combined Systems". Official policy is to encourage rehabilitation of existing urban heating systems, where this is viable, and construction of new systems. Encouragement is through the deregulation of small systems; no licences are needed and tariffs are not regulated. For larger units, the policy is also intended to encourage supply contracts with housing complexes; although these complexes generally have limited capability to assume payments and liabilities on behalf of occupants.

(v) Transport fuel

1. Practically all oil products are imported into Armenia by rail through Georgia; small amounts also arrive by truck. The PSRC does not set prices for petrol or diesel. The import and distribution of transport fuel is concentrated, with only seven enterprises operating in the petrol market in 2006: the top two had 84.5% market share of petrol sales and are classed as having dominant

positions based on the Law of Protection of Economic Competition. [27] In addition, the sector was identified by the State Commission for Protection of Economic Competition as being subject to fixed price changes. [28]

SERVICES

(i) Main features

1. The relative economic importance of Armenia's services sector increased from 59.2% of GDP in 2003 to 72.7% in 2008. This expansion was driven largely by construction services, and wholesale and retail trade. Trade in services has also expanded rapidly. Services exports increased by a nominal average of almost 26% per year over 2003-08, and services imports by around 29%. [29]

2. Armenia undertook sector-specific commitments in 11 of 12 sectors, or 97 of the 160 subsectors in the Services Sectoral Classification List (Table AVI.1) . [30] Important exceptions are postal services, and transportation of passengers and freight via air and rail. Market access and national treatment were left unbound with respect to the presence of natural persons, except for the temporary entry of persons covered in Armenia's horizontal commitments.

3. Armenia's list of GATS Article II MFN exemptions covers freight and passenger transportation by road, and audiovisual services related to the production and distribution of motion pictures and television programmes. All these measures are intended for an indefinite duration, except for audiovisual services regulated by bilateral agreements with a pre-determined duration.

4. Armenia bound some limitations to legal, telecommunications, financial, and transport services in its GATS Schedule of Commitments (see related sections below) . Nonetheless, Armenia's existing legal framework is in most cases (e.g. postal services, telecommunication and financial services) more liberal than its GATS commitments.

5. Armenia has not submitted an offer in the current services negotiations.

FINANCIAL SERVICES

(a) Market structure

1. Despite significant developments during the review period, Armenia's financial system continues to be small, and financial intermediation continues to be considerably below the CIS average. [31] In December 2008, the ratio of the financial sector's total assets to GDP was 30.2%; 93% of these assets were held by commercial banks, 6% by credit organizations, and 1% by insurance companies. [32] Total banking assets grew at a rate of 29% per year during 2003-08. The sector contributed 3.5% to Armenia's GDP and employed 0.9% of the workforce in 2008. [33]

2. From the mid 1990s until 2002, numerous banks were liquidated and the banking sector underwent considerable consolidation. In 2008, there were 22 commercial banks, 25 credit organizations, and 11 insurance companies functioning in Armenia. The concentration in the banking sector is relatively low as measured by the Herfindahl-Hirschman Index. [34] There were approximately 118 bank branches per million inhabitants in 2008. There is no State ownership in banking or insurance. The insurance sector is small if measured by the ratios of the value of total assets and total premiums to GDP, which were 0.3% and 0.2%, respectively, in 2008.

3. The financial sector seems to be sound, with relatively high capitalization, profitability, and liquidity; according to the authorities, regular stress testing also indicates its stability.

Nevertheless, the IMF warned that the acceleration of growth in bank deposits and credit may contribute to higher credit risk, and recommends improvement of corporate governance and strengthening of the deposit guarantee fund created in 2006 (see below) .

4. There is no significant provision of offshore financial services.

(b) Regulatory framework

1. The Central Bank of Armenia (CBA) is responsible for monetary policy (Chapter I(2)), and regulation and supervision of the entire financial system.[36] In 2006, the CBA took over responsibility for the regulation and supervision of insurance companies from the Insurance Inspectorate, and responsibility for the supervision of the securities markets from the Securities Commission. The CBA is responsible for the stability, liquidity, and solvency of the banking system, as well as the functioning of the payment and settlement systems. Moreover, by law only the CBA has the authority to issue regulations and grant licences for the operation of financial institutions (see below) .[37]

2. Concentration in the banking sector is monitored by the CBA, and a new Division on Competition Analysis was created within the CBA in 2009. However, the CBA continues only to provide support and to exchange information with Armenia's Competition Commission, which is legally responsible for anti-competitive practices and other competition policy issues (Chapter V(4)) .

3. Armenia has made substantial market access and national treatment commitments on financial services under the GATS (Table AVI.1) . The three most important restrictions concern: (i) the cross-border supply of insurance services (excluding those applied to marine and aviation transport), which was left unbound; (ii) the prohibition on branches of non-resident banks to accept deposits from Armenian nationals; and (iii) the reservation of settlement and clearing services for securities to Armenia's state-owned central depositary. The latter two are not applied in practice (see below) .

4. The CBA has signed memoranda of understanding concerning banking services with Cyprus, Georgia, Iran, the Russian Federation, and Ukraine.

Banking

1. Since its accession to the WTO in 2003, Armenia has taken steps to improve confidence in, and the stability of its banking sector. Amongst other things, it has modernized its legislation, created a deposit guarantee scheme, and raised minimum capital requirements. In order to harmonize its legislation with EC Directives and bring it into conformity with Basel II principles, new regulations have been issued and laws, such as the Law on Bankruptcy of Banks and Credit Institutions of 1996, have been amended. A deposit guarantee fund, based on mandatory quarterly contributions by all banks operating in Armenia (irrespective of the origin of capital), was created in 2004; local-currency deposits are guaranteed up to dram 2 million (some US$5,715), while foreign-currency deposits are guaranteed only up to dram 1 million.[38] In 2007, the CBA issued new regulation on banks' prudential standards that gradually raised the minimum total capital for a bank (new or already established) to dram 5 billion (some US$14.3 million) as of 1 January 2009.[39]

2. Bank licensing is a three-stage process: (i) the interested party requests a licence, submitting a set of documents to the CBA, including a three-year business plan; (ii) if all required documents have been submitted and reflect credible information, the CBA registers the bank or foreign bank subsidiary[40]; and (iii) a bank will be granted a licence within one year after registration, provided it has paid the minimum total capital and has complied with other legally specified requirements.

The law does not provide for any discriminatory treatment between national and foreign applicants. The holder of a bank licence is permitted to provide any financial service, except insurance. [41]

3. There are no ownership restrictions for the participation of foreign banks and other foreign investors in Armenia's banking sector. According to the legislation, foreign banks are allowed to establish a subsidiary, a branch or a representative office. However, the authorities noted that there are no foreign bank branches in Armenia. Subsidiaries of foreign banks are allowed to provide the same types of services as domestically owned banks. Contrary to Armenia's GATS commitments, branches of foreign banks are allowed to accept deposits from Armenian nationals; in which case, the CBA may set additional prudential requirements. Approximately 70% of the total capital of the banking system is owned by foreigners. [42] As confidence in Armenian banks was impaired in the recent past, due to connected lending and mismanagement, foreign ownership is seen as a conveyor of confidence in the system. [43]

4. In practice, there are no restrictions on the provision of cross-border banking services. Domestically established banks and corporations, as well as retail consumers, are allowed to borrow from and deposit with foreign banks located abroad. The only practical requirement is for foreign banks to obtain a licence with the CBA in order to provide cross-border services that involve the establishment of a bank branch in Armenia. In June 2009, domestically established financial institutions had a total of US$327 million in deposits and US$507 in debt with foreign banks abroad. Likewise, at the same date, the private sector had a relatively large (US$515 million) outstanding liability with foreign banks located abroad.

5. Banks are not allowed to provide insurance services, except for insurance agent services, and vice versa. Nevertheless, a holding company may own both a bank and an insurance company.

Insurance

1. In 2008-09, the National Assembly introduced amendments to the Law on Insurance and Insurance Activities of May 2007, which itself had replaced the Law on Insurance of 2004. During the review period, the CBA, which was empowered to supervise the insurance sector as of January 2006 (see above), issued new regulations concerning insurance activities, most importantly Regulation No. 3/01 of 30 October 2007. [44] This Regulation harmonizes the licensing procedures with those applied to other financial organizations (i.e. banks and credit organizations) and with the European standards of licensing.

2. The documents required by the CBA for registration and licensing are different for foreign and domestic insurance companies. Nevertheless, the objectives of the licensing process seem to be the same. To a large extent, the CBA relies on information provided by the supervisory authority in the foreign company's home country. All applications must be reviewed by the CBA within 30 days of submission.

3. Insurance licences may be issued for one or several classes of insurance activity defined in Article 7 of the Law. However, the same insurance company cannot provide life and non-life insurance simultaneously. The same investor, however, may obtain two separate licences for two separate insurance companies in order to provide life and non-life insurance. A reinsurance company may be simultaneously engaged in reinsurance of life and non-life insurance.

4. There are no foreign ownership restrictions in the provision of insurance services. Foreign insurance companies are allowed to establish subsidiaries, branches or representative offices in Armenia. Foreign ownership in insurance companies was 63% at end-September 2009. [45] There are no restrictions specific to foreign insurance companies, except those applied to representative offices: i.e. foreign insurance companies (and only those from WTO Member

countries) may only provide cross-border supply of insurance services that cover maritime shipping, civil aviation, spaceship launching (including satellites), international freight carriage, and reinsurance risks. [46]

5. Insurance intermediaries require a licence/permission and may only engage in insurance intermediation with licensed insurance companies. Only legal entities may apply for a licence to provide insurance brokerage services, while legal entities or natural persons may both apply for permission and registration as insurance agents. Professional qualification requirements apply to both national and foreign applicants, but there are no nationality restrictions for the provision of insurance intermediation activities.

Securities

1. Capital markets are still very small in Armenia. In 2008, the total value of transactions conducted in the securities markets totalled dram 821 billion (some US$2.4 billion), of which 96.8% were government securities, 2% were equities, and 1.2% were corporate bonds. The legislation currently applied is more liberal than Armenia's GATS commitments related to securities. Armenia's central depositary and stock exchange were demutualized [47] in 2007, subsequently privatized to the NASDAQ OMX Group in 2008, and since January 2009 operates under the name NASDAQ OMX Armenia. [48]

TELECOMMUNICATIONS

(a) Market structure

1. The Armenian telecommunications sector is still at a developing stage, mainly due to lack of investment during 1998-05. Although the telecom market was fully liberalized in 2007, new investments in the sector are still needed, as the inadequate quality of services, particularly of internet access, may be hindering business innovation and general economic development.

2. In 1998, ArmenTel, at that time Armenia's only telecom company, was partially privatized and granted a monopoly licence covering all telecom services for 15 years. Since then, the Government has imposed a series of fines on ArmenTel for its abuse of dominant position and for the poor quality of its services (see below) . In 2004, the Government renegotiated ArmenTel's licence, ending its monopoly in mobile telephony and internet access services. In 2005, a second mobile telephony licence (GSM) was granted to an Armenian company, which was subsequently sold to a Russian operator branded as VivaCell. In 2006, the State sold its remaining stake in ArmenTel to another Russian company branded as Beeline, which also acquired control over the rest of the company. In 2007, the Government eliminated the remaining exclusive rights enjoyed by Armentel on fixed telephony and international voice and data transmission services (by the end of 2009 there were three providers of international IP services and eight providers of voice services over fixed lines) . In 2009, the Government granted a third mobile telephony licence (also GSM) to a French company branded as Orange. When VivaCell entered the mobile services market prices dropped and the quality of services increased, the same was expected to happen when Orange began its operation in November 2009.

3. In 2008, telecommunications contributed 5% to Armenia's GDP. Between January 2003 and December 2008, the number of fixed telephone lines increased by around 8%, reaching a penetration rate of 20%. During the same period mobile subscriptions increased at an average annual rate of 44%, reaching penetration rate of 73% of inhabitants at the end of 2008. The authorities indicate that internet subscriptions have increased since liberalization of the market, reaching a total of 80,141; but there are no official statistics on the number of internet users.

(b) Regulatory framework

1. Armenia's GATS Schedule of Commitments covers virtually all basic and value-added services, for which it has agreed, with a few exceptions (i.e. reservations of monopoly rights), to impose no limitations on market access or national treatment for the first three modes of supply (Table AVI.1) . The GATS Schedule incorporates, under additional commitments, the telecommunications Reference Paper negotiated in the context of the extended negotiations. [49]

2. The Ministry of Transport and Communications is responsible for establishing policy for the telecom sector, while the Public Services Regulatory Commission (PSRC), an independent State body, is responsible for supervision and regulation. The authorities note, however, that the division of tasks between the two entities is not always clear. The PSRC consists of five members appointed by the President (upon nomination by the Prime Minister) for five years. Its funding must be approved by the Government but it should rely on obligatory fees collected by regulated entities. [50] The PSRC regulates the sector through Resolutions, which are in most cases only available in Armenian. [51]

3. The Law on Electronic Communications of 8 July 2005 is Armenia's main legislation for the telecom sector. Based on the Law, the PSRC has promulgated a number of regulations concerning activities in the telecom sector. The Law has provisions on competitive safeguards, and competition policy issues (such as the abuse of dominant position by a telecom operator), which are dealt with jointly by the PSRC and the Competition Commission (Chapter V(4)) . ArmenTel has been subject to various penalties, including fines for abuse of dominant position in mobile telephony in August 2005; for failing to provide VoIP services to two companies in 2007; and for predatory pricing of internet services in 2008.

4. Since the last of ArmenTel's monopoly rights were eliminated in 2007 (see above), there are no restrictions on the participation of foreign investors in Armenia's telecom sector. All providers of public telecommunication networks and services are required to obtain a licence with the PSRC before commencing activities. The assignation of the radio-electric spectrum is carried out via authorizations issued by the PSRC. It must act upon applications within six weeks of receipt, but it may, with notice to the applicant, extend this period for an additional three months. Licences may be renewed provided the licensee has operated within all the conditions of the original licence. [52]

5. Any provider of telecom networks and services, as defined in the Law, has the right and obligation to negotiate with other providers on interconnection for the provision of public telecom services. The PSRC regulates interconnection pricing by setting a maximum price for interconnection within the fixed network, and setting specific prices (which are reduced every six months) for interconnection on the mobile network. The PSRC may also impose additional access and interconnection pricing obligations on a provider with dominant position, if it considers that its access terms are discriminatory. Interconnection termination rates established by a dominant operator should be made publicly available. Disputes between service providers over interconnection terms may be submitted to the PSRC for resolution. Orders to change the interconnection agreement must be issued within a maximum of two months. During 2003-08, the PSRC received four requests for mediation of interconnection disputes; three were resolved through mediation, and one is still pending. Appeals of PSRC orders may first be reviewed administratively before they are brought before ordinary courts of law; at end 2009, no cases had been brought before the courts.

6. The pricing system for final consumers varies according to the service. The PSRC sets price caps for fixed telephony services, while prices for mobile phone and internet services are set freely by providers and only overseen by the PSRC. [53]

7. ArmenTel is still officially considered to have a dominant position in fixed public telephony and international IP transit service markets. [54] Armenian legislation does not require the unbundling of the local loop. However, the authorities noted that telecom providers are investing in wireless local loop technologies such as WiMAX. [55] Numeric portability is not legally required, but the authorities are analysing the issue.

8. Armenia has partially regulated the resale of telecom services, in particular, the PSRC has adopted regulations regarding the provision of voice over internet protocol (VoIP) services. Although the provision of VoIP services *per se* do not require a licence, companies that provide the termination of international voice calls must obtain a licence with the PSRC.

9. The PSRC may include universal service requirements in the licence of any operator or service provider. The legislation provides for the creation of a universal services fund based on services fees paid by all service providers; however, at end 2009, no fund had been established. On the other hand, the Government has created incentives for the provision of universal services, for example, by giving ArmenTel a discount on spectrum licences used to provide fixed telephony to rural areas via mobile technology. Cross-subsidies among telecom services are not allowed. [56]

(c) Postal services

1. Regular postal services are provided nationwide by a closed-stock company owned by the State but managed by a private company. Despite the *de facto* monopoly, Armenian legislation does not establish any exclusive rights to the state company. Thus, the postal service market is open to foreign investors, who have not shown interest so far.

2. Courier and other express postal services are also liberalized, and there are no restrictions on the participation of foreign investors.

TRANSPORT

(a) Overland transport

1. Armenia is land-locked, and borders Turkey, Georgia, Azerbaijan, and Iran; the borders with Turkey and Azerbaijan are completely closed. [57] It relies, therefore, on the north-south overland corridors for most of its trade (i.e. trade in goods for which airfreight is not feasible or cost effective) . [58] Three roads and one railway link Armenia to Georgia and one road links it to Iran. [59]

2. Armenia's strategy for 2009-19 is aimed at, *inter alia*, improving modal integration and upgrading its road infrastructure (see below), to facilitate international trade, economic development, and regional balance. Armenia participates in several international fora on transport aimed at creating corridors between regions and improving trade flows, including: the North-South Transport Corridor; the Transport Corridor Europe-Caucasus-Asia; the CIS Transport Coordination Council; the Black Sea Economic Cooperation Organization Working Group on Transport and Communications; the UNECE Trans-European Railway and Trans-European Motor Highway projects; the joint UNECE/UNESCAP Euro-Asian Transport Linkages project; the UNESCAP Asian Land Transport Infrastructure Development that includes the Asian Highway and the Trans-Asian Railway projects; and the International Transport Forum (former European Conference of the Ministers of Transport) . [60]

3. In the services auxiliary to all modes of transport, Armenia reserved customs clearance services to licensed customs agents established in Armenia.

Roads

1. Armenia's road network is relatively well developed. In 2007, it totalled 7,704 km of which 6,690 km were paved roads. However, road density, at 266.5 km per 1,000 km^2 (in 2005), remains low compared with neighbouring countries such as Azerbaijan (716 km) and Georgia (291.4 km) . [61]

2. Road transport remains the main means of moving passengers and freight (Table VI.6): around 90% of the volume of domestic freight transport is carried by road. However, in the north of the country, roads are impassable for large haulage trucks in winter, and haulage companies can only carry 20 and 40 foot containers from March to October. [63] Practically all of Armenia's international freight is transported by land and goes through the Georgian ports of Poti and Batumi on the Black Sea. [64] Both of these ports are about 700 km from the Armenian border, which takes about four days by road and 24 hours by rail. There is a twice weekly container train to Poti. In November 2009, transport costs for 20 and 40 foot containers from Yerevan to Poti are US$1,750 and US$2,080, respectively, by road and US$1,250 and US$1,900 by rail.

Overland transport

	2003	2004	2005	2006	2007
Total freight ('000 tonnes), of which:	7,061.0	6,734.9	8,280.8	9,676.4	10,296.1
Rail	2,125.5	2,629.6	2,612.3	2,719.6	2,983.7
Road	4,086.2	3,153.0	4,479.7	5,730.4	5,864.5
Freight revenue (dram million), of which:	10,038.4	10,585.4	11,584.4	14,422.7	16,946.2
Rail	7,787.7	8,715.7	8,040.6	8,936.6	10,375.3
Road	1,398.4	1,299.9	2,347.8	3,875.1	3,233.1
Total passenger flow (million), of which:	174.0	185.6	204.8	245.8	251.8
Rail	1.1	0.8	0.7	0.7	0.6
Road	147.5	158.6	174.0	214.0	216.0

Source: National Statistical Service of the Republic of Armenia (2008), *Statistical Yearbook of Armenia*; and information provided by the Armenian authorities.

3. Armenia does not have a road fund. Revenues colleted from excise duties on fuel, from tolls on heavy and oversized cargos, and on transit transportation, contribute to the general State budget and are not reserved for road construction or maintenance. [65] Road infrastructure is funded by the State budget, and foreign donors (World Bank, the U.S. Lincy Foundation, and the Asian Development Bank) have contributed in the past. The State budget allocation for roads is concentrated on road maintenance, and increased from US$15 million in 2004 to US$68 million in 2008, while foreign investment is concentrated on road construction, and is expected to total US$461 million for the 2000-11 period. The private sector is involved in road construction and maintenance but does not finance projects. Tenders that are to be funded under the State budget are implemented under the Law on Procurement (Chapter V(5)); and tenders financed by international financial institutions are implemented in accordance with the guidelines of those institutions.

4. The main domestic legislation for road transport is the Law on Road-Users Toll and the Automotive Roads Law. Under Government Decree No. 1720-N of December 2004, Armenia Roads SCJSC [66] was restructured to form Armenia Roads Directorate NCSO. [67] The Armenia Roads Directorate operates under the Ministry of Transport and Communication. Its main functions are to: provide technical assistance to the Ministry on road construction and road use; monitor the condition of roads, traffic intensity, etc.; prepare programmes for the rehabilitation of roads; and implement road rehabilitation programmes funded by international donors.

5. The Lifeline Road Network Programme, launched in 2004, is aimed at rehabilitating local roads and improving access from rural areas to the interstate and national road networks; it targets a total of 2,700 km local roads, including 784 km of high priority rural roads. Rehabilitation and maintenance of the existing road network, in particular reconstruction of bridges, is a high priority under Armenia's Poverty Reduction Strategy for 2004-15; total expenditure is dram 387.8 billion. [68] These improvements could encourage more rural producers to engage in foreign trade.

6. Public transport is provided by privately owned minibus companies. Foreign companies can provide public bus services. Like domestic companies, they must register in Armenia and apply for one of the competitions held by Yerevan Municipality for each new bus route. Public bus services are provided in Yerevan and throughout Armenia (although frequency is limited) . Most cities have taxi services [69]; taxi drivers, irrespective of their nationality, must be licensed by the Ministry of Transport and Communications. Public transport and taxi services are not subsidized.

Rail

1. The railway network is 827 km long; 726 km are operational. [70] The network is fully electrified and predominantly single-track. [71] Passenger and freight transport remains low, but rail still dominates international freight (60% market share by value) (Table VI.6) . Gold ore, cement, cement clinker, oil, construction materials, and wheat are the main commodities transported by rail.

2. Until 2008, Armenia Railways was a 100% government-owned joint-stock company. Following an international tender, Government decision No. 17A in January 2008 announced that Russian Railways JSC had won the tender. In February 2008, the Ministry of Transport and Communications and Russian Railways JSC signed a concession agreement, and in April 2008, the Ministry issued a licence to South Caucasus Railways, a subsidiary of Russian Railways, to operate Armenia's rail system. The licence concession covers rail freight and passenger services, rail rolling-stock, and rail infrastructure management. [72] The licence is for an initial period of 30 years, and may be extended after 20 years for a further 20 years.

3. Under the terms of the concession agreement, Russian Railways acquired the rolling-stock. Under the terms of the licence, South Caucus Railways can provide passenger and freight services and, in most circumstances, set tariffs. However, the Government can set: railway transport infrastructure usage tariffs during emergency situations; tariffs for international transport regulated by international agreements; and tariffs for strategic commodities (oil products, soft wheat, seeds, weapons, fertilizers, and chemicals) . [73]

4. The railway infrastructure remains state-owned. The authorities confirmed that Russian Railways is subject to ordinary tax provisions with no special tax relief provisions. There is an official subsidy for the loss-making passenger service, which is also cross-subsidized from the profitable freight business. Due to the vital importance of rail transport with Georgia, Armenia requested Russian Railways to adhere to Armenia's inter-state commitments on standards and interchange issues under the Organization for the Cooperation of Railways and related regional agreements; and it allows other rail operators (such as Georgian Railways) to use the network at

pre-determined access fees although Russian Railways holds exclusive rights to manage the infrastructure. [74]

5. South Caucasus CJSC has committed to invest US$572 million, of which, 30% will go to rolling-stock and the rest to improving infrastructure. The Asian Development Bank has also agreed to fund a feasibility study for the Armenia-Iran railway priority project; an additional feasibility study for the Vanadzor-Dilijan link is needed. Rehabilitation of the Yerevan-Tbilisi line has been in progress since 2008.

(b) Air transport

1. Armenia has two international airports: Zvartnots in Yerevan, and Shirak in Gyumi. While civil aviation companies may also operate from Erebuni airport, no passenger or freight services are operating. Since 1990, 12 local airports ceased operations and were transferred to the Ministry of Defence or to local self governing bodies. One additional local airport, which was included in the civil aviation system in 1990, also ceased to operate in 2006 due to lack of demand. International passenger flow has increased steadily since 2003. Despite increases in volume and revenue, the share of air freight in total freight transport remains low (Table VI.7) .

2. The legal framework for civil aviation is made up of international agreements signed by Armenia and the Law on Aviation of 2007, which replaced the Law on Aviation of 2000. The General Department of Civil Aviation (GDCA), the State regulatory body for aviation [75], elaborates and implements air transport policies, and administers and supervises aviation services. Its responsibilities include issuing certificates, permits, and licences for civil aviation activities, including certificates for aircraft, permits for operating commercial air transport, and licences for flight operations personnel, air traffic controllers, and aircraft maintenance personnel. [76] Armenia is a member of the International Civil Aviation Organization (ICAO), the European Civil Aviation Conference, the European Organization for the Safety of Air Navigation, and the Interstate Aviation Committee. [77]

Air transport indicators, 2003-09

	2003	2004	2005	2006	2007	2008	2009[a]
Total international passenger flow (million)	0.9	1.1	1.2	1.2	1.4	1.5	1.2
Total international air freight ('000 tonnes)	8.7	9.2	9.3	9.3	10.0	10.8	7.0
Air freight revenue (dram million)	1,398.4	1,299.9	2,347.8	3,875.1	3,233.1	4,274.5	2,580.5
Share of air freight in total freight transportation (%)	0.1	0.1	0.1	0.1	0.1	..	..
Share of air freight in total freight turnover (%)	0.3	0.5	0.5	0.5	0.5	..	..

.. Not available.

a From January to October.

Source: National Statistical Service of the Republic of Armenia (2008), *Statistical Yearbook of Armenia*; and information provided by the Armenian authorities.

3. Zvartnots International Airport is the main gateway to Armenia, with several international airlines and one domestically owned airline operating commercial flights to 48 destinations. [78] In 2008, it handled 372,179 passengers (98.4% of the total passenger flow) and 2,709 tonnes of freight (99.4% of total air freight) . [79]Zvartnots airport belongs to the State, but its management was handed over to a foreign private company (American International Airports LLC) via a 30-year concession contract in 2002. [80] The management company plans to invest some US$390 million during its concession to upgrade the airport. Its new passenger terminal, with a capacity of 2 million passengers per year, has been fully operational since 2007 and its cargo terminal handles 100,000 tonnes of freight annually. [81] Slot allocation procedures are regulated by GDCA and follow the respective EC Normative on the subject.

4. In 2007, Armenia International Airports CJSC was granted a management concession to operate the State-owned Shirak airport. [82] As a result, the airport's runway was completely renovated, and received a new certificate of operation from the ICAO.

5. All passengers departing from Armenia are charged with an exit tax of dram 10,000 (some US$29), which is levied at the moment of sale of the ticket. The following are exempt from the exit tax: children under 12 years of age; transit and transfer passengers; World War II veterans; and passengers of regional flights (within a radius of 450 km) .

6. Armenian Air Traffic Service (ARMATS), created in 1997, provides air navigation services (including traffic control, communication, navigation, and surveillance services) and aeronautical information services for Armenia's airspace, in compliance with international civil aviation standards. [83] ARMATS is a joint-stock company with 100% of its shares belonging to the State.

7. Armenian legislation does not restrict the participation of foreign investors in air transport services (either for passengers or cargo), thus, airlines may be fully owned by foreigners.

8. Armavia, Armenia's largest airline, has been operating commercial flights since 2002. [84] It carried 26% more passengers in 2008 (646,447 passengers) than in 2005. On the other hand, its market share decreased slightly, from 44.5% in 2005 to 42.9% in 2008. Its fleet consists of eight aircraft and it employs 480 people. [85]Armavia is privately owned; control is in the hands of an Armenian company that holds 70% of the shares, while the remaining 30% are held by a Russian partner company. When state-owned Armenian Airlines was liquidated in 2004, Armavia took over its licence to operate international flights. In 2005, Armavia also took over flights to Europe when Armenian International Airways ceased operations. [86]

9. Air Armenia is the only air cargo company based in Armenia; it is a private company founded in 2003. Since other airlines provide cargo services on their passenger flights, it is estimated that Air Armenia had a 59% market share of the air cargo shipments from and to Armenia in 2008. [87] It operates regular scheduled cargo flights from Yerevan to Frankfurt. There is no agreement with Germany in this respect; the decision to use Frankfurt as a logistics base was purely commercial, and shipments weighting over 10 tonnes do not usually transit through Frankfurt. [88] The cost of shipment depends on the weight and starts at €1.20/kg for the Yerevan to Frankfurt route and €1.8-2.4/kg for Frankfurt to Yerevan.

10. At the end of 2009, Armenia had 42 bilateral air services agreements in force, mainly with European and Middle Eastern partners. [89] Armenia signed a horizontal agreement on certain aspects of air services with the EU in December 2008, however for issues such as route rights and capacity determination, the bilateral agreements with EU Member states prevail. Another important bilateral air services agreement, in terms of traffic generated, was signed with the

United States in November 2008 and entered into force on 16 June 2009. The agreement with the Unites States can be classified as liberal [90] since it grants 3rd, 4th, and 5th freedoms of the air, and it establishes substantive ownership and effective control of airlines, multi-designation of points, free determination of capacity, and free pricing. [91]

(v) Professional services

(a) Legal services [92]

1. Armenia's new Law on the Profession of Advocates, enacted in 2004, provides for the establishment of the Chamber of Advocates (the Chamber) and the eligibility criteria for advocates. [93] The Chamber was established in 2005 and unified Armenia's bar unions (i.e. the Union of Advocates and the International Union of Advocates) . It is the regulatory authority responsible for, *inter alia*, licensing advocates, protecting their rights, and conducting disciplinary proceedings. Other associations are also active in capacity building for legal professionals, supporting the rule of law, improving awareness of Armenia's obligations under international legal treaties, and developing an independent judiciary power. [94]

2. Legal services are provided by advocates or non-advocate lawyers. Advocates are members of the Chamber, who are licensed by the Chamber after having passed a qualification examination. The exam, which was reintroduced in 2006, is set by the Chamber's Qualification Commission. Anyone with a law degree and two years experience in a legal position may apply to sit the examination. An advocate needs a licence to represent clients at civil, administrative, or criminal proceedings, while individuals have the right to represent themselves should they so wish. [95] Licences are issued for an indefinite period; however, the Chamber may suspend or withdraw them. Advocates pay fees to the Chamber, including the examination fee (dram 35,000), the licence fee (dram 50,000), and the membership fee (dram 3,000/month) . They are free to work independently or in firms. In 2008, there were 825 advocates in Armenia.

3. Non-advocate lawyers are not members of the Chamber. They work within private companies, governmental agencies, NGOs or independently, and can represent clients in civil and administrative cases only. Their activities are not regulated.

4. Foreign lawyers are allowed to practice as advocates in Armenia. They must have a licence from their home country and abide by the Law on the Profession of Advocates, the Charter of the Chamber of Advocate, and the Code of Conduct for Advocates. They have to be accredited to the Chamber but are not required to take the Chamber's qualification examination or language tests. Foreign lawyers use their home licence; where this has been withdrawn in their home country, they are removed from the list of advocates. They may not provide legal assistance on issues related to the State or state secrets. Although accredited to the Chamber of Advocates, they may not become members of the Chamber. Furthermore, in legal activities, notarising services are reserved to the State.

5. The enactment of the new Law on the Profession of Advocates in 2004 and the creation of the Chamber improved the provision of legal services in Armenia. However, it has been pointed out that two major concerns remain: firstly, a person with no educational or professional legal background can still assist and represent clients in civil and administrative cases; and secondly, legal services provision is still affected by the perception of endemic corruption. [96] These concerns are being addressed through structural and legal reforms, such as amendments to the Constitution and the judicial code.

(b) Accounting and auditing services

1. The legislative basis for Armenia's accountancy and other financial reporting requirements is the Law on Accounting, which entered into effect in 1998 and has been amended a number of times since then. Before December 2008, the statutory accounting standards used in Armenia were the Accounting Standards of the Republic of Armenia (ASRA), which were based on International Accounting Standards (IAS) of 2000 but were not updated. According to reports this created a standards gap between more recent IAS and the ASRA.[97]

2. This standards gap was addressed in the December 2008 Law on Making Amendments and Additions to the RA Law on Accounting. The following entities are, or will be, required to present their financial statements in compliance with International Financial Reporting Standards (IFRS): banks (from 1 January 2009); non-banking financial institutions [98] (from 1 January 2010); and other business entities (with effect from 1 January of the year following a six-month period after the IFRS and IFRIC interpretations have been officially adopted by the Government) . [99] The Amendment of December 2008 also requires all large companies to undergo an annual audit and publish their financial statements annually. [100] Entities with turnover of less than dram 100 million will apply accounting only for tax purposes; the Government Decree to bring this into force is expected in early 2010.

3. Implementation of IFRS requires their translation into Armenian. To this end, the Ministry of Finance has established the Official Translating Committee, composed of translators and accounting and audit professionals, which is responsible for translating IFRS and their guides and interpretations into Armenian.

4. Until August 2009, to be recognized by the Ministry of Finance, accountants and auditors had to meet its educational and professional experience requirements [101], and pass its certification exam. The certificates were valid for five years after which the accountants or auditors exams had to be repeated. Between 2006 and 2008, about 222 people sat the exam for the accountants certificate and 199 sat the exam for the auditors certificate. The pass rates were 38% and 26%, respectively. [102]

5. Since August 2009, under a government decree on accreditation of professional bodies, the Association of Accountants and Auditors of Armenia (AAAA) has been recognized as the professional association that represents both accountants and auditors. The AAAA was established in 1997 and became an associate member of the International Federation of Accountants (IFAC) in 2005. The AAAA has a certification scheme based on the Association of Chartered Certified Accountants. Under the Government decree on accreditation, all who have passed IFAC-recognized exams are recognized as certified accountants or auditors (as are those that had passed the Ministry of Finance's exam) . According to the authorities, the Government has stopped running its exams for accountants and auditors; the AAAA will continue to run its internationally recognized exams.

6. The AAAA's system of certification has three levels: certified bookkeeper; certified accountant; and certified auditor. As of June 2008 the AAAA had about 239 qualified bookkeepers, 20 qualified accountants and 11 qualified auditors. [103] There are no restrictions on non-Armenian individuals or enterprises setting up accountancy firms or audit companies in Armenia, provided they meet Armenian legislative requirements. In 2009, it was reported that there were 22 audit companies, including several international firms, and 11 private auditors in Armenia. [104]

7. As of November 2009, there were 189 qualified accountants and 106 auditors (including 32 with internationally recognized qualifications) . A number of foreign accountancy firms have established themselves in Armenia including three of the Big Four auditors.

(vi) Tourism

1. Tourism is estimated to have contributed 2.1% to GDP and 8.3% to employment in 2008.[105] Armenia's visitors come mainly from countries with large diaspora communities (e.g. Russia, Georgia, Iran, the United States, France, Germany, and Ukraine) . The main reason for visiting Armenia is, therefore, visiting friends and relatives (44.8%), followed by business/conference (22.4%) and leisure tourism (11.6%) . [106]

2. Armenia has good potential to attract tourism given its well preserved natural and cultural/historical attractions, including some UNESCO World heritage sites. It also has the potential to develop sport, adventure, and winter tourism. However, despite improvements in tourism indicators (Table VI.8), high flight costs and limited schedules, as well as high taxes on passengers [107], appear to have affected negatively tourism, which is also hampered by other factors such as underdeveloped infrastructure (transport and accommodation) .

3. Armenia's tourism policy and strategy are implemented by the Tourism Department at the Ministry of Economy. Under the 2008 Tourism Concept Paper, the objective is to increase the contribution of tourism to GDP to 12% by 2030, with a view to alleviating poverty and ensuring balanced development among the regions. The key policy targets are to increase: the number of visitors per year (to 3 million); tourism earnings (to US$3 billion); and tourism-related employment. These targets are to be met by: improving infrastructure and accessibility (e.g. expanding flight frequency and connections, and relaxing the entry and departure procedures); making Armenia a competitive tourist destination with unique and high quality tourism services and products; and training the workforce.

Selected tourism indicators, 2003-08

	2003	2004	2005	2006	2007	2008
Tourist arrivals	123,262	262,685	318,563	381,136	510,287	558,443
Revenue (US$ million)	90	188	240	307	333	..
Average spent per day (US$)	30	30	30	35	36	36
Rooms (No.)	2,455	2,638	2,914	3,109	3,654	4,195
Room occupancy (%)	25	25	22	22	25	..
Beds (No.)	..	..	..	..	..	8,376
Average length of stay (days)	15	15	17	17	20	20

.. Not available.

Source: Baghramyan M. and V. Ghushchyan (2008), "Implications of Armenian Dram Appreciation for the Competitiveness of Armenian IT, Tourism, and Food Processing Industries", *Armenian Journal of Public Policy*, Volume 3, No. 1, March; USAID, CAPS, Armenian Tourism Development Agency, and Armenian Development Agency (2008), *Armenian Tourism Industry: Investment Handbook*, August; and information provided by the Armenian authorities.

4. The two recently signed bilateral air services agreements with the EU and the United States support the objective of the Concept Paper by allowing for the expansion of the number of international flights; as does the Government's decision to grant concession contracts for the

management of Armenia's international airports (section (iv)(b) above) . In addition, the authorities noted that a Government Decree of 16 October 2008 adopted a programme for the sector that includes improving the legal framework regulating the tourism sector, improving the statistical system, and developing an efficient management model for State historical and cultural sites.

5. The Law on Tourism, adopted in 2003, is Armenia's main tourism-related legislation. It sets out the principles and objectives of the national policy as well as the Government's role in the implementation process and the provision of tourism services. The Government intends to review the law, based on best practices in international tourism legislation. [109]

6. The Armenian Tourism Development Agency (ATDA) was established in June 2000 to promote and market Armenia abroad, in order to more effectively meet the objectives of the Concept Paper (see above) . It was terminated in 2009, and the Government passed its functions to a wider reaching public organization, the National Competitiveness Foundation of Armenia.

7. Tourist guides must be licensed by the Ministry of Economy; licensing is subject to a levy (dram 3,000 examination fee and dram 10,000 annual fee) . [110] The current licensing examination is being reviewed by the Guild of Armenian Guides (GAG) to ensure compliance with the requirements of the World Federation of Tourist Guide Associations. [111] Any natural person, regardless of nationality or citizenship, may apply to obtain a tour-guide licence if they meet the requirements of: higher education with specialization in tourism, and minimum of two years of work experience as a tour guide. Although tour operators and travel agents do not require a specific licence, they must register at the State Registry of Legal Entities (Chapter V(1)) .

8. Accommodation establishments are certified, on a voluntary basis, by the Ministry of Economy. Certificates are valid for five years, renewable, and granted upon a site visit by the Classification Commission (composed of inspectors from various government agencies, consumers, architects, and representatives of the tourism sector) . Certification procedure fees vary from dram 150,000 (some US$430) for 1-star hotels, to dram 1,250,000 (some US$3,571) for 5-star hotels.

9. There are no restrictions on foreign investment in hotel services; FDI totalled US$19.3 million in 2007 (3% of total FDI) . Tourism activities are carried out mainly by SMEs with limited scope to invest significantly in the subsector. The level of public and private investment is currently low and will need to be increased by around US$2.5 billion to further develop the sector in accordance with the objectives of the Concept Paper. [112] The Government plans to actively encourage investment though bonds, bank guarantees, and special programmes in order to attract partnerships with the private sector and foreign donors. [113]

10. Armenia has been a member of the UNWTO since 1997. It has agreements on cooperation in tourism with members of the Black Sea Economic Cooperation, as well as with Argentina, Belarus, Bulgaria, China, Cyprus, Egypt, Greece, India, Iran, Kyrgyz Republic, Lebanon, Moldova, Poland, Romania, Russia, Syria, Ukraine, and United Arab Emirates.

INFRASTRUCTURES DEVELOPMENT AND INVESTMENT OPPORTUNITES

1. DRINKING WATER

CURRENT SITUATION

In the SDP, further reforms of water supply and sewerage systems aimed to enhance the reliability and efficiency of operations of those systems, reduce water losses and improve the quality of water supply and drainage services.

During the implementation of the SDP, the reliability of centralized water supply systems was improved significantly, especially in rural settlements (Table 10). Data presented reveals that the reliability of centralized water supply systems in rural settlements improved by 1.3 percentage points in 2011, compared to the level of 2008 and reached 93.7%.

As of 2011, transported potable water problem was solved for the households. If in 2008

1.1 percent of households was consuming transported water, the respective indicator according to 2011 data was 0 percent.

According to the results of the survey, the average daily duration of water supply in 2011 improved by around 3.6 hours, compared to the same indicator for 2008, and amounted to 16 hours per day thus reaching the 2012 target set by SDP.

Table 9. Access to drinking water in 2008-2017, %

Water supply source	Total population				Urban population				Rural population			
	2008	2009	2010	2011	2008	2009	2010	2011	2008	2009	2010	2011
Centralized water supply	97,0	97,5	97.5	97.5	99,4	99.6	99.5	99.5	92,4	93.6	93.5	93.7
Less than 1 hour	0,7	0.4	0.5	0.1	0,2	0.2	0.3	0.1	1,9	1.0	0.9	0.1
1-5 hours	31,3	30.0	26.6	18.6	31,2	26.8	23.7	16.4	31,4	36.5	32.4	23.3
6-12 hours	28,7	17.5	20.1	22.6	32,5	19.3	22.5	24.0	20,5	13.8	15.2	19.6
13-23 hours	5,7	3.8	4.3	5.5	5,9	4.9	3.9	5.3	5,3	1.4	5.2	5.8
24 hours	33,6	48.3	48.5	53.2	30,2	48.8	49.6	54.2	40,9	47.3	46.3	51.2
Water well, spring	1,2	1.6	1.4	1.3	0,1	0.2	0.2	0.1	3,2	4.3	3.6	3.6
Local source	0,6	0.5	1.0	1.1	0,2	0,2	0.3	0.4	1,2	1.3	2.5	2.6
Transported water	1,1	0.3	0.1	0.0	0,2	0,0	0.0	0.0	3,0	0.6	0.4	0.0
Other sources	0,1	0.1		0.1	0,1	0,0	-	0.0	0,2	0.2		0.1

280. The average daily duration of water supply in rural areas is also characterized by significant inequalities. In rural settlements serviced by Armenian Water Sewerage CJSC the average daily duration of water supply in 2012 amounted to 14.6 hours, while, for around one fourth of the rural population the average daily duration of water supply was five hours or less (Table 10).

MAIN DIRECTIONS OF PROGRAM POLICIES

The program plans to continue the reforms of drinking water systems in order to enhance the reliability and effectiveness of the operations of those systems and improve the quality of water supply and drainage services, at the same time focusing on mitigation of regional disparities.

Investment policy. Drinking water systems will continue to remain a priority for public investments. For the entire period of the program, annual investments in the system will amount to 0.4% of the GDP.

The targets for the investment policy will be the duration of services provided[29] and improvement of the quality of those services and mitigation of the existing regional disparities. The investment policy should also aim to enhance the efficiency of drinking water systems, focusing particularly on the issue of reducing water losses. In the sphere of wastewater removal of special importance are the reconstruction of wastewater removal systems in cities and major rural areas and construction of wastewater treatment plants for those systems.

The investment policy will adopt a special approach also to the around 560 rural communities, where water supply is not provided by specialized organizations possessing the relevant permits for water supply services provision. These communities will be included in the investment program of the government through their inclusion in the service area of already operating or future specialized organizations which have the corresponding permits for provision of water supply services. At the same time, water supply problems of communities, the inclusion of which in the service area of specialized organizations providing water supply services is technically difficult, or economically not viable, will not be ignored either.

Tarriff policy. Throughout the period of the program, the tariff policy will be aimed at gradually increasing tariffs to the levels of cost recovery, taking into account the affordability issues for households in the lowest income groups. The maximum level of affordable tariffs for water supply and wastewater disposal services will be defined[30], and the services provided with higher tariffs for poor families will be subsidized by the government to cover the difference.

Management reforms. Management reforms in the drinking water sector will continue by increasing the participation of the private sector. The government will encourage the widening of the service areas of specialized organizations with permits for provision of water supply services, as well as the establishment of new specialized organizations for provision of water supply services to rural communities which have been left out of the service areas of the operating specialized organizations. With this purpose country's water system comprehensive analysis will be conducted, including the rural areas currently out of service area.

[29] According to preliminary assessments, the proposed level will allow for increasing the average national indicator for continuous water supply by 0.5 hour annually.

[30] 2.5 percent of consumer expenditures of the poorest quintile of the population. The calculated daily consumption volume per capita is 70 L. According to the assessments in 2010, the affordable calculated tariff was 190 drams / cubic meter.

PROGRAM TARGET INDICATORS

287. The main target indicators for drinking water systems are presented in Table 10.

Table 10. Drinking water system main target indicators

Indicator	Base year	2014	2017	2021	2025
Transition indicator (published by EBRD)	2.67 (2013)	3.0	3.67	4.0	4.33
Water supply duration indicator improvement with respect to the base year, hours/day					
"Yerevan Water" CJSC service area (Includes city of Yerevan and adjacent 32 rural settlements)	23.0 (2012)	0.2	0.5	0.8	1.0
"Shirak Water and Sewerage" CJSC service area(Includes city of Gyumri and adjacent 36 rural settlements)	13.7 (2012)	1.0	2.5	4.5	6.3
"Lori and Sewerage" CJSC service area(Includes city of Vanadzor and adjacent 16 rural settlements)	12.1 (2012)	1.5	3.0	5.5	7.9
"Nor Akunq" CJSC service area(Includes city of Armavir and adjacent 10 rural settlements.)	22.4 (2012)	0.2	0.5	0.8	1.0
"Armenian Water and Sewerage" CJSC service area, including by group of cities and rural areas31	16.2 (2012)	0.9	2.2	3.4	4.5
Group of cities 1	22.6 (2012)	0.2	0.5	0.8	1.0
Group of cities 2	16.1 (2012)	0.8	2.0	3.0	3.9
Group of cities 3	12.1 (2012)	1.6	4.0	6.0	7.9
Rural areas	14.6 (2012)	1.0	2.5	4.0	5.4
Public investments level, % of GDP	0.37 (2012)	0.4	0.4	0.4	0.4

IRRIGATION

CURRENT SITUATION

288. The expansion of irrigated land areas was quite slow in recent years. In particular, compared to 2008, irrigated land areas in 2012 increased by only 1 percent and amounted to

130.7 thousand ha.

Table 11. Irrigated areas and volume of supplied water 2008-2012

	2008	2009	2010	2011	2012
Irrigated land serviced by WUAs, thous. ha	128.9	128.1	128.8	129.4	130.7
Volume of the supplied water, mln. cub. meters	576.7	412	396.5	415.3	472.1
Water consumption level, thous. cub. meters / ha	4.47	3.22	3.08	3.21	3.61

Source: State Water Committee of the Ministry of Territorial Administration.

289. During the recent period the volume of water used per hectare has decreased. In 2008 it amounted to 4.47 thous. cubic meters. In 2012, it reduced by around 19% down to 3.61 thous.

[31] The first group includes the cities with average daily water supply duration exceeding 20 hours in the base year, the second group includes the cities with average daily water supply duration of 10 to 20 hours in the base year, and the third group – cities with less than 10 hours of average daily water supply duration.

cubic meters. The decline in the per unit use of water mainly resulted from the changes in natural-climatic conditions and due to decrease in water losses in primary irrigation system.

290. At the same time, positive developments are recorded in recent years with regard to the indicators characterizing the level of satisfaction of water users with irrigation water supply services. In particular, in 2009-2011, the results of the representative sample survey of around 1500 water users revealed that the value of the satisfaction index of water user households with irrigation water supply services was around 50 in 2011, compared to 40 in 2009 (Table 12).

Table 12. Dynamics of satisfaction with irrigation water supply services 2009-2011

	2009	2011
Percent of h/hs which indicated that the irrigation water was supplied in timely manner in the total number of WU h/hs, %	57.2	70.8
Percent of h/hs which indicated that the irrigation water was supplied in enough quantity in the total number of WU h/hs, %	60.9	72.8
H/hs which have indicated that the irrigation water supply improved compared to the previous year, % of WU h/hs	17.0	12.2
H/hs which have evaluated the condition of the irrigation system in their village as very good and good, % of WU h/hs	23.5	35.7

WU's satisfaction with the irrigation water supply index (ISI)	39.7	47.9

Source: results of 2009 and 2011 survey of WUA member households (MCA Armenia SNCO/ AVAG Solutions Ltd).

MAIN DIRECTIONS OF PROGRAM POLICIES

Investment policy. Irrigation systems also will continue to remain a priority for public investments. For the entire period of the program, annual capital investments in the system will amount to 0.3% of the GDP. At the same time, the Government will take steps to ensure sufficient funding for the operation and maintenance expenses of the system.

The target of the investment policy will be the expansion of irrigated land areas and higher efficiency of the system. Expansion of irrigated land area is assumed to take place in the frames of existing irrigation systems.

Tariff and subsidy policy. The tariff policy will aim to gradually increase the current cost recovery level of the tariffs.

Provision of financial support to WUAs will be in the form of current grants in accordance with the relevant regulations for provision of public financial support[32].

Management reforms. Management reforms of the irrigation system will continue and will aim to further deepen the already formed participatory management schemes.

PROGRAM TARGET INDICATORS

The main target indicators for irrigation systems are presented in Table 13.

Table 13. Main target indicators for irrigation systems

Indicator	Base year	2017	2021	2025
Transition Indicator (EBRD)	2.67 (2013)	3.67	4.0	4.33
Irrigated land services by the WUAs, thous. ha	130 (2012)	132.4	135	138
Public capital investment level, % of GDP	0.18 (2012)	0.3	0.3	0.3
Tariff current cost (accrued), % recovery rate	46 (2012)	100	120	120

[32] Order of the government of Armenia No. 398-N dated 10 March 1211 "Regulating the process of provision of state financial support in the form of current grants to water user associations in 2012-2016".

2. TRANSPORT

CURRENT SITUATION

The Sustainable Development Program planned to increase the volumes of public resources allocated to the current operation and maintenance of motorways in order to prevent the accelerated deterioration of the road network and ensure safe, quick and easy transportation, and enhance the effectiveness of the use of allocated resources.

Public expenditures on road network operation and maintenance in 2007-2012 are presented in Table 14.

Table 14. State budget expenditures on road systems 2007-2012

	2007	2008	2009	2010	2011	2012
State budget expenditures on road systems33, mln. AMD	44243	41901	57792	32540	24647	29474
Percent of GDP	1.40%	1.17%	1.84%	0.93%	0.64%	0.73%

Source: Reports on execution of Armenia's state budget

299. As presented in the table, during the first years of the implementation of the sustainable development program, especially in 2009, state budget expenditures on road systems were increasing significantly, but a sharp decline was recorded in 2010-2012, as a result of the economic decline in 2009 caused by the financial crisis. Nonetheless, despite the decline, state budget expenditures on road systems as a share of the GDP was close to the target defined in the SDP (1% of the GDP in 2012).

MAIN DIRECTIONS OF PROGRAM POLICIES

The public expenditure policy in the sector will focus on increasing the volumes of public resources allocated to the current maintenance and capital repair of motorways, and enhancing the effectiveness of the use of those resources.

Starting from 2015 contributions to the sphere from consolidated budget will comprise around 1.4-1.5% of GDP annually on average, 85% of which will be aimed at road network[34], and the remaining 15% at other programs.

The primary target of the investment policy will be to repair segments of at least one traffic road connecting each settlement to the corresponding regional center, North-South road corridor construction, as well as roads and segments of roads with high economic effectiveness.

To increase effectiveness of budget allocations and strengthen program budgeting in the sector of road construction the government plans to implement modern management systems, among them:

[33] "Consolidated budget expenditures on road systems" article includes both current maintenance and capital investment expenditures. [34] According to preliminary estimations the offered amount of investments will enable recovering/rebuilding about 67% of road network of national significance annually (interstate, national and local).

1) Development of systems for program (unified) planning of operating and capital expenses in road building programs in the budget area;

2) Development and implementation of a methodology for determination of priorities in road building programs /directions to serve as the basis for medium-term expenditure planning and budget decision-making;

3) Improvement of the system for outcome planning and performance indicators, including contracts on works and services based on such indicators;

4) Development of mechanisms for evaluation of road maintenance /exploitation services;

5) Study and development of alternative approaches to financing of sector exploitation and investment programs.

Developments in civil aviation will be associated with "open air" policy declared by the Government of RA. The new policy envisages complete revision of institutional, legal and regulative bases of the sphere. As a result it is expected to have a competitive and sustainable air transportation services in Armenia. The reforms are directed towards improvement of air connection to and from Armenia, which will create additional possibilities for sector and general economy development and contribute to better national security. Expected positive effects of civil aviation reforms will be noticeable after some time, while usually airlines have got upto 2 years planning period. Though international experience shows that 2 years period is enough to obtain main expected outcomes.

In January 2013 kick-off ceremony of "North-South Railways" and "Southern highway of Armenia" projects has taken place. Connection of Armenian railway system to the Iranian railway network as well as construction of North-South road corridor have strategic implications for developing transit capacities of the Republic of Armenia and ensuring its food security. The Government of RA pays particular attention to these projects which will be implemented in the frames public-private partnership projects. In particular economic feasibility studies are planned to be implemented based on concession contracts and based on the results obtained also the construction process will be carried out by cooperation of public and private sectors.

The following programs and measures will be implemented in the transport sector.

1) Accessibility of common use transport, operation of buses with big seating capacity, improvement of transport station services, implementation of policies promoting development of nature-friendly transports (metro, electro-transport).

2) Big investment-requiring programs for construction of new metro stations, modernization and expansion of carriages, refreshment of trolley-bus parks, and improvement of the trolley power lines.

3) Measures on ensuring accessibility of transport means for disabled persons (slide platforms for wheelchairs on bus stops and pave ways, special vehicles with wheelchair lifters).

4) Program on construction of the new Vanadzor-Fioletovo railway.

5) Program on elimination of landslide consequences of Hrazdan-Ijevan railway Dilijan-Ijevan section and restart of communication.

6) Program of building a railway to Zvartnots airport, the international logistical center and the free economic zone to be created on airport's territory.

7) Telecommunications digitalization project[35]. 8) Project of launching Armenian space satellite.

PROGRAM TARGET INDICATORS

307. The main target indicators for the transport sector are presented in Table 15.

Table 15. Target indicators for transport sector					
Indicator	Base year	2014	2017	2021	2025

Transition Indicator (EBRD)	2.67 (2013)	3.0	3.67	4.0	4.33
Communities with at least one adequate road connecting them to the regional centre, % of total number of communities		30	50	80	90
Ratio of length of roads and segments in at least satisfactory condition to the overall length of roads of the same category, %	39%36 (2009)	45%	50%	57%	65%
Interstate	85% (2009)	89%	92%	96%	100%
State	34% (2009)	41%	47%	53%	60%
Local	10% (2009)	16%	21%	31%	45%
Level of public investments in road system, % of GDP	0.49 (2012)	1.4	1.1	1.0	1.0
Level of public investments in transport sector (excluding road system), % of GDP	0.14 (2012)	0.15	0.15	0.15	0.15
Level of public expenditures on current and winter maintenance of roads having state and interstate status, % of GDP	0.24 (2012)	0.21	0.25	0.25	0.25

3. ENERGY

CURRENT SITUATION

Currently, the energy system fully meets the domestic demand for electricity and maintains certain potential for electricity export.

Electricity is distributed and sold by a private company, and is produced by 6 independent large companies, one wind power plant, two cogeneration plants and numerous private small hydropower and micro plants.

During the implementation of the SDP, the government continued its policy for developing small hydropower plants. After 2008, 86 small hydropower plants started operations with a total design capacity of around 169.2 megawatts, producing average of 524.11 million kilowatt hours of electricity per annum. As of January 1st, 2014 electricity is produced by 154 small hydropower plants, with a aggregate design capacity of around 260 megawatts and actual average annual energy supply of around 720 mln. Kwt.hour.

In 2009 the Government of RA approved a "Development scheme for small hydropower plants", which envisages construction of additional 90 small hydropower plants with aggregate design capacity of around 110 megawatts (as of January 1st, 2012). As of 1st of January 2014,

[35] The project has been approved by point 34 of RA Government decree number 22 dated on 6 June, 2013. [36] Source: Fiscal consolidation and recovery, WB, June 2011

71 small hydropower plants are in construction phase with total design capacity of around 145 megawatts and expected annual average energy supply of around 515 mln. kWt.hour.

During the implementation of the SDP, the construction work on Iran-Armenia gas pipeline was completed and regular supply of gas from Iran started on 13 May 2009 together with the supply of electricity from Armenia to Iran, based on mutual agreement on the volumes and regimes, which are constantly growing.

ArmRusgasard CJSC has started the work for restoration of the underground storage of natural gas. The capacity of the underground gas storage facility has increased by around 1.8 times and, as of 2010, the volume of actually stored gas amounts to 132.7 million cubic meters. It is planned to increase the volume up to 140 million cubic meters. The volume of gas to be stored must be determined by the Government of RA.

Improvements have also been made to the electric energy systems, which has a key role in further strengthening of the reliability of the electricity system and promotion of regional cooperation, in particular:

1) As of 2010 with the assistance of international financial organizations 3 out of 14 electric energy sub-plants of 220 kw have been re-equipped fully and further 8 have been re-equipped partially.

2) In February of 2014 restoration of Gyumri-2 220 kw sub-plant has been completed and the project was implemented using loan fund provided by the KfW.

3) The work for restoration of 17 substations of 110 kilowatts implemented with the support of the Japanese government was completed in September 2010.

4) The work for the first phase of introduction of SCADA/communication system was completed in October 2010.

5) In 2010 and 2011 in Yerevan have been set in exploitation energetic blocks “Yerevan thermoelectrocentre” closed joint stock company and “ArmRusGazprom” of Hrazdan thermopower plant working with thermogas cycles of correspondingly 243.2 and 467 megawatt equipped with modern technologies.

MAIN DIRECTIONS OF PROGRAM POLICIES

315. During the implementation of the program, the main directions of the policy implemented in this sector will be as follows:

1) maximum use of own sources, specially renewable sources of energy;

2) further development of nuclear energy, in particular construction of new energy block and enhance in security of Armenian nuclear power station’s 2nd energy block and extension of its utilization period;

3) replacement of physically and morally depreciated power plants with those furnished

with new technologies; 4) diversification of energy supplies and regional integration; 5) promotion of energy efficiency in all sectors using energy resources; 6) Increase of the level of safety and reliability of the electroenergetic system.

For the entire period of the program, the level of annual public investment in the system (excluding large projects such as the construction of the new nuclear power plant) will amount to 0.3% of the GDP.

The new nuclear power plant with 1000 megawatts capacity (which is already provided for by the RA Law) will require an investment of USD 4-5 billion.

Targets of investment policy will include replacement of producing stations, construction of new producing and regulatory stations, maintenance and development of the electricity transportation system, also for integration with regional energy systems, as well as implementation of energy-saving measures and maximal use of renewable energy and alternative energy resources.

The following programs and activities will be implemented in the sphere of energy.

1) Full implementation of the SCADA /communication system;

2) Construction of new 400kW electric power lines on Armenia-Georgia and Armenia-Iran directions and interconnection of those systems with 220 kW energy networks. As well as construction of 400 kW sub-plant ensuring constant energy supply to Georgia.

3) Replacement of 220 kW sub-plants with those with the capacity of 450/500 kW; 4) Restoration and re-equipment of Vorotan hydropower plant; 5) Implementation of deep perforation activities in the geothermal systems discovered

during geophysical researches; 6) Institutional reforms of the sector, including implementation of a sustainable statistical system; 7) Implementation of quality and performance indicator standards for energy market participants.

PROGRAM TARGET INDICATORS

320. The main target indicators for the energy sector are presented in Table 16:

Table 16. Target indicators for energy sector

Indicator	Base year	2014	2017	2021	2025
Transition indicator (EBRD)	3.33 (2013)	3.67	4.0	4.33	4.67
Level of public investments, % of GDP	0.17 (2012)	0.3	0.3	0.3	0.3

REGIONAL DEVELOPMENT AND INVESTMENT OPPORTUNITES

SITUATION AND TRENDS

321. A country's regional socioeconomic development disparities are defined as deviations in social and economic development levels, which as a result hampers economic development and sustainable human development in both regions and the entire country. Nature and climate specifics of Armenia's region, uneven distribution of production forces and resources, as well as their economic development, social, demographic and cultural differences contribute to uneven development of territorial units. In the phase of transition to market economy (since early 2000s) these disparities have continuously deepened reaching alarming levels. Economic development has focused in Yerevan and in a limited number of regions (mainly Syunik and Kotayk), thus

creating clearly articulated differences in population wellbeing/poverty and human development indicators across regions of Armenia.

Table 17. Industrial per capita output at current prices in RA regions and Yerevan city between 2004 and 2012, thousand drams

		2004	2011	2012
Yerevan		217.0	399.4	424.2
Aragatsotn		45.4	152.0	147.0
Ararat		153.3	288.4	401.8
Armavir		96.6	146.4	167.1
Gegharkunik		81.3	74.1	92.0
Lori		113.2	260.5	339.7
Kotayk		213.5	370.4	569.3
Shirak		46.1	151.7	161.5
Syunik		582.6	1,166.6	1,401.4
Vayots Dzor		84.2	138.7	173.7
Tavush		32.8	47.0	60.8
Average for Marzes and Yerevan city		151.5	288.5	358.1
Index, 2004=100		100.0	190.5	194.7
	Characteristics of regional disparities			
Interval of disparity		549.9	1,119.5	1,340.6
Index, 2004 = 100		100.0	203.6	243.8
Average absolute aggregated deviation		101.9	192.7	248.1
Index, 2004=100		100.0	189.1	243.4

Source: Marzes of the Republic of Armenia and Yerevan City in Figures, NSS, 2010, 2012 and Demographic Handbook of Armenia, NSS, 2012

322. Economic development disparities across regions and Yerevan city continue growing for all main indicators. This means that the average regional (including Yerevan) indicator of per capita

industrial output has increased 1.9 times between 2004 and 2012. However the disparity interval[37] and the average absolute deviation[38] of the same indicator has increased

[37] The interval of inequality in regions and Yerevan is the difference between maximal and minimal values of per capita industrial output. [38] The average absolute aggregated deviation is the arithmetic mean of the absolute values of deviations of per capita industrial output in regions and Yerevan from their average.

about 2.4 times during that period. Per capita industrial production is the highest in Yerevan, Syunik and Kotayk marzes.

A similar picture is observed in agriculture gross produce indicator. The regional per capita indicator has increased 1.6 times between 2004 and 2012. However the regional development disparity indicators' growth is more rapid. The regional disparity interval has increased 1.7 times and the average absolute deviation 2.1 times. Compared with per capita volumes of industrial output, regional disparities of per capita agricultural produce are smaller and grow slowly. These are the highest in Gegharkunik, Ararat and Armavir marzes.

Analysis of territorial inequality aspects of other main economic indicators suggest that they all have increased, however the biggest growth is seen in services delivered to the population. The inequality media of this indicator and its mean absolute aggregated deviation across marzes between 2004 and 2012 has increased around 5.6 times, and the mean marz indicator has increased 3.4 times. In terms of these indicators Yerevan again appeared in the most favorable position.

Table 18. Per capita gross agriculture output at current prices in RA regions in 2004-2011, thousand drams

	2004		2011	2012
Yerevan	5.9		6.1	7.7
Aragatsotn	275.9		384.4	539.3
Ararat	242.4		320.6	416.5
Armavir	261.8		385.0	472.4
Gegharkunik	300.2		390.2	630.4
Lori	194.7		130.6	202.4
Kotayk	162.6		142.0	180.1
Shirak	171.5		198.4	329.8
Syunik	322.7		218.4	329.6
Vayots Dzor	424.7		202.5	301.8
Tavush	206.3		181.2	289.0

Average for Marzes, excluding Yerevan	256.3		255.3	369.1
Index, 2004=100	100.0		155.2	165.1
Regional disparity characteristics (excluding Yerevan)				
Interval of disparity	262.2		450.3	440.5
Index, 2004 = 100	100.0		171.8	168.0
Average absolute aggregated deviation	60.8		118.7	128.3
Index, 2004=100	100.0		195.3	211.0

Source: Marzes of the Republic of Armenia and Yerevan City in Figures, NSS, 2010, 2012, 2013 and Demographic Handbook of Armenia, NSS, 2012

Table 19. Per capita values of commissioning of fixed assets, retail trade turnover and services rendered to population in Yerevan city and Marzes (at current prices) in 2004 – 2012 and characteristics of their regional disparities

Indicators	Commissioning of fixed assets			Retail trade turnover			Services rendered to population		
	2004	2011	2012	2004	2011	2012	2004	2011	2012
Regional average (including Yerevan), thousand drams	28.5	76.1	79.0	115.7	187.6	197.5	39.6	119.1	132.8
Index, 2004=100	100.0	267.6	277.7	100.0	162.2	170.8	100.0	300.9	335.4
Interval of disparity, thousand drams	145.0	244.0	244.0	625.4	976.6	1,0409	137.8	671.2	763.3
Index, 2004=100	100.0	168.3	168.3	100.0	56.2	166.4	100.0	487.0	553.8
Average absolute aggregated deviation	22.7	61.7	65.9	98.0	153.0	163.9	21.6	106.4	120.8
Index, 2004=100	100.0	272.0	290.5	100.0	156.2	167.3	100.0	493.1	559.9

Source: Calculations based on NSS data.

325. According to estimates of the Ministry of Territorial Administration, per capita investments by all sources in Yerevan during 2011 -2012 have exceeded the indicator for marzes by 2.2 times. However, as opposed to 2007-2008, this difference has decreased around six times, which means that territorial inequality aspects have improved for this indicator.

Table 20. Per capita capital investments from all sources in Yerevan and marzes during 2008-2012 (thous. dram) and the related characteristics of regional disparities,

	2008	2009	2010	2011	2012
Total RA	234.6	142.5	153.6	123.2	126.2
Total marzes	44.9	79.4	98.9	87.2	89.5
Yerevan	595.6	262.5	257.6	191.7	196.0
Aragatsotn	46.6	51.7	217.0	89.1	156.1
Ararat	36.6	62.8	75.1	72.4	31.9
Armavir	23.1	35.3	48.5	60.7	50.2
Gegharkunik	21.6	77.8	54.9	70.8	50.5
Lori	22.5	50.5	72.3	79.8	47.5
Kotayk	57.7	104.6	122.5	99.3	144.4
Shirak	38.6	154.2	92.3	89.4	85.4
Syunik	130.8	106.1	200.9	93.3	104.2
Vayots Dzor	173.8	80.5	86.1	119.4	95.4
Tavush	31.4	60.4	119.4	167.2	255.6
Marzes average, including Yerevan	107.1	95.1	122.4	103.0	110.7
Marzes average, excluding Yerevan	58.3	78.4	108.9	94.1	102.1
	Characteristics of disparities				
Disparities' range	574.0	227.2	209.1	131.0	223.7
Index, 2004 =100	127.6	50.5	46.5	29.1	49.7
Average absolute deviation	105.2	44.9	56.1	30.8	56.3
Index, 2004 =100	135.4	57.7	72.1	39.6	72.4

Source: RA Ministry of Territorial Administration

326. Armenia does not officially publish its GDP indicators across marzes. Nonetheless, analysis of expert evaluations of marz GDPs witness that economic development is focused mainly in

Yerevan and Syunik marz, where the correlation of per capital GDP and the mean national indicator is the highest. In 2012, it made up approximately 152% of the mean national per capita GDP in Yerevan and 133% in Syunik. In other marzes it was lower than the national average – counting for around 67%. The most unfavorable situation was recorded in Lori, Tavoush, Vayots Dzor, Shirak and Tavush marzes, where the per capita GDP in 2012 shared 53%, 58%, 60% and 63% of the mean national figure correspondingly. Hence, advanced development of these marzes should be viewed as a priority goal of territorial development programs. During 2009-2012 the quickest economic growth was seen in the Syunik and Tavoush marzes.

Table 21. Per capita GDP ratio of Yerevan and Marzes to republican average, 2009-2011, %

	2009	2010	2011	2012	2012 Per capita GDP index (2009 = 100)
Total, RA	100.0	100.0	100.0	100.0	133.5
Yerevan	172.3	162.3	148.7	151.7	117.6
Aragatsotn	65.0	85.4	78.6	82.6	169.8
Ararat	68.2	74.2	73.8	71.1	139.2
Armavir	67.4	62.1	70.6	67.0	132.9
Gegharkunik	63.9	68.2	74.6	69.7	145.7
Lori	42.4	47.5	59.3	52.7	166.1
Kotayk	66.9	65.3	70.5	78.4	156.5
Shirak	57.6	54.4	65.0	59.7	138.4
Syunik	97.1	133.9	140.2	133.5	183.6
Vayots Dzor	52.1	55.1	59.5	57.7	147.8
Tavush	39.5	46.4	54.8	62.6	212.0

Source: Calculated and estimated based on NSS data

These economic development trends contribute to the increase of regional disparities in key social indicators, such as employment and poverty. Between 2004 and 2011 the interval of regional disparity as regards employment[39] has increased 1.4 and poverty -1.7 times[40]. Yerevan appeared in the most favorable situation vis-à-vis this indicator. Dominating part of the country's general economic growth is focused in Yerevan, which explains the highest nonagricultural employment and the lowest poverty rates.

Community-level development disparities should be explained by both objective specifics of communities (mainly geographic specifics -climate, nature) and their socioeconomic development pace. Socioeconomic development disparities of communities are due to fundamental factors like community population number, and sociodemographic composition, altitude above sea level, distance from the borderlines, distance from closest economic development center, availability and status of socioeconomic infrastructures, distance from in subnational and national roads, quantity and quality of farming lands, irrigation specifics, quantity of functioning industrial capacities, local financial resources, etc.

Some 5.35% of RA communities are urban and 94.64% are rural. Of them 16.5% are mountainous (1700-2000 m above sea level) and 12.2% high mountainous (2000m and higher above sea level), 20.5% are border communities. Equal development requires consideration of community population number. According to survey finings community population number is very closely co-related to the poverty level, i.e. the likelihood of poverty is higher among small communities. Out of the country's 915 communities 440 (438 rural and 2 urban) (or 48%) have population below 1000 people. Two hundred of 866 rural communities (or 23% of all communities) have population below 300. Urban communities are also rather inequal in terms of population number. In particular, 2 (4.1%) of 49 cities have below-1000 population, 6 cities

-1001-5000 population (12.2 % of total), 18 cities -5001-15000 population (36.7%). In total, 26 urban communities have below-15000 population (53% of urban communities). Regional

[39] Employment rate is the share of employed in the labor resources. [40] For detailed analysis of territorial inequalities of these indicators see relevant sections.

breakdown of the said factors shows strong differences, which in its turn affects development of regional disparities.

Table 22. Characteristics of communities in Armenia by Marz in 2012

	Number of communities	of which:		Number of border communities	Number of mountainous communities	Number of villages with population below 1000 persons
		Cities	Villages			
Yerevan	1	1		-	-	-
Aragatsotn	114	3	111	2	22	75
Ararat	97	4	93	9	2	18
Armavir	97	3	94	8		12
Gegharkunik	92	5	87	23	28	44
Lori	113	8	105	5	18	64
Kotayk	67	7	60		15	20
Shirak	119	3	116	15	50	68
Syunik	113	7	106	67	7	86

Vayouts Dzor	44	3	41	12	8	24
Tavush	62	5	58	47	1	27
Total	915	49	866	188	157	438

Source: NSS publications

Sharp differences in financial capacities of communities should be attributed to objective aspects as well as their economic development pace. These differences are reflected in the community socioeconomic infrastructures' development and maintenance, as well as unequal capacities for delivery of community services. Small communities, as a rule, have small budgets, and the revenues do not enable addressing not only community development issues, but even meeting population's basic social needs. This situation results in significant differences across communities as regards human development and poverty levels.

Summary analysis of RA regional development specifics reveals the following challenges, which once again confirms the need of a targeted regional development policy.

1) Deepening economic development regional disparities. 2) Deepening social development and wellbeing/poverty regional disparities. 3) Need for improvement of the quality, accessibility and effectiveness of infrastructures

and delivered local and public services in regions, particularly rural communities. 4) Need for coordination and improvement of effectiveness of public, donor and private investments in regional development and implementation of relevant programs. 5) Need for regional administration system reforms, in particular expansion of intercommunity cooperation and enlargement of communities. 6) Need for financial and institutional capacity building of regional administration and local self-government bodies. 7) Implementation of general methodology of complex local government development programs and the introductioin of their development practice. 8) Need for development of mechanisms for multi-dimensional credit assessment of socioeconomic development of administrative and regional units.

OBJECTIVES AND PRIORITIES

Further deepening of regional socioeconomic disparities will hamper the country's internal socioeconomic stability and even security and will promote undesirable migration from economically less developed regions. Hence, overcoming regional development disparities, ensuring even regional development and implementation of a targeted policy are seen as the country's regional development priority in both medium-and long-term term perspectives.

Targeted regional development policy should be geared at encouraging and promoting economic growth and social development outside the Yerevan city -in marzes and communities. It should ensure accelarated economic development for the most depressed territories and in the mid-term perspective enable to them to approach the average economic development level of the Republic. At the same time, this policy should ensure similar development paces across regions and their equal development in the long-term perspective.

Such development policy should include a number of fundamental activities that will promote economic and investment activities in the territories. Among those an essential role will be assigned to redirection of public and particularly private investments from Yerevan to regions – other cities and villages in order to promote development of regional growth poles. Promotion of economic growth in regions of Armenia will enable mitigating regional disparities in well-being, employment and human development. Thus, the policy should be targeted at complex development of Armenia's regions.

Regional growth poles can be developed in both urban and rural locations. They can cover certain individual communities and/or community groups. Those are the communities or groups where promotion and ensuring of advanced socioeconomic development rates will help to step up development of nearby communities and the general region. Hence, overcoming regional development disparities will require cooperation and consolidation of territorial units, particularly communities in order to jointly address socioeconomic development problems.

At the same time, the policy will include special support programs aimed at most vulnerable communities that have small objective capacities for advanced development.

Implementation of this development policy will require clear mechanisms for the assessment of development disparities and development of growth poles. In particular, a system of multidimensional assessment criteria for territories, communities and/or groups thereof, as well as the regions' socioeconomic development level will ne needed. The system will help revealing reasons and expressions of regional development disparities, identifying the most unfavorable (in terms of development) communities and areas on the one hand, and potential/emerging growth poles on the other hand. At the same time, implementation of the policy will require complex programs for socioeconomic development of areas, communities and their groups, which will enable evaluating the implementation impact on speeding up the territory's general development.

Meantime, implementation of the policy requires complex socioeconomic development programs of certain territories, communities and/or their groups, which will enable assessing their implementation impact on speeding-up the general development rates those territories.

The development policy must ensure also restoration and/or development of economic, productive and social infastructure predominantly in the territories (out of Yerevan) based on close cooperation with the private sector, as well as equal access to and affordability of basic services, giving the priority to communities and areas that lag behind in their development rate and are more vulnerable. It should ensure direction of public investment programs towards elimination of bottlenecks of economic, industrial and social infrastructures, which currently or in the near future may hinder socioeconomic development of the region or area.

Given the low socioeconomic growth rates of small and medium-size towns of Armenia, which have resulted in quite high poverty rates in these communities as opposed to the mean national, Yerevan and rural communities as well as migration, the targeted regional development policy should maximally contribute to their development. Economic development rates of those urban communities should, in medium-term perspective, gradually reach the mean national development level. Consequently, small and medium-size cities are considered a priority and main target of the policy aimed at mitigation of the regional development disparities.

Taking into consideration current specifics of economic development of rural areas, the policy on mitigation of development disparities across rural communities should be targeted at promotion of economic and investment activities, development of community and intercommunity infrastructures, access to and improvement of the quality community and public services, and improvement of community financial autonomy. At the same time of special importance are the issues related to the development and braodening of the application of the delegated authirities' institute.

The targeted complex policy on mitigation of regional disparities should ensure on the one hand radical improvement of regional business and investment environment, as well as of the quality of public administration and local government and on the other hand encourage and develop cooperation between the state, local governments and the private sector within the context of implementation of complex regional development programs.

Implementation of the policy requires improvements of regional development financial system, which implies coordination of public and donor/privet allocations for regional development. Actually, ad hoc funds can serve as financial tool for implementation of the complex regional development policy.

Ad hoc funds can serve as a general tool for implementation of a complex territorial development policy. The funds will be based on close cooperation with the public, donor and private sectors. Particularly, in medium-term perspective, it is appropriate to create a territorial development fund, which will enable addressing the following territorial development problems:

1) Contribute to improvement of the material and non-material wellbeing of the population and their employment;

2) Contribute to improvement of economic and investment activities in territories and development of territorial 'growth poles'.

3) Improve and develop the quality of local infrastructures and delivered community and public services, their accessibility and effectiveness.

4) Improve commitment and effectiveness of territorial socioeconomic development public, donor and private investment and programs,

5) Support implementation of territorial administration reforms, particularly expansion of inter-community cooperation,

6) Contribute to building local governments' financial and institutional capacities,

7) Support development of complex community and territorial development programs.

Prognosis on results of implementation of the territorial inequalities compensation policy suggest the following. If further development happens according to the base scenario (i.e. the said policy is not implemented), then based on the current economic development (20092011), the mean marz development rates will be retained, in the medium-term perspective the marz per capital GDP inequalities in 2017 will increase about 1.6 times, as opposed to 2011 and about 4 times in 2025. Half of marzes will ensure 60-70% of the mean national per capita GDP level.

Implementation of the complex territorial development policy will enable essentially improving the situation. Implementation of the policy, if the average development scenario is taken, envisages that the development rates of lagging marzes will accelerate so that their development level in medium-term perspectives will come closer to the average national development level. Meantime the current average annual growth of the most developed marzes will be retained during that period with almost similar proportions. According to defined targets, in 2017 the marz per capita GDP levels (excluding Yerevan), provided they show continuing growth, will approach the average national level and will share around 85% of it. In long-term perspective, in 2017 they will make up 85% of the average national per capita GDP, 90% in 2021 and 94% in 2025. This will help to the extent possible minimizing territorial development inequalities.

Table 23. Per capita GDP ratio of marzes and Yerevan to republican average, development base

and policy scenarios, %									
	Actual	Development base scenario				Policy scenario			
	2012	2015	2017	2021	2025	2015	2017	2021	2025
Total, RA	100.0	100.0	100.0	100.0	100.0	100.0	100.0	100.0	100.0
Yerevan	151.7	151.5	152.4	154.0	155.3	136.0	127.6	123.5	121.8
Aragatsotn	82.6	81.7	80.1	77.1	74.1	79.0	79.3	84.6	92.0
Ararat	71.1	71.4	71.0	70.2	69.7	74.3	81.1	84.1	87.1
Armavir	67.0	66.5	65.2	62.8	60.6	68.3	74.6	77.4	80.2
Gegharkunik	69.7	68.7	66.9	63.3	60.0	75.9	83.3	85.6	87.1
Lori	52.7	53.1	53.2	53.4	53.7	58.3	69.3	91.5	100.5
Kotayk	78.4	79.3	80.0	81.5	83.1	83.4	90.2	91.9	93.5
Shirak	59.7	59.3	58.5	56.9	55.4	61.4	70.4	79.7	85.6
Syunik	133.5	136.7	139.0	143.8	149.1	130.6	125.8	119.5	115.8
Vayots Dzor	57.7	57.3	56.7	55.4	54.2	62.7	71.6	79.6	83.3
Tavush	62.6	61.8	60.9	59.0	57.2	68.2	78.3	81.2	84.2
		Memorandum item							
Per capita GDP program targets in Armenia, thous. dram						1,684	2,037	3,054	4,612

EDUCATION AND SCIENCE SECTOR AND OPPORTUNITIES

EDUCATION

CURRENT SITUATION AND TRENDS

The education sector in Armenia is considered to be important as one of the preconditions for sustainable development of the country, reproduction and development of the human capital. Thus, developments in this sector are one of the development priorities of the country. Increasing the quality and effectiveness of education at all levels of the educational system, increasing the relevance of different levels to international standards and ensuring affordable/accessible education for all groups of the population are priorities for the development of the sector. In order to achieve the mentioned goals, reforms are implemented at all levels of education.

Based on the requirements for successful implementation of reforms in the education sector, the SDP planned to continuously increase public expenditures in the education sector, both by their nominal value of and as a percentage of GDP – ensuring the 4 percent of GDP target indicator by 2015. The economic decline, shrinking of the GDP and the narrowing of the resource base of the budget, limited the possibilities for maintaining expenditures on education to the planned volumes.

Table 38. The dynamics of the consolidated budget expenditures allocated to education sector in 20082013

	2008	2009	2010	2011	2012	2013
Consolidated budget expenditures on education, bln. AMD						
Actual	113.6[1]	121.1[1]	111.9[1]	122.4[1]	121.5[1]	122.1[2]
Consolidated budget expenditures on education to GDP, %	3.2	3.9	3.2	3.2	3.0	2.9
Consolidated budget expenditures on education to total consolidated budget expenditures, %	13.6	12.8	11.5	12.1	11.7	10.4

[1] *actual expenditures of Armenia's consolidated budget 2008-2012* [2] *planned expenditures of consolidated budget*

432. Analysis of the dynamics of public expenditures on the education sector reveals that consolidated budget public expenditures channeled to the education sector in 2008-2009, both by their nominal values and as a percentage of the GDP, had increased, but as a result of the crisis, they declined in 2010, and in 2011 returned to their nominal values of 2009. As a result, expenditures on education in 2013 amount to 2.9 percent of the GDP. The indicator for the share of expenditures on education as a percentage of GDP in Armenia in 2013 was 1.7 times lower than the average of the same indicator in 2010 for FSU and CCE countries (4.9 percent[48]) and around 2 times lower than the average for 2009 in 27 European Union countries

(5.4 percent[49]). In Armenia in 2008-2012, on average 12.3 percent of public expenditures were

[48] Source: TransMonee Database, UNICEF, 2012 [49] Source: Eurostat Database

channeled to education. It must be noted that the average indicator in 2008 for OECD countries amounted to 12.9 percent.

Table 39. Structure of expenditures of the consolidated budget on education 2011-2014, thousand AMD

	2011	2012	2013 preliminary	2014
	Actual	Actual	Actual	Planned
Total consolidated budget expenditures on education, of which:	122,436,067.9	121,474,278.1	122,110,757.3	147,525,224.8

Pre-school and elementary general education, including:	35,542,034.9	34,078,933.4	36,670,337.2	40,163,422.8
Pre-school education	10,693,784.9	11,985,410.5	13,225,044.3	14,062,678.9
Elementary general education	24,848,249.9	22,093,522.9	23,445,292.9	26,100,744.0
Secondary general education, including:	45,244,532.5	49,102,343.1	48,257,319.2	51,591,468.3
Basic general education	30,530,199.1	30,530,829.0	30,563,746.7	32,786,277.4
Secondary (complete) general education	14,714,333.4	18,571,514.1	17,693,572.5	18,805,190.9
Preliminary vocational (craftsmanship) and secondary vocational education, including:	5,083,154.2	5,375,467.2	6,182,089.9	8,716,477.2
Preliminary vocational (craftsmanship) education	1,906,069.7	2,028,182.0	2,306,510.8	2,865,068.2
Secondary vocational education	3,177,084.6	3,347,285.1	3,875,579.1	5,851,409.1
Higher education, including:	7,884,836.4	7,780,550.8	8,055,380.1	9,922,395.2
Higher professional education	7,290,951.2	7,128,593.6	7,367,944.8	9,100,794.4
Post-graduate professional education	593,885.2	651,957.2	687,435.3	821,600.8
Education, not classified by the levels, including:	7,715,361.1	7,866,189.2	8,712,617.7	9,691,110.5
Extracurricular education	6,640,342.0	6,851,628.7	7,647,863.2	8,490,560.6
Additional education	1,075,019.1	1,014,560.5	1,064,754.5	1,200,549.9
Supplementary services provided to education	20,242,328.6	16,598,812.2	13,549,005.5	26,541,053.6
Research and development activities in the sphere of education	264.0	740.0	60.0	0.0

Other Education (Not in the abovementioned items)	723,556.2	671,242.2	683,947.8	899,297.1

Source: Ministry of Finance of Armenia

433. General education is a program priority in the education sector. The major part of expenditures in the education sector is channeled to the general education programs[50] (82-83 percent). The decrease in expenditures on education by their nominal value (and as a percentage of GDP) has not resulted in lower expenditures per one beneficiary, particularly also in the general education sector. In the 3 tiers of general education – elementary, basic/lower secondary and complete general/upper secondary schools, the nominal values of annual public expenditures per pupil have continuously increased in 2008-2010. Annual public expenditure per one pupil enrolled in the general education system in 2011 amounted to 15.1 percent of the GDP per capita, or around 181,000 Armenian drams. Annual public expenditures per pupil are differentiated by levels of general education. In elementary school in 2011, they amounted to 15 percent of the per capita GDP, or around 179,000 Armenian drams, in basic school -to 16.5 percent of the per capita GDP or around 198,000 drams and they were the lowest in complete general/upper secondary school -13.1 percent of the per capita GDP or around 155,000 drams. Public expenditures per pupil in Armenia remain incomparably lower than the average for the European Union. In 2009, European Union countries annually spent on average around 22 percent of the per capita GDP per one pupil enrolled in elementary school and around 28 percent of the per capita GDP in general

[50] Formal basic education programs include elementary, basic and secondary (complete) general education (formal basic education, special education, etc.), as well as a number of programs envisaged within the framework of support to the implementation of general education programs.

secondary school, while the same indicators for Armenia in 2011 amounted to around 15 percent of the per capita GDP. Allocation of such small budgetary amounts to this sector hinders the entire process of reforms of the system and the ensuring of quality and accessible education for all groups of population.

There is a significant difference of public expenditures per pupil between preliminary and secondary vocational education and the upper secondary school[51]. At preliminary and secondary vocational education level, annual public expenditures in 2011 per one pupil in the public funded scheme was 2.2 times higher than the same expenditures per pupil in the upper secondary schools, amounting to around 31 percent of the per capita GDP, or 373,000 drams. At higher education level, annual public expenditures per student in the public funded scheme in 2011 amounted to 38 percent of the per capita GDP.

The most fundamental reform implemented in the general education sector is the formation of separately operating system of three-year upper secondary schools (grades 10 to 12) as the continuation of the general basic education. The purpose of establishing the system of the upper secondary schools is to improve the quality and effectiveness of education in this level, as well as give the possibility to their graduates to choose between further specialization and preliminary vocational education in accordance with their preferences. The establishment of upper secondary schools started in 2008. The number of high schools in Armenia during academic year 2011/12 was 104 and during 2012/13 – 108, which have 10th -12th grades. High schools are developed primarily in urban areas (their 95.5 are located in cities). 12-year education in rural areas is provided through secondary schools, which cover all levels of public education, including the high schools. During the 2012/13 academic year 812 secondary schools were functioning in the country, the overwhelming part of which, i.e. 86 % in rural areas. Those are mainly small schools

(830 of currently functioning 1,364 schools have 300 pupils, 410 have less than 100 pupils), with around half (particularly high schools) failing to deliver both high-quality and effective education.

The 12-year education is provided through both high schools and (mostly) secondary schools. However, the secondary school network does not enable on the one hand ensuring financial, material and human resources centralization on the level of high schools, and on the other hand, implementing quality pre-professional/stream education and ensuring smooth transition to higher educational establishments. Hence, emerging of high schools and ensuring high-quality pre-professional education require gradual reorganization of secondary schools into basic and high schools and ensuring maximum accessibility of high schools throughout the country.

At the same time, Armenia has a system of preliminary and secondary vocational education. As of 2011, the system includes 5052 preliminary and 101 secondary53 vocational educational institutions, which together with continuing the overall secondary education of their pupils also allow for obtaining specializations and qualifications. All preliminary and secondary vocational state educational institutions, in order to increase the accessibility of this educational programs, starting in the academic year of 2011-2012, admit students without entrance exams, only based on competition basis (with the exception of specializations in arts).

[51] At preliminary and secondary vocational and higher education levels, calculations are based on free-of-charge or

public-paid students, whose training is paid by public expenditures (public funded scheme). [52] State institutions: 25 preliminary and 20 secondary vocational educational institutions, 4 colleges, 1 higher educational institution

[53] Including 80 state institutions: 6 higher educational institutions, 73 secondary vocational institutions and one college

They have not only the public funded scheme/free of charge students, but also students, paying for the tuition. However, annual public expenditures per pupil in the upper secondary school are considerably lower compared to the same expenditures in preliminary and secondary vocational educational institutions, which creates risks for proper establishment and operation of upper secondary schools and the formation of the demand for their services.

Table 40. Annual public expenditures per pupil and per student in the public funded scheme in 2008-2011

	2008		2009		2010		2011	
	AMD	To per capita GDP, %	AMD	To per capita GDP, %	AMD	To per capita GDP, %	AMD	To per capita GDP, %
Elementary and general secondary education, including:	144,063	13.0	182,145	18.6	186,309	16.8	181,381	15.1
Elementary education	138,458	12.5	166,218	16.9	159,617	14.4	179,449	15.0

General secondary education, of which:	146,202	13.2	188,910	19.3	201,893	18.3	182,460	15.2
Basic education: basic/lower secondary school	140,946	12.8	192,569	19.6	203,465	18.4	198,150	16.5
General (complete) secondary education: upper secondary school	159,013	14.4	180,327	18.4	198,290	17.9	156,714	13.1
Preliminary vocational (craftsmanship) and secondary vocational education, including:	304,335	27.5	347,422	35.4	343,595	31.1	373,103	31.1
Preliminary vocational (craftsmanship) education	347,919	31.5	344,242	35.1	310,035	28.0	366,059	30.6
Secondary vocational education	282,337	25.6	349,414	35.6	368,451	33.3	377,460	31.5
Higher education	354,930	32.1	398,301	40.6	401,896	36.3	455,271	38.0

Source: calculated based on the consolidated budget figures and NSS "Social panorama of Armenia" 2008-2011

438. Study of the number of pupils who continue their education at upper secondary education level after graduating from the basic school reveals some important trends related to the operations of the upper secondary schools system. The enrollment rate in upper secondary school is lower than in the other levels of general education system and demonstrates the downward trend. According to official statistics, in the academic year of 2010/2011, enrollment rate in upper secondary school amounted to 84.4 percent, compared to 96.8 percent in elementary school and 91.6 percent in basic school[54]. And the enrollment rate in the academic year of 2011/2012 in elementary school constituted 99 percent, in basic school it was 91.8 percent and in upper secondary school it amounted to 72.8 percent[55]. This means that the share of pupils continuing their education in upper secondary school among graduates of the basic school has declined. In academic year of 2011/2012, in the 1st level of the upper secondary school (or grade 10), were enrolled only 70 percent of graduates from the 9th grade of the basic school in 2010/2011 (this is the coefficient of the transition from basic/lower secondary school to upper secondary school. In the academic year of 2010/2011, from about 39,000 pupils in the 9th grade graduating class of the basic school, around 27,000 continued their education in the 10th grade of upper secondary school). While in academic year of

[54] Source: "Social Panorama of Armenia in 2010", NSS 2011 [55]Source: "Social Panorama ofArmenia in 2011",NSS 2012

2006/2007, when the system of upper secondary schools was not yet introduced, the same indicator amounted to around 91 percent (it must be noted that the rate of transition from elementary school to basic school in 2008-2011 was 98-99 percent). Consequently, around 30 percent of graduates of the basic school, for one or another reason, have not used the educational services provided by upper secondary schools in 2011. At that, the reason behind this is not the difficult-to-access (physical-geographic) location of educational institutions delivering high school services, since as it was mentioned earlier, high school educational services are available in both urban and rural communities through secondary school system.

Table 41. Graduates of the basic school in the academic year of 2010/2011 and their further enrollment at different levels of the educational system

	Pupils	Percent in the total number of pupils enrolled in the last 9th grade of the basic school in 2010/11 academic year	Percent in the number of pupils received graduation certificates from basic school in 2011
Total number of pupils enrolled in the last 9th grade of the basic school in 2010/11 academic year	39,081	100.0	--
Of which:			
Received graduation certificates from basic school in 2011	37,756	96.6	100,0
Of which:			
Admitted to the other educational institutions in 2011/12 academic year	7,653	19.6	20.3
Admitted to upper secondary educational institutions in 2011/12 academic year	27,189	69.6	72.0
Did not appear in any level/institution of the educational system in 2011/12 academic year	2,914	7.4	7.7
Remained in the 9th grade	188	0.5	--
Studies are left unfinished	249	0.6	--
Emigrated	494	1.3	--
Other	394	1.0	--

Source: "Social Panorama of Armenia in 2011", NSS 2012

Of course, part of the graduates of the basic school prefers to continue their education in preliminary and secondary vocational educational institutions. In the academic year of 2010/2011, around 20 percent of pupils who received graduation certificates from basic school were admitted to other educational institutions. On the other hand, the number of pupils who leave the educational system at all after graduation from the basic school increases: part of the graduates of basic schools discontinued their education after graduating from the basic school. In the academic year of 2010/2011, 7.7 percent of basic school graduates did not continue their education at any other level in 2011/2012. Of course, part of them has seemingly emigrated, but there is a lack of information on that aspect. At the same time, the household living standard survey of 2010 reveals that it is basically the poorest segments of the population and the rural population that do not continue their education at upper secondary schools. In 2010, the rate of enrollment in upper secondary schools for the poorest decile of the population amounted to only 54 percent, and for the rural population it was around 53 percent[56]. This circumstance, in particular, creates poverty reproduction risks.

Although the number of population in the corresponding age group reduces because of the demographic trends, in 2007-2011 the preliminary and secondary vocational educational

[56] Source: "Republic of Armenia, Fiscal Consolidation and Recovery", WB, 2011

institutions had a steady rate of admitted students -on average 11-12 thousand students in the secondary vocational programs and 2-3 thousand students in the preliminary vocational programs. This is the evidence of the demand for services for those levels of the education system.

The aforementioned tendencies make the guaranteed free 12-year education of all population groups a serious challenge, if taken into consideration that part of vocational educational programs is implemented on paid basis. Hence, transition to universal 12-year education is a priority of public education. This means that the following are needed: a) ensure guaranteed free 12-year education (including vocational) in both high schools and vocational educational establishments for all basic education graduates, b) ensure correct planning of public expenditures in terms of the proportion of expenses related to high schools and vocational education.

In the general education system, increasing efficiency as a result of the reforms of the system is a priority. Thanks to the reforms of the general education sector, indicators characterizing the efficiency of the system showed positive trends in the beginning of 2000s, but they subsequently started to decline. In particular, the pupil/teacher ratio in 2006 amounted to 10.9. But in recent years, this indicator has started to decline again and amounted to 2 only 9.3 in 2012. Thus, the ratio of pupils/teachers is still far behind the international standard – in 2010, the average for the same indicator in the European Union countries was 12, and for OECD countries is amounted to 14.757. The same is true also for class density. It grew in the beginning of 2000s, and in 2005 amounted to 22 pupils in the class on average, compared to 20 in 2003, and reached the average for OECD countries in those years. But later, it started to decrease and in 2011 it amounted to 18.4. Of course this indicator is differentiated by different levels of the system. It was the highest in the elementary school in 2011 at 18.9, for the basic/lower secondary school it was 17.9 and the figure for upper secondary school was 18.2.

Regional distribution of these indicators reveals significant regional differences. The pupil/teacher ratio is the highest in Yerevan, Ararat and Kotayk regions (10.8, 10.1 and 10.0 respectively), and the lowest in Aragatsotn, Vayots Dzor, Syunik, Tavush and Lori regions (6.3, 6.6, 6.7 and 8.0 respectively). Class density indicator is also the highest in Yerevan, Kotayk, Ararat and Armavir regions (22.9, 20.4, 19.8 and 19.8 respectively) and the lowest in Aragatsotn, Syunik, Vayots Dzor regions (12.2, 12.7 and 13.0 respectively). There are also significant differences between urban and rural areas. In the academic year of 2011/2012, the pupil/teacher ratio for rural communities amounted to only 7.8, while it was 10.5 for urban communities. Consequently, the low level of average national indicators is explained by specific geographical characteristics, in particular the low level of this indicator of efficiency in rural schools. Taking into account the importance of protecting rural communities in general and remote, near border and small rural communities in particular, especially in conditions of the worsening demographic situation, the government will implement the policy for protection of schools in those communities and increasing the quality of educations to the extent possible. For such communities, other target values for the mentioned efficiency indicators should be defined, at the same time promoting high level of efficiency in rural schools. In this regard a special importance is attached to introduction of the practice of developing multi-set

[57] Source: Eurostat and OECD databases. It is noteworthy that the international data estimation methodology is based on the number of full-time employed teachers, which is different from data for Armenia which are calculated based on the absolute number of teachers. Note that during 2011/2012 academic year about 44% of general education school teachers in Armenia were employed at 0,75 workload rate, about 34% at 0,76-1 workload rate and 22% at more than 1 workload rate.

classes in small rural community schools, which in its turn translates into the need of training multi-profile teachers at higher educational establishments especially for upper secondary school.

Table 42. Pupil/teacher ratio and average density of classes in the general education institutions/schools in 2008-2011

			2010/11		2011/12	
				Total	Urban	Rural
Number of pupils	414,781	392,946	370,892	386,439	233,837	152,602
Average number of pupils per class	17.8	17.1	18.4	18.4	...	...
Number of teachers	42,601	41,512	41,402	41,757	22,284	19,473
Number of pupils per teacher (pupil/teacher ratio)	9.7	9.5	9.0	9.3	10.5	7.8
	Memorandum item					
Number of pupils per teacher (pupil/teacher ratio) in the preliminary vocational education system	7.3	7.2	6.8	5.3	...	...

Source: "Social Panorama of Armenia 2011", NSS 2012, "Regions and Yerevan in figures 2011", NSS 2011

Enhancing the qualifications of teachers through training courses, bringing their qualifications up to certain standards, and increasing their salaries on that basis, have crucial significance for the quality of general education. Since 2005, training courses are organized annually for around 20 percent of teachers. As a result, in the 5 years preceding 2011, 74 percent of teachers participated in training courses. At the same time, a new procedure for attestation of teachers was introduced in 2011, which will allow for differentiated financing and will create incentives for further improvement of qualifications. These measures will largely contribute to improving the quality of general education.

Correspondingly, salaries of teachers have been raised. In the beginning of 2000s, the average monthly remuneration for teachers grew continuously. In 2003-2006, it increased by around 3 times and amounted to about 58,000 drams in 2006 (for full time occupation). The ratio of the calculated annual average salary of one teacher to the GDP per capita in 2006 amounted to 0.85, compared to 0.43 in 2003. In 2009, the calculated average monthly salary of one teacher read the level of 116,300 drams -an increase of around 100 percent compared to 2006. Because of the decline in GDP and in order to maintain the level of salaries of teachers, the ratio of the calculated annual average salary of one teacher to the GDP per capita in 2009 amounted to 1.4. In 2011, the average calculated salary of one teacher increased to 117,500 drams, and the ratio of calculated annual salary of one teacher/GDP per capita constituted 1.3. All the mentioned indicators reveal that the efficiency of the general education needs significant further improvements. But the target values of the mentioned indicators of efficiency should be differentiated by type of settlement, in order to protect the low efficient schools of rural communities. At the same time, in order to promote the efficiency of rural schools, it is a priority to implement grant programs for enhancing the efficiency of those schools, which, in particular, will contribute to the normal process of integration of small rural schools.

Within the framework of the reforms of the formal basic education, special importance is attached to the issues of the management of the system, in particular the assets management, maintenance and operation. Considering that around 90 percent of expenditures on the educational sector are used for current expenditures, as well as taking into account the low level of efficiency indicators of schools, property and assets operations and maintenance become important issues. In particular, the planning of operation and maintenance costs of assets and the introduction of transparent mechanisms for their accountability become important issues.

With respect to enrollment indicators for other levels of the educational system, it must be noted that in preschool and specialization programs they are lower compared to the average of FSU and CCE countries, although an increase in the enrollment has been recorded in 20082011. In particular, in the academic year of 2010-2011, net enrollment in the preschool education amounted to 34 percent (in the age group of 3-6 years, the average for the same indicator in FSU and CCE countries is 59 percent58), compared to 29 percent in 2007-2008.

Although enrollment rates in specialization programs and higher educational institutions (tertiary education) show a tendency of increase, nevertheless they are much lower than the average for FSU and CCE countries and are highly polarized by living standard groups and by regions. According to the results of the Households Living Standards Survey conducted in 2010, the net enrollment rate of the poorest 10 percent of the population in tertiary education programs amounted to only 7.4 percent, and the same indicator for the richest 10 percent was

33.4 percent. In this regard, the issue is to enhance the accessibility of higher education for the poor groups of population and create equal opportunities for being admitted to higher educational institutions. To address this issue on 30 June 2011 the Government adopted the Strategy on Financing Higher Education in the Republic of Armenia. It defines reforms of higher education financing system, which provide for more targeted and effective state programs aimed at state financial support of students. For this purpose a number of student financial support programs will be introduced, including a) professional scholarship program, b) student financial support program, c) allowances for socially vulnerable and special group students, d) program on special scholarships for best progress students. At the same time, within the framework of the mentioned reforms, it is envisaged also to revise the relations of the state and higher educational institutions, especially as regards formation of tuition fees and student admission practices. In particular, it is envisaged to a) bring the amount of student scholarships and financial support in line with tuition fees, b) revise the current state policy of setting quotes of student admission and provide state quotes to professions of priority importance for the state.

At the same time, reforms of tertiary educational programs and additional training programs are underway and aim to improving the quality of preliminary and secondary vocational, as well as higher and continuing education, bringing these levels of education system in line with European standards, and increasing their competitiveness in international market.

Integration with the European higher education area assumes in-depth changes in the country's higher education system meeting requirements of Bologna process. The following components ensuring main requirements of Bologna process are already underway in higher educational establishments: a) introduction of the tri-level qualification system, b) introduction of the system of accumulation and transfer of academic credits at higher educational establishments in line with the European credit transfer system, c) establishment of the national system for professional education quality assessment and assurance in line with European standards, e) adoption of the national framework of education qualifications of the Republic of Armenia in line with European qualification framework, f) creation and implementation of the mobility organization system for students, academic and graduates, g) introduction of the system for cross-recognition of qualifications, diplomas and learning outcomes, h) expansion of students' participation in academic and management processes of higher educational establishments.

The integration to European common educational area includes also the preliminary and secondary vocational educational systems guided by Turin process. The preliminary and secondary vocational educational system reforms in Armenia are geared at updating the educational content, increasing of management effectiveness and strengthening of logistics in line with corresponding European trends. According to the requirements of the Turin process, state educational standards for 100 specialties and qualifications of vocational and secondary education were developed with the following revision of curricula. Over 1000 teachers and officers of production processes of vocational schools and colleges were trained annually. Also directors and vice-directors of vocational schools and colleges have undergone corresponding trainings. Efforts were put to promote social partnership in the field of primary and secondary vocational education and to strengthen links between vocational education system and employers.

One of the key directions of the European cooperation, Bologna and Turin processes is the additional and lifelong education, where comparatively recently the Ministry of Education and Science started putting efforts. In 2010 the Additional and Lifelong Education Division was established in the apparatus of the Ministry of Education and Science with a mandate to coordinate the field, address challenges, and implement activities ensuring ongoing development of the sector.

However, the sector of tertiary education continues facing challenges as per both the quality and efficiency of education. With this in view the Government plans to implement the Program on Expansion of the Process of Integration of Vocational Educational System of the Republic of Armenia into the European Higher Education Area, the purpose of which is to ensure further development of Armenia's secondary and higher technical and vocational system in line with goals of the new phase 2010-2020 of the European higher education area.

OBJECTIVES

Public education continues being a priority issue in the sphere of education. The public education program aims include:

[58] Source: TransMonee Database, UNICEF, 2012

1) Improvement of the quality of the general secondary education, its matching with internal standards and ensuring smooth transition to higher educational.

2) Implementation of functional, modern forms and methods (including electronic) of supervision of the quality of education and assessment of knowledge, as well as stage by stage implementation of their unified system.

3) Ensure equal access to high-quality guaranteed free 12-year secondary education for all population groups, transition from guaranteed minimum 9-year education to universal free 12-year education (including vocational).

4) Separation of the high and basic school systems, gradual reorganization of secondary schools system into basic and high schools, with the exception of those rural communities of marzes, where the geography conditions the need to preserve secondary schools.

5) Increase enrollment in upper secondary school, especially for poorer segments of the population;

6) Continuously improve the efficiency of the system and introduce and fully establish an effective system of management, including assets management.

The priorities for achieving the mentioned objectives are: continuous training of teachers, increase in their salaries through introduction of a differentiated system for their salaries depending on the results of the qualification exams and the category obtained.

In order to ensure the enhanced quality of general education and the implementation of the mission of upper secondary schools, it is necessary as a priority; to refurbish schools (and specially high schools) with day needed material-technical and educational-methodological basis (laboratory equipment, computers, Internet, quality textbooks and teachers manuals, electronic educational resources, etc.). The mentioned objectives require a significant increase in annual public expenditures per pupil.

For the proper establishment of upper secondary schools, it is necessary, as a priority, to develop the corresponding programs for the schools and ensure smooth transition to the higher levels, to introduce the system of the corresponding standards, to ensure diversity of specializations and to expand the possibilities for preliminary specialization, to organize qualification training courses for teachers. At this level of general education, annual public expenditures per pupil should significantly increase, and the difference in this indicator compared to preliminary and secondary vocational educational institutions should diminish.

From the viewpoint of creating equal initial opportunities for the senior group of children of 5-6 years of age, in preschool institutions, who are getting prepared to enter the general education system, it is a priority to improve the quality and accessibility of preschool educational services.

From the viewpoint of creating equal opportunities for children in vulnerable groups of population who need special conditions for studying in general education institutions, it is a priority to develop the inclusive education system in the general education and in the vocational education too, which will allow the children to at least receive quality basic education and to have a specialization.

Given the extreme importance of human resources for the country's long-term socioeconomic development, professional education should be the next priority during the program implementation. In terms of professional education the program envisages to:

1) Improve access to secondary and higher professional education for all population groups.

2) Improve the quality of professional education and bring it in line with demands of the labor market, promote employment of graduates.

3) Improve effectiveness of higher educational system, including structural changes, network review and improvement of the management system.

4) Balance public regulation and financing systems of higher educational establishments, expand autonomy and academic freedom of higher educational establishments, expand state higher educational establishments' organizational and legal status and ensure diversity.

5) Academic development of higher educational establishments, strengthening the research component in higher educational establishments, implementation of modern academic financing methods of higher educational establishments.

6) Continue reforms aimed at streamlining professional education in line with the country's strategic educational and scientific development goals, provisions of Bologna and Turin Agreements. Particularly a) promotion of mutual cognition and mobility, b) improvement of the system of accumulation and transfer of academic credits, c) integration of higher education and research activities, d) implementation of internal systems to improve the quality of professional education and institutional and program accreditation of public and non-public higher educational establishments, e) development of vocational and continuing educational systems . At the same time, improvement of the quality of higher education dwells on the following priorities: a) strengthening conditions for licensing of higher educational establishments in accordance with European standards and procedures, b) strengthening of the list of professions and granted qualifications and their harmonization with UNESCO and Eurostat classification, c) continuing internationalization of the higher education system through promotion of joint educational programs with European universities and joint granting of qualifications, which will definitely result in greater mobility of students and the faculty.

7) Higher education financing reform, including diversification of financing sources and mechanisms for higher educational establishments, improvement of targeting and effectiveness of state programs on student support, expansion of the volumes and forms of financial support of students, increase of state funding of higher education, promotion of higher education and business community cooperation, promotion of private investments, financing of innovative programs aimed at development of higher educational establishments and modernization of higher education.

In order to increase the efficiency and quality of the education, it is crucial to fight the corruption at all levels of education system.

Given the importance of the sector and the progress of reforms there is a need of increasing state support of the system by increasing public expenditures in the sector of education.

Moreover, demographic trends should be taken into account, which apparently demonstrate tangible decrease in the number of educational system's beneficiaries. With this regard, expenditures on education from the consolidated budget, should increase by such an amount that taking into account economic growth that at least by 2017 they amount to around 2.8% of GDP, 3.3% by 2021 and 3.7% by 2025. At the same time, to meet the targets set out for the sector, the structure of public expenditures in education per sub-sectors needs adjustment in terms of the proportion of expenditures in upper secondary schools, preliminary and secondary vocational education, as well as higher education.

SCIENCE

SITUATION AND TRENDS

Creation of country's economy competitive advantages based on the science and high technologies is the primary precondition for the development. Development of the industries based on sciences and high tech can result in qualitatively new factors of economic growth. Competitive advantage in modern economy is mostly achieved by differentiation relying on knowledge-based goods.

A number of steps were taken during the recent years aimed at ensuring advanced development of science, including improvement of the legislative framework regulating scientific and technical activities, as well as implementation of competition and program financing system of scientific programs and themes funded from the state budget. During 2008-2009 an independent scientific expertise system was created, which currently involves about 1,500 academicians both from the country and abroad.

Numerous internationally recognized profound works have been published by Armenian scientists or with their co-authorship in prestigious scientific journals. According to the SCOPUS

classification of countries, Armenia is highly ranked especially as regards publications in the sphere of natural sciences, such as mathematics, physics and astronomy, biology and chemistry. In 2011 Armenia ranked 41st among 140 countries in the fields of physics and astronomy and the 63rd in overall ranking.59

There are active international scientific organizations, laboratories and groups in Armenia. Particularly, local scientific organizations participate in broad-scale international scientific experiments aimed at regulation of essential scientific problems in international research centers or within the framework of scientific cooperation with LHC, HESS, JLab, DESY, JINR, etc. Programs implemented jointly with other countries or international organizations enable integrating the country's scientific human resources into the international scientific and educational community and create favorable conditions for participation in grant programs, thus essentially expanding financial resources provided by international organizations to Armenia. During 2012-2013 four scientific organizations of Armenia act as coordinators of the European Community's Seventh Framework Program (FP7/2007-2013) (total budget EURO 2 million). During the recent years international scientific cooperation has considerably developed. In particular, agreements have been signed and joint projects are being implemented with France, Belarus, Russian Federation and Germany. Apart from that, agreements have been signed for Armenia's participation in international organizations, as well as for founding branches of those organizations in Armenia.

Though in 2009 state funding of scientific and technical programs has increased more than 3 times in nominal terms compared with the 2001, the relative funding still lags keeping Armenia behind a number of developed and developing countries. Between 2008 and 2010 the state budget allocations to scientific and technical activities totaled 0.19%, 0.27% and 0.24% of GDP correspondingly. For comparison, in 2009 28 EU countries (including Croatia) spent on average 0.68 % of GDP60. It is noteworthy that in EU countries, on average 1/3 of gross expenditure on research and developments (R&D) is covered by the state and the rest is funded from private sources. Though there is no clear statistics on the share of private sector in research activities in Armenia, according to estimations, the difference between private funding of R&D costs in Armenia and the average EU figures is eminent. In this regard, one of the key steps towards expansion of funding in this sphere is the promotion of private sector participation in funding of research and development initiatives. The first steps are already in the place, namely biannual co-funding programs started in 2011 aimed at achievement of scientific results with the support of private sector. In 2011, at least 15% of funding of each program came from off-budget sources and in 2013 the figure reached 25%. For the future the private sector share is planned to reach 50%.

According to data provided by the Ministry of Education and Science, today around 80% of public allocations to the science are targeted at fundamental studies and only 20% at developments of applied nature. Whereas in US 16% of the funds are earmarked for fundamental studies, 26-28% for applied studies and 56-58% is spent on experimental and engineering works and technological developments.

In addition to the financial problem, among factors hampering development of knowledge-based economy is the lack of relevant environment favoring acquisition and dissemination of know-how, application of outdated technologies in a number of branches of industry, absence

[59] Source: SCImago Lab, www.schimagojr.com, indicators are taken from SCOPUS database. The classification is based on H index, which shows the number (h) of publications of the country that recieved at least (h) citations. [60] Source: OECD database

of stimulus to be involved in research and absence demand for high scientific qualification, as well as existence of economic monopolies.

Another key problem is about the human resources in science. After the collapse of the Soviet Union the country faced an overall aging of academic staff and in some areas elimination of the entire academic school. The absence of a targeted policy promoting effective reproduction of the country's scientific potential leads to insufficient turnover of generations of scientific and academic resources. There is significant drain of young specialists from science, which can create serious difficulties for development of science. To ensure effective changing of generations in science, the State Committee of Science of the Ministry of Education and Science has developed a program to attract young people in the sphere of science by aiming creation of relevant employment and socioeconomic conditions in order to use effectively the creative potential of young specialists, as well as to implement activities aimed at increasing attractiveness of science.

Lastly, the nowadays scientific and technical logistical basis and infrastructures limit opportunities to conduct researches meeting contemporary requirements and standards and do not contribute to effective utilization of available academic potential. Absolute majority of equipment is obsolete, which does not enable high-quality research activities, particularly of applied nature. At the same time, in 2013 the State Committee of Science of the Ministry of Education and Science has already initiated the annual program on modernization of the logistical basis and infrastructures in the sphere of science. Starting from 2013 tender-based financial support is provided aimed at the establishment of joint-use scientific hardware or laboratories.

The abovementioned challenges are reflected in the amount of innovations implemented in the economy. Though high technologies are considered a priority sphere and are aimed at promoting competitiveness throughout the entire economy, and certain progress is reported in different international reports during the past years, Armenia has not documented significant progress yet. Particularly, the 2012-2013 Global Competitiveness Report ranked Armenia 105th among 144 countries in terms of innovation (in the GCR 2011-2012 Armenia held 112nd position out of 142 countries).

In some cases the created applied scientific products are not competitive in the global innovations' market. This stems from objective and subjective reasons. The fact of not having developed infrastructures for academic studies leads to decline of competitiveness of applied scientific products.

Armenia has very few industrial large corporations which can act as a platform for the development of scientific and industrial unions thus boosting improvement of the industry process and increasing the share of private sector in funding of science. Besides, there is a need of creating scientific production associations through consolidation of mostly applied research organizations. The pioneer in this field is the "Haykensatechnologia" scientific production center created in 2010 in the sphere of biotechnology, which is comprised of the Biotechnology Institute, Microbiology Institute and the Microbial Depository Center. At the same time, the export policy of Armenia lacks in the component of creation and export of science-based value added, and there are no financial structures for commercialization of scientific products. Their creation is envisaged by the year 2020 which is a long period given today's dynamic changes.

In this regard, a significant step forward was the President's recommendation to prioritize technological innovations and the guarantee of granting privileges to companies creating innovative goods and services that will prove to be competitive in both domestic and external

markets. The government promises solid tax advantages for innovative and high tech-based programs (3-4 years exemption of profit tax, VAT deferral, etc.).

VISION

476. The development vision for science implies developing Republic of Armenia into a knowledge-based economy, which is competitive in the European scientific and technical community in terms of its fundamental and applied scientific research and development. Implementation of this vision requires:

1)	Development of a system for sustainable development of science and advanced technologies,
2)	Upgrading material and infrastructure base of scientific activities,
3)	Ensure stable growth of highly qualified workforce in scientific and technical fields,
4)	Attract young specialists to science and implement manageable and smooth change of academic generation,
5)	Ensure effective state sponsorship of fundamental academic studies and advanced development,
6)	Promote implementation of researches providing know-how applied in economy, as well as increase of the number of innovations and patents in scientific organizations,

7)	Develop harmonious system for development of science, technologies and innovation-based knowledge, promoting participation of private business in scientific events, ensure targeted application of gained knowledge in education and different spheres of economy, and								
8)	Considerably expand technologies.	international	cooperation	in	the	field	of	science	and
23.3.	OBJECTIVES								

STRUCTURAL AND TERRITORIAL OBJECTIVES

Development of science requires institutional reforms of the system. There is a need of optimization and structural reforms of scientific and technological activities, by uniting state organizations of similar scientific direction regardless of their legal subordination. According to the NSS data, in 2011 about 35 scientific research institutes functioned within the structure of various ministries. To improve their performance effectiveness, at least some of them can be moved under the Armenian Universities or relevant scientific organizations. On the one hand, this will promote close cooperation with research institutes, and on the other hand the research findings will be transformed into the policies of the ministries.

There is a tendency of reducing the number of research institutes. In 2011 only 72 out of 102 institutes functioning in 2005 were left, of which 9 were closed up between 2010 and 2011. This tendency is dictated both by optimization of scientific organizations and financial allocations to scientific and research establishments, their human resources and labor productivity. Their centralized management is more reasonable.

There is a need of establishing modern systems of organization and management of activities at scientific organizations, clearly outlining responsibilities and rights of directors and

academic boards, as well as limiting their term of office. Another important aspect is development and implementation of modern mechanisms for the evaluation of effectiveness of scientific organizations' activities, thus ensuring direct dependence of state funding of scientific organizations from achieved products and introducing performance-based incentives for scientific organizations demonstrating remarkable effectiveness. Implementation of such mechanisms should be coupled by individual incentive programs for scientists who have good performance (the first such competition was launched in 2013 by the State Committee of Science of the Ministry of Education and Science). This will not only improve social justice in the sector, but will also build confidence among young employees about their career development.

Another science -related problem is the almost absence of geographic distribution or it is very unequal. As of 2011 only 11 out of 72 scientific and technical organizations were located in regions. Three organizations function in each of Kotayk and Aragatsotn marzes, two organizations in Shirak, one in Ararat, one in Armavir and one in Syunik marzes.

The remaining regions do not have research institutes. The state policy should be targeted at boosting science in regions, since equal territorial development implies equal geographic development of science as well. Also, it should be considered that development of science in marzes of Armenia should not be an end in itself, but rather be based on economy specifics of the region. Later on, on the basis of these research centers, a program of establishing an technopark in each region can be implemented, thus creating innovation-based development opportunities for the region.

RESOURCES AND INFRASTRUCTURE

Development of science should be based on integration of science and identification of its development priorities. Armenia's scientific and technical development priorities between 2010 and 2014 are defined in the RA Government Decree 640-N of 27 May, 2010. They include the following: Armenology, humanities and socioeconomic studies, life sciences, renewable energy, new energy sources, leading technologies, information technologies, space studies, earth studies, environmental studies, fundamental sciences promoting essential applied studies. It is envisaged that these priorities will be reviewed every five years. In addition, development of science implies demand for managers with managerial skills in this filed, which will be a serious leverage for attraction of financial resources and funding of most competitive research teams.

Increase of financial allocations is one of the main priorities in science development. Particularly, science program is geared at increasing financial allocations to science and bringing scientists' wages to the level of average salary in the economy. The share of knowledge-and high technologies-based industries and services in the total GDP of the country should become dominating in some 10 to 15 years, as opposed to the current 2%.

Human resources are the basic factor of scientific development, hence there is a need of developing and implementing a program to attract and embed young specialists in science. Among key elements of these programs are improvement of working and socioeconomic conditions of young scientists, increasing scientists' career attractiveness, as well as individual and corporate incentives (for scientists and organizations) for those who effectively educate and train scientific human resources. In addition, annual grant programs supporting research activities by PhD students and biannual grant programs for young academic workers are implemented from 2011. It should be noted that improvement of career attractiveness of academic workers is extremely important. For that purpose the individual incentive mechanisms for scientists were adopted. A clear-cut scientist's professional career mechanism should be developed in the nearest future, envisaging transition from PhD to permanent employment, according to the model used in developed countries.

At the same time, the state order mechanism for education and training of human resources in the sphere of science should be reformed. Activities should be implemented in order to reform and streamline the content of PhD training and to improve the academic level of theses submitted. There is a need for transition to 4-year PhD programs and introduction of a modern system of granting academic degrees compatible with European scientific and educational standards. Creation of research universities in Armenia should be the first step towards implementation of modern methods of education of science and educational personnel. International experience suggests that research universities enable much more effective combination of educational and scientific components. The active scientific environment contributes to education of highly qualified specialists who meet modern requirements of science. It is more appropriate for our research universities to implement post-graduate /post-diploma/ higher education based on Master's degree and Bachelor-based (first degree) post-graduate, researcher programs. As analysis of Armenia science and higher education show, in the nearest future it is possible to open a technological research university on the basis of natural sciences. Secondly, there is a need of developing mechanisms for organization of targeted post-graduate education and post-doctoral courses at international lead scientific and educational centers.

One of the primary areas contributing to the development of science in Armenia is creation of developed infrastructures necessary for scientific activities, i.e. modern research laboratories, innovation centers, techno parks, which can not only implement various programs, but also serve as a solid platform for attracting reputable specialists and implementing joint projects.

Two approaches are considered for the development of consortium programs jointly with leading scientific and research organizations. First, relevant centers specialized in such programs should be opened, staffed with specialists experienced and skilled in implementation of such programs, preparation of applications and international cooperation. This task can be achieved by full use of the potential of Armenian Diaspora and scientists. The first step in this direction is the program on mobilization of the academic potential of the country by the State Science Committee of the Ministry of Education and Science.

Effective development of modern science and technologies requires better access to academic publications and information sources for scientists and all interested parties. Joint utilization and dissemination of knowledge and information is critical when speaking of modern science and technologies. Each university should have its information system to maintain data on academic projects implemented by the faculty. Such databases should include information reflecting products of academic and research activities conducted in a given field. At the same time, systems of library organizations enable preserving information on certain articles, persons, thematic catalogues, etc. There should be automated data collection from various sources which interprets into integration of information systems of academic researches. Relevant information systems are already available at some universities of Armenia (e.g. Yerevan State University), corresponding Agreements are concluded envisaging free access to international scientific and technical systems (Thomson Reuters, Springer), and a Virtual Science Library is created.

SCIENCE-ECONOMY RELATIONSHIP

Existing gaps between the science and industry should be bridged and restored. Innovations and achievement of new development levels should be the primary goal of any industrial enterprise activity. In this regard an important aspect is registration of new trademarks, new products, as well as granting patents for scientific discoveries, as well as implementation of their commercialization policy.

Creation of favorable economic environment and expansion of business opportunities is critical for scientific organizations.

Commercialization of science requires state support in implementation of applied studies. Addressing this type of scientific and technical issues should dwell on public-private cooperation mechanism by implementing co-funding programs jointly with the private sector. Such co-funding programs are already being implemented with 15% share of private sector in 2011 and 25% in 2013. In the future state budget allocations should be expanded and the share of off-budget resources should reach 50%. Besides, there is a need of public targeted programs geared at addressing specific problems of an economic sphere. These programs should be developed jointly by the responsible public agency and research institution responsible for scientific research and development of the concerned direction.

Implementation of an effective innovation system is critical for development of knowledge-based economy in the country. Research and developments require involvement of venture capital, creation of scientific and industrial centers, as well as establishment of business incubators and techno parks at universities.

Organization of modern industries in Armenia is important, as it will improve competitiveness of created academic products. Another important aspect is development of centers for commercialization of academic products. These centers should be specialized in two directions: (i) clearly define what producers' needs are (ii) present the standards/criteria to the academicians. At the end they should perform as mediators and ensure commercialization of the created products.

Innovative activities of SMEs should be encouraged actively. Importance is attached to diversification policy of locomotive and priority branches of industry (clusters), i.e. establishing clusters on the scientific platform with good academic potential, thus boosting development of the branch. On the other hand, industrial activities of SMEs should be promoted, since trade in Armenia's GDP has reached 12%, which proves largely commercial nature of SMEs.

Coordinated reforms in the sphere of management of intellectual property will be targeted at protecting products of intellectual activities and ensuring their marketing in Armenia and other countries. Among priority objectives are improvement of the legislative framework, training and education of national human resources, regular study of innovative activities according to economy branches, creation of a computerized information system on intellectual property and development of adequate infrastructures.

Tax policy should become one of the pillars preserving the country's intellectual and educational potential. Tax incentives should serve as an effective mean of maintaining and strengthening the country's intellectual potential.

IMPORTANT BUSINESS CONTACTS AND OPPORTUNITIES

U.S. COMPANIES WITH OFFICES IN ARMENIA[2]

CONSTRUCTION SERVICES AND MATERIALS

ESI Engineering & Construction Co., Inc.
ESI plans to build a series of hydro power plants in Armenia. Michael Roche, Construction Manager
55a Charents Street, Yerevan;
tel: (374-2) 553-539, or 151-646
Registered February 29, 1995 as a branch office of ESI Engineering &

Construction Co.,Inc., 777 South Flagler Dr., Suite 650 East Tower, West Palm Beach, FL 33401; tel: (407) 833-4040; fax: (407) 833-0011; Mr. Thomas Swiatowski, Project Administrator.

Hayshen
Construction, civil engineering, design, and cad
Henrik Tigranyan, Director
5 Nalbandian St., Apt. 11, Yerevan, Armenia 37501
Tel: (374-2) 523-983, 583-543, 580-070 fax: (374-2) 151-678
Founded in 1992 as a JV between HayArd Ltd., Armenia and Hybusiness (USA), Director - Vartkes Barsam

Huntsman Armenia Concrete Corporation
Manufacturing of prestressed concrete slabs
Mr. Hrach Tumanyan, Production Director
49 Artsakh St., Yerevan, Armenia, 375021
Tel: (374-2) 471-217, 54-33
Registered in 1990 as a JV between the Ministry of Construction and the Huntsman Corporation, 2000 Eagle Gate Tower, Salt Lake City, Utah 84111, Tel: (801)532-5200, fax: (801) 536-1581 (Jon Huntsman, President).

Armenian-American Housing-Manufacturing Ring Entity
Producer of artificial wall stone blocks, doors and windows frames, and wooden roof structures.
Koriun Gargaloyan, Director
53 Engels St., Maisyan Industrial District, Gumri 377516, Armenia; Tel: (374-269) 3-29-01.
Started in 1989, opened in 1991, as a joint venture between the American Assembly of America (60%) and the government of Armenia (40%).

Hill International Armenia
Construction management

---

[2] The following is a list of fully or partially U.S. owned companies, and representatives of U.S. firms in Armenia with the names of contact persons, a brief description of their activities, and the year and form of registration

Frederick Samelian, President
Greg Kahwajian, Director for Government & Public Affairs.
Renny Borhan, Project Manager.
Raouf Ghali, Financial Director.
5 Nalbandyan St., 2nd floor, Yerevan, Armenia; tel:(374-2) 529-871.
Founded April 21, 1995, as a subsidiary of Hill International, Inc., 4904 Petit Ave., Encino, CA 91436-1131; tel:(818) 981-1048, fax:(818) 981-3421.

EDUCATION

American University of Armenia (AUA)
Michael Kouchakdjyan, Director of Administration.
40 Marshall Baghramyan Ave., Yerevan, Armenia 275019;
Tel (374-2) 271-096, 270-309, 273-439; fax: (374-2) 151-048.
Established in 1991, as a JV between the University of California at Los Angeles, Armenian General Benevolent Union (USA), and the Ministry of Education of Armenia.

FOOD PROCESSING

Armenian Tomato Company
Processing and canning of fruits and vegetables.
Peter Petrosian, President (USA), Armand O. Ensanian, VP (USA)
Levon Tonyan, General Director (home address: 20 Tumanian St., Apt. 11, Yerevan, 375001, Armenia; tel: (374-2) 583-322 (h).
JV address: 4 Choban Kara Shosse, Ejmiadzin
Tel: (374-2)287-190.
Registered in May 1995, as a JV between the Ministry of Agriculture and P&E Food Production Technology Management, Inc. , 1066 Gridley Street, Bay Shore, NY 11706; tel: (516) 667-9339; fax: (516) 560-0611.

Armenian Sugar Company
Sugar-beet planting and processing
Mr. Peter Petrosian, President.
Registered in 1994, as a JV between the Ministry of Agriculture and P&E Food Production Technology Management, Inc. Tel: (516) 667-9339, fax: (516) 560-0611.

Coca-Cola Bottlers Armenia
3E-Tria Epsilon Group of companies (Greece) has built a Coca-Cola bottling line at the Yerevan Lemonade Plant The production started in June 1996.
Timos Matragas, Coordinator - Armenia.
Tria Epsilon Group of Companies. 9 Fragoklissias Str., 15125 Maroussi, Athens P.O.B. 65072, 154 10 Psychico, Athens, Greece. Tel: 689 5500-10, telex:221773 hbch, fax: 689 5515.

GAMES

Armenian Company of International Lottery & Gaming Instant lottery
Gagik Tchantchapanyan, Director
50 Nalbandian St., Apt. 103, Yerevan, Armenia 375010
Tel:(374-2) 589-913, 560-540, 587-289; fax: (374-2) 561-544
Founded in 1993, as a JV between the Armenian Trade Union Center (51%) and

International Communication Technologies, Inc., Executive office: 12555 W. Jefferson Blvd. #200, Los Angeles, California 90066, tel: (310) 301-7680, fax: (310) 301-7635, Robert Block, Chairman of the Board; SBU: International Lottery & Gaming, Corp., 419 Greenleaf, Glencol, IL 60022-1907, tel:(708)835-0046, fax:(708) 835-8861, Michael Siegl, President (49%).

GENERAL EXPORT/IMPORT/SALES

Arco
General import/export.
Ashot Rostomian, President, tel: (374-2)562-324, 5828-71.
Registered 1995, as a representation of Arco in USA, P.O. Box 873, Glendale, CA 91209-0873.
Corporate office: 600 W. Broadway, Suite 355, Glendale, CA 91204

Aramco
Wholesale distributor of commodities, consumer goods, and office supplies.
Levon Gevorkyan, President
18 Vardanants St., Yerevan, Armenia 375010
Tel: (374-2) 521-684; fax: (374-2) 527-650; telex: 243280 malg su.
Founded in 1995, as a JV between the concern Sigl (Armenia) and Segl International Export-Import, 1248 S. Glendale Ave., Suite AA, Glendale, CA 91205, Levon Gevorkyan, President

Arm Key
foodstuffs imports/sales
Viktor Saryan, Director
51 Komitas Street, Yerevan 375051 Armenia
tel: (374-2)238-010, 236-001; fax: (374-2)234-320
Founded in 1996, as a subsidiary of Cozy Foods (USA)
Battles Universal Armenia
General import-export
Christopher Principe, Chairman
25 Komitas Street, Yerevan Armenia
Tel: (374-2)27-30-02, 58-57-46
Registered in August 1995, as a JV with Battles Universal Inc., 200 Railroad Avenue, Greenwich, Connecticut 06830 USA; tel: (203)661-4141; fax: (203)661-2555.

Callister
Export of optical crystal products.
Rudik Oganessian, Director.
Khachik Khachatryan, Deputy Director
63 Barbyus Street, Apt. 17, Yerevan, Armenia 375058
Tel: (374-2)22-57-29, 22-11-22.
Registered on August 24, 1995, as representative of American-Armenian trade association, LLC., 2525 North 860 East, Provo, Utah 84604. Tel: (801)377-1815, fax: (801)377-1815. Registered in April 1995. Narine Sarkisyan, Manager-Member. Reed (Dick) R. Callister, Member.

Bellevue Trading Incorporated
General wholesale trading, import/export.
Pavel Martirosov, President.
20 Tigran Mets Avenue, Suite 331, Vanadzor 377200 Armenia.
Tel (374-57)2-92-83, or 2-23-56.
Registered on July 3, 1995, as subsidiary of Bellevue Trading Incorporated, 2705 California Ave., P.O. Box 16703, Seattle, Washington 90816.

Leus
General food and supermarket suppliers.
Leonid Golosinsky, President (USA).
Levon Lachinyan, Executive Director.
Vigen Tumanyan, Manager.
10 Tumanyan St., Suite 2, Yerevan 375010 Armenia.
Tel (374-2)58-40-94.
Registered in March 1996, as a subsidiary of Intertrust, Inc. 4240 Commercial Way, Glenview, IL 60025; tel/fax: 847-803-1482. The company is planning to engage in flour, wheat, sugar and other foods procurement for the government, as well as establish American-style supermarket, and consider investment opportunities in Armenian industries.

Erebuni
Import-export of food, construction materials and electronics, civil construction works
Hamlet Asryan, Director.
1 Charents St., Second floor, Yerevan, Armenia 375025
Tel: (374) 524-964, fax: (374) 524-964 or 151-789.
Founded in 1994 as a JV between Martin Co. and Champion International, 6233 Whittier Blvd., Los-Angeles, CA 90022, tel:(213) 722-4085, fax:(213) 720-748. Currently, Erebuni is not operating due to financial problems.

Phillip Morris
Tobacco products
Agaron Tatevosyan, Armenia Representative
Nerkin Zeitun, 2nd street, house 38, Yerevan, Armenia
Tel/fax: (374-2)64-55-28. Registered in 1996. Parent company: Phillip Morris Management Services, Kiev, Ukraine, tel: (380)290-79-41, 230-26-64, 290-09-93; fax: (380)230-26-65. Anna Kozorez, Investment Specialist.

Ralt Distribution LLC
Complete supermarket suppliers.
Mr. Ashot Rostomyam, CEO.
8 Hanrapetutyan Street, Suite 35
Yerevan 375010 Armenia
Tel: (374-2)566-741, fax: (374-2)151-094., E-mail: ralt@arminco.com.
Registered in March 1996, as a Subsidiary of Ralt Distribution based at 310 N. Harbor Blvd., Suite 100, Fullerton, CA 92634; tel: (714) 578-9478; fax: (714)578-1810.
Tim Luberski, President
Steve Chaussy, Chief Financial Officer
Peter V. Guidry Jr., Marketing

Sina
Retail sale of pharmaceutical, medical and orthopedic commodities.
Henrik Bakunts, President.
18 Vardanants St., Yerevan, Armenia 375010
Tel: (374-2) 521-684, 647-600; fax: (374-2) 647-600.
Founded in 1995 as a JV between Armenian Disaster Neurology Research Center (50%), Tech Insurance Company (30%) and Sigl Export-Import (20%), 1248 South Glendale Ave., Suite AA, Glendale, CA 91205.

Sexess Petroleum Corporation
International trading of cars, and general merchandise
Karapet Astvatsatryan, President.

41 Tavrizyan St., Yerevan, Armenia
Tel: (374-2) 274-004.
Established in 1993 as a subsidiary of Sexess Petroleum Corp, Glendale, California (same president).

Tigranes Worldwide
Distributor and retailer of U.S. cosmetics.
Richard Tigran Bezjian, President (USA).
Gurgen Balyan, Armenia Director.
20 Mashtotz Street, Yerevan Armenia 375002
Tel: (374-2)537-004.
Registered in November 1995, as a joint venture between Gurgen Balyan (Armenia) and Tigranes Worldwide, Inc., tel: (617)489-300, fax:(617)489-1486.

CONSUMER PRODUCTS

Goldex
Production of silver jewelry
Ara Tonoyan, Director.
Michael Minasyan, Director (USA)
21 Shoprony St., Yerevan, Armenia 375021.
Tel:(374-2) 650-941.
Founded in 1990, as a JV between Garfield Fin. Corp. (85%) and the Yerevan Institute of Laser Equipment (15%).

Golden Pair Corporation
Manufacturing of optical devices and wholesale trade.
Mr. Jirair Shamilyan, President
13 Vram Shapuh Arka Street, Yerevan, Armenia 375002
Tel:(374-2) 582-243, 617-201; fax: (374-2) 526-821, 612-360.
Founded on November 6, 1992 as a JV of Golden Pair Corp., 4659 Hollywood blvd., Hollywood, CA 90027, tel:(213) 665-2576; fax: (213) 665-0709

Haitex
Production of electric home appliances, plastic goods, instant lottery.
Levon Melikyan, Chairman of the Board
3A Hakobyan St., Yerevan, Armenia, 375033;
Tel: (374-2)221-021, fax:(374-2)151-073.
Established in 1990 as a JV.

Andok
Assembly and sale of optical equipments and glasses, biomedical services.
Martin Mirzoyan, Director.
20 Charentsy St., Suite 2-4, Yerevan, Armenia 375025
Tel: (374-2) 553-365, 564-746.
Founded 1993, as a subsidiary of Armenian Relief Society of Western USA Inc., 80 Bigelow Ave., Watertown, MA 02172; tel:(617)926-5892; fax:(617)926-4855.

Armentoy
Manufacturing of electric toys
Samvel Tumanyan, President.
Hakob Kukuryan, Executive Director.
12 Sevani St., Yerevan, Armenia 375023.

Tel: (374-2) 342-411, 567-652, 67-32; fax: (374-2) 567-652.
Registered in 1990, as a JV between Urarty Corporation (Armenia) and BMT Corporation (USA).

Tufenkian Armenia
Production and export of hand-made carpets and threads
James Tufenkian, President (USA).
Hambartsum (Garik) Chilingaryan, Manager.
21/1 Tumanyna St., Second Floor, Yerevan, Armenia
Tel:(374-2) 520-885, 511-259, fax:(374-2) 151-751.
Registered in July 1994 as a subsidiary of Tufenkian Export import Ventures, Inc.

PUBLISHING

Vertex Ventures, Ltd.
Publisher of Armenian Yellow Pages.
Assadour M. Ashdjian, President (USA).
3 Amiryan St., 3rd floor, Yerevan, Armenia
Tel:(374-2) 584-234, fax:(374-2) 583-197.
Registered in 1993 as a JV between the Yerevan City Council and Vertex Ventures, Ltd. (NY).

POSTAL SERVICES

DHL Worldwide Express-Armenia
Agent - Michael Yukhanayev, Director
36 Demirchyan St., Floor 1, Yerevan 3750002
1 Charentsy St., Yerevan 375025 Armenia
Tel: (374-2) 586-688, fax: (374-2) 528-158.
Founded in 1995.
Federal Express
Agent - Areg Khachatryan, Director
1 Charentsy St., Yerevan 375025 Armenia
Tel:(374-2)574-686, 574-859, fax:(374-39) 07155
Founded in 1995

SOFTWARE ENGINEERING

HPL Armenia
Software engineering.
David Y. Lepejian, President (USA)
Zaven Nalbandyan, Director.
Hovhannes Ghukasyan, Software Development Director.
22 Saryan Street, Yerevan, Armenia 375002
Tel:(374-2) 535-237.
Registered Feb 20, 1995 as a subsidiary of HPL Heuristic Physics Laboratories Inc., 1649 South Main St., Milpitas, California 95035 USA; tel:(408) 263-1475, fax:(408) 263-1584.

Hailink
Research and development in natural sciences and architecture, wireless communication networks, software and hardware engineering
Gagik Evoyan, Director.
24a Marshall Bagramian St., Yerevan, Armenia, 375019
Tel:(374-2) 521-664, 273-418; fax:(374-2) 521-664.

Founded in 1992 as a subsidiary of Cilink Corp., Hermosa Court 910, Sunnyvale, California, tel: 735-5800.

TELECOMMUNICATIONS

Armenia Telephone Company (Armentel)
Long-distance service, telecommunications, cellular, paging, etc.
Berry Hon, President (USA).
Grigor Poghpatyan, Chairman of the Board
Vahram Soghomonyan, Executive Director and VP
22 Saryan St., Yerevan, Armenia 375002
Tel: (374-2) 580-123,520-915, 151-000, 70-32; fax: (374-2) 151-001.
Registered in July 1995 as a JV between the Ministry of Communication (51%) and Trans-World Telecom America, 25200 La Paz Rd., Suite 210, Laguna Hills, CA 92653; tel: (714)837-2388, fax (714) 568-8874.

Armako
Production of video telephones, digital telephone switches, and other electronic devices
Don H. Coleman, President (USA).
Stepan Demirchyan, Chairman of the Board and CEO.
111 Raffi St., Yerevan, Armenia
Tel: (374-2) 738-323, 151-724; govt. Line: 50-44, fax: (374-2) 732-636, 151-724.
Founded in 1994, as a JV between MARS plant and ICT Group, 1255 West Jefferson Blvd., Suite 300, Los Angeles, CA 90066; tel: 310 301 7680; fax: 310 301 7635

TRAVEL SERVICES

Levon Travel Yerevan
Travel agent
Gary G. Titizian, President (USA).
Anahit Torosyan, Director.
10 Sayat Nova Blvd., Yerevan, 375009, Armenia
Tel: (374-2) 525-210, fax: (374-2) 151-133.
Founded in 1991 by Levon Travel Bureau, Inc., 7083 Hollywood Blvd., Los Angeles, CA 90028; tel:(213) 871-8711; fax: (213)462-7410.
Northwest Airlines/KLM (general sales agent)
10 Sayat Nova Blvd., Yerevan, 375009, Armenia
Tel: (374-2) 525-210, fax: (374-2) 151-133., E-mail: klm@arminco.com

Sidon Travel Armenia
Travel agent
Hrair Babayan, Manager (USA).
Ovanes Sinanian, Executive Director (USA).
19 Sayat Nova St., Yerevan, Armenia
Tel: (374-2) 522-967; fax: (374-2) 151-684.
Operating in Armenia since 1987 as an agent of Aeroflot (Russia). Re-registered in 1990 as a subsidiary of Sidon Travel and Tourism. Garo Avakian, President. 5825 Sunset Blvd., Suite 218, Los Angeles, CA 90028; tel: (213)266-9161; fax: (213) 466-2869.

OFFICIAL DISTRIBUTORS/DEALERS OF U.S. FIRMS

Dell Computer Corp.
(computers & peripherals)
Vallex F.M. Est., a subsidiary of a Netherland company with the same name, has become a dealer of Dell Computer Corp. in December 1995.
Mkrtich Martirosyan, Representative.
Sergey Solakhyan, Computer Salesman.
13 Moscovuan Street, Yerevan 375001 Armenia
Tel/fax: (374-2)56 09 00, e-mail: mart@vallex.arminco.com.

For Mars
(chocolate and candy bars).
Derjava-c, official distributor of Mars since 1995.
31/10 Mesrop Mashtots Ave., Yerevan, Armenia:
Tel:(374-2)530-058; fax: (374-2) 522-619.

For Proctor & Gamble.
(cleaning products, pampers)
"White" - distributor of P&G cleaning products.
Arman Zargaryan, Armenia Representative.
39 Tigran Mets Ave., Yerevan, Armenia,
Tel: (374-2)562-708, fax: (374-2)520-231.
Registered in November 1995, as distributor for Proctor & Gamble Tuketin Mallari Sanayi A.S., Halkali Caddessi No. 206-34620 Sefakoy - Istanbul, Turkey. Tel: (90-212)698-96-00; fax: (90-212) 697-44-62

For Rank Xerox
(photocopiers)
Computer Service Ltd.
1 Charents Street, Yerevan, Armenia
Tel: (374-2) 574-65, tel/fax: (374-2)575-37
Eduard Gabrielyan, President
Registered in January 1996 as an official dealer for
Xerox Buro Araclari Ticaret ve Servis A.S. Kasap Sokak, Konak Azxer Ishani No: 12, 80280/ Esentepe - Istanbul: tel: 0 212 - 274 93 54, fax: 0 212 - 267 12 80. Yervant Tirpan, Area Manager, Eurasia CBU.

For Reebok
(sports goods).
Armenian firm "Tigris" in 1995 became a dealer for Reebok. 29 Sayat Nova Street, Yerevan, Armenia: tel: (374-2)578-792

U.S. AND COUNTRY CONTACTS

COMMERCIAL SECTION * AMERICAN EMBASSY

18 Marshal Baghramyan St., Yerevan 375019 Armenia
Tel: (374-2)254-4661, 520-791, 151-144, Fax:(374-2)151-138,
Telex: 234137 AMEMY

U.S. address:
Eurasian-American Chamber of Commerce
Eurasian Investment Center

P.O. Bpox 15343
Washington, DC 20003
Ph: (202) 546-2130. Fax: (202) 546-3275
E-mail: rusric@erols.com

COMMERCIAL SECTION

AmEmbassy Yerevan
Department of State
Washington D.C. 20521-7020

attn: Andranik Hovhannisyan, Assistant Commercial Officer or
Armen Vahradyan, BISNIS representative

ARMENIAN TRADE AND INDUSTRY ASSOCIATIONS

ARMENIAN CHAMBER OF COMMERCE AND INDUSTRY

(President - Mr. Hamlet Hovhannisyan)
39 Hanrapetutyan St., Yerevan 375010, Armenia
Tel: (374-2) 56-54-38, Tlx: 243322 ALFASU, Fax: (374-2) 56-46-95. More than 360 private and state member-companies throughout Armenia. Business information support and business facilitation services.

THE ARMENIAN ENTREPRENEURS ASSOCIATION

(President - Ms. Hermine Haghdalyan)
19 Kievian St.,Yerevan, 375033, Armenia
Tel: (374-2)274-837, Fax:(374-2)566-468, or 151-069,
Tlx: 243368 BASIS SU.
The Association represents over 1,000 Armenian private businesses. Open to international contacts.

UNION OF ARMENIAN MERCHANTS

(President - Mr. Makich Demiryan)
13 Vardanants St., Yerevan, Armenia
Tel:(374-2)570-321, Tel & Fax: (374-2)151-734.
The Union is a trade association of of more than 400 retailers and wholesalers.

COUNTRY INDUSTRY, BUSINESS AND TRADE-RELATED GOVERNMENT AGENCIES

MINISTRY OF ECONOMY

Armen Yegiazaryan, Minister
I Government Bldg., Republic Square, Yerevan 375010
Tel:(374-2)527-342, Fax:(374-2)151-069

Foreign Investments Department

Aram Tarakhchyan, Director
Tel:(374-2)527-351, Fax:(374-2)524-332, 151-069

MINISTRY OF INTERNAL AFFAIRS

Vanik Siradeghyan, Minister
130 Nalbandyan St., Yerevan 375015
Tel:(374-2)560-908, Fax:(374-2)529-388

MINISTRY OF DEFENSE

Michael Harutyunyan, Minister
Ashtarak Shosse, Yerevan
Tel:(374-2)357-881

MINISTRY OF HEALTH

Ara Babloyan, Minister
8 Tumanyan Street, Yerevan 375001
Tel:(374-2)582-413, Fax:(374-2)151-097, 562-923

MINISTRY OF ENERGY AND FUEL

Miron Shishmanyan, Minister
2 Government Bldg., Republic Square, Yerevan 375010
Tel:(374-2)521-964, Fax:(374-2)151-089

MINISTRY OF INDUSTRY

Ashot Safaryan, Minister
2 Government Bldg., Republic Square, Yerevan 375010
Tel:(374-2)521-877, 520-579, Fax:(374-2)151-084, 523-564

MINISTRY OF CULTURE

Hakob Hakobyan, Minister
5 Tumanyan St., Yerevan 375001
Tel:(374-2)561-920, Fax:(374-2)523-922

MINISTRY OF LIGHT INDUSTRY

Rudolf Teimurazyan, Minister
4 Kochar St., Yerevan
Tel:(374-2)226-500, Fax:(374-2)227-363

MINISTRY OF EDUCATION

Ashot Bleyan, Minister
13 Movses Khorenatsy St., Yerevan 375010
Tel:(374-2)524-749, Fax:(374-2)567-164

MINISTRY OF COMMUNICATION

Grigor Poghpatyan, Minister
22 Saryan St., Yerevan 375002

Tel:(374-2)526-632, Fax:(374-2)151-446, 538-645

MINISTRY OF FOOD AND PROVISIONS

David Zadoyan, Minister
48 Nalbandyan St., Yerevan 375010
Tel:(374-2)529-611, 583-827, Fax:(374-2)564-683

MINISTRY OF FINANCE

Levon Barkhudaryan, Minister
I Melik Adamyan St., Yerevan 375010
Tel: (374-2)527-082, Fax:(374-2)151-154, 523-745

MINISTRY OF JUSTICE

Vahe Stepanyan, Minister
8 Khorhrdaranayin St., Yerevan 375010
Tel:(374-2)582-157, Fax:(374-2)582-449

MINISTRY OF EMPLOYMENT AND SOCIAL SECURITY

Ashot Yesayan, Minister
18 Isahakyan St., Yerevan 375025
Tel:(374-2)565-321, Fax:(374-2)563-075

MINISTRY OF CONSTRUCTION

Felix Pirumyan, Minister
3 Government Bldg., Republic Square, Yerevan 375010
Tel:(374-2)589-080, Fax:(374-2)523-200

MINISTRY OF TRADE

Levik Khachatryan, Minister
69 Teryan St.,Yerevan 375009
Tel:(374-2)562-591, Fax:(374-2)583-521

MINISTRY OF MATERIAL RESOURCES

Vahan Melkonyan, Minister
5 Hanrapetutyan St., Yerevan 375010
Tel:(374-2)538-082, Fax:(374-2)538-321

MINISTRY OF TRANSPORTATION AND COMMUNICATION

Henrik Kochinyan, Minister
10 Zakyan St., Yerevan 375015
Tel:(374-2)563-391, Fax:(374-2)525-268

MINISTRY OF NATURE AND ENVIRONMENTAL PROTECTION

Suren Avetisyan, Minister
37 Moskovyan St., Yerevan 375002
Tel:(374-2)530-741, Fax:(374-2)534-902, 538-613

MINISTRY OF AGRICULTURE

Ashot Voskanyan, Minister
2 Government Bldg, Republic Square, Yerevan 375010
Tel:(374-2)520-321, 524-641, Fax:(374-2)523-793

MINISTRY OF HIGHER EDUCATION AND SCIENCE

Vardges Gnuni, Minister
13 Movses Khorenatsy St., Yerevan 375010
Tel:(374-2)526-602, Fax:(374-2)525-317

MINISTRY OF FOREIGN AFFAIRS

Vahan Papazyan, Minister
10 Marshall Baghramyan St., Yerevan 375012
Tel:(374-2)523-531, 588-829, Fax:(374-2)151-042, 527-022

Vartan Oskanyan, Director, US/Canada Desk
Tel:(374-2)588-812, 588-814, 59-13

Minna Gurgenyan, Chief, Consular and Legal Section
Tel:(374-2)588-849

STATE ADMINISTRATION FOR NATURAL RESOURCES

Lasar Sargsyan, Chairman
46 Charents St., Yerevan 375025
Tel:(374-2)551-305, Fax:(374-2)550-488

STATE ADMINISTRATION FOR MINERALS AND GEOLOGY

Ashot Karapetyan, Chairman
46 Charents St., Yerevan 375025
Tel:(374-2)551-305, Fax:(374-2)550-822, Telex:243254

Customs:

CUSTOMS DEPARTMENT OF ARMENIA

Yerjanik Abgaryan, Chairman
35 Moskovyan St., Yerevan 375010
Tel:(374-2)533-538, Fax:(374-2)533-538

STATE TAXE ADMINISTARTION

Pavel Safaryan, Chairman
3 Movses Khorenatsy St, Yerevan 375015
Tel:(374-2)538-101, Fax:(374-2)151-967

PROTECTION OF INTELLECTUAL PROPERTY

ArmPatent (State Patent Office)
Sarkis Kantarjyan, Chairman
3 Government Bldg., Main Avenue, Yerevan 375010
Tel:(374-2)520-673, Fax: (374-2)580-631

DISPUTE SETTLEMENT

State Arbitrage (Economic Court)
Henrik Sarkisyan, Supreme Arbitrator
18 Paronyan St., Yerevan 375015
Tel:(374-2)532-411

SUPREME COURT OF ARMENIA

Tariel Barseghyan, Chief Justice
6 Khorhrdaranayin St., Yerevan 375010
Tel:(374-2)563-594, 583-231

STATE CHIEF PROSECUTOR'S OFFICE

Artavazd Gevorgyan, Chief Prosecutor
6 Khorhrdaranayin St., Yerevan 375010
Tel:(374-2)580-001

ADMINISTRATION FOR CIVIL AVIATION AND ARMENIAN AIRLINES

Shahen Petrosyan
Aviation Administration Bldg., Zvartnots Airport, Yerevan
Tel:(374-2)774-824, Fax:(374-2)151-123

ZVARTNOTS AIRPORT

Vagharshak Mnatsakanyan, Director
Aviation Administration Bldg, Zvartnots Airport, Yerevan
Tel:(374-2)773-097, Fax:(374-2)151-123

STATE ADMINISTRATION FOR RAILROADS

Vladimir Asryants, Chairman
50 Tigran Mets St., Yerevan 375005
Tel:(374-2)520-428, Fax:(374-2)573-630

STATE ADMINISTRATION FOR STATISTICS

Levon Davtyan, Director
3 Government Bldg., republic Square, Yerevan 375010
Tel:(374-2)524-213, Fax:(374-2)521-021, Telex:243497

MASS MEDIA

State Administration for Television and Radio

Tigran Hakobyan, Chairman
5 Alek Manukyan St., Yerevan 375025
Tel:(374-2)555-033, Fax:(374-2)551-513

Armenpress State Information Agency

Gevorg Hovhannisyan, Director
28 Isahakyan St., Yerevan 375015
Tel:(374-2)526-702, 526-702, Fax:(374-2)529-262

ARCHITECTURE AND CITY PLANNING

STATE ADMINISTRATION FOR ARCHITECTURE AND CITY PLANNING

Romeo Julakyan, Chairman
3 Government Bldg., Republic Square, Yerevan 375010
Tel:(374-2)526-234, Fax:(374-2)583-869

COUNTRY MARKET RESEARCH FIRMS

The Center for Business Research and Development (CBRD)
Stephan Karamardyan, Director
40 Marshall Baghramyan St., Yerevan 375019
Tel:(374-2)271-602, 151-049; Fax:(374-2)151-048
E-mail: AUA@adonis.ias.msk.su

TRANSCOM

Suren Shahinyan, Director
1/3 P. Byuzand St., Floor 6, Yerevan 375010
Tel: (374-2)271-827, 567-054; Fax: (374-2)151-048

LARGEST PRIVATE BANKS

ARMIMPEXBANK

2 Nalbandyan St., Yerevan, 375010
Tel:(374-2)589-906, 589-518, 564-617; Fax:(374-2)565-958
Chairman: Mr. Eduard Arabkhanyan
Corresponding Banks: Bank of America (Concord, CA), Bank of New York, Credit Lyonnais (New York); Creditanstalt Bankverein, Raiffeisenzentralbank A.G. (Vienna); Credit Lyonnais, Banque Francaise De L'orient, Deutsche Bank A.G. (Paris), Deutsche Bank A.G., Commerzbank (Frankfurt); Swiss Bank Corp., Union Bank of Switzerland, Credit Suisse (Zurich); Midland Bank, National Westminster Bank PLC (London); The Bank of Tokyo (Tokyo); Royal Bank of Canada (Toronto); ABN-Amro Bank (Amsterdam), Bank Brussels Lambert (Brussels); General Bank (Brussels); National Australia Bank (Sydney).

ArdShinBank (Industrial Construction Bank)
3 Deghatan St., Yerevan, 375010
Tel:(374-2)560-616, 528-513, Fax:(374-2)151-155, Telex:243349
Chairman: Mr. Karen Movsisyan
Corresponding Banks: Citibank, Bank of New York (New York).

ArmAgrobank (Agricultural joint stock commercial bank)
7a Movses Khorenatsu St., Yerevan, 375015
Tel:(374-2)534-342, Fax:(374-2)534-342
Chairman: Mr. Armen Arzumanyan
Corresponding Banks: The Bank of New York, Citibank, Republic National Bank of New York (New York); Deutsche Bank AG, Dresdner Bank AG, Commerzbank (Frankfurt); Credit Commerciale de France, Credit Agricole de France, Eurobank (Paris); Bank of Tokyo (Tokyo); Swiss Bank Corporation (Zurich); Bank Mees Pierson Amsterdam (Amsterdam); Bank Brussels Lambert (Brussels).
Visa Credit Card Service

ARMECONOMBANK

32 Garegin Njde, Yerevan, 375026
Tel:(374-2)440-511, 447-680, Fax:(374-2)562-705
Chairman: Mr. Vladimir Badalyan
Corresponding Banks: Banque Nationale de Paris (Paris); National Westminster Bank (London); Riggs National Bank of Washington, D.C. (Washington); Deutsche Bank (Frankfurt).

AVIABANK

1 P.Sevak St., Yerevan, 375014
Tel:(374-2)288-857, Fax:(374-2)281-940, Telex:243113
Chairman: Mr. Harutiun Vardanyan
Corresponding Banks:Credit Lyonnais (New York); Barklays Bank (London); Swiss Bank Corp. (Geneva); Credit Lyonnais (Paris), Dresdner Bank (Frankfurt), ABN Bank Amro (Vienna), MMKB (Moscow).

ARMSNUNDBANK

4 Spendiarov Dr.,Yerevan, 375002
Tel:(374-2)536-220, Fax:(374-2)563-220
Chairman: Mr. Hovik Melikyan
Corresponding Banks: Ukraina (Kiev), TverjuniversalBAnk (Moscow).

ANELIK BANK

4 Hrachya Kochar St., Yerevan, 375033, Armenia
Tel:(374-2)221-451, 226-526 Fax:(374-2)226-581
Chairman: Mr. Samvel Tsmatcyan
Corresponding Bank: Swiss Bank Corp.(Zurich), Mos BusinesssBank (Moscow).

AKUNK BANK

19a Koriun St., Yerevan, 375009
Tel:(374-2)520-792, 526-357 Fax:(374-2)526-867
Chairman: Mr. Grikor Vahanyan

ARMINVESTBANK

13 Vardanants St., Yerevan, 375010
Tel:(374-2)570-502, 570-350, Fax:(374-2)523-718
Chairman: Mr. Arthur Javadyan

ADANA BANK

5 Nalbandyan St., Yerevan, 375010
Tel:(374-2)589-017, 597-358 Fax:(374-2)633-591
Chairman: Mr.Karen Nersisyan
Corresponding Banks: Credo Bank (Saint Petersburg).

AREG BANK

11 Yerevan St., Abovian
Tel:(374-2)558-951 Fax:(374-39)07-033
Chairman: Mr. Ashot Arakelyan

Corresponding Banks: IncomBank (Moscow)

BANK FOR RECONSTRUCTION AND DEVELOPMENT

31 Moskovyan St., Yerevan, 375002
Tel:(374-2)530-156, 530-094, Fax:(374-2)530-156
Chairman: Alexander Griroryan
Corresponding Banks: Citibank (New York); Los Angeles Bank (Los Angeles).

CAPITAL BANK

38 Tamantsinery 4th Dr.,Yerevan, 375006
Tel:(374-2)484-610
Chairman: Mr. Kamo Poghosyan

CONVERSE BANK

49 Komitas St., Yerevan 375051
Tel:(374-2)281-015, 235-993 Fax:(374-2)285-082,
E-mail:convers.yerevan@rex.iasnet.com
Chairman: Mr. Smbat Nasibyan

CREDIT-YEREVAN BANK

2/8 Vramshapuh St., Yerevan 375002
Tel:(374-2)589-065 Fax:(374-2)580-083
Chairman: Mr. Martin Hovhanisyan
Corresponding Banks: Banque Nationale De Paris (Paris), Berlin Bank (Berlin).

DAVID BANK

16 Kievian St., Suite 609A, Yerevan, 375028
Tel:(374-2)262-831, 262-882, 275-809, 391-140, Fax:(374-2)353-900
Chairman: Mr. Azat Shahbazyan
Corresponding Banks: Inko Bank, Rossisky Credit (Moscow).

DELTA BANK

105 Raffu St., Yerevan, 375064
Tel:(374-2)533-924
Chairman: Mr. Arshak Karakhanyan

EREBUNI BANK

13 Khaghakh Don St., Yerevan 375087
Tel: (374-2)536-220
Chairman: Mr. Ph. Gevorkyan

ECHOBANK

36 Avetisyan St.,Suite #31, Yerevan 375012
Tel: (374-2)271-500, 271-510 Fax:(374-2) 271-510, 262-900
Chairman: Ms. Tamara Hovakymyan

ELITA BANK

16 Kievyan St., Yerevan 375028
Tel: (374-2)220-223, 223-478, 223-457, Fax:(374-2)226-163
Chairman: Mr. Sanasar Abazazyan
Corresponding Banks: Megeconomsberbank (Moscow).

FELIX BANK

38 Saryan St., Yerevan 375002
Tel:(374-2)589-062, (8852)280-702
Chairman: Mr. Barsegh Peplozyan

GLADZOR BANK

1/8 Charents St., Yerevan, 375025
Tel:(374-2)576-750, 551-515, Fax:(374-2)576-115
Chairman: Mr. Gagik Amaryan
Corresponding Banks: Stolichny, TverjunivesalBank (Moscow).

GARNI BANK

40 Hakhtanaky St., Abovyan
Tel:(374-61)21-334
Chairman: Mr. Grikor Aghadjanyan

GEVORG BANK

11 Hanrapetutyan Ave., Abovyan
Tel:(88261)25-877
Chairman: Mr. Suren Grigoryan

HaykhnayBank (Savings Bank)
28a Khorenatsu, Yerevan 375018
Tel:(374-2)520-458, 580-451, Fax:(374-2)560-766
Chairman: Mr. Hovhannes Mandakuny
Corresponding Banks: Banque Nationale de Paris (Paris), MegheconomBank, Sberbank (Moscow).

HAYKAP BANK

22 Saryan St., Yerevan, 375002
Tel:(374-2)532-080
Chairman: Mr. Hakob Terunyan
Corresponding Banks: Credit Lyonnais(Moscow), Sviaz Bank (Moscow)

HRAZDAN BANK

8 Spandaryan St., Hrazdan
Tel:(374-2)589-906
Chairman: Mr. Ashot Assatryan

LEND BANK

21 Nairy Zaryan St., Yerevan 375051

Tel:(374-2)399-060 Fax:(374-2)340-273
Chairman: Mr.Anushavan Khachikyan
Corresponding Banks: ABN Amro Bank, City Bank, Bank of New York (New York). Visa Credit Card Service via Incombank (Moscow).

LITSK BANK

P2 Dipol St., Kamo
Tel: (374-2)285-991
Chairman: Mr. Samvel Amirkhanyan

METS BANK

143 Artsakh St., Yerevan 375001
Tel:(374-2)525-310, Fax:(374-2)525-310
Chairman: Gagik Kafyan
Corresponding Banks: Commerzbank (Frankfurt)

PROMETEY BANK

19 Hracia Kochar St., Yerevan, 375012
Tel:(374-2)273-000, Fax:(374-2)274-818
Chairman: Emil Soghomonyan
Corresponding Banks: NevteGazStroy Bank (Moscow), Deutsche Bank (Frankfurt)

RIA BANK

12a Koriun St., Yerevan 375009
Tel:(374-2)560-132 Fax:(88539) 07057
Chairman: Mr. Viktor Virabyan
Corresponding Bank: Toko Bank (Moscow).

SIPAN BANK

37 Mashtots Ave., Yerevan 375002
Tel:(374-2)532-601, Fax:(374-2)532-601
Chairman: Mr. Volodia Hovsepyan
Corresponding Banks: MosGorStroyBank (Moscow)

SPURK BANK

2 Zaryan St., Yerevan 375002
Tel:(374-2)257-004, Fax:(374-2)228-155
Chairman: Mr. Samvel Sargisyan
Corresponding Banks: TverjuniversalBank(Moscow)

SPITAK BANK

2 Torosyan St., Spitak
Tel:(88269)4-58
Chairman: Mr. Boris Arakelyan

SEVAN BANK

24 Azatutyan St., Yerevan 375014

Tel:(374-2)288-747, Fax:(374-2)565-263
Chairman: Mr. Karen Manvelyan

SPACE BANK

1 Komeritmiutyan St., Yerevan
Tel:(374-2)533-419, Fax:(374-2)532-600, 240-985
Chairman: Mr. Armen Sukiasyan
Corresponding Banks: Alfa Bank (Moscow).

TRANSBANK

27 Tigranyan St., Yerevan 375014
Tel:(374-2)234-718
Chairman: Mr. Hrant Zazyan
Corresponding Banks: NA

INFORMATION ON INTERNATIONAL FINANCING

The Multilateral Develoment Bank Office
Brenda Ebeling, Director
14th & Constitutiona Avenue, NW
Washington DC 20007
Tel: 202-482-3399; Fax: 202-482-6179

AGRICULTURE - TRADE ASSISTANCE

U.S. Department of Agriculture
Foreign Agricultural Service
Trade and Promotion Office
Tel: 202-720-7420

GENERAL BUSINESS ASSISTANCE

Eurasian-American Chamber of Commerce
Eurasian-American Investment Center
P.O.Box 15343
Washington, DC 20003
Ph. (202) 546-2130. Fax: (202) 546-3275
E-mail: rusric@erols.com
Russian & NIS DataBank on Line: http://www.e-gate.net

COMMERCIAL BANKS AND INTERNATIONAL FINANCIAL INSTITUTIONS

COMMERCIAL BANKS

ADANA BANK
EXECUTIVE DIRECTOR: KAREN NERSESYAN
5 NALBANDYAN STREET
YEREVAN-10
TEL: (374-2) 567-109
FAX: (374-3) 907-157
E-MAIL: ADANA@MBOX.INTARNET.COM

AGRICULTURAL COOPERATIVE BANK OF ARMENIA
CHAIRMAN: STEPAN GISHYAN
1 BAYRONI STREET
YEREVAN-1
TEL: (374-2) 568-585
FAX: (374-2) 151-755
E-MAIL: ACBA@ARMINCO.COM

AKUNK BANK
CHAIRMAN: GAGIK VAHANYAN
19A KORYUNI STREET
YEREVAN-9
TEL: (374-2) 520-792
FAX: (374-2) 526-357
E-MAIL: ATLAS@ARMINCO.COM

ANELIK BANK
CHAIRMAN: SAMVEL CHEZMACHYAN
75 BAGHRAMYAN AVE.
YEREVAN-33
TEL: (374-2) 221-451
FAX: (374-2) 151-441
E-MAIL: ANELIK@ARMINCO.COM

ARDSHINBANK
EXECUTIVE DIRECTOR: LEVON FARMANYAN
3 DEGHATAN STREET
YEREVAN-10
TEL: (374-2) 528-513
FAX: (374-2) 151-155
E-MAIL: INTERNATIONAL@ARDSHIN.BANK.AM

AREXIMBANK
EXECUTIVE DIRECTOR: ARMEN KHANDKARYAN
20 TUMANYAN STREET
YEREVAN-1
TEL: (374-2) 580-506
FAX: (374-2) 583-131
E-MAIL: INFO@AREXIMBANK.AM

ARMAGROBANK
CHAIRMAN: EDWARD SANDOYAN
7A MOVSES KHORENATSI STREET
YEREVAN-15
TEL: (374-2) 585-790, 532-732
FAX: (374-2) 534-342
E-MAIL: AA@AGROBANK.AM

ARMECONOMBANK
EXECUTIVE DIRECTOR: ASHOT OSIPYAN
32/1 AMIRYAN STREET

YEREVAN-02
TEL: (374-2) 531-126
FAX: (374-2) 151-149
E-MAIL: ARMECO@ARMINCO.COM

ARMENIAN DEVELOPMENT BANK
CHAIRMAN: ALEXANDER GRIGORYAN
21/1 PARONYAN STREET
YEREVAN-15
TEL: (374-2) 530-094
FAX: (374-2) 533-233
E-MAIL: ROOT@ADB.INFOCOM.AMILINK

ARMIMPEXBANK
CHAIRMAN: BAGRAT ASATRYAN
2 NALBANDYAN STREET
YEREVAN-10
TEL: (374-2) 589-906
FAX: (374-2) 151-813
E-MAIL: OFFICE@IMPEX.BANK.AM

ARMINVESTBANK
CHAIRMAN: VARUZHAN AMIRAGYAN
13 VARDANANTS STREET
YEREVAN-10
TEL: (374-2) 523-718
FAX: (374-3) 907-210
E-MAIL: IBANK@DOLPHIN.AM

CONVERSE BANK
CHAIRMAN: SMBAT NASIBYAN
49 KOMITAS AVE.
YEREVAN-51
TEL: (374-2) 281-015
FAX: (374-3) 906-072
E-MAIL: CONVERSE.YEREVAN@REX.IASNET.RU

CREDIT-YEREVAN BANK
CHAIRMAN: MARTIN HOVHANNISYAN
2/8 AMIRYAN STREET
YEREVAN-10
TEL: (374-2) 589-065
FAX: (374-2) 151-820
E-MAIL: MAILCREYER@MAIL.CREYER.AM
ROZY@MAIL.CREYER.AM

CREDIT-SERVICE BANK
EXECUTIVE DIRECTOR: BORIS ARAKELYAN
15 TIGRAN METSI STREET
YEREVAN-10
TEL: (374-2) 527-794

FAX: (374-2) 525-701
E-MAIL: CREDIT@SERVICE-INFOCOM-EMAILK.NET

ECONOMINVESTBANK
EXECUTIVE DIRECTOR: KAREN DAVTYAN
2B ZAKYAN STREET
YEREVAN-10
TEL: (374-2) 535-113
FAX: (374-3) 907-215
E-MAIL: EKIM@SCI.AM

GLADZOR BANK
CHAIRMAN: GAGIK AMARYAN
1B CHARENTS STREET
YEREVAN-25
TEL: (374-2) 576-750
FAX: (374-2) 576-115
E-MAIL: GLADZOR@AMILINK.NET

HAYKAP BANK
EXECUTIVE DIRECTOR: EDUARD ARABKHANYAN
22 SARYAN STREET
YEREVAN-2
TEL: (374-2) 589-700
FAX: (374-3) 907-033
E-MAIL: HAYKAP@MBOX.AMILINK.NET

HAYKHNAYBANK (SAVINGS BANK)
EXECUTIVE DIRECTOR: HARUTYUN GHAZARYAN
46 NALBANDYAN STREET
YEREVAN-10
TEL: (374-2) 580-451
FAX: (374-2) 565-578
E-MAIL: AUTO@ISB.INFOCOM.AMILINK.NET

HSBC ARMENIA BANK
MANAGING DIRECTOR: GUY HARVEY-SAMUEL
2 KHORHRDARANI STREET
YEREVAN-10
TEL: (374-2) 587-095
FAX: (374-2) 151-858
E-MAIL: HSBC@ARMINCO.COM

INECOBANK
CHAIRMAN: AVETIS BALOYAN
17 TUMANYAN STREET
YEREVAN-1
TEL: (374-2) 563-725
FAX: (374-2) 565-974
E-MAIL: INECO@ACC.AM

INTERINVEST BANK
EXECUTIVE DIRECTOR: ASHOT YERANOSYAN
45 KHORENATSU STREET
YEREVAN-18
TEL: (374-2) 551-612
FAX: (374-2) 559-055
E-MAIL: BSEVAN@ARMINCO.COM

INTERNATIONAL COMMERCIAL BLACK SEA BANK (ARMENIA)
DEPUTY DIRECTOR GENERAL: ATANASIUS PIATAS
6 DEGHATAN STREET
YEREVAN-10
TEL: (374-2) 520-432
FAX: (374-2) 151-877
E-MAIL: ICBSB@ARMINCO.COM

LENDBANK
EXECUTIVE DIRECTOR: ANUSHAVAN KHACHIKYAN
8 YERVAND KOCHAR STREET
YEREVAN-70
TEL: (374-2) 542-588
FAX: (374-3) 907-035
E-MAIL: LEND@MBOX.AMILINK.NET

MELLAT BANK
EXECUTIVE DIRECTOR: ISSA CHABOK
1 PAVSTOS BUZANDI STREET
YEREVAN-10
TEL: (374-2) 581-791
FAX: (374-2) 151-811
E-MAIL: MELLAT@INFOCOM.AM

MENATEP-YEREVAN BANK
CHAIRMAN: ARA KITBALYAN
19A KORYUNI STREET
YEREVAN-9
TEL: (374-2) 529-471
FAX: (374-2) 529-471
E-MAIL: YEREVAN@MENATEP.INFOCOM.AMILINK.NET

PROMETEUS BANK
CHAIRMAN: EMIL SOGHOMONYAN
19 HRACHYA KOCHAR STREET
YEREVAN-12
TEL: (374-2) 273-000, 273-100
FAX: (374-2) 274-818
E-MAIL: NUNM@FREENET.AM

RIA BANK
CHAIRMAN: HARUTYUN MARGARYAN
39 HANRAPETUTYAN STREET

YEREVAN-10
TEL: (374-2) 587-264
FAX: (374-3) 907-057
E-MAIL: RIA@AICS.AM

SHIRAKINVEST BANK
EXECUTIVE DIRECTOR: MESROP KARAPETYAN
7 GAREGIN HZHDEH STREET
GYUMRI-377500
TEL: (374-69) 34-883
FAX: (374-69) 36-214
E-MAIL: SHIB@SHIRAK.AM

TRUSTBANK
CHAIRMAN: TIGRAN ARAKELYAN
10 ARTSAKHI STREET
YEREVAN-5
TEL: (374-2) 447-098
FAX: (374-2) 449-156
E-MAIL: TRUST@ARMINCO.COM

UNITED BANK
EXECUTIVE DIRECTOR: HOVSEP GALSTYAN
4 MOSKOVYAN LANE
YEREVAN-2
TEL: (374-2) 536-905
FAX: (374-3) 906-955
E-MAIL: UBANK@ARM.R.AM
HTTP://WWW.UBANK.AM

INTERNATIONAL FINANCIAL INSTITUTIONS

CAUCASUS ADVISORS LLC (MANAGER OF THE CAUCASUS FUND, FINANCED IN PART BY OPIC)
ARTAK MELKONIAN, MANAGING DIRECTOR OF ARMENIAN OPERATIONS
8 HANRAPETUTIAN STREET
YEREVAN-10
TEL: (374-2) 560-954, 587-418
FAX: (374-2) 587-418
E-MAIL: AMELKON@ACC.AM

EUROPEAN BANK FOR RECONSTRUCTION AND DEVELOPMENT
ALKIS DRAKINOS, HEAD OF YEREVAN RESIDENT OFFICE
ADDRESS: 20 BAGRAMYAN AVE.
YEREVAN-19
TEL.: (374-2) 540-425, 540-426, 540-427, 540-428
FAX: (374-2) 540-430
E-MAIL: DRAKINOA@EVN.EBRD.COM

INTERNATIONAL FINANCE CORPORATION
IRINA NIEDERBERGER, HEAD OF ARMENIA OFFICE

ADDRESS: 2 KHORHERTARANI STREET
REPUBLIC SQUARE
YEREVAN-10
TEL: (374-2) 599-546, 599-545, 599-543
FAX: (374-2) 599-544
E-MAIL: INIEDERBERGER@IFC.ORG

EURASIA FOUNDATION
EUGENE STAPLES, ACTING REGIONAL DIRECTOR
ADDRESS: 22 ISAHAKIAN STREET SUITE 11
YEREVAN-9
TEL: (374-2) 585-598, 566-789, 565-147, 561-626, 151-824
FAX: (374-2) 151-824, 585-598
E-MAIL: EURASIA@EURASIA.AM

WORLD BANK
OWAISE SAADAT, RESIDENT REPRESENTATIVE
ADDRESS: 2 KHORHERTARANI STREET
REPUBLIC SQUARE
YEREVAN-10
TEL: (374-2) 505-060, 520-992, 523-992
FAX: (374-2) 151-883, 151-788
ABUNIATYAN@WORLDBANK.ORG

SHOREBANK ADVISORY SERVICES (SHORE OVERSEAS CORPORATION)
JENNIFER O'NEIL, COUNTRY MANAGER
15 PARPETSU STREET SUITE 3
YEREVAN-10
TEL: (374-2) 537-310, 537-360
FAX: (374-2) 151-806
E-MAIL: SAFARM@ARMINCO.COM
JONSAF@ARMINCO.COM

IMF RESIDENT REPRESENTATIVE OFFICE
GEORGE ANAYOTOS, RESIDENT REPRESENTATIVE
1 MELIK-ADAMYAN STREET SUITE 326
YEREVAN-10
TEL: (374-2) 528-532, 528-960
FAX: (374-2) 151-703
E-MAIL: GANAY@ARMINCO.COM

KEY CONTACTS

UNION OF BANKS OF ARMENIA
CHAIRMAN: ARMEN YEGHIAZARYAN
19A KORYUNI STREET
YERAVAN-9
TEL: (374-2) 527-731
FAX: (374-2) 567-589
E-MAIL: ABA@ARMINCO.COM

CENTRAL BANK OF ARMENIA
CHAIRMAN: TIGRAN SARGSYAN
6 NALBANDYAN STREET
YEREVAN-10
TEL: (374-2) 583-841
FAX: (374-2) 580-052
E-MAIL: INFO@CBA.AM
HTTP://WWW.CBA.AM

MINISTRY OF FINANCE AND ECONOMY
MINISTER: LEVON BARKHUDARYAN
1 MELIK-ADAMYAN STREET
YEREVAN-10
TEL: (374-2) 595-304
FAX: (374-2) 524-282 OR 151-069
E-MAIL: STAFF@MF.GOV.AM

AMERICAN EMBASSY, YEREVAN
COMMERCIAL SECTION
18 BAGHRAMIAN AVE.
YEREVAN-19
TEL: (374-2) 151-551
FAX: (374-2) 151-550
E-MAIL: ISAYANGX@YEREVANB.US-STATE.GOV
HTTP://WWW.ARMINCO.COM/EMBUSA/COMMERCIAL/FRAME.HTM
CONTACT: GEORGE ISAYAN, BISNIS REPRESENTATIVE IN ARMENIA

KEY CUSTOMS CONTACTS AND CERTIFICATION AGENCIES IN ARMENIA

THE CENTRAL CUSTOMS BODY IN ARMENIA IS THE DEPARTMENT OF CUSTOMS, WHICH BECAME A PART OF THE MINISTRY OF STATE REVENUES OF ARMENIA IN JULY 1999. THE TERRITORY OF ARMENIA IS DIVIDED INTO FOUR CUSTOMS REGIONS. IT INCLUDES FOUR REGIONAL CUSTOMS OFFICES AND 11 CUSTOMS POSTS.

CUSTOMS DEPARTMENT OF THE MINISTRY OF STATE REVENUES CONTACT: SUREN ADAMYAN, HEAD OF FOREIGN RELATIONS DEPARTMENT
3 MOVSES KHORENATSI STREET
YEREVAN-15
TEL: (374-1) 538-192
FAX: (374-1) 537-125

ARARAT REGIONAL CUSTOMS OFFICE
10 ISAKOV AVENUE
YEREVAN-82
TEL: (374-1) 545-300
FAX: (374-1) 541-090

GUGARK REGIONAL CUSTOMS OFFICE

44 MOSKOVYAN STREET
VANADZOR-377200
LORI PROVINCE
TEL: (374-1) 288-637
FAX: (374-1) 537-125

SHIRAK REGIONAL CUSTOMS OFFICE
3 TBILISI HIGHWAY
GYUMRI-377500
SHIRAK PROVINCE
TEL: (374-1) 285-614
FAX: (374-1) 537-125

SYUNIK REGIONAL CUSTOMS OFFICE

SISIAN-YEREVAN HIGHWAY SIXTH KILOMETER
SISIAN-378010
SYUNIK PROVINCE
TEL: (374-1) 285-826
FAX: (374-1) 537-125

LIST OF MAJOR CUSTOMS POSTS

BAGRATASHEN CUSTOMS POST (ARMENIAN-GEORGIAN BORDER)
TEL: (374-66) 21-980
FAX: (374-1) 537-125

AYRUM CUSTOMS POST (ARMENIAN-GEORGIAN BORDER, RESPONSIBLE FOR RAILROAD
TRANSPORTATION ONLY)
TEL: (374-66) 21-980
FAX: (374-1) 537-125

MEGHRI CUSTOMS POST (ARMENIAN-IRANIAN BORDER)
TEL: (374-2) 285-452
FAX: (374-1) 537-125

YEREVAN-ZVARTNOTS INTERNATIONAL AIRPORT CUSTOMS POST
TEL: (374-1) 593-566
FAX: (374-1) 541-090

LIST OF CERTIFICATION AGENCIES

DEPARTMENT OF STANDARDIZATION, CERTIFICATION AND METROLOGY OF ARMENIA
BORIS SAHAKYAN, HEAD OF FOREIGN RELATIONS DEPARTMENT
49/2 KOMITAS AVE.
YEREVAN-51
TEL: (374-1) 234-375
FAX: (374-1) 285-620
E-MAIL: SARM@SARM.AM

NATIONAL INSTITUTE OF STANDARDS
MELKON GASPARYAN, DIRECTOR
49/2 KOMITAS AVE.
YEREVAN-51
TEL: (374-1) 235-623
FAX: (374-1) 285-620
E-MAIL: GASPARYAN@SARM.AM

YER-TEST - CENTER FOR TESTING AND CERTIFICATION
GURGEN AZATYAN, DIRECTOR
49/2 KOMITAS AVE.
YEREVAN-51
TEL: (374-1) 281-033
FAX: (374-1) 285-620
E-MAIL: AZATYAN@SARM.AM

METROLOG - CENTER FOR METROLOGY
VLADIMIR HAKOBYAN, DIRECTOR
49/2 KOMITAS AVE.
YEREVAN-51
TEL: (374-1) 234551
FAX: (374-1) 285-620
E-MAIL: SARM@SARM.AM

PAREN (CERTIFICATION OF FOOD PRODUCTS)
ROBERT SUKHUDYAN, DIRECTOR
4 GORVETKAYI STREET
YEREVAN-23
TEL/FAX: (374-1) 524-687

DRUG AND MEDICAL TECHNOLOGY AGENCY OF ARMENIA
DR. EMIL GABRIELIAN, DIRECTOR
15 MOSKOVYAN STREET
YEREVAN-1
TEL: (374-1) 585-235
FAX: (374-1) 151-697
E-MAIL: ADMIN@PHARM.AM

FOR ADDITIONAL INFORMATION PLEASE CONTACT
AMERICAN EMBASSY, YEREVAN
COMMERCIAL SECTION
18 BAGHRAMIAN AVE.
YEREVAN-19 ARMENIA
TEL: (374-1) 151-551
FAX: (374-1) 151-550
E-MAIL: ISAYANGX@STATE.GOV
http://WWW.ARMINCO.COM/EMBUSA/COMMERCIAL/FRAME.HTM

ENERGY SECTOR CONTACTS

GOVERNMENT ENTITIES

MINISTRY OF ENERGY
2ND GOVERNMENT BUILDING
YEREVAN-10
TEL: (374-1) 521-964
FAX: (374-1) 521-964
CONTACT: KAREN GALUSTYAN, MINISTER

ENERGY COMMISSION
18 ISAHAKYAN STREET
YEREVAN-25
TEL: (374-1) 592-544
FAX: (374-1) 525-563
E-MAIL: ECA@ARMINCO.COM
CONTACT: VARDAN MOVSISYAN, CHAIRMAN

ENERGY AND NATURAL GAS SUPPLIERS

ARMENERGO STATE CLOSED JOINT STOCK COMPANY
27 ABOVYAN STREET
YEREVAN-09
TEL: (374-1) 151-721, 521-781, OR 592-231
FAX: (374-1) 151-721 OR 521-781
E-MAIL: PROJECT@PROJECT.R.AM
CONTACT: KAREN KARAPETYAN, GENERAL DIRECTOR
TRANSMISSION OF ELECTRICITY, AS WELL AS DESIGN AND CONSTRUCTION OF POWER PLANTS, AND PRODUCTION OF RELAY DEVICES FOR PROTECTION OF ELECTRIC CABLES

ARMROSGASPROM ARMENIAN-RUSSIAN JV
43 TBILISYAN KHECHUGHI
YEREVAN-94
TEL: (374-1) 286-531
FAX: (374-1) 286-462
CONTACT: ROLAND ADONTS, EXECUTIVE DIRECTOR

POWER GENERATING EQUIPMENT SUPPLIERS

ARM ITERA ENERGY ARMENIAN-AMERICAN JV
5 PARUIR SEVAKI STREET
YEREVAN-44
TEL: (374-1) 281-660
FAX: (374-1) 288-954
CONTACT: VAHE HARUTYUNYAN, GENERAL DIRECTOR

DVIN CONCERN STATE CLOSED JOINT STOCK COMPANY

67 ARSHAKUNYATS STREET
YEREVAN-61
TEL: (374-1) 442-674
FAX: (374-1) 442-674
E-MAIL: DVINCON@NETSYS.AM

RESEARCH & DEVELOPMENT

ARMENIAN RESEARCH INSTITUTE OF ENERGY
127 AMARANOTSAYIN STREET
YEREVAN-47
TEL: (374-1) 655-449
FAX: (374-1) 151-697
CONTACT: TIGRAN GNUNI, DIRECTOR
PRIMARY INTEREST - CONTROL OF ENERGY SYSTEMS; DEVELOPMENT OF STRATEGIC POLICY AND POWER SAVING MEASURES IN THE ENERGY SECTOR; DEVELOPMENT OF ENERGY
STANDARDS

ARMENRGOSETPROYEKT (ELECTRICITY TRANSMISSION/DISTRIBUTION - RESEARCH/DESIGN)
129 AMARANOTSAYIN STREET
YEREVAN-47
TEL: (374-1) 650-987
FAX: (374-1) 286-531
CONTACT: YURI AVAKYAN, DIRECTOR
DEVELOPMENT/PRODUCTION OF ELECTRICITY CONTROL AND MEASUREMENT DEVICES. AS
WELL AS AUTOMATED MANAGEMENT SYSTEMS FOR ELECTRICITY TRANSMISSION AND DISTRIBUTION SECTOR

ARMHYDROENERGOPROYEKT INSTITUTE
33A MOSKOVYAN STREET
YEREVAN-02
TEL: (374-1) 532-312
FAX: (374-1) 286-531
CONTACT: ARMEN GRIGORYAN, DIRECTOR
DESIGN OF HYDRO-POWER PLANTS

INTERNATIONAL ORGANIZATIONS

ENERGINVEST
ELECTRICITY TRANSMISSION AND DISTRIBUTION PROJECT
(ETDP) PROJECT IMPLEMENTATION OFFICE
67 HANRAPETUTYAN STREET
YEREVAN-10
TEL: (374-1) 592-648
FAX: (374-1) 151-809, 523-372
CONTACT: RUBEN HOVHANNISYAN, DIRECTOR
IMPLEMENTATION OFFICE FOR THE ETDP - FUNDED BY THE WORLD BANK/JAPANESE GOVERNMENT

EUROPEAN BANK FOR RECONSTRUCTION AND DEVELOPMENT
20 BAGHRAMYAN AVE.
YEREVAN-19
TEL.: (374-2) 540-425, 540-426, 540-427, 540-428
FAX: (374-2) 540-430
E-MAIL: RO-YEREVAN@EBRD.COM

U.S. AGENCY FOR INTERNATIONAL DEVELOPMENT
MISSION TO ARMENIA
18 BAGHRAMYAN AVE
YEREVAN-19
TEL: (374-1) 569-656
FAX: (374-1) 151-131
E-MAIL: BPRIMM@USAID.GOV
CONTACT: BARRY PRIMM, HEAD OF ECONOMIC RESTRUCTURING AND ENERGY OFFICE

WORLD BANK
2 KHORHERTARANI STREET
REPUBLIC SQUARE
YEREVAN-10
TEL: (374-2) 505-060, 520-992, 523-992
FAX: (374-2) 151-883, 151-788
ABUNIATYAN@WORLDBANK.ORG
CONTACT: OWAISE SAADAT, RESIDENT REPRESENTATIVE

LARGEST OIL PRODUCT IMPORTERS AND DISTRIBUTORS

ARAX CONTRACT
40 TIGRAN METSI STREET
YEREVAN-5
TEL: (374-1) 567-043
FAX: (374-1) 582-043
CONTACT: EDUARD SARKISYAN, DIRECTOR

FLASH
30 YEZNIK KOGHBATSU STREET
YEREVAN-2
TEL: (374-1) 582-884
FAX: (374-1) 582-884
E-MAIL: FLASHARM@FREENET.AM
WEB SITE: HTTP://WWW.FLASH.AM
CONTACT: BARSEGH BEGLARYAN, PRESIDENT

MIKA LIMITED
4 TERYAN STREET
YEREVAN-10
TEL: (374-1) 523-370
FAX: (374-1) 562-459
CONTACT: MIKHAYIL BAGDASAROV, PRESIDENT

VYAK
NOR GHYUGH VILLAGE
KOTAYK PROVINCE
TEL: (374-22) 25-285
FAX: (374-22) 26-693
E-MAIL: VYAK@ARMINCO.COM
CONTACT: SUREN MKHITARYAN, EXECUTIVE DIRECTOR

FOR ADDITIONAL INFORMATION PLEASE CONTACT
AMERICAN EMBASSY, YEREVAN
COMMERCIAL SECTION
18 BAGHRAMIAN AVE.
YEREVAN-19
TEL: (374-1) 151-551
FAX: (374-1) 151-550
EMAIL: ISAYANGX@YEREVANB.US-STATE.GOV
HTTP://WWW.ARMINCO.COM/EMBUSA/COMMERCIAL/MAIN.HTM

FOOD PROCESSING

GOVERNMENT ENTITIES

MINISTRY OF AGRICULTURE OF ARMENIA
2 GOVERNMENT BUILDING
REPUBLIC SQUARE
YEREVAN-10
TEL: (374-1) 520-641
FAX: (374-1) 523-793
CONTACT: ZAVEN GEVORGYAN, MINISTER

AGRIBUSINESS DEVELOPMENT CENTER
12 VAGHARSHIAN STREET
YEREVAN-12 ARMENIA
TEL: (374-1) 505-995
FAX: (374-1) 277-647
EMAIL: ADC@MBOX.AMILINK.NET
CONTACT: ARMEN DAVTYAN, DIRECTOR

INDUSTRY ASSOCIATIONS

AGRARIAN-PEASANT UNION OF ARMENIA
13A VARDANANTS STREET
YEREVAN-10
TEL: (374-1) 542-121
FAX: (374-1) 542-121
CONTACT: HRACHYA BERBERYAN, EXECUTIVE DIRECTOR

ARMENIAN WINE-PRODUCERS UNION
42/55 YEZNIK KOGHBATSU STREET
YEREVAN-02
TEL: (374-1) 537-259
FAX: (374-1) 537-259

CONTACT: AVAG HARUTYUNYAN, PRESIDENT

ARMENIAN FARMERS ASSOCIATION
43A PUSHKIN STREET
SUITE 30A
YEREVAN-02
TEL: (374-1) 538-053
FAX: (374-1) 538-053
CONTACT: HAYKUHU LAMBARYAN, PRESIDENT

INTERNATIONAL DEVELOPMENT ORGANIZATIONS

ACDI/VOCA (VOLUNTEERS IN OVERSEAS COOPERATIVE
ASSISTANCE)
39 TUMANYAN STREET
YEREVAN-02
TEL: (374-1) 531-253
FAX: (374-1) 151-124
EMAIL: VOCA@ARMINCO.COM
CONTACT: ARTASHES GHANDILYAN, DIRECTOR

U.S. DEPARTMENT OF AGRICULTURE'S MARKETING ASSISTANCE
PROJECT
74 TERYAN STREET
YEREVAN-09
TEL: (374-1) 525-562
FAX: (374-1) 151-696
EMAIL: MAP@USDA.AM
WEB SITE: WWW.USDA.AM
CONTACT: CRAIG INFANGER, PROJECT COORDINATOR AND DIRECTOR

FOOD PROCESSING COMPANIES

1) CANNERIES AND FRUIT JUICE PRODUCERS

ARTASHAT CANNERY
AUGUST 23RD STREET
ARTASHAT
ARARAT PROVINCE
TEL: (374-35) 26-275
FAX: (374-35) 21-308
CONTACT: SERGO KARAPETYAN, PRESIDENT

ARTASHES CANNERY
VILLAGE OF DZORAGHPYUR
KOTAYK PROVINCE
TEL: (374-1) 644-710 OR (374-9) 403-123
FAX: (374-1) 644-710
CONTACT: ARTASHES GASPARYAN, PRESIDENT

EUROTERM
15A AMIRYAN STREET

YEREVAN-02
TEL: (374-1) 538-445
FAX: (374-1) 537-571
EMAIL: EUROTERM@ACC.AM
CONTACT: ARMEN ARSENYAN, DIRECTOR

MAP JSC (WINERY AND CANNERY)
LENUGHI VILLAGE
ARMAVIR PROVINCE
TEL: (374-1) 581-405
FAX: (374-37) 66-219
CONTACT: ALEXAN PETROSYAN

MEGHRI CANNERY
26 GORTSARANAYIN STREET
MEGHRI
SYUNIK PROVINCE
TEL: (374-860) 34-60
FAX: (374-860) 34-60
CONTACT: GRISHA GRIGORYAN

SARDARAPAT-ARMAVIR CANNERY
OFFICE IN YEREVAN
11A KTYEVYAN STREET
YEREVAN-19
TEL: (374-1) 227-065
FAX: (374-1) 521-871
EMAIL: SARDARAPAT@TPA.AM
CONTACT: ASHOT ADULYAN, DIRECTOR

2) DAIRIES, INCLUDING ICE-CREAM PRODUCERS

ASHTARAK-KAT JSC
6 HRACHYA NERSISYAN STREET
YEREVAN-14
TEL: (374-1) 287-261
FAX: (374-1) 285-912
EMAIL: ASHKAT@ACC.AM
CONTACT: ASHOT APOYAN, DIRECTOR

SHANT PLUS
12 LENINAKANI STREET
YEREVAN-12
TEL: (374-1) 350-777
FAX: (374-96) 06-561
EMAIL: SHANT@LX2.YERPHI.AM
WEB SITE: WWW.SHANT.AM
CONTACT: MANVEL GHARIBYAN, DIRECTOR

TAMARA
1 NAIRI STREET
CITY OF ABOVIAN
KOTAYK PROVINCE

TEL: (374-1) 281-624
FAX: (374-22) 36-606
EMAIL: TAMBOR@ARMINCO.COM
CONTACT: BORIS OGANESYAN, PRESIDENT

3) CHEESE PRODUCERS

AMASIA CHEESE FACTORY
TOWN OF AMASIA
SHIRAK PROVINCE
TEL/FAX: (374-460) 35-756
CONTACT: NORAYR SHABOYAN, OIRECTOR

ASHOTSK CHEESE FACTORY
MAYISYAN VILLAGE
ASHOTSK REGION
SHIRAK PROVINCE
TEL/FAX: (374-1) 727-031
CONTACT: GEORGI BAGHDASARYAN, DIRECTOR

DUSTER MELANYA FAMILY ENTERPRISE
346 KIROV STREET
TOWN OF TASHIR
LORI PROVINCE
ARMENIA
TEL/FAX: (374-54) 21-594
CONTACT: RUBEN HARUTYUNYAN, OWNER

STEPANAVAN LIPO CHEESE FACTORY
1 YERITASARDUTSIAN STREET
TOWN OF STEPANAVAN
LORI PROVINCE
TEL/FAX: (374-56) 22-244
CONTACT: ARARAT DOKHOLYAN, EXECUTIVE DIRECTOR

4) WINE PRODUCERS

ARARAT COGNAC-WINE-VODKA COMPANY
9 ADMIRAL ISAKOV AVENUE
YEREVAN-10
PHONE: (374-1) 525-810, (374-9) 407-035 (CELL PHONE)
FAX: (374-1) 525-810
EMAIL: ZAVENIN@CS.COM
CONTACT: ZAVEN GUIRAGOSSIAN, CEO, GENERAL DIRECTOR

ARENI JSC
ARENI VILLAGE
VAYOTS DZOR PROVINCE
TEL: (374-1) 560-014
FAX: (374-1) 151-696
CONTACT: RAFAYEL SIMONYAN, OIRECTOR

GINETAS

39 LEVONYAN STREET
YEGHEGNADZOR
VAYOTS DZOR PROVINCE
TEL: (374-1) 560-014
FAX: (374-1) 151-696
CONTACT: VAROAN KHALATYAN, DIRECTOR

GREAT ARARAT
4 MOVSES KHORENATSU STREET
YEREVAN-15
TEL: (374-1) 522-172
FAX: (374-1) 522-172
EMAIL: GREATVALLEY@INFOCOM.AM
CONTACT: TIGRAN ARZAKANTSYAN, PRESIDENT

IJEVAN WINERY JSC
9 YEREVANYAN STREET
IJEVAN
TAVUSH PROVINCE
TEL/FAX: (374-1) 225-429, (374-63) 33-953
FAX: (374-63) 34-233
CONTACT: AVETIS GALSTYAN, PRESIDENT

KIMLEY
ARENI VILLAGE
VAYOTS DZOR PROVINCE
TEL: (374-1) 560-014
FAX: (374-1) 151-696
CONTACT: MIKAYEL GRIGORYAN, DIRECTOR

TAPERAKAN VILLAGE
ARARAT PROVINCE
TEL: (374-1) 560-014
FAX: (374-1) 151-696
CONTACT: MIHRAN MANASERYAN, DIRECTOR

VEDI-ALKO
VEDI VILLAGE
ARARAT PROVINCE
TEL: (374-34) 23-111, 24-843
FAX: (374-1) 288-020 OR (374-34) 23-192
CONTACT: MANVEL GHAZARYAN, PRESIDENT

YEREVAN BRANDY FACTORY
2 TSOVAKAL ISAKOVI AVENUE
YEREVAN-82
TEL: (374-1) 540-000
FAX: (374-1) 151-298
CONTACT: PIERRE LARRETCHE, PRESIDENT AND GENERAL DIRECTOR

5) MINERAL WATER BOTTLERS

BJNI JSC

8 GORTSARANAYIN STREET
CHARENTSAVAN
KOTAYK PROVINCE
TEL: (374-26) 43-600
FAX: (374-26) 43-600
EMAIL: SIL@ARMINCO.COM
WEB SITE: WWW.SIL.AM
CONTACT: VAGHINAK POGHOSYAN, EXECUTIVE DIRECTOR

COCA-COLA BOTTLERS ARMENIA
3RD LANE AZATUTYAN
YEREVAN-52
TEL: (374-1) 280-552
FAX: (374-1) 151-434
EMAIL: RECEPTION@ARMINCO.COM
CONTACT: ANGELOS RORIS, MANAGING DIRECTOR

JERMUK JSC
I GORTSARANAYIN STREET
TOWN OF JERMUK
VAYOTS DZOR PROVINCE
TEL: (374-87) 21-117
FAX: (374-87) 21-119
CONTACT: ARMEN TER-STEPANAYAN, EXECUTIVE DIRECTOR

JERMUK GROUP
18 ARSHAKUNYATS STREET
YEREVAN-23
TEL: (374-87) 21-221
FAX: (374-87) 21648
CONTACT: ANASTASTAS ARSENYAN, EXECUTIVE OIRECTOR

6) BREWERIES

ABOVIAN BREWERY
10 ABOVIAN STREET
TOWN OF ABOVIAN
KOTAYK PROVINCE
TEL: (374-1) 285-293
FAX: (374-1) 151-220
CONTACT: GABRIYEL ZAKARYAN, EXECUTIVE DIRECTOR

YEREVAN BREWERY
8 TSOVAKAL ISAKOVI AVENUE
YEREVAN-82
TEL: (374-1) 583-654 OR (374-1) 541-238
FAX: (374-1) 583-654
CONTACT: ASHOT BAGHDASARYAN, GENERAL MANAGER

7) MEAT PROCESSING COMPANIES

ATENK
59A TSARAV AGHPYURI STREET
YEREVAN-52

TEL: (374-1) 629-100
FAX: (374-1) 151-377
CONTACT: ARAMAYIS BILYAN, OIRECTOR

BARI SAMARATSI
22-NO STREET OF NOR ARESH
#117
YEREVAN-20
TEL: (374-1) 474-794
FAX: (374-1) 458-015
CONTACT: HOVHANNES HOVAKIMYAN, DIRECTOR

ETALON G.A.M.A.
1/3 PAVSTOS BYUZAND STREET
YEREVAN-10
TEL: (374-1) 521-280
FAX: (374-1) 589-626
EMAIL: ETALON@NETSYS.COM
CONTACT: ARSEN GALSTYAN, PRESIDENT

GEGHARD
JRVEZH VILLAGE
KOTAYK PROVINCE
TEL: (374-1) 634-849
FAX: (374-1) 151-165
CONTACT: ALBERT VARDANYAN, DIRECTOR

8) POULTRY PRODUCTION

JRARAT POULTRY FACTORY
ECHMIADZIN REGION
ARMAVIR PROVINCE
TEL: (374-9) 404-274 OR (374-1) 271-400
FAX: (374-1) 271-400
CONTACT: MYASNIK GRIGORYAN, PRESIDENT

LUSAKERT POULTRY FACTORY JSC
NOR GEGHI VILLAGE
KOTAYK PROVINCE
TEL: (374-1) 280-821
FAX: (374-1) 258-665 OR 542-465
EMAIL: LUSAKERT@INFOCOM.AM
CONTACT: MHER BAGRATYAN, PRESIDENT

YEREVAN POULTRY FACTORY JSC
45 SHIRAKI STREET
YEREVAN-86
TEL: (374-1) 548-877 OR 467-636
FAX: (374-2) 467-515
EMAIL: ERPOUL@ARMINCO.COM
CONTACT: AVETIS AVETISYAN, DIRECTOR

9) CONFECTIONERY PRODUCTION

GRAND CANDY ARMENIAN-RUSSIAN JV
31 MASISI STREET
YEREVAN-61
TEL: (374-1) 446-373
FAX: (374-1) 445-633
EMAIL: GCANDY@ARMINCO.COM
CONTACT: ARMINE HOVHANNISYAN, EXECUTIVE DIRECTOR

MAJOR PC HARDWARE VENDORS AND INTERNET SERVICE PROVIDERS

MAJOR PC HARDWARE VENDORS

BI-LINE
50 KHANJIAN STREET,
YEREVAN-1, ARMENIA
TEL: (374-2) 578-825
FAX: (374-3) 907-077
E-MAIL: INFO@BI-LINE.AM
URL: HTTP://WWW.BI-LINE.AM
CONTACT: ARTAK ZAKARYAN, DIRECTOR

UNICOMP
33 SAYAT-NOVA STREET,
YEREVAN-1, ARMENIA
TEL: (374-2) 541-474
FAX: (374-2) 541-474
E-MAIL: UNICOM@ARMINCO.COM
CONTACT: ARMEN BALDRYAN, DIRECTOR

NOVA
24B BAGHRAMYAN AVE.,
YEREVAN-19, ARMENIA
TEL: (374-2) 584-441
FAX: (374-2) 568-508
E-MAIL: ASHOT@NOVA.AM
URL: HTTP://WWW.NOVA.AM
CONTACT: VARUZHAN MELIKYAN, DIRECTOR

ARES COMPUTERS
23 SAYAT-NOVA STREET,
YEREVAN-1, ARMENIA
TEL: (374-2) 561-104
FAX: (374-2) 584-476
E-MAIL: GTGGTG@ARMINCO.COM
URL: HTTP://WWW.ARES.AM
CONTACT: KARINE STEPANYAN, DIRECTOR

KHARTIYA

HANRAPETUTYAN SQUARE, UNIONS BUILDING,
YEREVAN-10, ARMENIA
TEL: (374-2) 561-425
FAX: (374-2) 561-425
E-MAIL: XARTIA@XAR.AM
URL: HTTP://WWW.XAR.AM
CONTACT: HRACHYA ABOVYAN, PRESIDENT

MIGMA
15 SAYAT-NOVA STREET,
YEREVAN-1, ARMENIA
TEL: (374-2) 564-849
FAX: (374-2) 521-356
E-MAIL: MIGMACOMP@HOTMAIL.COM
CONTACT: GRIGOR BARSEGYAN, DIRECTOR

VALLEX
9 NALBANDYAN STREET,
YEREVAN-10, ARMENIA
TEL: (374-2) 560-900
FAX: (374-2) 526-690
E-MAIL: VALLEX@VALLEX.AM

COMPUSYS
3 BAGHRAMYAN AVE.,
YEREVAN-19, ARMENIA
TEL: (374-2) 563-081
FAX: (374-2) 563-081
E-MAIL: ARMINE@FLAVIUS.ARMINCO.COM
CONTACT: MHER TOVMASYAN, DIRECTOR

COMPUTER-SERVICE
1 CHARENTS STREET
YEREVAN-25, ARMENIA
TEL: (374-2) 575-137
FAX: 9374-2) 151-668
E-MAIL: COMPS@ARMINCO.COM

LANS
49 KOMITAS AVE.,
YEREVAN-51, ARMENIA
TEL: (374-2) 230-510
FAX: (374-2) 282-951
E-MAIL: LANS@LANS.AM
URL: HTTP://WWW.LANS.AM
CONTACT: ARSHAVIR GYULKHASYAN, DIRECTOR

FINE
18 TUMANYAN STREET,
YEREVAN-1, ARMENIA
TEL: (374-2) 568-178

FAX: (374-2) 568-178
E-MAIL: FINE@FREENET.AM
CONTACT: HAIK HAYRAPETYAN, DIRECTOR

CIT
6/1 ABELYAN STREET,
YEREVAN-38, ARMENIA
TEL: (374-2) 350-390
FAX: (374-2) 351-230
E-MAIL: CIT@CIT.AM
URL:HTTP://WWW.CIT.AM
CONTACT: GAGIK KARAPETYAN, DIRECTOR

MAJOR INTERNET SERVICE PROVIDERS IN ARMENIA

ARMINCO
28 ISAHAKYAN STREET,
YEREVAN-9, ARMENIA
TEL: (374-2) 563-674
FAX: (374-2) 285-082
E-MAIL: POSTMASTER@ARMINCO.COM
HTTP://WWW.ARMINCO.COM
CONTACT: ANDRANIK ALEXANYAN, MANAGING DIRECTOR

ARMCOMPUTER CENTER
28 NALBANDYAN STREET,
YEREVAN-10, ARMENIA
TEL: (374-2) 569-702
FAX: (374-2) 569-701
E-MAIL: ADMIN@ACC.AM
HTTP://WWW.ACC.AM
CONTACT: VAHRAM MKHITARYAN, MANAGING DIRECTOR

INFOCOM
22 SARYAN STREET,
YEREVAN-2, ARMENIA
TEL: (374-2) 531-039
FAX: (374-2) 528-856
E-MAIL: BIT@MBOX.AMILINK.NET
HTTP://WWW-ANI.AMILINK.NET
CONTACT: ARTAK GABRIYELYAN, PRESIDENT

KEY CONTACTS

MINISTRY OF TRANSPORTATION AND COMMUNICATIONS
ADDRESS: 10 ZAKYAN STREET, YEREVAN-375015, ARMENIA
TEL: (374-2) 563-391
FAX: (374-2) 523-200
CONTACT: GAGIK GRIGORYAN, HEAD OF FOREIGN RELATIONS DEPARTMENT

ARMENIA TELEPHONE COMPANY (ARMENTEL)
ADDRESS: 22 SARYAN STREET,
YEREVAN-02, ARMENIA
TEL: (374-2) 549-100
FAX: (374-2) 151-001
CONTACT: IOANIS LAMBRIANOS, EXECUTIVE DIRECTOR
(NOTE: THIS GREEK OWNED CLOSED JOINT STOCK COMPANY HAS A MONOPOLY ON ALL WIRE TELECOMMUNICATIONS INCLUDING INTERNET CHANNELS.)

AMERICAN EMBASSY, YEREVAN
COMMERCIAL SECTION
18 BAGHRAMIAN AVE.
YEREVAN
TEL: (374-2) 151-551
FAX: (374-2) 151-550
E-MAIL: ISAYANGX@YEREVANB.US-STATE.GOV
HTTP://WWW.ARMINCO.COM/EMBUSA/COMMERCIAL/FRAME.HTM
CONTACT: GEORGE ISAYAN, BISNIS REPRESENTATIVE IN ARMENIA

U.S.- OWNED SOFTWARE DEVELOPMENT COMPANIES

BOOMERANG SOFTWARE
CONTACT: GURGEN BALYAN, DIRECTOR
ADDRESS: 6/1 ABELYAN STREET, 5TH FLOOR, YEREVAN-38
PHONE/FAX: (374-1) 350-570, 350-488
E-MAIL: OFFICE@BS.AM

BRIENCE
CONTACT: HOVHANNES AVOYAN, DIRECTOR
ADDRESS: 9 ALEK MANUKYAN STREET, YEREVAN-70
PHONE: (374-1) 512-045
FAX: (374-1) 512-112
E-MAIL: HAVOYAN@AM.BRIENCE.COM

CREDENCE SYSTEMS ARMENIA LLC
CONTACT: MANUK GEVORGYAN, DIRECTOR
ADDRESS: 48 MAMIKONYANTS STREET, YEREVAN-51
PHONE: (374-1) 530-433, 530622
FAX: (510) 217-9448
E-MAIL: MANUK_GEVORGYAN@CREDENCE.AM

EPSILON LOGIC
CONTACT: NAZIK KHUDAVERDYAN, DIRECTOR
ADDRESS: 4 TIGRAN METSI STREET, YEREVAN-10
PHONE/FAX: (374-1) 587-740, 587-710, 586-775
E-MAIL: NAZIK@E-LOGIC.COM

EPYGI LABS AM LLC
CONTACT: HAROUTUN AKILIAN, DIRECTOR
ADDRESS: 41 ARASHAKUNIANTS STREET, YEREVAN - 26

PHONE: (374-1) 442-160, (374-9) 403-799
FAX: (374-1) 442-155
WEBSITE: WWW.EPYGI.COM

HAILINK
CONTACT: GAGIK EVOYAN, DIRECTOR
ADDRESS: 24A MARSHALL BAGRAMYAN AVE., YEREVAN-19
PHONE: (374-1) 521-664, 151-037
FAX: (374-1) 151-037
E-MAIL: GAGIKE@FOROF.SCI.AM

HI-TECH GATEWAY
CONTACT: HAKOB MANUCHARYAN, GENERAL MANAGER
ADDRESS: 1 CHARENTSI STREET, YEREVAN-25
PHONE: (374-1) 573-770, 576-253
FAX: (374-1) 573-770
E-MAIL: HAKOB@HI-TECK.COM

HPLA LLC
CONTACT: ANDRANIK HOVHANNISYAN, MANAGING DIRECTOR
ADDRESS: 49/3 KOMITAS STREET, FLOOR 9, YEREVAN-51
PHONE: (374-1) 238-550, 234-581, 238-309
FAX: (374-1) 151-974
E-MAIL: ANDREW@ARM.HPL.COM
WESITE: WWW.HPL.COM

INFINITE TECHNOLOGIES CORPORATION
CONTACT: KHOREN KOTANJYAN, DIRECTOR
ADDRESS: 54V KOMITAS AVE., YEREVAN-51
PHONE: (374-1) 234-889
E-MAIL: KHOREN@ITC.AM

LEDA SYSTEMS, INC. ARMENIAN BRANCH
CONTACT: HOVIK MUSAELYAN, GENERAL DIRECTOR
ADDRESS: 60 CHELYUSKINTSINERY STREET, YEREVAN-18
PHONE: (374-1) 540-169, 540-868
FAX: (374-1) 530-777
EMAIL: HMUSAYELYAN@FYS.WEB.AM
WEBSITE: WWW.LEDASYS.COM

MOSAIC AM
CONTACT: FELIX KARAPETYAN, DEPUTY DIRECTOR
ADDRESS: 37 ISRAYELYAN STREET, YEREVAN-15
PHONE: (374-1) 586-389
FAX: (374-1) 586-389
E-MAIL: OFFICE@MOSAIC.AM

SYNERGY INTERNATIONAL SYSTEMS
CONTACT: SERGEY ZIGELYAN, DIRECTOR
ADDRESS: 6 KORYUNY STREET, SUITE 4, YEREVAN-09
PHONE: (374-1) 567-681
FAX: (374-1) 567-681
E-MAIL: SZIGELYAN@ARM.SYNYS.COM

WEBSITE: WWW.SYNISYS.COM

VIRAGE LOGIC INTERNATIONAL YEREVAN
CONTACT: HAKOP TUVALYAN, DIRECTOR
ADDRESS: 12 VAGHARSHYAN STREET, YEREVAN-33
PHONE: (374-1) 271-580, 272-772
FAX: (374-1) 271-580
E-MAIL: NLUCY@VIRAGELOGIC.AM
WEBSITE: WWW.VIRAGELOGIC.COM

THIS REPORT WAS PREPARED BY GEORGE ISAYAN, BISNIS REPRESENTATIVE IN ARMENIA.

FOR ADDITIONAL INFORMATION PLEASE CONTACT
AMERICAN EMBASSY, YEREVAN
COMMERCIAL SECTION
18 BAGHRAMIAN AVE.
YEREVAN-19
TEL: (374-1) 151-551
FAX: (374-1) 151-550
E-MAIL: ISAYANGX@STATE.GOV OR GEORGE@USIS.AM
HTTP://WWW.ARMINCO.COM/EMBUSA

INTERNET

INTERNET CONNECTIVITY

Internet connectivity is offered by the following two main Internet providers through cable radio modem channels, or direct satellite connections.

Arminco Global Communications
A. Alexanian, CEO
26 Isahakian St., Yerevan-9, Armenia
Tel: (374-2) 526-326
Fax: (374-2) 285-082
Email: postmaster@ arminco.com
support@arminco.com
Website: http: //www. arminco.com

Infocom
A.Gabrielaian, CEO
22 Saryan St., Yerevan-2, Armenia
Tel: (374-2) 530-369
Fax; (374-2) 528-858
E-mail: postmaster@mtd.Armenia.su

NOTE:
Infocom has become part of the Greek-owned "Armenia Telephone Company" (Armentel), which holds an exclusive license for almost all types of fixed and mobile services in the territory of

Armenia. Armentel can be reached at 2 Aharonyan St., Floor 9, Yerevan-14, Armenia Tel: (374-2) 580-123
Fax: (374-2) 151-001

Lsoft
24 Pavstos Byuzand St., Yerevan, Armenia
Tel: (374-2) 564-517
Fax: (374-2) 151-441
e-mail: efanel@arminco.com
Contact: Larisa Lalayan, President
Software Products:
"LSbank" LAN based banking system for the Armenia central bank
"LS Minfin" LAN based database for the Armenian Treasury
"LS Finance" LAN based database for Armenian Airlines

CEDIT
Hovhannes Aboyan, Director
5 Hanrapetutian Bldg B, Floor 4, Yerevan-10, Armenia
Tel: (374-2) 529-432
Fax; (374-2) 151-548
E-mail: havoyan@www.cedit.amilink.net
Software Products:
JavaPro, a tool for financial trading system
Automated financial trading system
A system for trading, settlement, and analysys of currency, bonds, and other securities and futures traded on the Yerevan Stock Exchange

Migma
Grigor Barseghyan, Director
15 Sayat Nova Street, Yerevan, Armenia
Tel: (374-2) 564-849
Fax: (374-2) 521-356
Software Products:
Multimedia Programs

MAJOR ELECTRONICS COMPANY

MARS Plant (Stepan Demirchyan, Director)
111 Raffi St.
Yerevan, Armenia
Tel: (374-2) 738-323, 151-724
Govt. line: 50-44
Fax: (374-2) 732-636, 151-724
(production/assembly of electronic and electrical components/devices)

Transistor R&D Company - Ashtarak Plant (Aram Vardanyan, Director)
41 Arshakunyats Ave.
Yerevan 375026
Tel: (374-1) 405-617, (374-2)560188
Fax: (374-2)151-705. (production/assembly of electronic and electrical components/devices)

Radiophysics Measureement Institute -RMI (Dr. Paris Herouni, Director)
49/4 Komitas Ave., Yerevan-14, Armenia.

Tel: (374-2)234-990
Tel/fax: (374-2) 151-401
E-mail: herouni@sci.am. (laboratory research and production of electronic components and devices)

Ministry of Industry and Trade
Haik Gevorkian, Minister
5 Hanrapetutyan St., Yerevan-10
Tel:(374-2)538-082
Fax:(374-2)588-321, 151-081

INVESTMENT LEADS

Industry: Electronics
Company: Resistor

Resistor was founded in 1966 and privatized in 1996. The company specializes in manufacturing resistors. The company owns production facilities with 100,000 sq. ft., which include assembling units, metal processing units, and storage space. Before the collapse of the Soviet Union, the defense industry was the plant's main customer. In 1992, the company began developing a new client base. Currently, the company exports to several Russian electronic companies. Resistor employs 50 highly qualified engineers and support staff. All existing equipment is in good working condition. There is a research and development group affiliated with the plant that developed a number of innovative designs in the automotive and electrical engineering sectors.

Resistor seeks a U.S. partner to restructure existing production facilities to assemble and export U.S.- designed electronic devices. The company expects an American partner to supply modern technology and equipment and provide marketing assistance. Resistor will contribute its facilities, space, and highly qualified and inexpensive workforce.

Contact: Yuri Atayan, Executive Director
1 Karchikian Street
Echmiadzin, Armenia
Tel: +374-59-53-423
Fax: +374-59-54-501

Industry: Electronics
Company: Aghavni

SUPPLEMENTS

STARTING JULY 15, 2005, AT 00:00 HOURS ARMENIA'S AREA CODES WILL CHANGE. THE NEW AREA CODE FOR LAND LINES TO YEREVAN WILL BE 1. TO CALL YEREVAN FROM OVERSEAS, CALLERS MUST DIAL (374-1)+NUMBER. TO CALL CELLULAR PHONES FROM OVERSEAS, CALLERS MUST DIAL (374-9)+NUMBER.

ARMENIA LAWS AND REGULATIONS AFFECTING BUSINESS

06/27/01	Licensing Law
04/26/01	Law on the State Registration
01/01/01	Customs Code
12/05/00	Amendments to the Tax Law
12/05/00	Protection of Economic Competition
07/28/00	Securities Market Regulations
08/01/00	Law on Excise Tax
06/19/2005	Law on Procurement
05/31/2005	Law on Trademarks
01/12/2005	Law on Copyright and Neignboring Rigts
12/15/99	Law on Firm Names
11/09/99	Law On The Conformity Assessment Of Products And Services To Normative Requirements
04/14/99	Law on Property Registration
12/28/98	Law on Customs Fees
12/28/98	Law on Environmental Protection and Payments for Environmental Damage
12/15/98	Law on Customs Duties
09/01/98	Criminal Procedure Code
08/07/98	Civil Procedure Code
06/17/98	Law on Adopting a New Civil Code
05/19/98	Law on Accounting Records
05/05/98	Law on Arbitration and Arbitration Courts
03/18/98	Law on Tax Privileges for State Procurement, Clearing Shipments, and Goods and Services Provided Under Inter-Governmental Agreements

02/17/98	Law on Telecommunications
02/03/98	Law on Transportation
02/03/98	Law on Intellectual Property Protection for Microchip Technologies
02/03/98	Law on Tax Privileges for Energy Sector Enterprises
01/01/98	Law on Land Tax
12/27/97	Law on Property Tax
12/27/97	Law on State Duties
12/27/97	Law on Income Tax
12/10/97	Law on the Privatization and Denationalization of State Owned Enterprises and Unfinished Construction Projects (periodically amended)
11/27/97	Law on Profit Tax
07/19/97	Law on Duties
06/24/97	Law on Excise Tax
06/15/97	Law on Value Added Tax
06/10/97	Law on Brand Names
06/10/97	Law on Trademarks
05/27/97	Methodology Unification Law
05/27/97	Standardization and Certification Law
05/12/97	Law on Taxes
05/12/97	Law on Customs Duties
05/01/97	Law On The Bankruptcy And Financial Reorganization Of Legal Entities, Enterprises Lacking Legal Entity Status, And Entrepreneurs
11/19/96	Insurance Law
11/16/96	Law on Bank Secrecy
06/30/96	Law on Banks and Banking Activities
06/30/96	Law on the Central Bank
06/29/96	Bank Bankruptcy Law
06/11/96	Law on State Duties
05/13/96	Copyright Law
05/06/96	Joint Stock Company Law
04/30/96	Advertisement Law

11/15/95	Mortgage Law
06/15/95	Bankruptcy Law
05/19/95	Basic Principles for Retail Trade
07/31/94	Foreign Investment Law
06/17/94	Law on the Status of Foreign Citizens
04/27/94	Law on Land Tax
12/27/93	Individual Businessmen Law
09/08/93	Law on the Circulation of Securities
09/02/93	Law on the State Register of Enterprises
08/31/93	Law on Commodities Exchange
08/27/93	Customs Code
08/21/93	Law on Patents
06/29/93	Law on the Privatization of State and Public Housing Stock
03/02/93	Water Code
03/19/92	Lithosphere Code
03/14/92	Law on Enterprises and Entrepreneurial Activity
01/29/91	Land Code
10/31/90	Law on Ownership in the Republic of Armenia
01/22/90	Law on Farms and Collective Farms (amended 3/30/92)

ARMENIA: LEGAL AND BUSINESS CONSULTING COMPANIES

ARAX CONSULTING GROUP
A. POGHOSYAN, PRESIDENT
21 MASHTOTSI AVE., 4TH FLOOR
SUITE 34
TEL: +374 (1) 529-418, 564-013, 151-865
FAX: +374 (1) 529-418, 151-865
EMAIL: ARAX@ARMINCO.COM
WWW.ARMINCO.COM/HOMEPAGES/ARAX

ABG CONSULTING
A. GULKANYAN, DIRECTOR
22/4 MARSHAL BAGHRAMYAN AVE.
YEREVAN-19
TEL/FAX: +374 (1) 527-571
EMAIL: ABG@ARMINCO.COM

AMERIA
A. MKRTCHYAN, EXECUTIVE DIRECTOR
6-2 MARSHAL BAGHRAMYAN AVE.
YEREVAN-19
TEL: +374 (1) 524-040
FAX: +374 (1) 151-800
EMAIL: AMERIA@AMERIA.AM
WWW.AMERIA.AM

AMIOT EXCO ARMENIA
A. PINARBASI, DIRECTOR
10 VARDANANTS STREET
YEREVAN-10
TEL: +374 (1) 586-373
FAX: +374 (1) 584-419
EMAIL: AMYOT@ARMINCO.COM

AUDIT SERVICE AUDITING & CONSULTING COMPANY
G. DAVTYAN, DIRECTOR
16 KIYEVYAN STREET
SUITES 501, 502, 507-509
YEREVAN-28
TEL: +374 (1) 262-831
FAX: +374 (1) 262-831

DEVELOPMENT PROGRAMS
T. ARAKELYAN, CHAIRMAN
4-12 DEGHATAN STREET
YEREVAN-10
TEL: +374 (1) 568-421
FAX: +374 (1) 568-421
EMAIL: TARON@DP.ARMINCO.COM
WWW.DP.AM

HAI CONSULT ENTERPRISES SUPPORT CENTER
G. MAKARYAN, EXECUTIVE DIRECTOR
5 AGATANGEGHOS STREET, 3RO FLOOR
YEREVAN-10
TEL: +374 (1) 528-709
FAX: +374 (1) I51-057
EMAIL: CONSULT@FEENET.AM

INTERNATIONAL LEGAL CONSULTING (ILC) LLC
E. KHACHATOURIAN, MANAGING DIRECTOR
I9 SAYAT-NOVA AVE., SUITE 200
YEREVAN-1
TEL: +374 (1) 595-655
FAX: +374 (1) 566-735
EMAIL: EKHACH@ARMINCO.COM

KPMG ARMENIA
A. KUCHUKYAN, EXECUTIVE DIRECTOR

8 HANRAPETUTYAN STREET
TEL: +374 (1) 584-754, 566-762, 586-379
FAX: +374 (1) 151-986, 151-989
EMAIL: KPMG@ARMINCO.COM

SED MARSED CONSULTING COMPANY
T. JRBASHYAN, EXECUTIVE DIRECTOR
25/27 NALBANDYAN STREET, SUITE 2
YEREVAN-1
TEL: +374 (1) 522-734
FAX: +374 (1) 565-625
EMAIL: TJRBASHYAN@HOTMAIL.COM
WWW.SED-MARSED.AM

TER-TACHATYAN LEGAL AND BUSINESS CONSULTING
A. TER-TACHATYAN, DIRECTOR
13 MASHTOTSI AVE.
YEREVAN-2
TEL: +374 (1) 534-591, 534-399
FAX: +374 (1) 534-591
EMAIL: TLEGAL@ARMINCO.COM

AMERICAN EMBASSY, YEREVAN
COMMERCIAL SECTION
18 BAGHRAMIAN AVE., YEREVAN-19
TEL: +374 (1) 151-551
FAX: +374 (1) 151-550
EMAIL: ISAYANGX@STATE.GOV
HTTP://WWW.ARMINCO.COM/EMBUSA

COMMERCIAL BANKS AND INTERNATIONAL FINANCIAL INSTITUTIONS IN ARMENIA

COMMERCIAL BANKS

ADANA BANK
EXECUTIVE DIRECTOR: KAREN NERSESYAN
5 NALBANDYAN STREET
YEREVAN-10
TEL: (374-2) 567-109
FAX: (374-3) 907-157
E-MAIL: ADANA@MBOX.INTARNET.COM

AGRICULTURAL COOPERATIVE BANK OF ARMENIA
CHAIRMAN: STEPAN GISHYAN
1 BAYRONI STREET
YEREVAN-1
TEL: (374-2) 568-585
FAX: (374-2) 151-755
E-MAIL: ACBA@ARMINCO.COM

AKUNK BANK
CHAIRMAN: GAGIK VAHANYAN
19A KORYUNI STREET
YEREVAN-9
TEL: (374-2) 520-792
FAX: (374-2) 526-357
E-MAIL: ATLAS@ARMINCO.COM

ANELIK BANK
CHAIRMAN: SAMVEL CHEZMACHYAN
75 BAGHRAMYAN AVE.
YEREVAN-33
TEL: (374-2) 221-451
FAX: (374-2) 151-441
E-MAIL: ANELIK@ARMINCO.COM

ARDSHINBANK
EXECUTIVE DIRECTOR: LEVON FARMANYAN
3 DEGHATAN STREET
YEREVAN-10
TEL: (374-2) 528-513
FAX: (374-2) 151-155
E-MAIL: INTERNATIONAL@ARDSHIN.BANK.AM

AREXIMBANK
EXECUTIVE DIRECTOR: ARMEN KHANDKARYAN
20 TUMANYAN STREET
YEREVAN-1
TEL: (374-2) 580-506
FAX: (374-2) 583-131
E-MAIL: INFO@AREXIMBANK.AM

ARMAGROBANK
CHAIRMAN: EDWARD SANDOYAN
7A MOVSES KHORENATSI STREET
YEREVAN-15
TEL: (374-2) 585-790, 532-732
FAX: (374-2) 534-342
E-MAIL: AA@AGROBANK.AM

ARMECONOMBANK
EXECUTIVE DIRECTOR: ASHOT OSIPYAN
32/1 AMIRYAN STREET
YEREVAN-02
TEL: (374-2) 531-126
FAX: (374-2) 151-149
E-MAIL: ARMECO@ARMINCO.COM

ARMENIAN DEVELOPMENT BANK
CHAIRMAN: ALEXANDER GRIGORYAN
21/1 PARONYAN STREET
YEREVAN-15

TEL: (374-2) 530-094
FAX: (374-2) 533-233
E-MAIL: ROOT@ADB.INFOCOM.AMILINK

ARMIMPEXBANK
CHAIRMAN: BAGRAT ASATRYAN
2 NALBANDYAN STREET
YEREVAN-10
TEL: (374-2) 589-906
FAX: (374-2) 151-813
E-MAIL: OFFICE@IMPEX.BANK.AM

ARMINVESTBANK
CHAIRMAN: VARUZHAN AMIRAGYAN
13 VARDANANTS STREET
YEREVAN-10
TEL: (374-2) 523-718
FAX: (374-3) 907-210
E-MAIL: IBANK@DOLPHIN.AM

CONVERSE BANK
CHAIRMAN: SMBAT NASIBYAN
49 KOMITAS AVE.
YEREVAN-51
TEL: (374-2) 281-015
FAX: (374-3) 906-072
E-MAIL: CONVERSE.YEREVAN@REX.IASNET.RU

CREDIT-YEREVAN BANK
CHAIRMAN: MARTIN HOVHANNISYAN
2/8 AMIRYAN STREET
YEREVAN-10
TEL: (374-2) 589-065
FAX: (374-2) 151-820
E-MAIL: MAILCREYER@MAIL.CREYER.AM
ROZY@MAIL.CREYER.AM

CREDIT-SERVICE BANK
EXECUTIVE DIRECTOR: BORIS ARAKELYAN
15 TIGRAN METSI STREET
YEREVAN-10
TEL: (374-2) 527-794
FAX: (374-2) 525-701
E-MAIL: CREDIT@SERVICE-INFOCOM-EMAILK.NET

ECONOMINVESTBANK
EXECUTIVE DIRECTOR: KAREN DAVTYAN
2B ZAKYAN STREET
YEREVAN-10
TEL: (374-2) 535-113
FAX: (374-3) 907-215
E-MAIL: EKIM@SCI.AM

GLADZOR BANK
CHAIRMAN: GAGIK AMARYAN
1B CHARENTS STREET
YEREVAN-25
TEL: (374-2) 576-750
FAX: (374-2) 576-115
E-MAIL: GLADZOR@AMILINK.NET

HAYKAP BANK
EXECUTIVE DIRECTOR: EDUARD ARABKHANYAN
22 SARYAN STREET
YEREVAN-2
TEL: (374-2) 589-700
FAX: (374-3) 907-033
E-MAIL: HAYKAP@MBOX.AMILINK.NET

HAYKHNAYBANK (SAVINGS BANK)
EXECUTIVE DIRECTOR: HARUTYUN GHAZARYAN
46 NALBANDYAN STREET
YEREVAN-10
TEL: (374-2) 580-451
FAX: (374-2) 565-578
E-MAIL: AUTO@ISB.INFOCOM.AMILINK.NET

HSBC ARMENIA BANK
MANAGING DIRECTOR: GUY HARVEY-SAMUEL
2 KHORHRDARANI STREET
YEREVAN-10
TEL: (374-2) 587-095
FAX: (374-2) 151-858
E-MAIL: HSBC@ARMINCO.COM

INECOBANK
CHAIRMAN: AVETIS BALOYAN
17 TUMANYAN STREET
YEREVAN-1
TEL: (374-2) 563-725
FAX: (374-2) 565-974
E-MAIL: INECO@ACC.AM

INTERINVEST BANK
EXECUTIVE DIRECTOR: ASHOT YERANOSYAN
45 KHORENATSU STREET
YEREVAN-18
TEL: (374-2) 551-612
FAX: (374-2) 559-055
E-MAIL: BSEVAN@ARMINCO.COM

INTERNATIONAL COMMERCIAL BLACK SEA BANK (ARMENIA)
DEPUTY DIRECTOR GENERAL: ATANASIUS PIATAS
6 DEGHATAN STREET
YEREVAN-10
TEL: (374-2) 520-432

FAX: (374-2) 151-877
E-MAIL: ICBSB@ARMINCO.COM

LENDBANK
EXECUTIVE DIRECTOR: ANUSHAVAN KHACHIKYAN
8 YERVAND KOCHAR STREET
YEREVAN-70
TEL: (374-2) 542-588
FAX: (374-3) 907-035
E-MAIL: LEND@MBOX.AMILINK.NET

MELLAT BANK
EXECUTIVE DIRECTOR: ISSA CHABOK
1 PAVSTOS BUZANDI STREET
YEREVAN-10
TEL: (374-2) 581-791
FAX: (374-2) 151-811
E-MAIL: MELLAT@INFOCOM.AM

MENATEP-YEREVAN BANK
CHAIRMAN: ARA KITBALYAN
19A KORYUNI STREET
YEREVAN-9
TEL: (374-2) 529-471
FAX: (374-2) 529-471
E-MAIL: YEREVAN@MENATEP.INFOCOM.AMILINK.NET

PROMETEUS BANK
CHAIRMAN: EMIL SOGHOMONYAN
19 HRACHYA KOCHAR STREET
YEREVAN-12
TEL: (374-2) 273-000, 273-100
FAX: (374-2) 274-818
E-MAIL: NUNM@FREENET.AM

RIA BANK
CHAIRMAN: HARUTYUN MARGARYAN
39 HANRAPETUTYAN STREET
YEREVAN-10
TEL: (374-2) 587-264
FAX: (374-3) 907-057
E-MAIL: RIA@AICS.AM

SHIRAKINVEST BANK
EXECUTIVE DIRECTOR: MESROP KARAPETYAN
7 GAREGIN HZHDEH STREET
GYUMRI-377500
TEL: (374-69) 34-883
FAX: (374-69) 36-214
E-MAIL: SHIB@SHIRAK.AM

TRUSTBANK
CHAIRMAN: TIGRAN ARAKELYAN

10 ARTSAKHI STREET
YEREVAN-5
TEL: (374-2) 447-098
FAX: (374-2) 449-156
E-MAIL: TRUST@ARMINCO.COM

UNITED BANK
EXECUTIVE DIRECTOR: HOVSEP GALSTYAN
4 MOSKOVYAN LANE
YEREVAN-2
TEL: (374-2) 536-905
FAX: (374-3) 906-955
E-MAIL: UBANK@ARM.R.AM
HTTP://WWW.UBANK.AM

INTERNATIONAL FINANCIAL INSTITUTIONS

CAUCASUS ADVISORS LLC (MANAGER OF THE CAUCASUS FUND, FINANCED IN PART BY OPIC)
ARTAK MELKONIAN, MANAGING DIRECTOR OF ARMENIAN OPERATIONS
8 HANRAPETUTIAN STREET
YEREVAN-10
TEL: (374-2) 560-954, 587-418
FAX: (374-2) 587-418
E-MAIL: AMELKON@ACC.AM

EUROPEAN BANK FOR RECONSTRUCTION AND DEVELOPMENT
ALKIS DRAKINOS, HEAD OF YEREVAN RESIDENT OFFICE
ADDRESS: 20 BAGRAMYAN AVE.
YEREVAN-19
TEL.: (374-2) 540-425, 540-426, 540-427, 540-428
FAX: (374-2) 540-430
E-MAIL: DRAKINOA@EVN.EBRD.COM

INTERNATIONAL FINANCE CORPORATION
IRINA NIEDERBERGER, HEAD OF ARMENIA OFFICE
ADDRESS: 2 KHORHERTARANI STREET
REPUBLIC SQUARE
YEREVAN-10
TEL: (374-2) 599-546, 599-545, 599-543
FAX: (374-2) 599-544
E-MAIL: INIEDERBERGER@IFC.ORG

EURASIA FOUNDATION
EUGENE STAPLES, ACTING REGIONAL DIRECTOR
ADDRESS: 22 ISAHAKIAN STREET SUITE 11
YEREVAN-9
TEL: (374-2) 585-598, 566-789, 565-147, 561-626, 151-824
FAX: (374-2) 151-824, 585-598
E-MAIL: EURASIA@EURASIA.AM

WORLD BANK

OWAISE SAADAT, RESIDENT REPRESENTATIVE
ADDRESS: 2 KHORHERTARANI STREET
REPUBLIC SQUARE
YEREVAN-10
TEL: (374-2) 505-060, 520-992, 523-992
FAX: (374-2) 151-883, 151-788
ABUNIATYAN@WORLDBANK.ORG

SHOREBANK ADVISORY SERVICES (SHORE OVERSEAS CORPORATION)
JENNIFER O'NEIL, COUNTRY MANAGER
15 PARPETSU STREET SUITE 3
YEREVAN-10
TEL: (374-2) 537-310, 537-360
FAX: (374-2) 151-806
E-MAIL: SAFARM@ARMINCO.COM
JONSAF@ARMINCO.COM

IMF RESIDENT REPRESENTATIVE OFFICE
GEORGE ANAYOTOS, RESIDENT REPRESENTATIVE
1 MELIK-ADAMYAN STREET SUITE 326
YEREVAN-10
TEL: (374-2) 528-532, 528-960
FAX: (374-2) 151-703
E-MAIL: GANAY@ARMINCO.COM

KEY CONTACTS

UNION OF BANKS OF ARMENIA
CHAIRMAN: ARMEN YEGHIAZARYAN
19A KORYUNI STREET
YERAVAN-9
TEL: (374-2) 527-731
FAX: (374-2) 567-589
E-MAIL: ABA@ARMINCO.COM

CENTRAL BANK OF ARMENIA
CHAIRMAN: TIGRAN SARGSYAN
6 NALBANDYAN STREET
YEREVAN-10
TEL: (374-2) 583-841
FAX: (374-2) 580-052
E-MAIL: INFO@CBA.AM
HTTP://WWW.CBA.AM

MINISTRY OF FINANCE AND ECONOMY
MINISTER: LEVON BARKHUDARYAN
1 MELIK-ADAMYAN STREET
YEREVAN-10
TEL: (374-2) 595-304
FAX: (374-2) 524-282 OR 151-069
E-MAIL: STAFF@MF.GOV.AM

AMERICAN EMBASSY, YEREVAN

COMMERCIAL SECTION
18 BAGHRAMIAN AVE.
YEREVAN-19
TEL: (374-2) 151-551
FAX: (374-2) 151-550
E-MAIL: ISAYANGX@YEREVANB.US-STATE.GOV
HTTP://WWW.ARMINCO.COM/EMBUSA/COMMERCIAL/FRAME.HTM
CONTACT: GEORGE ISAYAN, BISNIS REPRESENTATIVE IN ARMENIA

INFORMATION FOR BUSINESS TRAVEL AND OPERATIONS

BUSINESS CUSTOMS

Many Armenians, despite decades of Soviet rule, managed somehow to preserve their historically inherited entrepreneurial spirit. However, foreigners working in Armenia, will encounter a layer of oriental traditions and approaches sometimes combined with remnants of the Soviet working mentality.

In general, foreigners should be aware that in many cases, every stage of their contacts/negotiations with Armenian businessmen may be accompanied by much wining and dining. The giving of gifts, home visits, and visits to historic sites in the countryside are also not unheard of.

Foreigners should not be discouraged by belated replies to their inquiries, letters, and faxes, or by the lack of a reply. Reliable international communication is very expensive and often not accessible for many Armenians. This, along with the remnants of Soviet working habits, means that many Armenians answer only correspondence that is of vital interest to them. The need to respond promptly is, however, gradually becoming accepted in the Armenian business community.

Due to differences in interpretation and understanding of some business terminology (some of which is very new for Armenia), U.S. businessmen are strongly encouraged to make absolutely sure that the content of their communications/negotiations/agreements with an Armenian partner is adequately understood.

Information resources in Armenia are mainly concentrated in the hands of state ministries and agencies, employees of which, below the top management level, have no incentive to work effectively. Often, they are unwilling to provide necessary information.

Corruption is a widespread and growing phenomenon in the majority of state organizations in Armenia, including such controlling bodies as the police and the customs department. Though foreigners are largely exempt, there may be cases where officials will delay approval of your application to rent an office from a state agency, for transportation, licensing, and let you know directly or indirectly that a good "tip" may fix things immediately. When this happens, U.S. businessmen should feel free to consult with the U.S. Embassy's Commercial Section.

TRAVEL ADVISORY AND VISAS

Americans travelling to Armenia should obtain an entry visa from the Armenian Embassy in Washington or from the Ministry of Foreign Relations of Armenia immediately upon arrival. Visas are valid for the following periods:

Visas obtained without an invitation.................21-days
Visas obtained with an official invitation period specified in the invitation
Transit visa..3 days
Multi-entry and multi-entry transit visas one year

Payment of the visa processing fee is from $20 to $200 depending on the type of the visa, and should be made with a certified check or money order to the Armenian Embassy.

For more information contact:

Consular Department. Embassy of the Republic of Armenia., 1660 L Street. N.W., Floor 11, Washiungton DC 20036; Tel: 202-628-5766, Fax: 202-628-5769
from 10 a.m. to noon, Monday through Friday.

Travellers to Armenia are strongly encouraged to bring with them as much cash as possible in crisp new bills. Credits cards and checks are not accepted. A few banks have started to cash travellers checks.

HOLIDAYS

Jan 1-2	New Year
Jan 6	Christmas
Apr 7	Motherhood and Beauty Day
April 24	Genocide Memorial Day
May 9	Victory Day (WW II)
May 28	Independence Day
July 5	Constitution Day
Sep 21	Referendum Day
Dec 7	Earthquake Memorial Day

BUSINESS INFRASTRUCTURE

LANGUAGE

Armenian ("Hayeren") is the official language of the country and is used in documents. The majority of the population and business circles speaks Russian as well. English or French are mandatory third languages in the majority of schools, and local universities produce a significant number of English language specialists - finding an interpreter or translator does not represent a problem.

HOTELS:

Hotel Armenia ****
One Amiryan Street, Yerevan 375010
Tel: (374-2)525-393, 560-844, 569-040; Fax: (374-2)151-802

Hotel Hrazdan ****
72 Pionerakan St., Yerevan, 375002
Tel: (374-2)535-332, 535-302; Fax: (374-2)537-095
(reservations require governmental permission)

Hotel Ani ***
19 Sayat-Nova Ave, Yerevan, 275010
Tel: (374-2)520-775, 582-638, Fax:(374-2)520-545

Hotel Dvin ***
40 Paronyan St., Yerevan, 375002
Tel: (374-2)536-343; Fax:(374-2)151-528

Hotel Erebuni***
26/1 Nalbandyan St., Yerevan, 375010
Tel: (374-2)564-943, 584-834

Restaurants & Clubs:

Dzoragyugh,
1 Paronyan St.,
Yerevan. Tel: (374-2)537-670

Krakov,
27 Tumanyan St.,
Yerevan. Tel: (374-2)562-020

Ararat,
Republic Square,
Yerevan. Tel: (374-2)527-382

Sunk,
11A Kievian St.,
Yerevan. Tel: (374-2)227-519

Kars,
Tel: (374-2)635-596, 636-583

Armenian Kitchen,
Tel: (374-2)480-303, 482-961

Downtown Jazz Club,
3 Pushkin Street, Yerevan

Tavush Music Club,
7 E.Kochar St., Yerevan;
Tel:(374-2)553-366

Telecommunications:

The regular Armenian telephone network currently belongs to the Ministry of Communication. Direct-dial long distance phone calls cannot be made outside of the NIS. One must call the operator and reserve a call/fax transmission. This telephone system is old and unreliable.

However, those who wish reliable international direct-dial telephone/fax communication have an opportunity to subscribe to a special, and more expensive, long-distance service which uses AT&T equipment and satellite connection via Washington with the rest of the world. At present this service is primarily used by key government institutions, foreign missions and leading firms in Yerevan.

To subscribe contact: AT&T Service, Long Distance Telephone Exchange, Azatutyan Avenue, Yerevan, 375044, Armenia: tel:(374-2)288151, 151-002, fax:(374-2)151-333.

To subscribe to international telex services contact the Ministry of Communication, 22 Saryan Street, Yerevan, 375022, Armenia; Tel:(374-2)526-632, fax:(374-2)151-446

E-mail services are rendered by two companies, based in Yerevan:

ARMINCO,
51 Mashtots Avenue,
Yerevan, 375009, Armenia;
tel:(374-2)526-
326, 281-425, Fax:(374-2)285-082; E-mail: root@arminco.com (Internet)

INFOCOM,
22 Saryan Street,
Yerevan, 375022,
Armenia; Tel & fax:
7(8852)528-856, or 151-926;
E-mail:infocom.mgmt@alliance-partners.sprintintl.net

Public Transportation:

Armenia has a quite developed public transportation system which includes buses, trolley buses, trams, vans - "route taxies", and a subway (Metro) in Yerevan. Taxis are available in the capital and a few major cities. The present rates in Yerevan are (June 1995):

Trolley, Tram, Metro - 20 drams/ride
Urban Bus - 25 drams/ride (30-50 drams for private buses)
Mini-Van - 50 drams/ride (100 drams for private vans)
Taxi - 200 drams/km

Besides a number of flights to many NIS cities, regular weekly flights connect Armenia with Paris, Amsterdam, Athens, Thesaloniki, Burgas (Bulgaria), Sofia, Beirut, Tehran, and Fujairah (UAE), through which further connections are made with the rest of the world. For reservations contact the following travel agents:

Levon Travel Yerevan
(Director - Ms. Ahahit Torosyan)
10 Sayat-Nova Street, Yerevan 375001
Tel: (374-2)582-831, 525-909, 525-210
Fax: (374-2)151-133
American-Armenian Joint Venture. divisions in the USA:

Saberatour-Sevan
(Director - Mr. Ruben Avetisyan)
37 Hanrapetutyan Street, Yerevan 375010
Tel: (374-2)525-448, 528-548
Fax: (374-2)564-030
Branch of "Saberatour"(Paris) and "Sevan" (Lyon)

Sidon Travel & Tourism, Inc. (Armenian Branch)
(Director - Mr. Hrair Babayan)
19 Sayat Nova St., Hotel Ani, Floor 1, Yerevan 375001
Tel: (374-2)522-967
fax: (374-2)151-684

Continental
(Director- Mr. Sergey Barsegyan)
1/3 Abovyan Street, Yerevan 375001
Tel: (374-2)533-852, 564-582, 582-726
Fax: (374-2)
AEROFLOT agent - Russia

LOGISTICS

U.S. business representatives willing to visit Armenia may contact:
ARAX Travel and Logistics Co., ltd.,
Hotel Yerevan, 14 Abovian Street, Suite 200, Yerevan 375001
Tel: (374-2)529-418, fax: (374-2)151-048.

Arax offers the following services: hotel and travel arrangements; apartment rental, accommodations throughout the country, office space rental; car/van rental with driver; airport pick-up/delivery; interpreters and tour assistants/tour escorts; meeting arrangements and secretarial services; guided trips throughout Armenia; video services. Arax accepts all major credit cards, such as American Express, Visa, Eurocard, Mastercard, Diners Club International, and JCB.

SHIPPING TO AND FROM ARMENIA:

Rail transportation:

Of the four railroad routes connecting Armenia with the outside world via Georgia, Azerbaijan, and Turkey, only the line from Armenia to Georgia continues to operate. From Yerevan, the line passes through Gyumri and Vanadzor, two major Armenian cities, enters Georgia and reaches the Black Sea ports of Batumi and Poti. The port of Poti is suitable for handling container shipments. The port of Batumi is largely used for shipments of oil and oil products. Average delivery time from Yerevan to these Black Sea ports is 4 days (700 km). The railroad owns a number of warehouses located along its routes. In Yerevan, it has six large warehouses, each 20 by 80 meters, as well as numerous open storage sites.

For more information and to contract shipments directly, contact:

Cargo Transportation Department.
State Railroads Administration
(Chairman - Mr. Vladimir Asryants)
50 Tigran Metsi St., Yerevan, 375005, Armenia
Tel: (374-2) 573-234 (cargo dept), 520-428 (chairman)
Fax: 7(8852)573-630

Air transportation:

Armenia has 6 civil airports with artificial field surfacing. Armenian Airlines - the only official Armenian air carrier - does not possess its own cargo planes. In 1992, the City Council of Yerevan purchased two Russian IL-76 cargo aircraft, which mainly serve the government export and import programs, and bring in humanitarian aid. A few companies, however, lease cargo planes in Russia or Ukraine for international shipment of goods to and from Armenia. Yerevan's Zvartnots Airport can handle all types of planes, including the largest cargo aircraft. Under the EBRD loan, a modern cargo terminal is being constructed at Zvartnots Airport to handle international and national cargo shipments.

The following local companies can be contracted for cargo air shipments:
Commercial Center of Civil Aviation Administration
Zvartnots Airport Admin bldg., Room 6, Yerevan 375042
Tel:(374-2)282-641, 774506, 772362
Fax: (374-2)282-641

Yerevan Avia Corporation
1/3 Byuzandi Street, Yerevan 375010
Tel: (374-2)527-864, 580-121, 561-461
Fax: (374-2)567-511, 151-799

NAAVI Air Transportation Company
20 E. Kokhbatzu Street, Yerevan 375010

Tel: (374-2)564-978, 582-653, or 562-809
Fax: (374-2)562-653

IMAC Italian-Armenian Joint Venture
28 Isaahakyan Street, Floor 3, Yerevan 375009
Tel: (374-2)529-983, 529-740
Fax: (374-2)561-548

Motor transportation:

Armenia has 7,705 km of roads, of which 7,454 are paved. International cargo routes in use are those connecting Armenia with the Georgian sea ports of Batumi and Poti, and a low-capacity pontoon bridge connecting the Meghri region of Armenia (in the South) with Iran. A permanent bridge to replace the pontoon bridge is now under construction. It is hoped that the new bridge will alleviate some of Armenia's international cargo transportation needs.

For tracking/freight forwarding services (private sector), contact:

Apaven, Ltd.
(Director - Mr. Arsen Kazaryan)
P.O.Box 386, Yerevan 375010
Tel:(374-2)350-160; Fax:(374-2)350-131, 151-502
Telex: 243329 ROBOT SU

Zakinturtrans Joint Stock Company
(General Director - Mr. Henri Ter-Markossian)
I Paruyr Sevak St., Yerevan, 375044
Tel: (374-2)285-342, fax:(374-2)282-000
(international cargo transportation/freight forwarding)

For information on state companies which provide motor transportation services, contact:
Cargo Transportation Department
Ministry of Transportation
(Director - Mr. Ashot Stepanyan)
10 Zakyan Street, Yerevan 375010
Tel: (374-2)523-862, Fax: (374-2)525-268

SELECTED GOVERNMENT AND BUSINESS CONTACTS

U.S. Embassy - Yerevan
Ambassador: The Honorable Michael Lemmon
Econ/Commercial Officer: Jeffrey Horwitz
18 Baghramyan Street, Yerevan, Armenia 375019
Tel: +374 (1) 151-551; 524-661; 520-791
Fax: +374 (1) 151-550
Telex: 234137 AMEMY
Website: www.arminco.com/embusa/

BISNIS Representative: George Isayan
Email: Isayangx@state.gov
U.S. & Foreign Commercial Service (USFCS) Commercial Specialist: Mher Avetyan
Email: mher.avetyan@mail.doc.gov
Commercial Assistant: Armine Yeghiazarian
Email: yeghiazara@state.gov

U.S. Mailing Address:
Commercial Section
American Embassy, Yerevan
Department of State
Washington, DC 20521-7020

Embassy of the Republic of Armenia in the United States
Ambassador: The Honorable Arman Kirakossian
2225 R Street, NW
Washington, DC 20058
Tel (202) 319-1976
Fax (202) 319-2982
Website: www.armeniaemb.org

Consulate General of the Republic of Armenia
Consul General: Armen Melkonian
50 North La Cienega Blvd., Suite 210
Beverly Hills, CA 90211
Tel: (310) 657-6102, 657-7320
Fax: (310) 657-7419
Email: consulate@erols.com

TRADE ASSOCIATIONS AND CHAMBERS OF COMMERCE

U.S. Armenia Business & Investment Association
3600 Winfield Lane, NW, Washington, DC 20057-2385
Tel: (202) 342-2582; Fax: (202) 342-9861
Email: info@usabia.org
Website: www.usabia.org
Armenia office:
19 Khanjian St., Yerevan 375010
Tel: +374 (1) 542-272
Email: ada@ada.am

American Chamber of Commerce In Armenia
Hotel Armenia, 1 Amirian St., Yerevan-10
Tel: +374 (1) 599-450
Email: amcham@acc.am

Armenian Chamber of Commerce and Industry
Mr. Samvel Sharbatian, President
29/1 Sayat Nova Yerevan 375001, Armenia
Tel: +374 (1) 56-54-38, Fax: +374 (1) 56-50-71
Email: chamber@arminco.com

The Union of Armenian Industrialists and Entrepreneurs
Mr. Aram Vardanyan, Chairman
41 Arshakunyants Ave., Yerevan 375026, Armenia
Tel: +374 (1) 56-29-23, Fax: +374 (1) 56-29-21, Mobile: +374 (9) 40-56-17
Email: umba@arminco.com

Union of Armenian Merchants
Mrs. Zolvard Gevorkian, President Demiryan
Yerevan, Armenia
Tel: +374 (1) 24-19-20
The Union is a trade association of more than 100 retailers and wholesalers

Association of Accountants of Armenia
Ms. Hasmik Hovsepyan, CEO
5 Hanrapetutyna St., 7th floor, room 614-615, Yerevan-10;
Tel: +374 (1) 538-403, 538, 162

Association of Banks of Armenia
Bagrat Asatryan, President
23/1 Amiryan St., Yerevan-02
Tel: +374 (1) 533-343, Fax: +374 (1) 528-811

Union of Banks of Armenia
Armen Yeghiazaryan, Chairman
19A Koryuni Street, Yerevan-9
Tel: +374 (1) 527-731
Fax: +374 (1) 567-589
E-mail: aba@arminco.com

Real Estate Association of Armenia
Gagik Poghosyan, President
22 Nairi Zaryan St. Yerevan-51
Tel: +374 (1) 254-792, 255-331, Fax: +374 (1) 254-995;
Email: postmast@aaango.armenia.su

Securities Market Members Association
Avetik Maikogluyan, Chairman
8/1 Chekhov St., Suite 7, Yerevan Armenia
Tel: +374 (1) 463-818

Association of Armenian Importers of Building Materials
Mr. Ruben Shahmuradian, President
65 Orbeli Yekhbayrneri St., Yerevan
Tel: +374 (1) 226-498; Fax: +374 (1) 151-475

Armenian Tourism Association
Arthur Voskanyan, Chairman
27 Amiryan Street, Yerevan-02, Armenia
Tel: +374 (1) 534-501; Fax: +374 (1) 563-927; E-mail: nta@freenet.am

Armenian Jewelers' Association

E-mail: aja@ada.am, aja@freenet.am;
Website: www.aja.am

Association of Goldsmiths and Jewelers of Armenia
Emil Grigoryan, Chairman of the Board
12 Arshakunyats St, Yerevan-10
Tel: +372 (2) 525-321, Fax: +374 (2) 525-713
Email: goldjew@infocom.am

Association of Armenian Freight Forwarders
Meruzhan Smbatyan, Chairman
50 Tigran Metsi Street, Yerevan-5
Tel: +374 (1) 552-698
Fax: +374 (3) 906-878
E-mail: sms@mbox.armlink.net

MARKET RESEARCH AND BUSINESS INFORMATION FIRMS

Spyur Information Service (Company Register of Armenia, Yellow Pages of Armenia)
Ashot Grigoryan, Director
Pavstos Buzandi St. 1/3, 7th floor, Yerevan 375010 Armenia
Tel: +374 (1)590-000, 563-505; Tel/Fax: +374 (1) 563-635
Email: info@spyur.am
Web sites: www.spyur.am; www.yellowpages.am

Silk Road Investments, Inc.
Tim Jemal, President
19 Khanjian St., Yerevan 375010
Tel: +372 (1) 54-11-33; Fax +374 (1) 54-22-72; e-mail: silkroad@ada.am

The Center for Business Research and Development (CBRD)
Michael Kouchakdjian, Director
40 Marshall Baghramyan St., Yerevan 375019
Tel: +374 (1) 271-602, 151-049; Fax: +374 (1)151-048
E-mail: AUA@adonis.ias.msk.su

ABSC - Armenian Business Support Center
Samvel Gevrogyan, Executive Director
24 Moskovian St., Apt. 2, Yerevan 375002 Armenia
Tel/Fax: +374 (1) 151-934, 528-279, 528-654, 561-064
Email: sgc@absc.static.amilink.net

Sed-Marsed Consulting CJSC
Tigran Jrbashyan, CEO
25/27 Nalbandyan, Suite 2, Yerevan-01
Tel: +374 (1) 522-734, 565-625; Fax: +374 (1) 565-625
E-mail: sedmar@arminco.com

ACCOUNTING FIRMS

KPMG Armenia (resident full service office)
8 Hanrapetutyan St., Yerevan-10 Armenia
Tel: +374 (1) 151-986; Fax: +374 (1) 151-989
Website: www.am.kpmg.net

AMYOT-Armenia
Mr. Tigran Mkrtchyan, Director
3 Isahakyan St, Yerevan-9 Armenia
Tel: +374 (1) 586-373, 522-401, Tel/Fax: +374 (1) 151-870; e-mail: amia@arminco.com

STOCK EXCHANGES

Yerevan Stock Exchange
Mr. Sedrak Sedrakyan, President
22 Saryan Street, Yerevan-22, Armenia

Tel: +374 (1) 535-823, 536-162; Fax: +374 (1) 525-801, 151-148

"Adamand" Yerevan Stock and Commodity Exchange
Mr. Suren Kaplanyan, Director
5 Hanrapetutyan St., Yerevan-33, Armenia
Tel: +374 (1) 271-936; Fax: +374 (1) 276-921

Gyumri Stock Exchange
Samvel Mkhitaryan, Director
244 Abovyan St., Gyumri 377504, Armenia
Tel: +374 (69) 23109; Tel/fax: +374 (69) 21023

LAW FIRMS

Arax Consulting Group (Affiliate of Vedder Price)
Mr. Ashot Poghosyan, President
21 Mashtots Ave., Suite 33, Yerevan, Armenia
Tel: +374 (1) 52-94-18, 56-40-13, 53-22-77
Fax: +374 (1) 15-18-65
Email: arax@arminco.com
URL: www.arminco.com/homepages/arax

Vedder Price, Kaufman, Kammholz&Day
805 Third Avenue, New York, New York 10022-2203
Phone: 212-407-7700; Fax: 212-407-7799
Email: vkrikorian@vedderprice.com

INSURANCE COMPANIES

Armenian Financial Insurance Company (financial)
Mr. Levon Mamikonyan, Managing Director
22 Saryan St., Yerevan-22, Armenia
Tel: +374 (1) 531-311; Tel/fax: +374 (1) 151-548
Email: imamik@yse.armenia.su

ARAX LLC (contracts, expropriation)
Mr. Ashot Poghosyan, President
21 Mashtots Ave, Suite 33, Yerevan, Armenia
Tel: +374 (1) 529-418, 564-013, or 589-856; Fax: +374 (1) 151-865 or 529-418
Email: arax@arminco.com
URL: www.arminco.com/homepages/arax

HSBC Insurance (Armenia)
Jonathan Stark, General Manager
3 Komitas Avenue, Yerevan 375033, Armenia
Tel: +374 (1) 269-308; Fax: +374 (1) 151 305, 151 886

Main Administration for State Insurance (life, property)
Mr. Sanasar Ananyan, Director
6 Abelyan St., Yerevan-38, Armenia
Tel: +374 (1) 340-644, or 345-456

MICA Insurance Company (medical, life)
Mr. Michael Yeroyan, Deputy Director
4 Tigran Metsi Ave., Room 203
Yerevan-10, Armenia
Tel/fax: +374 (1) 566-003

"DIAGNOSTIKA" JSC (medical)
Mr. Haik Nikoghosyan, President and CEO
6/1 Markaryan St., Achapnyak, Yerevan-73, Armenia
Tel: +374 (1) 343-247, 287-411; Fax: +374 (1) 151-639, 287-411
Email: haik@diagnost.arminco.com

FREIGHT FORWARDERS

Apaven Armenian-Georgian J/V
Arsen Ghazaryan, General Director
6/1 Abelyan Street, Yerevan-10
Tel: +374 (1) 351-180
Fax: +374 (1) 351-240
Email: international@apaven.r.am

Armtransexpeditor (Armtrex) Armenian-Georgian J/V
Meruzhan Smbatyan, Chairman
50 Tigran Metsi Street, Yerevan-5
Tel: +374 (1) 552-698
Fax: +374 (3) 906-878
Email: sms@mbox.amilink.net

LTT Interforwarders
Vladimir Papoyan, Director

80 Tigran Metsi Street, Yerevan-5
Tel/fax: +374 (1) 575-325

Nomad Express Armenian-Belgian J/V
Vahram Jotyan, Director
1 Baghramyan Avenue, Suite 53, Yerevan-19
Tel: +374 (1) 523-540 +374 (1) 402-445
Fax: +374(3) 231-0981 (antwerp)
Email: nomadexpress@acc.am

Sati-Armenia
Norayr Melkom-Melkomyan, General Director
21 Mashtots Avenue, Yerevan-2
Tel: +374 (1) 539-900, 531-022
Fax: +374 (1) 539-900, 531-120
Email: root@sati.arminco.com

Seaborne International Armenian-American J/V
Eva Troyan, Manager
8 Hanrapetutyan Street, Yerevan-10
Tel: +374(1) 566-699, 566-599
Fax: +374 (1) 151-538
Email: seaman@arminco.com
In the United States:
Seaborn International Inc.
Steve Robinson, President
11222 La Sienega Blvd., Suite 620, Inglewood, CA 90304 USA
Tel: (310) 338-8666, 216-4225 or (800) 662-6722; Fax: (310) 216-1124
E-mail: sar@seaborne-intl.com,
Website: www.seaborne-intl.com

Trans-Alliance Ltd.
Sarkis Martirosyan, Director
5 Nalbandyan Street, Yerevan-10
Tel: +374 (1) 529-598
Fax: +374 (3) 906-979
Email: serv@transa.infocom.amilink.net

Transimpex
Gagik Azatyan, Director
1 Pushkin Street, Suite 18, Yerevan-10
Tel/fax: +374 (1) 589-144
Email: tripex@arminco.com

Transkal Cargo Services
Erdal Sarap, Director
116-15 Nalbandyan Street, Yerevan-1
Tel: +374 (1) 585-768, 585-799
Fax: +374 (1) 585-799, 585-799
Email: trskal@arminco.com

Unitrans International Ltd.
Vakhtang Vardanyan, Director
37 Mashtots Street, Apt. 3 Yerevan 375002
Tel: (374 1) 53-94-25, 53-94-26, 53-08-48
Fax: (374 1) 53-94-27
Email: unitrans@arminco.com

COURIER DELIVERY SERVICE PROVIDERS

EMS
Vahagn Sarkisyan, Manager
22 Saryan Street, Yerevan-2
Tel/fax: (374-1) 539-613

YUMAX - DHL Representative
Emma Beluyan, Executive Director
36 Demirchyan Street, Suite 1a, Yerevan-2
Tel: (374-1) 528-058, 586-688
Fax: (374-1) 528-158
E-mail: dhlevn@arminco.com
Website: www.dhl.com/wrd

Argotour - Fedex Representative
Martun Makaryan, Director
1 Charentsi Street
Yerevan-25
Tel: (374-1) 574-686, 574-859
Fax: (374-3) 907-184
Website: www.fedex.com/am

TNT
David Alsikyan, Manager
1 Koryuni Street, Yerevan-25
Tel: (374-1) 545-525
Fax: (374-1) 521-886
E-mail: tntarm@freenet.am
veran@arminco.com

UPS Express Haik Armenian-American J/V
Hambartsum Kupelyan, President
35 Komitas Avenue, Suite 410, Yerevan
Tel: +374 (1) 258-706, 259-191
Fax: +374 (3) 906-211

MAJOR PC HARDWARE VENDORS

Bi-Line
Artak Zakaryan, Director
50 Khanjian Street, Yerevan-1, Armenia
Tel: (374-1) 578-825
Fax: (374-3) 907-077
E-mail: info@bi-line.am
Website: http://www.bi-line.am

Unicomp
Armen Baldryan, Director
33 Sayat-Nova Street, Yerevan-1, Armenia
Tel: (374-1) 541-474
Fax: (374-1) 541-474
E-mail: Unicom@arminco.com

Nova
Varuzhan Melikyan, Director
24B Baghramyan Ave., Yerevan-19, Armenia
Tel: (374-1) 584-441
Fax: (374-1) 568-508
E-mail: ashot@nova.am
Website: http://www.nova.am

Ares Computers
Karine Stepanyan, Director
23 Sayat-Nova Street, Yerevan-1, Armenia
Tel: (374-1) 561-104
Fax: (374-1) 584-476
E-mail: gtggtg@arminco.com
Website: http://www.ares.am

Khartiya
Hrachya Abovyan, President
Hanrapetutyan Square, Unions Building, Yerevan-10, Armenia
Tel: (374) (1) 561-425
Fax: (374) (1) 561-425
E-mail: xartia@xar.am
Website: http://www.xar.am

Migma
Grigor Barsegyan, Director
15 Sayat-Nova Street, Yerevan-1, Armenia
Tel: +374 (1) 564-849
Fax: +374 (1) 521-356
E-Mail: migmacomp@hotmail.com

Vallex
9 Nalbandyan Street, Yerevan-10, Armenia
Tel: (374-1) 560-900
Fax: (374-1) 526-690
E-mail: vallex@vallex.am

Compusys
3 Baghramyan Ave., Yerevan-19, Armenia
Tel: (374-1) 563-081
Fax: (374-1) 563-081
E-mail: armine@flavius.arminco.com
Contact: Mher Tovmasyan, Director

Computer-Service
1 Charents Street, Yerevan-25, Armenia
Tel: (374-1) 575-137
Fax: (374-1) 151-668
E-mail: comps@arminco.com

Lans
49 Komitas Ave., Yerevan-51, Armenia
Tel: (374-1) 230-510
Fax: (374-1) 282-951
E-mail: lans@lans.am
Website: http://www.lans.am
Contact: Arshavir Gyulkhasyan, Director

Fine
18 Tumanyan Street, Yerevan-1, Armenia
Tel: (374-2) 568-178
Fax: (374-1) 568-178
E-mail: fine@freenet.am
Contact: Haik Hayrapetyan, Director

Cit
6/1 Abelyan Street, Yerevan-38, Armenia
Tel: (374-1) 350-390
Fax: (374-1) 351-230
E-mail: cit@cit.am
Website: http://www.cit.am
Contact: Gagik Karapetyan, Director

INTERNET SERVICE PROVIDERS

Arminco
A. Alexanian, Managing Director
28 Isahakian St., Yerevan-9, Armenia
Tel: +374 (1) 563-674; Fax: +374 (1) 285-082
Email: postmaster@ arminco.com, support@arminco.com
Website: http://www.arminco.com

Armcomputer Center
Vahram Mkhitaryan, Managing Director
28 Nalbandyan Street, Yerevan-10
Tel: (374-1) 569-702
Fax: (374-1) 569-701
E-mail: admin@acc.am
Website: http://www.acc.am

Infocom
Artak Gabrielaian, President
22 Saryan St., Yerevan-2, Armenia
Tel: +374 (1) 531-039
Fax: +374 (1) 528-856
E-mail: bit@mbox.amilink.net
Website: http://www.ani.amilink.net

BUSINESS ASSISTANCE AND PROMOTION ORGANIZATIONS

Eurasia Foundation
Small Business Loan Program
22 Isahakyan Street, Suite 11, Yerevan 375009 Armenia
Tel: +374 (1) 58-55-98, 55-67-89, 56-16-26, 56-51-47
Fax: +374 (1) 15-18-24, 58-55-98
E-mail: eurasia@eurasia.am
Website: www.efcaucasus.org

International Executive Service Corps
Stephanie Brennan, Country Director
5 Tamanian, Apt. 5, Yerevan, Armenia 375009
Tel: +374 (1) 56-40-20, 52-50-97/52-51-97
Fax: +374 (1) 151-766
E-mail: sbrennan@iesc.org, iesc@arminco.com
Website: www.iesc.org

IREX Armenia
Ms. Zara Oganessian, IREX Country Director
17 Marshal Baghramian Ave. Union of Armenian Architects, 2nd floor, Yerevan, Armenia
Tel: +374 (1) 56-37-81; Tel/Fax: 151-116
E-mail: irex@irex.arminco.com
Website: www.irex.am
IREX Branch office - Gyumri
82a Akhurian Street, Gyumri, Armenia
Tel/Fax: +374 (69) 3-59-49
E-mail: eurasia@shirak.am

Peace Corps Armenia
Bill Benjamin, Country Director
33 Charents Street, Yerevan, 375025 Armenia
Tel: +374 (1) 524-450, 551-365
Tel/Fax: +374 (1) 151-117
E-mail: pcarm@am.peacecorps.gov

Trade Point Armenia
(UNCTAD/UNTPDC program for trade efficiency and for development of Armenian small and medium-sized enterprises)
Admiral Isakov Ave. 10, Yerevan 375082, Republic of Armenia
Tel./Fax: +374 (1) 568 474; Tel: +374 (1) 568-474, 568-098
E-mail: vjh@tpa.am
Website: www.tpa.am

Shorebank Advisory Services, Caucasus SME Finance Program
Jennifer O'Neil, Country Manager
15, Parpetsu St., Suite 3 - 2nd Floor, Yerevan, Armenia
Tel: +374 (1) 53-73-10, 53-73-60; Fax: +374 (1) 15-18-06
E-mail: safar@arminco.com; jonsaf@arminco.com

Armenian Development Agency
Vahagn Movsissyan, Executive Director
7 Charentsi Str., Yerevan, 375025, Armenia
Tel/Fax: +374 (1) 542-272; e-mail: ada@ada.Am
Website: www.ada.am

Agribusiness Development Center
12 Vagharshian Street, Yerevan-12, Armenia
Tel: +374 (1) 505-995; Fax: +374 (1) 277-647
E-mail: Adc@Mbox.Amilink.Net

U.S. AND INTERNATIONAL FINANCIAL INSTITUTIONS

Overseas Private Investment Corporation
1100 New York Avenue, N.W., Washington, DC 20527; Tel: (202) 336-8620,
Fax: (202) 408-5142, Telex: 493-8219

OPIC Caucasus Fund
Mr. Peter Aldrich, Chairman
AEW International
53 State Street, 16th Floor, Boston, MA 02109
Tel: (617) 261-9300; Fax: (617) 261-9333

Caucasus Advisors LLC (OPIC Caucasus Fund Representative Office in Armenia)
Mr. Artak Melkonyan, Managing Director of Armenian Operations
8 Hanrapetutyan St., Yerevan-10, Armenia
Tel/Fax: +374 (1) 560-954, 587-418
E-mail: amelkon@acc.am

USAID/Caucasus Regional Office
10 Aigedzor Street, Yerevan-19
Tel: +374 (1) 227-448, 151-955; Fax: +374 (1) 151-131.

The European Bank for Reconstruction and Development (EBRD)
One Exchange Square, London EC2A 2EH, United Kingdom
Lindsay Forbes, Country Director
Tel: +44 (171) 338-6198; fax: +44 (171) 338-6599
EBRD Armenia Field Office
Alkins Drakinos, Head of Resident Office
20 Baghramyan Ave., Yerevan-19, Armenia
Tel: +374 (1) 540-425; Fax: +374 (1) 540 430
E-mail: drakinoa@evn.ebrd.com

World Bank Office
Owaise Saadat, Resident Representative
Republic Square, 2 Khorhertarani Street, Yerevan-10
Tel: +374 (1) 15-16-86, 520-992, 523-992;
Fax: +374 (1) 151-833, 151-788
E-mail: abuniatyan@worldbank.org

IFC Office
Irina Niederberger, Head of Armenia Office
Republic Square, 2 Khorhertarani Street, Yerevan-10
Tel: +374 (1) 599-546, 599-545 599-543;
Fax: +374 (1) 599-544
E-mail: eneiderberger@ifc.org

Eurasia Foundation
Eugene Staples, Acting Regional Director
22 Isahakian Street, Suite 11, Yerevan-9
Tel: (374-1) 585-598, 566-789, 565-147, 561-626, 151-824
Fax: (374-1) 151-824, 585-598
E-mail: Eurasia@Eurasia.am

Shorebank Advisory Services (Shore Overseas Corp.)
Jennifer O'Neil, County Manager
15 Parpetsu Street, Suite 3, Yerevan-10
Tel: (374-1) 537-310, 537-360
Fax: +374 (1) 151-806
E-mail: safarm@arminco.com, jonsaf@arminco.com

IMF Resident Representative Office
George Anayotos, Resident Representative
1 Melik-Adamyan Street, Suite 326, Yerevan-10
Tel: +374 (1) 528-532, 528-960
Fax: +374 (1) 151-703
E-mail: ganay@arminco.com

BANKS WITH CORRESPONDING U.S. BANKING ARRANGEMENTS

Armimpexbank
2 Nalbandyan St., Yerevan, 375010
Tel:(374-2)589-906, 589-518, 564-617; Fax:(374-2)565-958
Chairman: Mr. Eduard Arabkhanyan
Corresponding Banks: Bank of America (Concord, CA),
Bank of New York,
Credit Lyonnais (New York);
Creditanstalt Bankverein,
Raiffeisenzentralbank A.G. (Vienna);

Credit Lyonnais, Banque Francaise De L'orient,
Deutsche Bank A.G. (Paris),
Deutsche Bank A.G.,
Commerzbank (Frankfurt);
Swiss Bank Corp.,
Union Bank of Switzerland,
Credit Suisse (Zurich);
Midland Bank,
National Westminster Bank PLC (London);
The Bank of Tokyo (Tokyo);
Royal Bank of Canada (Toronto);
ABN-Amro Bank (Amsterdam),
Bank Brussels Lambert (Brussels);
General Bank (Brussels);
National Australia Bank (Sydney).

ArdShinBank (Industrial Construction Bank)
3 Deghatan St., Yerevan, 375010
Tel:(374-2)560-616, 528-513, Fax:(374-2)151-155, Telex:243349
Chairman: Mr. Karen Movsisyan
Corresponding Banks: Citibank, Bank of New York (New York).

ArmAgrobank (Agricultural joint stock commercial bank)
7a Movses Khorenatsu St., Yerevan, 375015
Tel:(374-2)534-342, Fax:(374-2)534-342
Chairman: Mr. Armen Arzumanyan
Corresponding Banks: The Bank of New York, Citibank, Republic National Bank of New York (New York); Deutsche Bank AG, Dresdner Bank AG, Commerzbank (Frankfurt); Credit Commerciale de France, Credit Agricole de France, Eurobank (Paris); Bank of Tokyo (Tokyo); Swiss Bank Corporation (Zurich); Bank Mees Pierson Amsterdam (Amsterdam); Bank Brussels Lambert (Brussels).
Visa Credit Card Service was introduced.

ArmEconomBank
32 Garegin Njde, Yerevan, 375026
Tel:(374-2)440-511, 447-680, Fax:(374-2)562-705
Chairman: Mr. Vladimir Badalyan
Corresponding Banks: Banque Nationale de Paris (Paris); National Westminster Bank (London); Riggs National Bank of Washington, D.C. (Washington); Deutsche Bank (Frankfurt).

Aviabank
1 P.Sevak St., Yerevan, 375014
Tel:(374-2)288-857, Fax:(374-2)281-940, Telex:243113
Chairman: Mr. Harutiun Vardanyan
Corresponding Banks:Credit Lyonnais (New York); Barklays Bank (London); Swiss Bank Corp. (Geneva); Credit Lyonnais (Paris), Dresdner Bank (Frankfurt), ABN Bank Amro (Vienna), MMKB (Moscow).

Bank for Reconstruction and Development
31 Moskovyan St., Yerevan, 375002
Tel:(374-2)530-156, 530-094, Fax:(374-2)530-156
Chairman: Alexander Griroryan
Corresponding Banks: Citibank (New York); Los Angeles Bank (Los Angeles).

Lend Bank
21 Nairy Zaryan St., Yerevan 375051
Tel:(374-2)399-060 Fax:(374-2)340-273
Chairman: Mr.Anushavan Khachikyan
Corresponding Banks: ABN Amro Bank, City Bank, Bank of New York (New York). Visa Credit Card Service via Incombank (Moscow).

SELECTED FOREIGN COMPANIES AND JOINT VENTURES IN ARMENIA

HAITEX
3 A.Hakobyan St., Yerevan, 375033, Armenia
Tel: (374-2)221-021, Fax:(374-2)151-073
Mr. Levon Melikyan, Chairman of the Board
Production of electric home appliances, plastic goods, instant lottery.
Established in 1990 as a joint venture.

Levon Travel Yerevan
10 Sayat Nova St., Yerevan, Armenia
Tel: (374-2)525-210, 394-825, 151-133
Fax: (374-2)151-684
Mr. Anahit Torosyan, Director
Travel agent. Joint Venture. Founded in 1991.

Sidon Travel Armenia
19 Sayat Nova St., Yerevan, Armenia
Tel: (374-2)520-593, 522-967
Fax: (374-2)151-684
Mr. Vladimir Boryan, Manager
Travel agent. Joint Venture.

Armentoy
12 Sevani St., Yerevan, 375023, Armenia
Tel: (374-2)342-411, 567-652
Fax: (374-2)567-652
Mr. Samvel Tumanyan, President
Toys mfg. Joint Venture.

Huntsman Armenian Concrete Corporation
49 Artsakh St., Yerevan 375021, Armenia
Tel: (374-2)471-217
Mr. David Horn, Chairman of Board
Mfg of prestressed slabs. Joint Venture between the Huntsman Chemical Corporation(USA) and the Ministry of Construction of Armenia.

5. Vertex Ventures Ltd.
3 Amiryan St., Floor 3, Yerevan, Armenia
Tel:(374-2)584-234
Fax:(374-2)583-197
Mr. Assadour M. Ashdjian, President
Publisher of Armenian Yellow Pages. Joint Venture

HPL Armenia
44 Narekatsi Street, Avan 3
Yerevan, Armenia
Tel:(374-2)535-237
FAX: N/A yet.
Mr. Zaven Nalbandyan, Director
Mr. Hovhannes Ghukasyan, Software Development Director
Software engineering. Registered on Feb 20, 1995, as a subsidiary of HPL Heuristic Physics Laboratories Inc. (David Y. Lepejian, President and CEO),1649 South Main Street, Milpitas, California 95035 USA; tel:(408)263-1475, fax:(408)263-1584.

Tufenkian Armenia
17 Aram Khachatryan, #74
Yerevan 375012 Armenia
Tel:(374-2)261-827, 270-826
Fax:(374-2)151-048 (AUA)
Mr. Hambartsum (Garik) Chilingaryan, Manager
Hand-made carpets and threads mfg & export. Registered in July 1995 as a subsidiary of Tufenkian Export Import Ventures, Inc., N.Y. President - Mr. James Tufenkian.

Hill International Armenia
5 Nalbandyan Street, Second Floor
Yerevan Armenia
Tel:(374-2)529-871
Mr. Frederick Samelian, President
Mr. Greg Kahwajian, Government & Public Affairs
Construction Management. Founded on April 21, 1995, as a subsidiary of Hill International, Inc., 4904 Petit Avenue, Encino, CA 91436-1131; tel: (818)981-1048, fax: (818)981-3421.

GOLDEX
21 Shoprony St., Yerevan, 375021 Armenia.
Tel:(374-2) 650-941
Mr.Ara Tonoyan, Director
Silver jewelry production. Founded in 1990, as Joint Venture between the American company Garfield Fin. Corp., Director Michael Minasyan (85%) and the Yerevan Institute of Laser equipment (15%).

Hailink
24a M.Bagramian St.,Yerevan 375019 Armenia.
Tel:(374-2) 521-664, 273-418
Fax:(374-2) 521-664
Director:Mr.Gagik Evoyan
Research and development in natural sciences and architecture, wireless communication networks, software and hardware engineering. Founded in 1992 as a subsidiary of CILINK Corp., Hermosa Court 910, Cunnyvale, California, tel: 735-58-00.

Andok
20 Charentsy St., suite # 2-4, Yerevan 375025 Armenia.

tel: (374-2) 553-365, 564-746
Director:Mr.Martin Mirzoyan
Assembly and sell of optical equipments and glasses, biomedical services. Founded in 1993 as a subsidiary of Armenian Relief Society of Western U.S.A. Inc., 80 Bigelow Avenue, Waterdown, MA 02172, U.S.A., tel:(617)926-5892,fax:(617)926-4855.

Hayshen
5 Nalbandian St., apt.11, Yerevan 375010 Armenia.
tel: (374-2) 523-983, 583-543, 580-070
fax: (374-2) 151-678
Director: Henrik Tigranyan
Construction and civil engineering, design, CAD. Founded in 1992 as a Joint Venture between HAYARD Ltd., Armenia and HAYBUSINESS (USA), Director Vartkes Barsam.

13. Golden Pair Corporation
13 Vram Sapu Arka Street, Yerevan, 375002 Armenia
tel:(374-2) 582-243, 617-201
fax: (374-2) 526-821, 612-360.
President: Mr. Jirayr Shamilyan
Optical devices mfg, wholesale trade. Founded on November 6,1992, as a Joint Venture of Golden Pair Corp., 4659 Hollywood Blvd. Hollywood, CA 90027, tel:(213) 665-2576, fax: (213) 665-0709

DHL Worldwide Express
1 Charentsy St., Yerevan 375025 Armenia
tel: (374-2) 574-869
fax: (374-2) 574-686
Director: Michael Yukhanayev
Representative in Armenia by UMAX ltd. Founded in 1995.

Armako
111 Raffu st., Yerevan Armenia.
tel: (374-2) 738-323, 151-724
fax: (374-2) 732-636, 151-724
Chairman: Stepan Demirchyan
Production of radio, video and other electronic devices. Founded in 1994 as a Joint Venture between ICT group (USA) and "MARS" plant (Armenia).

Armenian Company of the International Lottery and Gaming
50 Nalbandian St., apt. 103,Yerevan 375010 Armenia.
tel: (374-2) 589-913, 560-540, 587-289
fax: (374-2) 561-544
Director:Gagik Tchantchapanyan

Instant Lottery. Founded in 1993 as a Joint Venture between the Armenian Trade Union Center (51%) and International Communication technologies, Inc., Executive office, 12555 W. Jefferson Blvd. #200, Los Angeles, California 90066, tel: (310) 301-7680, fax: (310) 301-7635, Robert Block, Chairman of the Board; SBU: International Lottery & Gaming, Corp. 419 Greenleaf, Glencol, IL 60022-1907, tel:(708)835-0046, fax:(708) 835-

8861, Michael Siegl, President (49%).

Sina
18 Vardanants St.,Yerevan 375010 Armenia.
tel: (374-2) 521-684, 647-600
fax: (374-20 647-600
President: Henrik Bakunts
Retail Sale of pharmaceutical, medical and orthopedic commodities.
Founded in 1995 as a Joint Venture between Armenian Disaster Neurology Research Center (50%), TECH insurance company (30%) and Sigl Export-Import, 1248 S.Glendale Ave., Suite AA, Glendale CA 91205, President Gevorkyan (20%),

ESI Engineering & Construction Co., Inc.
31 Moskovian Street, Apt. 29
Yerevan 375002 Armenia
Tel: (374-2)533-293
Ms. Karine Manukyan, Office Manager
Will build a hydro power plant in Amasia, Armenia. Registered on February 29, 1995 as a branch office of ESI Engineering & Construction Co., 777 South Flagler Drive, Suite 650 East Tower
West Palm Beach, Florida 33401; Tel: (407) 833-4040; Fax: (407) 833-0011; Mr. Thomas N. Swiatowski, Project Administrator

2. Armenian Tomato Company
20 Tumanian St., apt. 11, Yerevan Armenia.
tel: (374-2) 583-322
Processing and cannery of fruits and vegetables. Joint Venture.

Armenian Sugar Company
Tel: (516) 667-9339 (U.S.A.)
Fax: (516) 560-0611 (U.S.A.)
Mr. Peter Petrosian, President
Sugar and fruit processing. Joint Venture.
Newly established. Planning to start operations in 1995.

ARCO
4. International Import Export-Mailing Address: P.O. Box 873, Glendale, CA 91209 - 0873, Corporate Office: 600 W. Broadway, Suite 355, Glendale, CA 91204, President Ashot Rostomian, founded in 1995, office is not available yet, intends to act in Moscow.

5. ARAMCO
18 Vardanants St., Yerevan 375010 Armenia.
tel: (374-2) 521-684
fax: (374-2) 527-650
telex: 243280 MALG SU
President: Mr. Levon Gevorkyan
Wholesale distribution. Founded in 1995 as a joint venture between the Concern Sigl and Segl International Export-Import 1248 S. Glendale Ave., Suite AA, Glendale CA 91205, President Gevorkyan.

Erebuni
1 Charents St.,second floor, Yerevan 375025 Armenia.
tel: (374) 524-964
fax: (374) 524-964 or 151-789
Director: Hamlet Asryan
Import-export of food, construction materials and electronics, civil construction. Founded in 1994 as a Joint Venture between Martin Co. and Champion International, 6233 Whittier Blvd., Los-Angeles, California 90022, tel:(213)722-4085, fax:(213)72-0748, Not operating yet due to financial/credit problems with the American partner.

Ahaton
10 Hanrapetutian St.,Yerevan 357010 Armenia.
tel: (374-2) 563-832
fax: (374-2) 151-502
Director: Aharon Gabrelyan
Import-Export, production of lenses. Founded in 1994 as a Joint Venture with the American Resident Mr.Christopher Sahakyan, Washington DC. 5139, Yuma St. N.W. 20016 tel:(202) 966 6887, fax:(202) 966 6889.

Lunar Travel
10 Shahsuvarian St., apt.4, Yerevan
Tel:(374-2) 231-814
Mail services - Armenian Representative.

Medium
6 Kasian St., apt.19, Yerevan
Tel:(374-2) 277-361
Joint Venture. Repair of optical, photo and movie devices.

Hayinform
17 Gvardiakanery St., Yerevan
tel: (374-2) 235-161
Director:Mr. Ashot Sahakyan
Information service for the industrial network of NIS. Founded in 1991 as a joint venture between MEMCO Ltd.(USA) and GOSSTANDART, Armenia. Never stared operations on various reasons including electricity shortages.

Amarak
1a Zakyan St.,suite # 20 Yerevan 375002 Armenia.
tel:(374-2) 531-950
Director: Nver Pogosyan
Import/Export, Tourism - Joint venture. Founded in 1993.

Enterprise, Ltd
39 Komeritmiutyan St., Ashtarak Armenia.
Tel: NA
Cattle breeding

Rubin
13 Mikoyan St., Yerevan, Armenia.
tel: (374-2) 633-561
Jewelry and Gem Stones production. Joint Venture.

U.S. AND COUNTRY CONTACTS

U.S. EMBASSY TRADE RELATED OFFICIALS

Country Address: American Embassy - Commercial Section
18 Marshal Baghramyan Avenue, Yerevan 375019, Armenia
Tel: (374-1) 524-661, 520-791, 151-551
Fax: (374-1)151-550
E-mail: Yerevan.Office.Box@mail.doc.gov
Web: http://www.csarmenia.com

U.S. Address: American Embassy Yerevan, Commercial Section,
Department of State, 7020 Yerevan Place, Washington D.C. 20521-7020

Attn:
David Gehrenbeck, Economic/Commercial Officer,
Mher Avetyan, FCS Commercial Specialist,
George Isayan, BISNIS representative, or
Armine Yeghiazarian, Commercial Assistant

ARMENIAN TRADE AND INDUSTRY ASSOCIATIONS

American Chamber of Commerce in Armenia
Mr. Tom Samuelian, President
Ms. Nanik Melkonian, Executive Director
Hotel Armenia
1 Amirian Street, Republic Square, Yerevan
Tel: (374-1) 599 187
E-mail: amcham@arminco.com

The Union of Manufacturers and Businessmen of Armenia
Mr. Arsen Khazarian, Chairman
41 Arshakunyants Ave., Yerevan 375026, Armenia
Tel: (374-1) 560-188
Fax: (374-1) 151-705

Union of Armenian Merchants
Mr. Makich Demiryan, President
12 Vagharshyan St., Yerevan, Armenia
Tel:(374-1) 273-603, 277623, 570-321
Fax: (374-1) 273-540

Association of Accountants of Armenia
Ms. Hasmik Hovsepyan, CEO
5 Hanrapetutyna St., 7-th floor, room 614-615, Yerevan-10
Tel: (374-1) 538-403
Fax: (374-1) 538,162

Association of Banks of Armenia
Armen Yeghizarian, President
23/1 Amiryan St., Yerevan-02
Tel: (374-1) 533-343
Fax: (374-1) 528-811

Real Estate Association of Armenia
Gagik Poghosyan, President
22 Nairi Zaryan St. Yerevan-51
Tel: (374-1) 254-792, 255-331
Fax: (374-1) 254-995
E-mail: postmast@aaango.armenia.su

Securities Market Members Association
Avetik Maikogluyan, Chairman
8/1 Chekhov St., Suite 7, Yerevan, Armenia
Tel: (374-1) 463-818

EXPORT AND INVESTMENT PROMOTION AGENCIES

Armenian Development Agency (ADA)
Vahagn Movsisian, Director
9 Khangyan Street, Yerevan - 10
Tel:- (374-1) 542-272
Fax: (374-1) 542-272
E-mail: ada@ada.am

COUNTRY GOVERNMENT AND TRADE-RELATED GOVERNMENT OFFICES

President
Robert Kocharian, President
President's House
26 Marshal Baghramian Ave.
Yerevan 375019
Tel: (374-1) 588-734, 588-712, 588-793 (Protocol)
Fax: (374-1) 561-581, 151-152

Prime Minister
Andranik Markarian, Prime Minister
1st Government House

Republic Square
Yerevan 375010, Armenia
Tel: (374-1) 520-360
Fax: (374-1) 151-036, 523-219

MINISTERS:

Ministry of Agriculture
Zaven Gevorgian, Minister
48 Nalbandyan Street
Yerevan 375010
Tel: (374-1) 524-641
Fax: (374-1) 151-583

Chief of Staff of the Cabinet
Manouk Topazian, Minister
1st Government House
Republic Square
Yerevan 375010, Armenia
Tel: (374-1) 520-360
Fax: (374-1) 151-036, 523-219

Ministry of Coordination of Production Infrastructure
David Zadoyan, Minister
1st Government House
Republic Square
Yerevan 375010
Tel: (374-1) 520-321
Fax: (374-1) 151-036

Ministry of Culture, Youth, And Sports
Roland Sharoyan, Minister
5 Tumanian Street
Yerevan 375001
Tel: (374-1) 529-349
Fax: (374-1) 523-922

Ministry of Defense
Serge Sargisian, Minister
36 Gevorg Chaush Street
Yerevan 375088
Tel: (374-1) 520-481
Fax: (374-1) 151-445

Ministry of Education and Science
Eduard Ghazarian, Minister
13 Movses Khorenatsi Street
Yerevan 375010
Tel: (374-1) 526-602, 524-998
Fax: (374-1) 580-403

Ministry of Energy
Karen Galustian, Minister
2nd Government House
Republic Square
Yerevan 375010
Tel: (374-1) 521-964
Fax: (374-1) 151-687, 526-365

Ministry of Environmental Protection
Murad Muradian, Minister
35 Moskovian Street
Yerevan 375002
Phone: (3742) 521-099
Fax: (3742) 533-372

Ministry of Finance and Economy
Vardan Khachatrian, Minister
1 Melik Adamian Street
Yerevan 375010
Tel: (374-1) 595-255
Fax: (374-1) 524-282, 151-069

Ministry of Foreign Affairs
Vardan Oskanian, Minister
2nd Government House
Republic Square
Yerevan 375010
Tel: (374-1) 523-531, 527-022, 151-157
Fax: (374-1) 521-796, 151-042

Ministry of Health
Ararat Mkrtchian, Minister
8 Tumanian Street
Yerevan 375001
Tel: (374-1) 582-413
Fax: (374-1) 151-097

Ministry of Industry and Trade
Karen Chshmaritian, Minister
5 Hanrapetutian Street
Yerevan 375010
Tel: (374-1) 522-884
Fax: (374-1) 151-081, 526-577

Ministry of Interior
Haik Harutiunian, Minister
130 Nalbandian Street
Yerevan 375015
Tel: (374-1) 560-952, 521-682
Fax: (374-1) 520-310

Ministry of Justice
David Harutiunian, Minister
8 Khorhrdarani Street

Yerevan 375010
Tel: (374-1) 582-157
Fax: (374-1) 523-417

Ministry of National Security
Karlos Petrosian, Minister
104 Nalbandian Street
Yerevan 375015
Tel: (374-1) 529-733
Fax: (374-1) 525-891

Ministry of Social Welfare
Razmik Martirosian, Minister
69 Terian Street
Yerevan 375009
Tel: (374-1) 526-831
Fax: (374-1) 526-831

Ministry of State Property Management
David Vardanian, Minister
2nd Government House
Yerevan 375010
Tel: (374-1) 521-877
Fax: (374-1) 526-557

Ministry of State Revenues
Ervand Zakharian, Minister
3 Khorenatsi Street
Yerevan 375015
Tel: (374-1) 539-195
Fax: (374-1) 538-226

Ministry of Territorial Administration
Hovik Abrahamian, Minister
Tel: (374-1) 525-274, 521-265
Arthur Arustamian, Assistant to the Minister
Tel: (374-1) 522-893

Ministry of Transportation and Communications
Andranik Manoukian, Minister
10 Zakian Street
Yerevan 375015
Tel: (374-1) 563-391
Fax: (374-1) 560-528

Ministry of Urban Development
David Lokian, Minister
Tel: (374-1) 589-080
Artyom Tarzian, Assistant to the Minister
Tel: (374-1) 565-180

PROTECTION OF INTELLECTUAL PROPERTY

Patents and Industrial Designs:
Agency: Armenian Patent and Trademark Office, Government Bldg. 3, Central Avenue, Yerevan 375010; tel: (374-1) 520-673; fax: (374-1) 151 823; e-mail: patent@arminco.com
Head: Prof. Sarkis L. Khantardjian, President.

Trademarks:
Agency: Armenian Patent and Trademark Office, Government Bldg. 3, Central Avenue, Yerevan 375010; tel:(374-1) 520-673; fax: (374-1) 151 823; e-mail: patent@arminco.com
Head: Prof. Sarkis L. Khantardjian, President.

Copyrights:
Agency: National Copyright Agency (NCA), 19A Koryun St., Yerevan 375009; tel:(374-1)527-350, 529-492; fax:(374-39) 06-873
Head: Vladimir M. Kostandian, Chief. NCA was established by in December 27, 1994.

DISPUTE SETTLEMENT

Economic Court, Henrik Sargsian, Supreme Arbitrator,
18 Paronian St., Yerevan 375015; Tel: (374-1) 532-411

Court of Cassation, Henrik Danielian, Chairman
6 Khorhrdaranayin St., Yerevan 375010; Tel: (374-1) 563-594, 583-231

TRANSPORTATION

Main Administration for Civil Aviation and Armenian Airlines, Hovhanes Yeritsian, Director General, Aviation Administration Bldg., Zvartnots Airport, Yerevan; Tel: (374-1) 774-824, Fax: (374-1)151-123

Zvartnots Airport, Valeri Harutunian, Director
Aviation Administration Bldg, Zvartnots Airport, Yerevan; Tel: (374-1) 773-097, Fax: (374-1) 151-123

State Administration for Railroads
50 Tigran Mets St., Yerevan 375005; Tel: (374-1) 520-428, Fax: (374-1) 573-630

COUNTRY MARKET RESEARCH FIRMS

BSC - Business Support Center, 24 Moskovain Street, apt. 2, Yerevan 375002 Armenia, Tel/Fax: (374-1) 588 654, 561 064, 528 279, 151-934; e-mail: bsc@bsc.am. An EU/TACIS initiated project that provides consulting to local and foreign private companies.

SED-MARSED consulting company. (CEO- Tigran Jrbashyan) 25/27 Nalbandyan, Suite 2, Yerevan-01; tel: (374-1) 565 625, 522 734; fax: (374-1) 565 625. A consulting company, which specializes in financial advise and auditing.

Hai-Consult (Executive Director - Gagik Makaryan), 4 Tigran Mets, room 2, 2nd floor, Yerevan-10, Armenia; tel: (374-1)589-337, 562-318; fax: (374-1) 151-822; e-mail: veneto@arminco.com. A consulting and auditing company.

Amyot Exco (Executive Director - Armand Pinarbasi), 18 Vardanats, Yerevan 375010, Armenia; tel: (374-1) 522 401, 586 373; fax: (374-1) 584 419, 584 459; e-mail: amyot@arminco.com. An affiliate of the Grand Thorton consulting company.

KPMG Armenia (Executive Director - Alan Kuchukian), 8 Hanrapetsusian, Yerevan 375010, Armenia, tel: (374-1) 566 762, 584 754, 586 379; fax: (374-1) 151 986, 151 989. An affiliate of KPMG's London office.

CENTRAL BANK OF ARMENIA

Central Bank of Armenia
Tigran Sargsian, Governor
6 Nalbandian Street, Yerevan 375010 Armenia
Tel: (374-1) 583-841, Fax: (374-1) 560-441, or 151-107
Web: http://www.cba.am

COMMERCIAL BANKS

Adana Bank, 5 Nalbandian St., Yerevan, 375010; Tel: (374-1) 567-109, 585-980, 562-216 Fax: (374-1)585-980. Chairman: Mr. Karen Nersisian. Correspondent Banks: Credo Bank (Saint Petersburg).

Agricultural Cooperative Bank of Armenia, 16 Vardanants St., Yerevan, 375010; Tel: (374-1) 570-227, 565-858, Fax: (374-1)151-755. Chairman: Mr. Stepan Gichian.

Akunk Bank, 19a Koriun St., Yerevan, 375009; Tel: (374-1) 520-792, 526-357 Fax: (374-1) 526-357. Chairman: Mr. Grigor Vahanian.

Anelik Bank, 4 Hrachya Kochar St., Yerevan, 375033, Armenia; Tel: (374-1) 221-451, 226-526; Fax: (374-1) 226-581. Chairman: Mr. Samvel Tsmatchian. Correspondent Bank: Bank Trust Company (New York), SWIFT (New York), Swiss Bank Corp. (Zurich), MosBusinessBank (Moscow).

Ardshinbank (Industrial Construction Bank), 3 Deghatan St., Yerevan, 375010; Tel: (374-1) 560-616, 561-247, 567-631, 581-403, Fax: (374-1) 151-155, 561-247. Chairman: Mr. Levon Farmanian. Correspondent Banks: Citibank, Bank of New York (New York).

Armagrobank (Agricultural joint stock commercial bank), 7a Movses Khorenatsu St., Yerevan, 375015; Tel: (374-1) 535-347, Fax: (374-1) 535-347. Chairman: Mr. Armen Arzumanyan. Correspondent Banks: The Bank of New York, Citibank, Republic National Bank of New York (New York); Deutsche Bank AG, Dresdner Bank AG, Commerzbank (Frankfurt); Credit Commerciale de France, Credit Agricole de France, Eurobank (Paris); Bank of Tokyo (Tokyo); Swiss Bank Corporation (Zurich); Bank Mees Pierson Amsterdam (Amsterdam); Bank Brussels Lambert (Brussels). Visa Credit Card Service is available.

Armeconombank, 23/1 Amiryan St., Yerevan, 375002; Tel: (374-1) 562-705, 531-115, Fax: (374-1) 562-705, 151-149. Chairman: Mr. Armen Martirosian. Correspondent Banks: Banque Nationale de Paris (Paris); National Westminster Bank (London); Riggs National Bank of Washington, D.C. (Washington); Deutsche Bank (Frankfurt).

Armenian Development Bank, 21/7 Paronyan St., Yerevan, 375015; Tel: (374-1) 530-094, 531-832, 537-552, Fax: (374-1) 530-312. Chairman: Alexander Griroryan. Correspondent Banks: Citibank (New York); Los Angeles Bank (Los Angeles).

Armimpexbank, 2 Nalbandyan St., Yerevan, 375010; Tel: (374-1) 589-906, 564-319; Fax: (374-1) 565-958; Chairman: Mr. Eduard Arabkhanyan. Correspondent Banks: Bank of America (Concord, CA), Bank of New York, Credit Lyonnais (New York); Creditanstalt Bankverein, Raiffeisenzentralbank A.G. (Vienna); Credit Lyonnais, Banque Francaise De L'orient, Deutsche Bank A.G. (Paris), Deutsche Bank A.G., Commerzbank (Frankfurt); Swiss Bank Corp., Union Bank of Switzerland, Credit Suisse (Zurich); Midland Bank, National Westminster Bank PLC (London); The Bank of Tokyo (Tokyo); Royal Bank of Canada (Toronto); ABN-Amro Bank (Amsterdam), Bank Brussels Lambert (Brussels); General Bank (Brussels); National Australia Bank (Sydney).

Arminvestbank, 13 Vardanants St., Yerevan, 375010; Tel: (374-1) 523-718, 523-929 Fax: (374-1)151-545. Chairman: Mr. Arthur Javadyan.

Converse Bank, 49 Komitas St., Yerevan 375051; Tel: (374-1) 281-015, 235-301, 271-610; Fax: (374-1-39) 06-072, E-mail:convers.yerevan@rex.iasnet.com. Chairman: Mr. Smbat Nasibyan.

Credit Service Bank, 15 Tigran Mets St., Yerevan, 375032; Tel: (374-1) 772-962, 770-410, Fax: (374-1) 770-410. Chairman: Mr. Boris Arakelian.

Credit-Yerevan Bank, 2/8 Amiryan St., Yerevan 375010; Tel: (374-1) 589-065, 563-652 Fax: (374-39) 06-891. Chairman: Mr. Martin Hovhanisyan, Correspondent Banks: Republic National Bank of New York (New York), The Bank of New York (New York), City Bank (London), Banque Nationale De Paris (Paris), Berlin Bank (Berlin).

David Bank, 23 Halabyan St., Yerevan, 375038; Tel: (374-1) 391-081, Fax: (374-1) 391-365. Chairman: Mr. Azat Shahbazyan. Correspondent Banks: Inko Bank, Rossisky Credit (Moscow).

Erebuni Bank, 13 Khaghakh Don St., Yerevan 375087; Tel: (374-1) 577-256, 577-249, Fax: (374-1) 577-256. Chairman: Mr. Gagik Lopojyan.

Gladzor Bank, 1/8 Charents St., Yerevan, 375025; Tel: (374-1) 576-750, 574-681, 551-515, 576-596; Fax: (374-1) 576-115. Chairman: Mr. Gagik Amaryan. Correspondent Banks: Stolichny, TverjunivesalBank (Moscow).

Haykap Bank, 22 Saryan St., Yerevan, 375002; Tel: (374-1) 532-080, 536-798, 566-729, Fax: (374-1-39) 07-033. Chairman: Mr. Grigor Terunyan. Correspondent Banks: American Express (Federal Bank in Cyprus), Bank of New York (Moscow), Credit Lyonnais(Moscow), Sviaz Bank (Moscow).

HaykhnayBank (Savings Bank), 20 Mikoyan St., Yerevan 375018; Tel: (374-1) 644-600, 635-853, 634-060 Fax: (374-1) 634-060. Chairman: Mr. Hovhannes Mandakuny. Correspondent Banks: Banque Nationale de Paris (Paris), MegheconomBank, Sberbank (Moscow).

HSBC Armenia Bank, 1 Amirian St., Yerevan 375010; Tel: (374-1) 563229, Fax: (374-1) 151-717. CEO: Charles Gregory.

INEKO Bank, 17 Tumanian St., Yerevan; Tel: (374-1) 563-725, 560-751, Fax: (374-1) 565-974; Chairman: Mr. Stepan Tonakanyan. Correspondent Banks:Republic National Bank (New York), Bank of New York (New York).

Mellat, 1 Pavstos Byuzand St., Yerevan 375010; Tel: (374-1) 581-354; Chairman: Morteza Nizami.

Menatep-Yerevan, 19a Koriun St., Tel: (374-1) 529-471, 589-512, Fax: (374-1) 529-471. Chairman: Mr. Ara Kitbalyan.

Prometeus Bank, 19 Hrachia Kochar St., Yerevan, 375012; Tel: (374-1) 273-000, Fax: (374-1) 274-818. Chairman: Emil Soghomonyan. Correspondent Banks: NevteGazStroy Bank (Moscow), Deutsche Bank (Frankfurt).

Ria Bank, 12a Koriun St., Yerevan 375009; Tel: (374-1) 560-132, 585-536 Fax: (374-39) 07057. Chairman: Mr. Viktor Virabyan. Correspondent Bank: Bank of America (New York), Toko Bank (Moscow).

Rossiyski Kredit Armenia Bank, 20 Tumanian St., Yerevan; Tel: (374-1) 580-506, 583-982, 526-731.

Sevan Bank, 3 Bagramian St., Yerevan 375019; Tel: (374-1) 273-971, Fax: (374-1) 273-892. Chairman: Mr. Ashot Eranosyan.

ShiraklnvestBank, 7 Garegin Njdeh St., Gyumri, 377500; Tel: (374-69) 2-20-69, Fax: (374-69) 3-62-14. Chariman: Mr. Ara Kitbalyan.

Sipan Bank, 37 Mashtots Ave., Yerevan 375002; Tel: (374-1) 534-722, Fax: (374-1) 532-601. Chairman: Mr. Volodia Hovsepyan. Correspondent Banks: MosGorStroyBank (Moscow).

TrustBank, 10 Artsakh St., Yerevan 375005; Tel: (374-1) 521-544, Fax: (374-1) 521-544. Chairman: Mr. Tigran Arakelyan. Correspondent Banks: AUDI (New-York).

United Bank, 4 Spendiarov Dr.,Yerevan, 375002; Tel: (374-1) 536-905, 535-543; Fax: (374-1-39) 06-955, Chairman: Mr. Hovsep Galstian.

AUDIT FIRMS

KPMG Armenia (resident full service office)
Mr. Alan Kutchukian, Managing Director
8 Hanrapetutyan St.
Yerevan-10 Armenia
Tel: (374-1) 566-762 or 584-754
Tel/Fax: (374-1) 151-985 or 151-989

AMYOT EXCO-ARMENIA
Mr. Armand Pinarbasi, Director
3 Isahakyan St
Yerevan-9 Armenia
Tel: (374-1) 586-373, 522-401
Tel/Fax: (374-1)151-870
E-mail: amia@arminco.com

INSURANCE COMPANIES

Armenian Financial Insurance Company (financial services)
(Mr. Levon Mamikonian, Managing Director)
22 Sarian St.
Yerevan-22, Armenia
Tel: (374-1) 531-311
Tel/fax: (374-1)151-548
E-mail: imamik@yse.armenia.su

ARAX LLC (contracts, expropriation)
(Mr. Ashot Poghosian, President)
21 Mashtots Ave, Suite 33
Yerevan, Armenia
Tel: (374-1) 529-418, 564-013, 589-856
Fax: (374-1)151-865 or 529-418
E-mail: arax@arminco.com.
Internet Page:
http://www.arminco.com/homepages/arax

"DIAGNOSTIKA" JSC (medical)
(Mr. Haik Nikoghosian, President and CEO)
6/1 Markarian St., Achapniak
Yerevan-73, Armenia
Tel: (374-1) 343-247, 287-411
Fax: (374-1)151-639, 287-411
E-mail: haik@diagnost.arminco.com

Main Administration for State Insurance (life, property)
(Mr. Sanasar Ananian, Director)
6 Abelyan St.
Yerevan-38, Armenia
Tel: (374-1) 340-644, or 345-456

MICA Insurance Company (medical, life)
(Mr. Michael Yeroyan, Deputy Director)
4 Tigran Mets Ave., room 203
Yerevan-10, Armenia
Tel/fax: (374-1) 566-003

Prime Insurance Brokers
(Mr. Artavazd Yakhshibekian, Chairman)
P.O.Box 1
Yerevan-09, Armenia
Tel: (374-1) 526-431
Fax: (374-1)526-441

INFORMATION ON INTERNATIONAL FINANCING

Multilateral Development Bank Operations (MDBO)
U.S. Department of Commerce
USA Trade Center, Ronald Reagan Building, Mezzanine Level (14th Street Entrance) Washington, DC 20054
Tel: (202) 482-3399
Fax: (202) 482-3914
Web: http://www.usatrade.gov/mdbo

AGRICULTURE - TRADE ASSISTANCE

U.S. Department of Agriculture
Foreign Agricultural Service
Trade and Promotion Office
Washington, D.C. 20250
Tel: 202-720-7420

USDA Marketing Assistance Project (Dr. Craig Infanger, Director)
74 Terian Street
Yerevan 375009
Tel: (374-1) 525-975, 529-607, 578-390
Fax: 151-696
Web site: www.usda.am

MASS MEDIA

State Administration for Television and Radio
Tigran Hakobyan, Chairman
5 Alek Manukyan St., Yerevan 375025
Tel:(374-2)555-033, Fax:(374-2)551-513

Armenpress State Information Agency
Gevorg Hovhannisyan, Director
28 Isahakyan St., Yerevan 375015
Tel:(374-2)526-702, 526-702, Fax:(374-2)529-262

Architecture and City Planning

State Administration for Architecture and City Planning
Romeo Julakyan, Chairman
3 Government Bldg., Republic Square, Yerevan 375010
Tel:(374-2)526-234, Fax:(374-2)583-869

COUNTRY MARKET RESEARCH FIRMS

The Center for Business Research and Development (CBRD)
Stephan Karamardyan, Director
40 Marshall Baghramyan St., Yerevan 375019
Tel:(374-2)271-602, 151-049; Fax:(374-2)151-048
E-mail: AUA@adonis.ias.msk.su

Transcom
Suren Shahinyan, Director
1/3 P. Byuzand St., Floor 6, Yerevan 375010
Tel: (374-2)271-827, 567-054; Fax: (374-2)151-048

LARGEST PRIVATE BANKS

Armimpexbank
2 Nalbandyan St., Yerevan, 375010
Tel:(374-2)589-906, 589-518, 564-617; Fax:(374-2)565-958
Chairman: Mr. Eduard Arabkhanyan
Corresponding Banks: Bank of America (Concord, CA), Bank of New York, Credit Lyonnais (New York); Creditanstalt Bankverein, Raiffeisenzentralbank A.G. (Vienna); Credit Lyonnais, Banque Francaise De L'orient, Deutsche Bank A.G. (Paris), Deutsche Bank A.G., Commerzbank (Frankfurt); Swiss Bank Corp., Union Bank of Switzerland, Credit Suisse (Zurich); Midland Bank, National Westminster Bank PLC (London); The Bank of Tokyo (Tokyo); Royal Bank of Canada (Toronto); ABN-Amro Bank (Amsterdam), Bank Brussels Lambert (Brussels); General Bank (Brussels); National Australia Bank (Sydney).

ArdShinBank (Industrial Construction Bank)
3 Deghatan St., Yerevan, 375010
Tel:(374-2)560-616, 528-513, Fax:(374-2)151-155, Telex:243349
Chairman: Mr. Karen Movsisyan
Corresponding Banks: Citibank, Bank of New York (New York).

ArmAgrobank (Agricultural joint stock commercial bank)
7a Movses Khorenatsu St., Yerevan, 375015
Tel:(374-2)534-342, Fax:(374-2)534-342
Chairman: Mr. Armen Arzumanyan
Corresponding Banks: The Bank of New York, Citibank, Republic National Bank of New York (New York); Deutsche Bank AG, Dresdner Bank AG, Commerzbank (Frankfurt); Credit Commerciale de France, Credit Agricole de France, Eurobank (Paris); Bank of Tokyo (Tokyo); Swiss Bank Corporation (Zurich); Bank Mees Pierson Amsterdam (Amsterdam); Bank Brussels Lambert (Brussels).
Visa Credit Card Service

ArmEconomBank
32 Garegin Njde, Yerevan, 375026
Tel:(374-2)440-511, 447-680, Fax:(374-2)562-705
Chairman: Mr. Vladimir Badalyan
Corresponding Banks: Banque Nationale de Paris (Paris); National Westminster Bank (London); Riggs National Bank of Washington, D.C. (Washington); Deutsche Bank (Frankfurt).

Aviabank
1 P.Sevak St., Yerevan, 375014
Tel:(374-2)288-857, Fax:(374-2)281-940, Telex:243113
Chairman: Mr. Harutiun Vardanyan
Corresponding Banks:Credit Lyonnais (New York); Barklays Bank (London); Swiss Bank Corp. (Geneva); Credit Lyonnais (Paris), Dresdner Bank (Frankfurt), ABN Bank Amro (Vienna), MMKB (Moscow).

ArmSnundBank
4 Spendiarov Dr.,Yerevan, 375002
Tel:(374-2)536-220, Fax:(374-2)563-220
Chairman: Mr. Hovik Melikyan
Corresponding Banks: Ukraina (Kiev), TverjuniversalBAnk (Moscow).

Anelik Bank
4 Hrachya Kochar St., Yerevan, 375033, Armenia
Tel:(374-2)221-451, 226-526 Fax:(374-2)226-581
Chairman: Mr. Samvel Tsmatcyan
Corresponding Bank: Swiss Bank Corp.(Zurich), Mos BusinesssBank (Moscow).

Akunk Bank
19a Koriun St., Yerevan, 375009
Tel:(374-2)520-792, 526-357 Fax:(374-2)526-867
Chairman: Mr. Grikor Vahanyan

Arminvestbank
13 Vardanants St., Yerevan, 375010
Tel:(374-2)570-502, 570-350, Fax:(374-2)523-718
Chairman: Mr. Arthur Javadyan

Adana Bank
5 Nalbandyan St., Yerevan, 375010
Tel:(374-2)589-017, 597-358 Fax:(374-2)633-591
Chairman: Mr.Karen Nersisyan
Corresponding Banks: Credo Bank (Saint Petersburg).

Areg Bank
11 Yerevan St., Abovian
Tel:(374-2)558-951 Fax:(374-39)07-033
Chairman: Mr. Ashot Arakelyan
Corresponding Banks: IncomBank (Moscow)

Bank for Reconstruction and Development
31 Moskovyan St., Yerevan, 375002
Tel:(374-2)530-156, 530-094, Fax:(374-2)530-156
Chairman: Alexander Griroryan
Corresponding Banks: Citibank (New York); Los Angeles Bank (Los Angeles).

Capital Bank
38 Tamantsinery 4th Dr.,Yerevan, 375006
Tel:(374-2)484-610
Chairman: Mr. Kamo Poghosyan

Converse Bank
49 Komitas St., Yerevan 375051
Tel:(374-2)281-015, 235-993 Fax:(374-2)285-082,
E-mail:convers.yerevan@rex.iasnet.com
Chairman: Mr. Smbat Nasibyan

Credit-Yerevan Bank
2/8 Vramshapuh St., Yerevan 375002
Tel:(374-2)589-065 Fax:(374-2)580-083
Chairman: Mr. Martin Hovhanisyan
Corresponding Banks: Banque Nationale De Paris (Paris), Berlin Bank (Berlin).

David Bank
16 Kievian St., Suite 609A, Yerevan, 375028
Tel:(374-2)262-831, 262-882, 275-809, 391-140, Fax:(374-2)353-900
Chairman: Mr. Azat Shahbazyan
Corresponding Banks: Inko Bank, Rossisky Credit (Moscow).

Delta Bank
105 Raffu St., Yerevan, 375064
Tel:(374-2)533-924
Chairman: Mr. Arshak Karakhanyan

Erebuni Bank
13 Khaghakh Don St., Yerevan 375087
Tel: (374-2)536-220
Chairman: Mr. Ph. Gevorkyan

EchoBank
36 Avetisyan St.,Suite #31, Yerevan 375012

Tel: (374-2)271-500, 271-510 Fax:(374-2) 271-510, 262-900
Chairman: Ms. Tamara Hovakymyan

Elita Bank
16 Kievyan St., Yerevan 375028
Tel: (374-2)220-223, 223-478, 223-457, Fax:(374-2)226-163
Chairman: Mr. Sanasar Abazazyan
Corresponding Banks: Megeconomsberbank (Moscow).

Felix Bank
38 Saryan St., Yerevan 375002
Tel:(374-2)589-062, (8852)280-702
Chairman: Mr. Barsegh Peplozyan

Gladzor Bank
1/8 Charents St., Yerevan, 375025
Tel:(374-2)576-750, 551-515, Fax:(374-2)576-115
Chairman: Mr. Gagik Amaryan
Corresponding Banks: Stolichny, TverjunivesalBank (Moscow).

Garni Bank
40 Hakhtanaky St., Abovyan
Tel:(374-61)21-334
Chairman: Mr. Grikor Aghadjanyan

Gevorg Bank
11 Hanrapetutyan Ave., Abovyan
Tel:(88261)25-877
Chairman: Mr. Suren Grigoryan

HaykhnayBank (Savings Bank)
28a Khorenatsu, Yerevan 375018
Tel:(374-2)520-458, 580-451, Fax:(374-2)560-766
Chairman: Mr. Hovhannes Mandakuny
Corresponding Banks: Banque Nationale de Paris (Paris), MegheconomBank, Sberbank (Moscow).

Haykap Bank
22 Saryan St., Yerevan, 375002
Tel:(374-2)532-080
Chairman: Mr. Hakob Terunyan
Corresponding Banks: Credit Lyonnais(Moscow), Sviaz Bank (Moscow)

Hrazdan Bank
8 Spandaryan St., Hrazdan
Tel:(374-2)589-906
Chairman: Mr. Ashot Assatryan

Lend Bank
21 Nairy Zaryan St., Yerevan 375051
Tel:(374-2)399-060 Fax:(374-2)340-273
Chairman: Mr.Anushavan Khachikyan
Corresponding Banks: ABN Amro Bank, City Bank, Bank of New York (New York). Visa Credit Card Service via Incombank (Moscow).

Litsk Bank
P2 Dipol St., Kamo
Tel: (374-2)285-991
Chairman: Mr. Samvel Amirkhanyan

Mets Bank
143 Artsakh St., Yerevan 375001
Tel:(374-2)525-310, Fax:(374-2)525-310
Chairman: Gagik Kafyan
Corresponding Banks: Commerzbank (Frankfurt)

Prometey Bank
19 Hracia Kochar St., Yerevan, 375012
Tel:(374-2)273-000, Fax:(374-2)274-818
Chairman: Emil Soghomonyan
Corresponding Banks: NevteGazStroy Bank (Moscow), Deutsche Bank (Frankfurt)

Ria Bank
12a Koriun St., Yerevan 375009
Tel:(374-2)560-132 Fax:(88539) 07057
Chairman: Mr. Viktor Virabyan
Corresponding Bank: Toko Bank (Moscow).

Sipan Bank
37 Mashtots Ave., Yerevan 375002
Tel:(374-2)532-601, Fax:(374-2)532-601
Chairman: Mr. Volodia Hovsepyan
Corresponding Banks: MosGorStroyBank (Moscow)

Spurk Bank
2 Zaryan St., Yerevan 375002
Tel:(374-2)257-004, Fax:(374-2)228-155
Chairman: Mr. Samvel Sargisyan
Corresponding Banks: TverjuniversalBank(Moscow)

Spitak Bank
2 Torosyan St., Spitak
Tel:(88269)4-58
Chairman: Mr. Boris Arakelyan

Sevan Bank
24 Azatutyan St., Yerevan 375014
Tel:(374-2)288-747, Fax:(374-2)565-263
Chairman: Mr. Karen Manvelyan

Space Bank
1 Komeritmiutyan St., Yerevan
Tel:(374-2)533-419, Fax:(374-2)532-600, 240-985
Chairman: Mr. Armen Sukiasyan
Corresponding Banks: Alfa Bank (Moscow).

Transbank
27 Tigranyan St., Yerevan 375014
Tel:(374-2)234-718
Chairman: Mr. Hrant Zazyan
Corresponding Banks: NA

INFORMATION ON INTERNATIONAL FINANCING

The Multilateral Develoment Bank Office
Brenda Ebeling, Director
14th & Constitutiona Avenue, NW
Washington DC 20057
Tel: 202-482-3399; Fax: 202-482-6179

AGRICULTURE - TRADE ASSISTANCE

U.S. Department of Agriculture
Foreign Agricultural Service
Trade and Promotion Office
Tel: 202-720-7420

GENERAL BUSINESS ASSISTANCE

Eurasian-American Chamber of Commerce
Eurasian-American Investment Center
P.O.Box 15343
Washington, DC 20053
Ph. (202) 546-2130. Fax: (202) 546-3275
E-mail: rusric@erols.com

COMMERCIAL BANKS IN ARMENIA

AKUNK BANK Chairman: Grigor VAHANYAN 1/21 Bagramian Street Yerevan Telephone: (3741) 526357 Fax: (3741) 520792 E-mail: atlas@arminco.com	AGRICULTURAL COOPERATIVE BANK OF ARMENIA Chairman: STEPAN GICHYAN 1 Bayron Street Yerevan Telephone: (3741) 568585 Fax: (3741) 151755 E-mail: acba@arminco.com Internet: http://www.acba.am
ARDSHINBANK Executive Director: LEVON FARMANYAN 3 DEGHATAN Street Yerevan Telephone: (3741) 528513 Fax: (3741)151155 E-mail: office@ardshin.bank.am Internet: http://www.ardshin.bank.am/	ANELIK BANK Chairman: SAMVEL CHEZMACHYAN 75 Baghramyan Street Yerevan Telephone: (3741) 221451 Fax: (3741) 226581 E-mail: anelik@arminco.com, Internet: http://www.anelik.am/
ARMAGROBANK Chairman: KAREN DAVTYAN 7a Movses Khorenatsi Street Yerevan Telephone: (3741) 534342 Fax: (3741) 535347 E-mail: head-office@agrobank.am Internet: http://www.agrobank.am	AREXIMBANK Executive Director: ARMEN KHANDKARYAN 20 Tumanyan Street Yerevan Telephone: (3741) 583131 Fax: (3741) 580506 E-mail: info@areximbank.am Internet: http://www.areximbank.am

ARMENIAN DEVELOPMENT BANK Chairman: ALEXANDER GRIGORYAN 21/1 Paronyan Street Yerevan Telephone: (3741) 531832 Fax: (3741) 533233 E-mail: info@armdb.com	ARMECONOMBANK Executive Director: ASHOT OSIPYAN 23/1 Amiryan Street Yerevan Telephone: (3741) 538904 Fax: (3741)151149 E-mail: armeco@arminco.com Internet: http://www.aeb.am
ARMINVESTBANK Chairman: VARUZHAN AMIRAGHYAN 13 Vartanants Street Yerevan Telephone: (3741) 570502 Fax: (3741) 07210 E-mail: root@invest.b.infocom.amilink.net	ARMIMPEXBANK Chairman: BAGRAT ASATRYAN 2 Vazgen Sargsyan Street Yerevan Telephone: (3741) 589906 Fax: (3741) 565958 E-mail: jav@impex.infocom.amilink.net Internet: http://www.impex.bank.am
ARMSAVINGSBANK Executive Director: SEDA PETROSYAN 46 Nalbandyan Street Yerevan Telephone: (3741) 580451 Fax: (3741) 565578 E-mail: savebn@mbox.amilink.net	ARMCOMMUNICATIONBANK Executive Director: HARUTYUN MESROPYAN 30 Eznik Kokhbacu Street Yerevan Telephone: (3741) 581934 Fax: (3741) 534497 E-mail: haykap@mbox.amilink.net
ARTSAKHBANK Chairman: KAMO NERSISYAN 30 D. Sasounci Street Stepanakert Telephone: (3741) 285872 Fax: (3741) 288943 E-mail: artsakh@nktel.net	CONVERSE BANK Chairman: SMBAT NASIBYAN 49 Komitas Street Yerevan Telephone: (374-1) 281015 Fax: (3741) 06195 E-mail: www.converse.r.am
CREDIT-Yerevan BANK Chairman: HAKOP MALKASYAN 2/8 Amiryan Street Yerevan Telephone: (3741) 589065 Fax: (3741) 06868 E-mail: ss@mbox.creyer.amilink.net	CREDIT-SERVICE BANK Executive Director: TIGRAN MIRZOYAN 15 Tigran Mets Street Yerevan Telephone: (3741) 585331 Fax: (3741) 525701 E-mail: credit@service-infocom-email.net
GLADZOR BANK Chairman: GAGIK AMARYAN 1B Charents Street Yerevan Telephone: (3741) 576750 Fax: (3741) 506447 E-mail: gladzor@amlink.net	HSBC ARMENIA BANK Managing Director: CHARLES BERNARD GREGORY 9 Vazgen Sargsyan Street Yerevan Telephone: (3741) 563229 Fax: (3741) 527078 E-mail: hsbc@arminco.com
INECOBANK Chairman: AVETIS BALOYAN 17 Tumanyan Street Yerevan Telephone: (3741) 565974 Fax: (3741) 545166 E-mail: incobank@incobank.am Internet: http://www.inecobank.am	INTERNATIONAL INVESTMENT BANK Executive Director: ASHOT ERANOSYAN 45 Khorenatsu Street Yerevan Telephone: (3741) 559055 Fax: (3741) 525955 E-mail: bsevan@arminco.com
INTERNATIONAL COMMERCIAL BLACK SEA BANK (ARMENIA) Deputy Director General: GORGE PETRUCOS 6 Deghatan Street Yerevan	"ITB" INTERNATIONAL TRADE BANK Chairman: ARA KITBALYAN 19a Koryun Street Yerevan Telephone: (3741) 588512 Fax: (3741) 529471 E-mail: yerevan@menatep.infocom.amilink.net

Telephone: (3741) 520432 Fax: (3741) 151878 E-mail: cbgam@arminco.com	
LENDBANK Executive Director: ANUSHAVAN KHACHIKYAN 8 Errvand Kochar Street Yerevan Telephone: (3741) 558970 Fax: (3741) 07035 E-mail: lend@mbox.amlink.net	MELLAT BANK Executive Director: ISSA JHAHREMANI TCHABOK 6 Amiryan Street Yerevan Telephone: (3741) 581791 Fax: (3741) 151811 E-mail: mellat@infocom.am
PROMETEY BANK Chairman: EMIL SOGHOMONYAN 44/2 Hanrapetutian Street Yerevan Telephone: (3741) 562036, 521705 Fax: (3741) 545719 E-mail: nunm@freenet.am	SHIRAKINVEST BANK Executive Director: MESROP KARAPETYAN 7 Garegin Hzdeh Street GYUMRI Telephone: (269) 34883 Fax: (269) 36214 E-mail: shib@shirak.am
UNIBANK Chairman: VARDAN ATAYAN 12 Amiryan Street Yerevan Tel: (374-1) 535132, 539870 Fax: (3741) 533032 E-mail: unibank@unibank.am	

INTERNATIONAL FINANCIAL INSTITUTIONS:

CAUCASUS ADVISORS LLC (MANAGER OF THE CAUCASUS FUND, FINANCED IN PART BY OPIC) ARTAK MELKONIAN MANAGING DIRECTOR OF ARMENIAN OPERATIONS Address: 8 Hanrapetutyan Street Yerevan Telephone: (3741) 560954, 587418 Fax: (3741) 587418 E-mail: amelkon@acc.am	EUROPEAN BANK FOR RECONSTRUCTION AND DEVELOPMENT ALKIS DRAKINOS, HEAD OF YEREVAN RESIDENT OFFICE Address: 20 Baghramyan Street Yerevan Telephone: (3741) 540425, 540426, 540427, 540428 Fax: (3741) 540430 E-mail: drakinoa@evn.ebrd.com
INTERNATIONAL FINANCE CORPORATION ARUSYAK SARGSYAN, OFFICE MANAGER Address: 2 Khorhertarani Street Republic Square Yerevan Telephone: (3741) 545241, 545242, 545243 Fax: (3741) 599542 E-mail: asargsyan@ifc.org, Internet: http://www.ifc.org	EURASIA FOUNDATION EUGENE STAPLES, ACTING REGIONAL DIRECTOR Address: 22 Isahakian Street, SUITE 11 Yerevan Telephone:(3741) 585598, 566789, 565147, 561626, 151824 Fax: (3741) 151824, 585598 E-mail: eurasia@eurasia.am

WORLD BANK OWAISE SAADAT, RESIDENT REPRESENTATIVE Address: 2 Khorhrtarani Street Republic Square Yerevan Telephone: (3741) 505060, 520992, 523992 Fax: (374-1) 151883, 151788 E-mail: abuniatyan@worldbank.org	SHOREBANK ADVISORY SERVICES (SHORE OVERSEAS CORPORATION) JENNIFER O'NEIL, COUNTRY MANAGER 15 Parpetsu Street, SUITE 3 Yerevan Telephone: (3741) 537310, 537360 Fax: (3741) 151806 E-mail: safarm@arminco.com jonsaf@arminco.com

IMF RESIDENT REPRESENTATIVE OFFICE GEORGE ANAYOTOS, RESIDENT REPRESENTATIVE 1 Melik Adamyan Street, SUITE 326 Yerevan Telephone: (3741) 528532, 528960 Fax: (3741) 151703 E-mail: ganay@arminco.com

OTHER FINANCIAL INSTITUTIONS:

UNION OF BANKS OF ARMENIA Chairman: ARMEN YEGHIAZARYAN 19A Koryuni Street YERAVAN Telephone: (3741) 527731 Fax: (3741) 567589 E-mail: aba@arminco.com	CENTRAL BANK OF ARMENIA Chairman: TIGRAN SARGSYAN 6 Nalbandyan Street Yerevan Telephone: (3741) 583-841 Fax: (3741) 580052 E-mail: info@cba.am Internet: http://www.cba.am
MINISTRY OF FINANCE AND ECONOMY MINISTER: VARDAN KHACHATRYAN 1 Melik Adamian Street Yerevan Telephone: (3741) 595304 Fax: (3741) 524282 OR 151069 E-mail: staff@mf.gov.am	AMERICAN EMBASSY, Yerevan Commercial Section GEORGE ISAYAN, BISNIS REPRESENTATIVE IN ARMENIA 18 BAGHRAMIAN Street Yerevan Telephone: (3741) 151551 Fax: (3741) 151550 E-mail: Isayangx@yerevanb.us-state.gov Internet: http://www.arminco.am/embusa/cons.htm

BASIC TITLES ON ARMENIA

IMPORTANT!
All publications are updated annually!
Please contact IBP, Inc. at ibpusa3@gmail.com for the latest ISBNs and additional information

title
Armenia A "Spy" Guide - Strategic Information and Developments
Armenia A Spy" Guide"
Armenia Banking & Financial Market Handbook
Armenia Banking & Financial Market Handbook
Armenia Business and Industrial Directory
Armenia Business and Industrial Directory
Armenia Business and Investment Opportunities Yearbook
Armenia Business and Investment Opportunities Yearbook
Armenia Business and Investment Opportunities Yearbook Volume 1 Strategic Information and Opportunities

title
Armenia Business Intelligence Report - Practical Information, Opportunities, Contcts
Armenia Business Intelligence Report - Practical Information, Opportunities, Contcts
Armenia Business Law Handbook - Strategic Information and Basic Laws
Armenia Business Law Handbook - Strategic Information and Basic Laws
Armenia Business Law Handbook - Strategic Information and Basic Laws
Armenia Business Law Handbook - Strategic Information and Basic Laws
Armenia Company Laws and Regulations Handbook
Armenia Constitution and Citizenship Laws Handbook - Strategic Information and Basic Laws
Armenia Country Study Guide - Strategic Information and Developments
Armenia Country Study Guide - Strategic Information and Developments
Armenia Country Study Guide - Strategic Information and Developments Volume 1 Strategic Information and Developments
Armenia Customs, Trade Regulations and Procedures Handbook
Armenia Customs, Trade Regulations and Procedures Handbook
Armenia Diplomatic Handbook - Strategic Information and Developments
Armenia Diplomatic Handbook - Strategic Information and Developments
Armenia Ecology & Nature Protection Handbook
Armenia Ecology & Nature Protection Handbook
Armenia Ecology & Nature Protection Laws and Regulation Handbook
Armenia Energy Policy, Laws and Regulation Handbook
Armenia Export-Import and Business Directory
Armenia Export-Import and Business Directory
Armenia Export-Import Trade and Business Directory
Armenia Export-Import Trade and Business Directory
Armenia Financial Laws and Regulations Handbook
Armenia Financial Laws and Regulations Handbook
Armenia Foreign Policy and Government Guide
Armenia Foreign Policy and Government Guide
Armenia Government and Business Contacts Handbook
Armenia Government and Business Contacts Handbook
Armenia Immigration Laws and Regulations Handbook - Strategic Information and Basic Laws
Armenia Industrial and Business Directory
Armenia Industrial and Business Directory
Armenia Internet and E-Commerce Investment and Business Guide - Strategic and Practical Information: Regulations and Opportunities
Armenia Internet and E-Commerce Investment and Business Guide - Strategic and Practical Information: Regulations and Opportunities
Armenia Investment and Business Guide - Strategic and Practical Information
Armenia Investment and Business Guide - Strategic and Practical Information
Armenia Investment and Business Guide - Strategic and Practical Information
Armenia Investment and Business Guide - Strategic and Practical Information
Armenia Investment and Trade Laws and Regulations Handbook
Armenia Labor Laws and Regulations Handbook - Strategic Information and Basic Laws

title
Armenia Land Ownership and Agriculture Laws Handbook
Armenia Mineral & Mining Sector Investment and Business Guide - Strategic and Practical Information
Armenia Mineral & Mining Sector Investment and Business Guide - Strategic and Practical Information
Armenia Mining Laws and Regulations Handbook
Armenia President and Political System Handbook
Armenia President Handbook: Strategic and Political Information
Armenia Privatization Programs and Regulations Handbook
Armenia Privatization Programs and Regulations Handbook
Armenia Recent Economic and Political Developments Yearbook
Armenia Recent Economic and Political Developments Yearbook
Armenia Recent Economic and Political Developments Yearbook
Armenia Starting Business (Incorporating) in....Guide
Armenia Tax Guide
Armenia Tax Guide
Armenia Taxation Laws and Regulations Handbook
Armenia Telecom Laws and Regulations Handbook
Armenia Telecommunication Industry Business Opportunities Handbook
Armenia Telecommunication Industry Business Opportunities Handbook
Armenia Transportation Policy and Regulations Handbook
Armenia Wine Industry Investment and Business Opportunities Yearbook

WORLD COMPANY LAWS AND REGULATIONS LIBRARY

Ultimate directories for conducting export-import operations in the country. Largest exporters and importers, strategic government and business contacts, selected export-import regulations and more...

Price: $149 each

TITLE

Afghanistan Company Laws and Regulations Handbook
Albania Company Laws and Regulations Handbook
Algeria Company Laws and Regulations Handbook
Andorra Company Laws and Regulations Handbook
Angola Company Laws and Regulations Handbook
Anguilla Company Laws and Regulations Handbook
Antigua and Barbuda Company Laws and Regulations Handbook
Antilles (Netherlands) Company Laws and Regulations Handbook
Argentina Company Laws and Regulations Handbook
Armenia Company Laws and Regulations Handbook
Aruba Company Laws and Regulations Handbook
Australia Company Laws and Regulations Handbook
Austria Company Laws and Regulations Handbook
Azerbaijan Company Laws and Regulations Handbook
Bahamas Company Laws and Regulations Handbook
Bahrain Company Laws and Regulations Handbook
Bangladesh Company Laws and Regulations Handbook
Barbados Company Laws and Regulations Handbook
Belarus Company Laws and Regulations Handbook
Belgium Company Laws and Regulations Handbook
Belize Company Laws and Regulations Handbook
Benin Company Laws and Regulations Handbook
Bermuda Company Laws and Regulations Handbook
Bhutan Company Laws and Regulations Handbook
Bolivia Company Laws and Regulations Handbook
Bosnia and Herzegovina Company Laws and Regulations Handbook
Botswana Company Laws and Regulations Handbook
Brazil Company Laws and Regulations Handbook
Brunei Company Laws and Regulations Handbook
Bulgaria Company Laws and Regulations Handbook
Burkina Faso Company Laws and Regulations Handbook
Burundi Company Laws and Regulations Handbook
Cambodia Company Laws and Regulations Handbook
Cameroon Company Laws and Regulations Handbook
Canada Company Laws and Regulations Handbook
Cape Verde Company Laws and Regulations Handbook
Cayman Islands Company Laws and Regulations Handbook
Central African Republic Company Laws and Regulations Handbook
Chad Company Laws and Regulations Handbook
Chile Company Laws and Regulations Handbook
China Company Laws and Regulations Handbook
Colombia Company Laws and Regulations Handbook
Comoros Company Laws and Regulations Handbook
Congo Company Laws and Regulations Handbook
Congo, Democratic Republic Company Laws and Regulations Handbook
Cook Islands Company Laws and Regulations Handbook
Costa Rica Company Laws and Regulations Handbook
Cote d'Ivoire Company Laws and Regulations Handbook
Croatia Company Laws and Regulations Handbook
Cuba Company Laws and Regulations Handbook
Cyprus Company Laws and Regulations Handbook
Czech Republic Company Laws and Regulations Handbook
Denmark Company Laws and Regulations Handbook
Djibouti Company Laws and Regulations Handbook
Dominica Company Laws and Regulations Handbook
Dominican Republic Company Laws and Regulations Handbook
Ecuador Company Laws and Regulations Handbook
Egypt Company Laws and Regulations Handbook
El Salvador Company Laws and Regulations Handbook

Equatorial Guinea Company Laws and Regulations Handbook
Eritrea Company Laws and Regulations Handbook
Estonia Company Laws and Regulations Handbook
Ethiopia Company Laws and Regulations Handbook
Falkland Islands Company Laws and Regulations Handbook
Faroes Company Laws and Regulations Handbook
Fiji Company Laws and Regulations Handbook
Finland Company Laws and Regulations Handbook
France Company Laws and Regulations Handbook
Gabon Company Laws and Regulations Handbook
Gambia Company Laws and Regulations Handbook
Georgia Company Laws and Regulations Handbook
Germany Company Laws and Regulations Handbook
Ghana Company Laws and Regulations Handbook
Gibraltar Company Laws and Regulations Handbook
Greece Company Laws and Regulations Handbook
Greenland Company Laws and Regulations Handbook
Grenada Company Laws and Regulations Handbook
Guam Company Laws and Regulations Handbook
Guatemala Company Laws and Regulations Handbook
Guernsey Company Laws and Regulations Handbook
Guinea Company Laws and Regulations Handbook
Guinea-Bissau Company Laws and Regulations Handbook
Guyana Company Laws and Regulations Handbook
Haiti Company Laws and Regulations Handbook
Honduras Company Laws and Regulations Handbook
Hungary Company Laws and Regulations Handbook
Iceland Company Laws and Regulations Handbook
India Company Laws and Regulations Handbook
Indonesia Company Laws and Regulations Handbook
InternationalCompany Laws and Regulations Handbook
Iran Company Laws and Regulations Handbook
Iraq Company Laws and Regulations Handbook
Ireland Company Laws and Regulations Handbook
Israel Company Laws and Regulations Handbook
Italy Company Laws and Regulations Handbook
Jamaica Company Laws and Regulations Handbook
Japan Company Laws and Regulations Handbook
Jersey Company Laws and Regulations Handbook
Jordan Company Laws and Regulations Handbook
Kazakhstan Company Laws and Regulations Handbook
Kenya Company Laws and Regulations Handbook
Kiribati Company Laws and Regulations Handbook
Korea, North Company Laws and Regulations Handbook
Korea, South Company Laws and Regulations Handbook
Kosovo Company Laws and Regulations Handbook
Kuwait Company Laws and Regulations Handbook
Kyrgyzstan Company Laws and Regulations Handbook
Laos Company Laws and Regulations Handbook
Latvia Company Laws and Regulations Handbook
Lebanon Company Laws and Regulations Handbook
Lesotho Company Laws and Regulations Handbook
Liberia Company Laws and Regulations Handbook
Libya Company Laws and Regulations Handbook
Liechtenstein Company Laws and Regulations Handbook
Lithuania Company Laws and Regulations Handbook
Luxembourg Company Laws and Regulations Handbook
Macao Company Laws and Regulations Handbook
Macedonia Company Laws and Regulations Handbook
Madagascar Company Laws and Regulations Handbook
Madeira Company Laws and Regulations Handbook
Malawi Company Laws and Regulations Handbook
Malaysia Company Laws and Regulations Handbook
Maldives Company Laws and Regulations Handbook
Mali Company Laws and Regulations Handbook
Malta Company Laws and Regulations Handbook
Man Company Laws and Regulations Handbook
Marshall Islands Company Laws and Regulations Handbook
Mauritania Company Laws and Regulations Handbook
Mauritius Company Laws and Regulations Handbook
Mayotte Company Laws and Regulations Handbook
Mexico Company Laws and Regulations Handbook
Micronesia Company Laws and Regulations Handbook
Moldova Company Laws and Regulations Handbook
Monaco Company Laws and Regulations Handbook
Mongolia Company Laws and Regulations Handbook
Monserrat Company Laws and Regulations Handbook
Morocco Company Laws and Regulations Handbook
Mozambique Company Laws and Regulations Handbook
Myanmar Company Laws and Regulations Handbook
Namibia Company Laws and Regulations Handbook
Nauru Company Laws and Regulations Handbook
Nepal Company Laws and Regulations Handbook
Netherlands Company Laws and Regulations Handbook
New Caledonia Company Laws and Regulations Handbook
New Zealand Company Laws and Regulations Handbook
Nicaragua Company Laws and Regulations Handbook
Niger Company Laws and Regulations Handbook
Nigeria Company Laws and Regulations Handbook
Niue Company Laws and Regulations Handbook
Northern Mariana Islands Company Laws and Regulations Handbook
Norway Company Laws and Regulations Handbook
Oman Company Laws and Regulations Handbook
Pakistan Company Laws and Regulations Handbook
Palau Company Laws and Regulations Handbook

Palestine Company Laws and Regulations Handbook
Panama Company Laws and Regulations Handbook
Papua New Guinea Company Laws and Regulations Handbook
Paraguay Company Laws and Regulations Handbook
Peru Company Laws and Regulations Handbook
Philippines Company Laws and Regulations Handbook
Pitcairn Islands Company Laws and Regulations Handbook
Poland Company Laws and Regulations Handbook
Polynesia French Company Laws and Regulations Handbook
Portugal Company Laws and Regulations Handbook
Qatar Company Laws and Regulations Handbook
Romania Company Laws and Regulations Handbook
Russia Company Laws and Regulations Handbook
Rwanda Company Laws and Regulations Handbook
Saint Kitts and Nevis Company Laws and Regulations Handbook
Saint Lucia Company Laws and Regulations Handbook
Saint Vincent and The Grenadines Company Laws and Regulations Handbook
Samoa (American) Company Laws and Regulations Handbook
Samoa (Western) Company Laws and Regulations Handbook
San Marino Company Laws and Regulations Handbook
Sao Tome and Principe Company Laws and Regulations Handbook
Saudi Arabia Company Laws and Regulations Handbook
Scotland Company Laws and Regulations Handbook
Senegal Company Laws and Regulations Handbook
Seychelles Company Laws and Regulations Handbook
Sierra Leone Company Laws and Regulations Handbook
Singapore Company Laws and Regulations Handbook
Slovakia Company Laws and Regulations Handbook
Slovenia Company Laws and Regulations Handbook
Solomon Islands Company Laws and Regulations Handbook
Somalia Company Laws and Regulations Handbook
South Africa Company Laws and Regulations Handbook
Spain Company Laws and Regulations Handbook
Sri Lanka Company Laws and Regulations Handbook
St. Helena Company Laws and Regulations Handbook
St. Pierre & Miquelon Company Laws and Regulations Handbook
Sudan Company Laws and Regulations Handbook
Suriname Company Laws and Regulations Handbook
Swaziland Company Laws and Regulations Handbook
Sweden Company Laws and Regulations Handbook
Switzerland Company Laws and Regulations Handbook
Syria Company Laws and Regulations Handbook
Taiwan Company Laws and Regulations Handbook
Tajikistan Company Laws and Regulations Handbook
Tanzania Company Laws and Regulations Handbook
Thailand Company Laws and Regulations Handbook
Togo Company Laws and Regulations Handbook
Tonga Company Laws and Regulations Handbook
Trinidad and Tobago Company Laws and Regulations Handbook
Tunisia Company Laws and Regulations Handbook
Turkey Company Laws and Regulations Handbook
Turkmenistan Company Laws and Regulations Handbook
Turks & Caicos Company Laws and Regulations Handbook
Tuvalu Company Laws and Regulations Handbook
Uganda Company Laws and Regulations Handbook
Ukraine Company Laws and Regulations Handbook
United Arab Emirates Company Laws and Regulations Handbook
United Kingdom Company Laws and Regulations Handbook
United States Company Laws and Regulations Handbook
Uruguay Company Laws and Regulations Handbook
Uzbekistan Company Laws and Regulations Handbook
Vanuatu Company Laws and Regulations Handbook
Vatican City Company Laws and Regulations Handbook
Venezuela Company Laws and Regulations Handbook
Vietnam Company Laws and Regulations Handbook
Virgin Islands, British Company Laws and Regulations Handbook
Wake Atoll Company Laws and Regulations Handbook
Wallis & Futuna Company Laws and Regulations Handbook
Yemen Company Laws and Regulations Handbook
Serbia Company Laws and Regulations Handbook
Zambia Company Laws and Regulations Handbook
Zimbabwe Company Laws and Regulations Handbook

www.ingramcontent.com/pod-product-compliance
Ingram Content Group UK Ltd.
Pitfield, Milton Keynes, MK11 3LW, UK
UKHW051509290926
15471UKWH00008B/1519